Early Childhood Care and Education in Canada

Edited by
Larry Prochner and Nina Howe

Early Childhood Care and Education in Canada

UBC Press · Vancouver · Toronto

Printed in Canada on acid-free paper

ISBN 0-7748-0771-7 (hardcover)
ISBN 0-7748-0772-5 (paperback)

Canadian Cataloguing in Publication Data

Main entry under title:

Early childhood care and education in Canada

Includes bibliographical references and index.
ISBN 0-7748-0771-7 (bound); ISBN 0-7748-0772-5 (pbk)

1. Early childhood education – Canada.
2. Child care services – Canada. I. Prochner, Larry Wayne, 1956- . II. Howe, Constance Nina, 1951-
LB1139.3.C3E27 2000 372.21'0971 C99-911203-1

This book has been published with the help of a grant from the Humanities and Social Sciences Federation of Canada, using funds provided by the Social Sciences and Humanities Research Council of Canada.

UBC Press acknowledges the financial support of the Government of Canada through the Book Publishing Industry Development Program (BPIDP) for our publishing activities.

Canadä

We also gratefully acknowledge support of the Canada Council for the Arts for our publishing program, as well as the support of the British Columbia Arts Council.

UBC Press
University of British Columbia
2029 West Mall
Vancouver, BC V6T 1Z2
(604) 822-5959
Fax: 1-800-668-0821
E-mail: info@ubcpress.ubc.ca
www.ubcpress.ubc.ca

We dedicate this volume to the pioneers of early childhood care and education in Canada for their work on behalf of children and families, as teachers, volunteers, and researchers. We would like to thank our spouses, Barb and Bill, and our children, Isabel, Ana, and Nick, for their support.

Contents

Illustrations and Tables

Illustrations

Tables

Early Childhood Care and Education in Canada

Introduction

Formal programs for the care and education of young children in Canada have a history that goes back almost 200 years. Nonetheless, issues surrounding services for our youngest Canadians continue to be hotly contested as the current century comes to a close. As one commentator noted, the history of programs for young children in North America has a "complicated and distinctive character, one filled with various strains and tensions" (Schickedanz 1995, 6). This character is reflected in the present: the expanding ecology of early childhood education is one of the defining features of the field in late-twentieth-century North America (Peters and Klinzing 1990). Early childhood care and education (ECCE) in Canada is striking for its tremendous diversity – some would say fragmentation – on such key issues as curriculum, financing, and teacher education. The range of programs and philosophies included in the rubric of ECCE can be overwhelming for parents, practitioners, academics, researchers, and policy makers alike.

The diversity of the field is evident in the vocabulary used to describe programs and services. While some of the historical terms are infrequently used today, others remain in current practice with different meanings. Terms used to describe educational programs included *infant schools, nursery schools, preschools, play schools,* and *kindergartens*. Programs designed primarily for the purpose of caring for children in the temporary absence of their parents included the *crèche, day nursery, day care, child care, foster home care,* and *family home day care*. The entire enterprise, from an educational standpoint, was termed nursery education beginning in the 1920s and, later, *early childhood education*. From the 1920s, child study was the term used to describe the primarily psychological study of children and families. Because child study was an applied field from the outset, it was closely linked to developments in nursery school and parent education. In this book some attention is paid to public school kindergarten as an early childhood setting, primarily in relation to historical developments (e.g., teacher education). However, because school-based programs are better documented in the existing literature and more uniform in their character, we chose to focus on child day care in its various forms.

Variation within ECCE is reflected in the multidisciplinary nature of this volume. In creating the collection, we set out to document what we determined to be key issues in the field: What programs are currently available to parents and what are their origins? How have adults been prepared to work in these programs? What do the adults do with the children? What policies guide the programs? How has the field reflected on itself through research? We believe that the book will be of interest to students, teachers, and researchers in child study, early education, policy studies, and history. The authors of the essays in the collection include psychologists, sociologists, historians, teacher educators, and social policy analysts, as well as those who place themselves within several of these areas. Some authors are parents who have experienced the challenge of finding good child care, the early morning rush to the child care centre and then to work, and the daily contact with teachers and other parents at a centre. Some authors have also been teachers who know firsthand the labour and rewards of teaching young children. We believe that the result is a book that brings together points of view seldom presented on the same stage: historians, policy analysts, educators, and researchers sit side by side. There are missing voices, however, leaving a challenge for work in this area in the future. Examples are voices of children and teachers, representatives of minority cultures, and Aboriginal peoples.

Our assumption is that an understanding of history has a critical role to play in current conceptions of issues. For this reason, the first five chapters tell the story of the care and education of young children in Canada, and the field of child study in general, from a historical standpoint; the remaining chapters describe features of the present landscape and suggest a vision for the future. In their review of child study history in Canada, Rooke and Schnell (1991, 200) noted that child care and policy related to children and families were striking for their absence in the historiography of childhood in Canada. Further, what we do know is sometimes plain wrong, as Hewes (1997) pointed out in a provocatively titled paper, "Fallacies, phantasies, and egregious prevarications in early childhood education history." The authors in this collection take a step toward rectifying this, and in doing so they demonstrate that care and education services for young children have a long history. The history is not interpreted as a series of purposeful steps that reach a point in the present in which answers to our questions are clear. Instead, the past – both recent and distant – is revealed as a complex entanglement of issues, as Susan Prentice terms the situation in her essay in this book. The fragmentation of current services has its roots in a fragmented historical development. The means of balancing children's interests, parents' interests, and society's interests have never been *less* clear than in the present, as Richardson described in her postmodern view of the history of childhood in Canada at the end of the twentieth century: "As the century closes we are faced with our restructured and seemingly endangered family, confusing sexualities, fractured public schools, problematic health care and an apparent rebellion against answers from the past including the efficacy of the welfare state. We have turned an ambivalent eye on the poor, weak, and young, once the recipients of our benefactions. Wariness about the future and growing disbelief in inevitable progress through science is reflected in an ambiguity about the identity we have thrust on the child in time" (1996, 392-3).

As Nina Howe points out in her concluding chapter, "there are no simple answers" or formulas for the one best way to serve the diverse needs of children and families in Canada. Yet we believe that the essays in this collection contribute to a creative reframing of the questions.

Organization

We believe that this collection of essays represents a critical approach to ECCE in Canada that reflects the international trend to re-examine early childhood services in fresh ways (Hayden 1999; Kagan and Cohen 1996; Taylor and Woods 1998). The collection begins with a survey of historical developments in child care and early education in Canada, from the infant schools of the early nineteenth century to the renewal of interest in ECCE as a social reform issue in the 1960s. It is important to note that the historiography of ECCE in Quebec is different from that in English Canada. Of particular relevance to this book, as historian and sociologist Turmel (1997) has pointed out, Quebec had no Child Study Movement similar to that in English Canada. The essays by Donna Varga, Mary Wright, and Kathleen Brophy share a concern with the role of adults in early childhood programs and how best to prepare them for this role. In Chapter 2, Varga examines the history of teacher education, with a focus on the different "tracks" that developed for kindergarten teachers and child care providers. Wright's rich description of the influence of academic child study on the history of early education sets the scene for Brophy's history of child development laboratories. In Chapter 5, Alan Pence and Allison Benner present an original analysis of child care research over the past three decades that indicates where we have come from and what work remains to be done. Taken together, the chapters in Part 1 provide the narrative of the development of ECCE in Canada. Some themes in this story include the nature of change, the source of ideas, and the interaction of various ECCE contexts.

First, development occurred as incremental change periodically interrupted by big events – for example, the birth of the Dionne quintuplets and their impact on child study research in Canada. Another theme is that ideas have many sources. Programs developed in local contexts but were influenced by national and international developments. Both individuals and ideas crossed borders – for example, the spread of the kindergarten movement in the early part of the twentieth century. A third theme is the interaction of ideas in different contexts. An action in one context had a reaction in another. And the reaction sometimes resulted in the modification of the original idea – for example, the interplay of government policy and research, or teacher education and life in kindergarten classrooms.

Chapters 6 to 10 provide a set of current contexts in ECCE. Ellen Jacobs describes the range of child care programs currently available to families in Canada, and Nina Howe, Jacobs, and Lisa Fiorentino summarize the main approaches to the early childhood curriculum. Both these chapters reflect historical themes noted above – particularly, the multiple sources of ideas and the interplay of ideas in different contexts. A central factor in child care quality is the child care provider, which is the focus of Chapter 8 by Donna White and Davina Mill. White and Mill pay particular attention to the importance of routine interactions between children and adults. In Chapter 9, Martha Friendly details the history of child care as a social policy issue on the national stage – which unfolds as a story of disappointment. She illustrates the way that largely incoherent federal and provincial policies have led to a "non-system" of child care in Canada. One of the outcomes is a permissive approach to free market child care. In Chapter 10, Susan Prentice provides a critical look at the politics of child care auspice and the impact of such politics on quality. In concluding the collection, Howe analyzes the historical and current social issues in ECCE described in the chapters, and offers a vision of early childhood care and education in Canada for the future.

References

Hayden, J. 1999. *Early childhood landscapes: Cross national perspectives on empowerment and restraint.* New York: Peter Lang.

Hewes, D. 1997. Fallacies, phantasies, and egregious prevarications in early childhood education history. Paper presented at the annual meeting of the National Association for the Education of Young Children, Anaheim, CA, 14 Nov. ERIC document no. ED 414058.

Kagan, S., and N.E. Cohen. 1996. *Reinventing early care and education: A vision for a quality system.* San Francisco: Jossey-Bass.

Peters, D.L., and D.G. Klinzing. 1990. The content of early childhood teacher education programs: Child development. In *Early childhood teacher preparation,* ed. B. Spodek and O. Saracho, 67-82. New York: Teachers College Press.

Richardson, T. 1996. Ambiguities in the lives of children: Postmodern views on the history and historiography of childhood in English Canada. *Paedagogica Historica* 32(2):363-93.

Rooke, P.T., and R. Schnell. 1991. Canada. In *Children in historical and comparative perspective: An international handbook and research guide,* ed. J.M. Hawes and N.R. Hiner, 179-216. Westport, CT: Greenwood Press.

Schickedanz, J.A. 1995. Early education and care: Beginnings. *Journal of Education* 177(3):1-7.

Taylor, J., and M. Woods, eds. 1998. *Early childhood studies: An holistic introduction.* London: Arnold.

Turmel, A. 1997. Historiography of children in Canada. *Paedagogica Historica* 33(2):509-20.

Part 1
Historical Contexts

1

A History of Early Education and Child Care in Canada, 1820-1966

Larry Prochner

Describing the history of child study, Hawes and Hiner (1991) observed, "Clio's newest offspring is robust, but it is clearly still in its infancy" (3). The historical study of early childhood care and education (ECCE) is one component of a critical approach to child study. Current developments and issues are informed by a context that includes developments in the past (Ferguson, Pence, and Denholm 1987, 200). Yet child study history is a "truly marginal sub-specialty" in Canada, as described in a survey of the literature by Rooke and Schnell (1991, 179). They described it as a field "fraught with ambiguity, conceptual confusion, and incompleteness" (179), with child care and nursery school history particularly "undeveloped" areas (200). In fact, a small body of literature on ECCE and related services did exist by 1991 (Corbett 1989; Desjardins 1991; Dumont-Johnson 1980; Schulz 1978; Simmons 1984; Sutherland 1976), and additional work has been completed since that time (Prentice 1993; Prochner 1996a, 1996b, 1997; Varga 1993, 1997). This chapter builds on this literature by presenting a national picture of the history of formal care and education programs for young children in Canada. The emphasis is on child care and preschool, from the opening of the first infant schools in the nineteenth century to the revival of interest in early care and education in the mid-1960s. The aim is to further our understanding of current developments in programs and policies by reviewing their evolution over the past 150 years. This is, admittedly, an ambitious task. The chapter presents a possible history of care and education for young children based on sources located in public and private archives, research libraries, newspapers, and various secondary sources. It is not an exhaustive inventory of programs. Rather, programs were selected to represent the type and range of initiatives characteristic of different periods. The history is divided into three parts: a review of the European programs that served as the inspiration and model for those in Canada; the story of early education in

Canada; and finally, child care programs for wage-earning parents.

"Whatever [the ladies of the society] have attempted, has been done only with a desire to ameliorate the condition of those who are early exposed to vice, or to give the young mind a greater store of purer and more enlarged ideas" (Montreal Infant School Society 1831, 7). These words, contained in the first report of the Montreal Infant School Society in 1831, capture the spirit of early education in Canada, not only in the nineteenth century, but also throughout most of the twentieth century. At the heart of all the programs was the belief that there are significant benefits, for both individuals and society, from providing children with formal education or out-of-home care. The corollary to this idea is that some children are at risk from the care they receive in their homes and communities. Most of the models of early intervention that developed in Europe, which were based on this key premise, eventually became part of the Canadian and US experience. However, there are important differences in the way they developed in each case. Patterns of immigration, industrialization, and the nature of private charity all played a role in creating a specifically Canadian history of preschool and child care. Nineteenth-century Canada consisted of indigenous peoples and a settler population spread over a vast geographic area. A handful of small cities served as the first stopping place for immigrant families from Great Britain and Europe. Canada was not heavily industrialized compared with the United States, even by the end of the nineteenth century, and the family was still the centre of the economy. The dominance of the English-Christian tradition in schools and charitable institutions meant that many of the programs for children took on the job of assimilating newcomers into the language and values of the Anglo majority.

As Rooke (1977) has indicated, "the aim of child study history is not to make an issue of whether such and such a practice originated in X, and was transferred to Y or Z, but to establish the distinctive Canadian mentality which led to a particular response" (167). Not all types of programs were established everywhere in Canada either simultaneously or in the same way. Following settlement patterns, the first classes that opened for children under the age of seven were infant schools in Eastern Canada. As immigration increased in the 1840s and 1850s, and cities in the east underwent rapid population growth, a greater range of institutional programs were established, including those in orphanages, foundling homes, and nurseries. A similar phenomenon occurred in Western Canada in the early twentieth century.

Another feature revealed in the history of Canadian child care and education is that most of the privately sponsored programs, ranging from charity kindergartens and nursery schools to day nurseries, were organized and headed by women. With the exception of public school kindergartens, almost all programs for preschoolers prior to the Second World War were in the hands of private charity. State support for the working poor is a relatively recent development. Groups of women under many different banners, including church groups, local branches of the Canadian Council of Women, the Women's Christian Temperance Union, and the Red Cross, volunteered their time, energy, and expertise to ease the burden of poor wage-earning women by providing their children with care and education during their absence.

A further feature noted in the history is the debate over the role of parents as opposed to the state or private charity in providing education and care for young children. In general, child care was provided as a social service for poor families. It was considered justifiable only insofar as it helped families in times of critical need. If it appeared that mothers were employed outside the home by choice and not necessity, the sponsors of nursery services, and later the professional staff that managed them, were generally critical. One of the most damning charges that could be made against a day nursery was that mothers used the service to provide themselves with leisure time. A Hamilton journalist, Joseph Tinsley, posed the question to the manager of the Hamilton Crèche in 1904:

> *Tinsley:* I suppose mothers who wish to spend a day at the beach or leave the city, or have a desire to get rid of their offspring for an hour or so, leave babies in charge of the matron?
> *Manager:* Oh, dear, no! We watch very closely all our customers. The children, in all cases, belong to women who have to work for a living (Tinsley 1904).

The view that parents were primarily responsible for early education was also part of the debate over kindergartens in public schools. Even at the end of the twentieth century, compulsory attendance in kindergartens is required in only one province in Canada, New Brunswick. Schools have historically had difficulty in accommodating all those children whose attendance was compulsory, and many school boards have seen the kindergarten as a frill to be eliminated in the effort to balance budgets and ease overcrowding. The kindergarten program has been made to prove its worth, not once, but time and time again. Current developments in child care and preschool in Canada reflect some of these historical debates. There is still no national plan directing child care policy across all provinces and territories, and kindergarten continues to have an ambiguous place in schools. Nonetheless, it remains at the forefront of what governments regard as either key social reforms (adding preschool or child care programs) or basic cost-cutting measures (taking them away).

The European Tradition

Early Education

Formal programs aimed at the education and care of young children were rare in Europe prior to the late eighteenth century. From the earliest times, the family and community assumed joint responsibility for children's upbringing. The first examples of programs for children under the age of seven – called infant schools – were directed at poor children. They were preventive in nature, meaning their aim was to decrease crime, ignorance, disease, and political instability through early intervention. They incorporated ideas from both Jean-Jacques Rousseau and John Locke. From Rousseau, the earliest programs (e.g., Robert Owen's) adopted the principle of play as the natural business of children. Even later and more structured infant schools recognized children's need to play and, as a result, introduced recess into their daily schedules. The modern playground had its origins in the infant school of the 1830s. The schools also incorporated Locke's optimistic view of early education and human potential. Locke's sensationalist approach to learning (knowledge comes first through the senses) had a profound influence on the early infant schools. Their promoters believed that a child's future was limited only by a teacher's imagination and the richness of the school environment.

John Frederic Oberlin, who was a Lutheran minister, established one of the first infant schools in Europe in 1770 in the Alsace region of France. The school operated on a part-time basis as an educational experiment and a mission of the church. Children were taught basic hygiene, social manners, nature studies, and such practical skills as knitting. Oberlin hoped that some of the school culture acquired by the children would be carried back into their homes to influence their parents. As Singer (1992) observed in her analysis of the history of child care and the influence of psychology, Oberlin's "knitting schools" contained themes found in most subsequent preschools over the next two centuries: they were envisioned as a means of social reform, they stressed the importance of early intervention, and they were inconsistent in their attitude toward the role of teachers and mothers. With reference to the last point, while Oberlin placed great importance on the educative and nurturant value of maternal affection and care, he did not believe that the children could receive maternal care from their own mothers. Instead, this care would be attained through contact with young women trained in mothering in a special setting away from the home.

Other examples of programs for young children of working parents are scarce during this period. An exception is the refuge for infants established in Paris in 1800 by Adelaide de Pastoret. Pastoret was a member of the political and intellectual élite living in post-revolution Paris. Distressed by the plight of the young children of working mothers and inspired by Oberlin's example, she established a refuge for the infant children of wage-earning mothers. The refuge had the luxury of heat and was furnished with twelve cribs. While Pastoret may have planned for only twelve children, many more actually attended. The Irish writer Maria Edgeworth visited in late 1802 and reported seeing twenty-eight children. The matron, Soeur Françoise, oversaw the operation of the *asile* (or refuge), while a "family woman" was employed as a combination wet-nurse and housekeeper. In some cases mothers returned to the *asile* several times a day to nurse their babies and all the children returned to their homes at night. This latter point was critical to the idea of the refuge as a daytime only care facility, for Pastoret "did not wish to destroy the tie of natural affection" (Edgeworth in Colvin 1979, 39). The refuge was austere and lacked any of the luxuries found in the homes of wealthier Parisians. There was a conscious desire to avoid spoiling the children during their daily stay at the refuge. "Nothing in [the] house was above the condition of the children," noted Edgeworth, "nothing could tend to give them ideas that might make them discontented with their lot" (Edgeworth in Colvin 1979, 39-40). The *asile* was a short-lived experiment, but the reasons for its demise and even the date of its closure are unclear. One account stated that the two staff found the work exhausting and soon quit. Another suggested that the effort was not understood by the citizens of Paris at the time. However, that a temporary refuge would have existed at all at the beginning of the nineteenth century is remarkable. The preferred child care option for all but the poorest mothers was the use of a wet-nurse. Pastoret targeted the most impoverished women for her service, many of whom were day labourers in the markets of Paris with few options for child care.

Maria Edgeworth made Pastoret's refuge the subject of a novella titled *Madame de Fleury,* which was published in 1809. As a result, although Pastoret's *asile* was no longer open, the idea gained widespread attention in Great Britain. Edgeworth may have inspired the industrialist and social reformer Robert Owen to open the first infant school in England in 1816. He called the school the Institution for the Formation of Character. Owen built the school for the children of workers in his cotton factory in New Lanark, Scotland. The rational infant school was based on the egalitarian principles of Rousseau and was an attempt to raise children above their circumstances. The school admitted children over the age of one. Like Rousseau, Owen rejected the use of books until children reached the age of ten or twelve. The primary occupation of the children was play, and it was through the structuring of children's amusements that their characters were to be formed. Along with social reform, the school offered practical benefits to Owen. He maintained that the school led to decreased theft in the factories and created a ready supply of trained workers. As a result of his efforts, "all the houses in the village, with one hundred and fifty acres of land around it, formed parts of the establishment, all united, and working together as one machine, proceeding day by day with the regularity of clockwork" (Owen [1857] 1967, 135-6). The schools were suited to Owen's business as well as his humanitarian interests as a means of quieting worker discontent at a time when resistance to industrialism was sometimes violent.

For the first teachers of the New Lanark school, Owen chose the "simple-minded kind-hearted" James Buchanan and the seventeen-year-old Molly Young, "who of the two, in natural powers of mind, had the advantage over her new companion" (Owen [1857] 1967, 139). Young was responsible for the babies, and Buchanan took charge of the older children. Owen personally trained them in the methods of the infant school. Both teachers were instructed never to beat or threaten the children, but rather "to speak to them with a pleasant countenance, and in a kind manner and tone of voice" (Owen [1857] 1967, 139).

In 1819, Buchanan moved to London to become the teacher at the first infant school in that city. While in London, Buchanan convinced Samuel Wilderspin, a school teacher, of the benefits of infant schools. Wilderspin became superintendent of a school himself and founded the Infant School Society to promote the system. This school and the many infant schools that followed departed from Owen's plan, instead undertaking to apply the monitorial system of schooling devised by Joseph Lancaster and Andrew Bell in the early nineteenth century. While infant schools grew in number and flourished in the 1820s, they became increasingly rigid and subject-

Infant school playground, England, c. 1820

oriented as they strove to achieve both efficiency and moral purpose. They typically housed 200 or more children from approximately two to six years of age, all in a single room. To manage the large numbers, children were contained in galleries or tiers of seats, and older children were trained as monitors. The schools had playgrounds attached to them, and the children were permitted to play within the restrictions of the program. As a result, play usually involved leading the children in a series of movement exercises. Wilderspin became the self-appointed leader of the Infant School Movement and published books on his system. Infant schools were then both popularized and standardized, as similar institutions were established abroad through the influence of organizations such as the Home and Colonial Infant School Society.

Part of the success of Wilderspin's system was his promotion of the infant school as a means of reducing crime, a call repeated by advocates of preschools in the twentieth century (Schweinhart and Weikart 1997). He pointed to the moral neglect of children by working mothers as a major contributor to juvenile delinquency. Wilderspin was generally critical of the ability of working class parents to nurture their young. Moreover, he viewed the root cause of crime to be the immorality of the family itself. He noted, "As appalling as the effects of juvenile delinquents are, I think we may discover a principal cause of them in the present condition and habits of the adult part of the laboring classes" (Wilderspin 1825, 38).

Wilderspin believed, as did Oberlin, in the power of infant education (i.e., through infant schools) as a form of parent education. Accordingly, as a result of their experience in the infant school, his hope was that children would "rise up to cultivate and humanize their parents" (Wilderspin 1825, 17). Infant schools briefly flourished before succumbing to problems of inadequate funding, poor promotion, and the popularization of the idea that young children's minds were harmed by early academic instruction, which caused undue "mental excitement." At the same time, educators such as Pestalozzi and, later, Froebel, stressed that mothers were the first and natural teachers of children. Early education for the masses in infant schools, featuring recitations from the Bible by several hundred youngsters, did not fit within this maternal model. The success of the kindergarten in North America followed the decline of the infant school. Although the kindergarten developed partly as an alternative to the rigid structure of the infant school, it borrowed some of its most powerful ideas. The horticultural metaphor of children as plants and teachers as gardeners was also a favourite of Wilderspin's.

The kindergarten was not conceived as a preschool in the modern, secular sense. It was tied to Froebel's understanding of the workings of the universe and the proper path to religious and spiritual growth. This metaphysical dimension of the kindergarten was part of its original appeal. However, it later became its downfall, when it was seen to be out of fashion with modern, scientific thinking. By the twentieth century, Froebel's "old-fashioned" notions were criticized by North American psychologists, educators, and philosophers. In addition, teachers in overcrowded, urban schools in Canada and the United States in the 1880s and 1890s had difficulty following the exacting techniques of the original kindergarten program. In the early twentieth century, the kindergarten was competing with supporters of the nursery school for a similar clientele. The nursery school evolved out of British and continental experiments aimed at giving children from poor backgrounds a head start. The persons most closely associated with its early history are Margaret and Rachel Macmillan and Maria Montessori. Margaret Macmillan's innovative "camp school" at Deptford, England, bore little resemblance to current nursery schools, which are typically half-day programs for children three to four years old. When the camp opened in 1911, it took in a group of girls aged six to fourteen (Steedman 1990) for an overnight stay. They ate their evening meal at the camp, bathed, and slept at night in tents or the open air. After breakfast, they went to school and from school they returned to their own homes. The camp experience was designed as a therapeutic intervention to strengthen the girls' bodies, which reflected the Macmillans' understanding of the ideas of Seguin and sensory education. A Baby Camp for children under five started in 1914. This approach to nursery education was disseminated through a training school in Deptford and through books, articles, and lectures by Margaret Macmillan.

Another promoter of the nursery school as a cure for social ills was Maria Montessori. Montessori was an Italian doctor and educator who developed a system of education based on carefully prescribed methods. Some aspects of Montessori's system were the same as Froebel's, including a grounding in the philosophy of idealism, the use of specialized teaching materials to support educational objectives, and a concern for the spiritual growth of young children. Although Rousseau's influence on Montessori is evident, her approach to education was far more psychological than that of her predecessors. In this respect, her system was equally a product of the twentieth century. She focused on the development of individuals, which was to be achieved through carefully planned interaction with materials. Montessori's system also incorporated the earlier work of Jean-Marc Gaspard Itard and Edouard Seguin with training intellectually and physically disabled children (Montessori [1912] 1967). She believed that all children could reach their social, moral, and intellectual potential if they had appropriate experiences in a prepared environment.

When Montessori began her work with poor families in a slum tenement in Rome in 1907, she was trying to do more than give children an academic head start. Her program, which took place in what she called a Children's House, was aimed at supporting wage-earning mothers by providing day care and training children in hygiene, practical skills, and social manners. The Children's House was part of the community, and the director lived on site. The Children's House was thus similar to settlement houses in Great Britain and North America at the turn of the century. Like many other prominent early childhood educators, Montessori was concerned about the lack of supervision for young children of wage-earning mothers. Left to their own devices within the degrading conditions of the slum, the tenement children became "ignorant vandals" (Montessori in Braun and Edwards 1972, 116). The Children's House offered an orderly, hygienic, safe, and stimulating alternative to life on the street. The Montessori system is another example of a preventive program that aimed to protect children from a disorderly and adult-controlled world. While Montessori's system was largely ignored in North America until the early 1960s, and the British nursery school was regarded as too focused on health and hygiene, the nursery school was identified by child psychologists and the Child Study Movement as having a key role in children's mental health. The role of the nursery school in the Child Study Movement in Canada is described in detail in Chapters 3 and 4 of this book.

A visit to a model crèche, Paris, 1846

Child Care

The divisions between child care facilities and those that had an educational mandate were not always clear. Many child care services offered some type of educational program. This took the form of practical domestic skills for young girls – sewing, cooking, and child care – second language learning, Bible study, and modified kindergarten programs. The infant schools of the nineteenth century and the charity kindergartens and nursery schools in the twentieth doubled as child care services. Nonetheless, the history of child care is distinct from that of early education in that it is based on a tradition of child and maternal welfare, and its roots are in health and social welfare rather than education. Although the first infant day care is generally regarded to be Pastoret's refuge, described above, the Crèche Movement, initiated by Jean Firmin Marbeau in Paris in 1844, had a greater influence on day care in North America (Prochner 1996a). Americans who visited model crèches in Paris were inspired to establish similar institutions on their return, although few crèches were constructed on such a grand scale as the one in the illustration taken from a book promoting the crèche idea.

The aim of the crèche in France and North America was to enable mothers of young children to earn a wage outside the home by providing child care for their children. The institutions, called nurseries, day nurseries, or crèches in Canada and the United States, were linked to poverty and the notion that the poor should be encouraged to help themselves through their own labour.

Early Education in Canada

Infant Schools

One of the first infant schools in Canada was opened in Montreal, on St. Dominique Street in 1828, by "several ladies of the city" (Montreal Infant School Society 1831, 4). It offered care and instruction for poor children, according to Lancaster's Infant School system. In 1829, the women opened a boarding department for children who needed longer term care; during the first year, they boarded twenty children. A second charity infant school opened on the western part of the island, in St. Anne, prior to 1831, along with several private schools. This extension of the infant school from the poor to the wealthy was consistent with developments in the United States in cities such as New York and Boston. As the Montreal Infant School Society (1831) explained in its report, "though originally introduced for the poorer classes, the system of instruction is equally calculated to produce correct principles in the children of all classes" (6). Infant schools were well attended almost from their creation, and the

Montreal school was followed by similar schools in Charlottetown, Halifax, Quebec City, and Toronto (Phillips 1957). The Quebec City school was opened in 1834 by the British and Canadian Infant School Society, and in its first year it accommodated 100 to 150 children each day. In its report, the Society emphasized that boys and girls, Protestants and Catholics attended the school in equal numbers. The Montreal and Quebec City schools did not stress their role as a support for wage-earning mothers. The greater portion of their reports promoted the educational function of the schools. The British and Canadian Infant School Society expanded on the need for teachers to treat children in a kindly manner as a way of meeting its educational aims: "Inasmuch as the fundamental principle of the Infant School system is love, it should be the constant endeavour of the Teacher to win the affection of the children, and then cause them to feel pleasure in submission to his will" (British and Canadian Infant School Society 1834, 4).

While few very young children were accommodated in common schools in the first-half of the nineteenth century in Canada, overcrowding meant that there was a "need to get rid of the youngest and oldest students, or, second best, to separate them" (Prentice 1977, 150). If the youngest children, usually those under seven years old, were to have their own schools, the model available at mid-century was the infant school. In Newfoundland, an infant school was established in 1854 in the fishing community of Greenspond to relieve severe overcrowding in the main school building (Winsor 1979). One hundred and fifty of the youngest children were placed in the infant school under the direction of a teacher trained in St. John's, leaving the main school with 120 older pupils. Elsewhere in the Atlantic provinces, infant schools were opened as charity services for poor families, with a combined focus on moral education and basic custodial care, in the spirit of the Montreal and Quebec schools, described above. An article in the Halifax newspaper the *Nova Scotian,* on 8 February 1832, lauded the infant school as a "nursery of knowledge," and stressed the importance of such schools for the poor and the benefits for young children who are "not yet formed." Infant schools as a charity service lasted until the late nineteenth century in New Brunswick and Nova Scotia, and therefore did not follow the pattern of the Infant School Movement in the United States, which was a quickly diminishing force by the end of the 1830s. As late as 1852, an infant school opened near Kingston in Portsmouth, Ontario. The Portsmouth school looked after young children and taught their mothers to read. In New Brunswick, infant schools were called Madras Schools, in honour of the system established in India by Andrew Bell in the late eighteenth century. Most Madras Schools in New Brunswick were administered by a philanthropic organization called the National Society for the Promotion of Education for the Poor, established in 1820. By 1843, there were eight Madras Schools in New Brunswick with a total enrolment of 1,000 children. The annual report for the year noted that most were from the "indigent class" (National Society for the Promotion of Education for the Poor 1843, 2).

In Nova Scotia, an infant school was opened in Halifax by a group of wealthy citizens in a room of Dalhousie College in 1833. The Halifax Infant School was directed by a female teacher, called the "lady manager," according to a report by the *Nova Scotian* on 20 April 1837. The school enrolled about 100 children per day, ranging in age from two to six. The age range expanded over the years, by 1862 including children eighteen months to ten years old. Children were taught Bible lessons and were provided with food, shelter, and clothing. Meanwhile, their parents "at their work [had] the comfort of knowing their children [were] comfortably lodged and protected from harm and also receiving all the instruction suitable to their tender years in a manner that amuses while it instructs the child" (Halifax Infant School Society 1856). The service was offered free of charge. The larger social benefit was derived from helping poor parents "to leave their homes and seek employment that they could not otherwise obtain" (Halifax Infant School Society 1853).

Private Kindergartens

Infant schools developed for several different reasons. In Greenspond, Newfoundland, an infant class grew out of the common school as a result of overcrowding. In communities throughout the Atlantic provinces and in Ontario and Quebec, they were established as charities for poor children. A small number of private infant schools opened for children from wealthy families. However, their development was sporadic and by the 1870s, most had succumbed to a maternalist ideology that called for mothers to be in sole charge of early education and that held the belief that young children were harmed by the overstimulation of their fragile minds. The few remaining infant schools, mostly run by charities in the Atlantic provinces, were joined by an alternative form of early education, Froebel's kindergarten.

In Montreal and Toronto there was a gap of several decades between the closing of the infant schools and the founding of the first private kindergartens. In New Brunswick, the Madras Schools coexisted for a short time with private kindergartens for children from wealthy families, which opened in Fredericton, Moncton, and Saint John. By the 1870s, the idea was well established that all young children could benefit from a formal early education, and mothers needed some assistance (but not replacement) in the complex task of child rearing. The kindergarten was perfectly suited to meet this need in a way that respected the contemporary thinking about the nature of children. Rote instruction and the teaching of large numbers of very young children in a single class were discarded in favour of a child-centred approach, which by the 1880s, would be known as the New Education. The spread of the kindergarten philosophy in North America was accomplished in the beginning by teachers trained in Froebel's methods in Germany. The first kindergarten in North America was established in 1856, by Margarethe Schurz in her home in Watertown, Wisconsin. In Canada, the first kindergarten was opened in the Wesleyan Methodist Church in Charlottetown in 1870 (Olsen 1955). Private kindergartens were common in larger towns and cities by the end of the 1870s. Ada Marean, who was the director of the first kindergarten established by the Toronto School Board in 1883, had first taught in a private kindergarten in Saint John in 1878.

Kindergartens soon moved beyond their middle- and upper-class clientele to be adopted as a vehicle of mission work and social reform. The kindergarten was well suited to this because of the religious quality of the philosophy and the focus on home and family. Kindergartens with a social reform or mission orientation were known as Free Kindergartens, simply meaning that they were available free of charge. The Free Kindergarten Movement took root in the late 1870s in large cities in the United States, under the direction of leaders such as Pauline Agassiz Shaw in Boston and Alice Putnam in Chicago (Beatty 1995). Free Kindergartens served a similar need as infant schools in the 1830s, by combining early schooling with a custodial service for young children from poor families. The Free Kindergarten Movement was influential in the day nursery field, and kindergartens became established in many day nurseries long before nursery schools were common in more progressive centres in the 1920s.

The best-known Free Kindergartens in Canada were run by the Winnipeg Free Kindergarten Association, established in 1892. The Association was a non-sectarian organization led by middle- and upper-class women who believed that the social reform aspects of the kindergarten could provide relief for the poor of Winnipeg's north end. The kindergarten served a largely non-English-speaking immigrant population. The Association worked to assimilate the newcomers by immersing their children in Anglo-Canadian culture. Part of the Free Kindergarten idea was that preschools were effective in quieting the discontent of the working class by teaching children not to question the values of the political and social élite. Kindergartens would "keep children off the streets and bend their faculties in the right direction" (Winnipeg Free Kindergarten Association 1908, 9). The managers and teachers believed the homes of immigrant families to be poor child-rearing environments. In 1908, the directress of the kindergarten spoke of "homes where the children grow up like weeds, with such environments as tend to develop only the lower nature of the child" (Winnipeg Free Kindergarten Association 1908, 9). Because poverty was regarded as the result of "shiftlessness or sinful indulgence," it made sense to remove the children from their homes for a few hours a day to expose them to the kindergarten culture (Winnipeg Free Kindergarten Association 1910, 8).

The first kindergarten organized by the Winnipeg Association was located in a storefront at the corner of Logan and Ellen Streets. In the late 1890s, it moved into the Swedish Lutheran Church. The Association purchased the church, but when it was found to be inadequate for their needs, it was demolished and a new building was constructed on the site in 1903. Prior to the Compulsory School Attendance Act in 1916, the kindergarten accepted children from the ages of six to eight. After the introduction of the Act, it moved to accept younger children, aged four and five, since children aged six and older were required to attend school. In the early years of the twentieth century, the kindergarten was attended by up to seventy children per session. This success led the managers to open a second kindergarten in 1907, in a church on Sherman Street, a short distance away. In 1908 it was moved to Alexander Avenue and named the Froebel School. In 1917 this branch school was discontinued. The Association believed that the key benefits of the kindergarten were that it shielded the children "from the hurtful influences of the street" and awakened in them "a love for school – an important item

Free Kindergarten, Swedish Lutheran Church, Winnipeg, 1899

when there [was] no compulsory school law" (*History of the Winnipeg Free Kindergarten* 1910). In some cases, school-aged children were responsible for looking after younger siblings during the day, preventing the older children from attending school. The Association played a role in helping these young caregivers to attend school by providing a kindergarten program for preschoolers. On one occasion, the deaconess learned of a ten-year-old girl who was not able to attend school because she was responsible for her two younger brothers. The Association arranged for her to attend school for two full days and three half days, while her brothers were in the kindergarten.

The Winnipeg Association was devoted to using traditional kindergarten methods, which was evident in their naming a branch in honour of Froebel. From the beginning, the Association hired only trained teachers. Most were educated in schools in Chicago, which at the time was the heart of kindergarten-teacher education in the American Midwest. After the First World War, the kindergarten on Ellen Street gradually shifted from its Froebelian roots until it resembled a semi-structured play school, as the managers sought to follow "modern educationists" (Kindergarten Settlement Association 1921). The program expanded to include unit work on themes (e.g., Eskimos), which were repeated yearly. However, the Kindergarten Settlement Association (the Winnipeg Free Kindergarten Association changed its name in 1915) resisted the more progressive aspects of kindergarten work in the 1920s. Following a study leave to visit kindergartens in New York City in 1926, including the one at Teachers College, the Association's teacher concluded that she was not sure of the usefulness of the new methods with poor children who seemed "lost in the freedom." She believed that "children love the organized rhythm and singing games" of the traditional kindergarten (Kindergarten Settlement Association 1926, 12).

The Winnipeg Free Kindergarten Association was not the only organization to provide poor children with kindergarten education in Canada, or even in Winnipeg. One of the first services offered by the Methodist All People's Mission, when it was established in Winnipeg's north end in 1889, was a class for immigrant children under the direction of Daisy Gordon. The kindergarten first operated in a tent and later moved into a roughly built structure at the back of the church. Kindergartens opened later in the Stella and the Sutherland Missions, which were branches of the All People's Mission. The Mission became well known throughout Western Canada for its community work under the direction of J.S. Woodsworth. The aims of the mission kindergartens matched those of the secular Kindergarten Settlement Association – namely, to teach English to the new immigrants; to care for the children while their mothers worked outside the home; and to offer religious training, kindergarten training, and

All People's Mission Kindergarten, Winnipeg, 1904

training in "Canadian homemaking" (All People's Mission of the United Church of Canada 1928). The kindergarten was viewed as a feeder program for Sunday School, and was a weekday version of Sunday School evangelism. The teachers in the mission kindergartens were trained kindergartners, and some taught in both mission and free kindergartens. Other mission kindergartens were established for Japanese and Chinese children in British Columbia by the Anglican, Baptist, Catholic, and United Churches.

Some mission kindergartners became leaders in nursery education. Florence Bird, who led United Church mission kindergartens in British Columbia, was the first president of the Vancouver Kindergarten Teachers

International Kindergarten, New Westminster, BC, c. 1920

Miss Elizabeth Baker's kindergarten class in Oriental Home, Victoria, BC, 1915

Association when it started in 1932. The free and mission kindergartens played an important role in the development of preschool education in the early twentieth century. At a time when public school kindergartens were rare, the free and mission kindergartens offered a small number of children the benefit of a well-planned educational program. But their assimilationist character ignored the home language and culture of the children, as did the public school kindergartens. Another category of kindergartens was developed to serve specific populations of children or cultural or religious groups. For example, in 1934 the Jewish community in Montreal opened a kindergarten to promote religious education and early schooling for Jewish children. Its purpose was the opposite of the assimilationist mission kindergartens. A pamphlet described the Talmud Torah Kindergarten in this way: "In the budding minds of our very young the beginning of knowledge and pride in Judaism is carefully implanted. This first step is important as it is the foundation of the work which, step by step, finally sends out into the social, political and business world an enthusiastically loyal Jew and good citizen filled with love for his race and faith" (Talmud Torah Schools 1937).

Starting in the early years of the twentieth century, many private schools for the children of the élite incorporated kindergartens and embraced the latest innovation in progressive education. The photograph of the kindergarten class in St. Margaret's School, a private school in Victoria, British Columbia, in the 1920s, shows children working at

St. Margaret's School kindergarten, Victoria, BC, c. 1920

Froebelian tasks. Private kindergartens, and nursery schools and play schools for younger children were another form of preschool education from the earliest years of the twentieth century. The curriculum was sometimes limited, centring on "courteous speech, taking turns, and playing fair" (Olsen 1955, 84). These schools, which were attended by a very small number of preschool children, were often located in the home of the teacher or, in some cases, the home of a wealthy family who employed a teacher for their own children and those of their friends or neighbours. Some were operated by trained kindergarten teachers and, later, by

Central Neighbourhood House Preschool, Toronto, 1929

graduates of child study programs providing expertise in nursery school education.

Beginning in the 1930s, graduates from St. George's School for Child Study in Toronto established nursery schools in church basements, community centres, and private homes in communities across Canada. Miss Idell Robinson's Nursery School and Kindergarten, which opened in Winnipeg in 1934, was the first nursery school west of Toronto. Robinson was a graduate of St. George's, and her school had the "enthusiastic support and interest" of St. George's director, Dr. William Blatz (Paterson 1966, 119). Some of the first nursery schools that were established for poor children in Toronto, known as charity or free nursery schools, were also staffed by graduates from St. George's. They joined existing charity nursery schools operated by settlement houses, such as the one at Central Neighbourhood House in Toronto. These included the Metropolitan Nursery School and the Woodgreen Nursery School, which were both opened in Toronto in 1937 as United Church missions. The Woodgreen school was reorganized in 1948 under the guidance of Anne Harris, who was later to marry Blatz. The souvenir program of the opening day ceremonies lauded it as "Canada's Foremost Nursery School."

Public School Kindergartens

The kindergarten was a basic element of the New Education Movement, which emphasized learning through doing rather than by lecture or through books (Stamp 1982). Whereas the Old Education used techniques such as recitation and rote learning, the New Education curriculum provided for children to learn by manipulating concrete objects that represented the real world. Other components of the New Education were manual education and domestic science. Public school kindergartens were also promoted by supporters such as James Hughes, chief inspector for public schools in Toronto, as an important force in social reform. In this respect, the public school kindergarten was not unlike its counterpart in the field of mission or charity work.

The first kindergarten in a public school in Canada opened in Toronto in 1883, in the Louisa Street School. It is often claimed that Toronto was the second city in North America to establish a kindergarten within a public school system, the first being St. Louis, Missouri, in 1872. Toronto was actually one of a number of communities to establish kindergartens in public schools in this period. Kindergartens were part of public schools in New Orleans from the late 1870s (Wheelock and Aborn 1935; *History of the kindergarten movement* 1939; *History of the kindergarten movement* 1940) and were opened in public schools in San Francisco, California, in 1880; Newport, Rhode Island, in 1882; Portland, Maine, in 1883; and New

Haven, Connecticut in 1884. Ontario was also not the first jurisdiction to pass legislation for funding kindergartens in public schools. Vermont enacted permissive legislation permitting "all towns and school districts to aid kindergarten schools" in 1886 (Wheelock and Aborn 1935, 35).

The Toronto kindergartens were part of the general movement in the 1880s by progressive school boards to provide a specialized program for very young children at public expense. They admitted children from five to seven years old. The wide age range was a feature of early public school kindergartens in Canada, but it was narrowed over time. Kindergartens were popular with parents and well attended, and by 1895 there were kindergartens in forty public schools (Corbett 1989, 47). In addition to carrying out the higher aims of the New Education Movement for a child-centred education, kindergartens served the purpose of removing the youngest children from the first grade level to relieve overcrowding and offer them a program more suited to their developmental level.

In Quebec, kindergartens were first proposed as a solution to the old problem of "very small children" – those under the age of five – being sent to school. In his report in 1872, the inspector for the Protestant Board of School Commissioners for the City of Montreal (PBSCCM) was moved to write the following: "The large number of very small children that seek admission into the schools demonstrates the need of establishments in which children who have not yet attained the legal school age can be cared for, provided with healthy and instructive amusement and be

Kindergarten under the auspices of the Protestant School Board, Montreal, 1913

trained into habits of cleanliness, order, cheerful obedience, and mutual forbearance, love and helpfulness" (Robins 1872).

The situation was made worse by the Quebec school law, which made public schooling available to children from the age of five. The PBSCCM complained that as a result, "many more infants [younger than five] are sent to school, especially during the summer months, to get rid of them from home, and the little that they learn in the summer is forgotten during the winter" (PBSCCM 1877). Nothing was done until 1885, when a special Preparatory Class was opened for children aged five to seven. The youngest children still attended, but the course of study was different from the old curriculum: "The daily session is for the forenoon only, from 9 to 12, and the instruction given is entirely oral ... It is, in fact, a modified kindergarten" (PBSCCM 1886, 10). The course of studies in the Preparatory Class was regarded over time as a poor match for the children's abilities, and a true kindergarten was introduced in the High School for Girls in 1891. At this time, the school board sent one of its teachers to St. Paul, Minnesota, for training in kindergarten methods. The next year, a second kindergarten opened in Lorne School, and both were filled to capacity. By the end of the decade, almost all schools under the Protestant Board had kindergarten departments.

The key development in the 1890s was the division of the wide age range in the Preparatory Class into three separate levels: Kindergarten (age five), Preparatory Class (age six), and Transition Class (age seven). The Kindergarten and Preparatory Classes were not required, but were recommended "for the benefit of very young children who are unable to enter upon the regular First year work" (PBSCCM 1899, 6-7). The variability in school-starting age was partly due to a lack of a compulsory school law. Schooling was not compulsory in Quebec until 1943. The kindergarten program was markedly different from that of other levels. It consisted of Scripture reading and moral lessons, morning talks, songs and games, the weather record, and Froebel's gifts and occupations. The Preparatory Class did not include any Froebel work, but instead five hours a week were devoted to reading, language, and stories, in addition to calisthenics, songs, marches, drawing, and writing (1 hour 40 minutes); numbers, forms, and colour (3 hours 20 minutes); and Scripture and moral lessons (1 hour 40 minutes). The Transition Class, which was the first regular level of schooling, included reading and spelling (4 hours 45 minutes per week), writing (1 hour), language lessons (1 hour), object lessons (1 hour 20 minutes), Scripture lessons (1 hour 40 minutes), arithmetic (2 hours), drawing (2 hours), singing (50 minutes), and physical training (1 hour 15 minutes).

Other communities in Canada introduced kindergartens as part of the public school system in this period, and for similar reasons. In 1889, a

Miss Hamilton's kindergarten class, Dartmouth, NS, 1909

kindergarten was established in Dartmouth, Nova Scotia, by the Board of School Commissioners, who called it the "first free public kindergarten east of the St. Lawrence River" (Payzant 1993, 19). The teacher, Mary Ann Hamilton, had started teaching in Dartmouth schools in 1866; she came to the kindergarten when it first opened. Just as in many public school kindergartens, she trained apprentice teachers in her classroom. Hamilton used strict Froebelian methods and worked with as many as ninety children at a time. The photograph above shows Hamilton and her class along with her apprentice in 1909. A bust of Froebel can be seen resting on a book on Hamilton's right. When she retired in 1916, after a career that spanned five decades, the kindergarten department of the Dartmouth School Commission closed, apparently for economic reasons. In subsequent years, five-year-olds were admitted into a "grade-primary," with a program similar to the Transition Class in Montreal.

Across the harbour from Dartmouth, the Halifax Board of School Commissioners first discussed introducing kindergartens in 1888, the same year that the province made attendance at school compulsory for children aged seven to fourteen. A kindergarten opened three years later in 1891. By the next year there was a kindergarten in almost every school in the city. Children who were one year younger than compulsory school age were eligible to attend, but large numbers of children younger than six years old also attended. The enrolment varied from school to school, ranging from as few as ten to more than sixty in a class. In the beginning, the Halifax Board operated its own training school for kindergarten teachers (see Chapter 2). However, a private individual opened a kindergarten department with a model kindergarten as a private venture within the Nova Scotia Normal School in Truro. The Truro School Board took over kindergarten-teacher preparation in 1900, and in 1907 the kindergarten department of the Truro School Board was absorbed within the Normal School. However, because almost all kindergartens in the province were located in the communities of Dartmouth, Halifax, and Truro, the kindergarten department in the Normal School never had more than a few students.

The first kindergartens in public schools in Western Canada opened in Regina, Saskatchewan, in 1891, only eight years after the founding of the city. At that time the settlement was a gathering of tents around the little railroad station. However, it was made the capital of the North-West Territories, a fact that sparked its subsequent growth. Nonetheless, it was still a small city in 1891, with a population of 1,681. Kindergartens in Regina were originally full-day programs, but as enrolment increased, the school board changed this to two half-day sessions in 1899. They also narrowed the age range to ease overcrowding. Even so, children from four and a half to six and a half could attend (Neely 1946). The Regina School Board came to be viewed as experts in kindergarten work in Western Canada. When the authorities in Lethbridge, Alberta, planned to introduce a kindergarten into its school system, they wrote to Regina officials to ask about their experience.

Kindergartens in the public schools of Halifax, Montreal, Regina, and Toronto have continued from their beginnings in the nineteenth century to the present day. Elsewhere in Canada, kindergartens have been more vulnerable to shifting economic and educational priorities. In New Brunswick and Newfoundland there was no provincial support for kindergartens in public schools until recent times, a situation that did not seem to generate any great debate. In Newfoundland, kindergartens were opened in public schools in the late 1960s, and in New Brunswick in 1985. The different timing in the introduction of kindergarten in schools across provinces partly rested in the fact that kindergartens were largely an urban phenomenon, even in Ontario. It was simply too difficult for young children in rural areas to walk great distances to school. When the government of Saskatchewan provided funding for kindergartens in the 1940s, rural schools were not eligible. Nonetheless, there was a modest expansion of kindergartens in Western Canada in the period from 1891 to the First World War. Except for the Regina kindergartens, they all succumbed to hard economic times and disappeared from Western schools by the 1920s. They did not reappear until after the Second World War, and it was not until the 1960s that they reached their earlier numbers. A national survey of preschools in the late 1950s by the Canadian Education Association found that the only cities outside Ontario to have kindergartens in public schools were Halifax, Montreal, Regina, Vancouver, Victoria, and Winnipeg (Canadian Education Association 1965). Although the survey omitted a number of kindergartens in small towns in British Columbia, it highlighted the decline of the public school kindergarten in Canada between the world wars, from their strength in the 1890s.

A pattern of early introduction of kindergartens followed by their termination after a fairly short period was repeated in Nipean, Manitoba (1899-1915), Dauphin, Manitoba (1912-5), Lethbridge, Alberta (1907-24), Edmonton (1913-21), and elsewhere on the Prairies. In Moose Jaw, Saskatchewan, a kindergarten was opened in a public school in 1906 and continued until 1934 (Olsen 1955, 49). This pattern was common in many communities in the American Midwest and the Southern and Southeastern states, where the history of kindergartens was described as "here and there" and "now and then" by one historian (*History of the kindergarten movement* 1939, 31). The relatively short life of the kindergarten on the Canadian Prairies meant that kindergarten-teacher training developed late in local normal schools. One of the chronic problems of kindergartens in the west was the difficulty of securing teachers, who were either brought in from Eastern Canada or the United States, or recruited from primary classrooms. Many kindergarten teachers, who were trained in big cities, were reluctant to settle in small, isolated communities (Neely 1946).

However, the main reasons that kindergartens survived or failed were to be found in the decisions of school trustees and administrators, who often acted in pragmatic ways to cope with overcrowding in schools or with budget shortfalls by eliminating aspects of schools regarded as frills. The kindergarten fell into that category, as did other subjects such as music. The kindergartens in western provinces were also vulnerable to the growing criticism of the New Education Movement. Even in Ontario, the Kindergarten Movement had "faltered since the early enthusiasm of the 1880s" (Stamp 1982, 71). Kindergartens had not lived up to their promise as a vehicle for social and educational reform. Nonetheless, as kindergarten attendance declined in Ontario, new kindergartens were still being opened in the west. In Lethbridge, the school board took a pragmatic view. The board viewed the kindergarten as a worthwhile experiment, but at the same time, when it built a separate school for a kindergarten, the board required the architect to make sure that it could easily be converted into a residence (Lethbridge School District No. 51 1985). In the spring of 1907, the district principal in Lethbridge conducted a survey to determine the number of children who would be six years old in September (compulsory school age was seven years). A sufficient number of children were located, and a teacher from Ontario was hired. The class began in temporary quarters in September 1907, while the "Kindergarten School" was being completed. From about 1912, however, enrolment decreased, reaching a low in 1919, when the age of admission for both kindergarten and grade 1 was set at six years. The kindergarten was terminated in 1924, and the Kindergarten School turned into a residence.

Not much is known about the daily operation or curriculum of kindergartens in Western Canada in this period, other than that it was based on a Froebelian understanding of child development, with the addition of Bible lessons, music, games, and manual training. This was the case in the kindergartens in Edmonton, which were established in January 1913 and discontinued in 1921. Sufficient records of the Edmonton kindergartens exist for us to understand some of the reasons for the early introduction and subsequent termination of kindergartens in the west. During the 1910s, Edmonton kindergartens showed a steady increase in numbers, from four in 1913 to eight in 1920. They accepted children from age four to six, but most were five at the beginning of the school year. The program operated in two sessions, from 9 a.m. to 11 a.m. and 1:30 p.m. to 3:30 p.m. Each class was staffed by a trained kindergarten teacher and one assistant. The kindergartens were equipped with Froebel's gifts, as well as motherplay pictures, weaving slats, tapestry needles, scissors, work tiles and tile pegs, crêpe paper, beads, shoe laces, and paper sewing cards. All kindergarten classrooms were equipped with tables with one-inch squares inscribed on the top for use with parquetry squares.

Kindergarten School, Lethbridge, Alberta, c. 1920

Despite their growth in numbers and popularity with parents, the kindergartens never had the full support of the school trustees. Part of the problem was the unpopularity of the man who introduced them into the schools, James McCaig, the superintendent of Edmonton Public Schools. McCaig was known as a proponent of the New Education. He urged the school board to go beyond "the 3 R's" to include music, household science, manual training, and kindergarten. Although the curriculum did expand to include this broader program, the school trustees did not have confidence in McCaig. Furthermore, they felt that the way McCaig had been selected as superintendent had not followed proper procedures. They did not believe he was a good moral example. He frequented beer halls while on the job, and the news of his drinking habits was reported in the local paper. In the end it was his "moral indiscretion" with a teacher that led to his resignation in October 1913.

With McCaig gone, the progressive components of the curriculum were open to fresh debate. In the fall of 1915, the school trustees tried to eliminate music along with the kindergarten, arguing that it was a cost-cutting measure. However, kindergartens were very popular with parents. Attendance had increased to seventy children per session by 1915. The kindergarten program continued. The bid to close the kindergartens was renewed in 1920, brought on by overcrowding in the schools and economic difficulties. Their proposed closure was condemned by community leaders and private citizens in letters to the school board. Kindergartens were promoted as providing early religious instruction and training for the body and mind. Supporters asserted that closing them would be an injustice to children, who were themselves unable to raise objections; that kindergartens were relatively cheap to operate; and that teachers in later grades found children who had attended kindergarten were easier to teach. The trustees responded that they had never approved kindergartens in principle and that they "object[ed] to public money to supply this sort of day nursery" (Support for Kindergartens 1920). This last point was challenged by a mother who replied, "Our Kindergarten teachers are well trained in particular work, and the average Canadian mother has more intelligence than to regard a Kindergarten as a 'Day Nursery'" (Madill 1921). Nevertheless, the kindergartens were closed, and the arguments used by the trustees echoed the reasons heard for and against kindergartens in cities and towns across Canada. On the one hand, supporters promoted kindergartens as a way to give children a good start in life and in schooling. In short, kindergartens were an investment in the future. On the other hand, critics contended that they were costly and that the returns on the investment were not easy to determine.

The growth of kindergartens in public schools was stagnant across

Canada until the 1940s. At the start of the Second World War, the only public school kindergartens outside the province of Ontario were located in Halifax, Montreal, and Regina. By the end of the war, kindergartens had opened in Calgary, Vancouver, Victoria, and Winnipeg. They were created out of a heightened awareness of the welfare of young children that was brought on by wartime conditions, combined with an increase in the number of mothers working for pay. These same conditions stimulated the growth of private kindergartens, nursery schools, day nurseries, and boarding homes. Calgary's first public school kindergarten began as just such a charity endeavour. The Calgary Stagette Club, a philanthropic women's group, founded a preschool in a poor area of the city in 1939, in a move to "keep children off the streets" (Olsen 1955, 59). Called the Tom Thumb Kindergarten, it was located in a classroom in the Calgary School Board's James Shortt School. The Stagette Club lacked the financial resources to maintain it as more than a demonstration program, and they asked the school board to take it over, which it did it in 1941. More kindergartens were opened by the board over the next decade. However, in 1954 all the kindergartens were closed because of overcrowding in schools, a shortage of teachers, and a study by a local academic who concluded that the benefits of kindergarten do not last beyond grade 4 (Seguin 1977, 58). As was the case in Edmonton thirty years before, there was a strong public protest over this decision, but it had little impact on the closings. However, the public school kindergarten programs did have an impact on subsequent developments in preschool education in Calgary. There was a carry-over of standards from public school kindergartens to the private kindergartens that developed to take their place following their closure (Olsen 1955). In addition, the Calgary Public School Board assisted parents in forming community-run kindergartens, which marked the start of a "community kindergarten movement" (Seguin 1977, 59).

In Winnipeg, the Free Kindergarten Association worked for decades to put kindergartens in public schools, but school trustees were never receptive to the idea. Despite this, from the early 1890s, the Association ran kindergartens in two public schools in classrooms rented from the board. Appeals were made to the school board in 1914, and again in 1920, at which time the board agreed to pay the salary of a teacher for one term. This arrangement continued until the end of the decade. The official history of the Winnipeg School Division attributed the slowness of the board to sponsor kindergartens on a larger scale to the usual reasons: it was experimental, there were not enough trained kindergarten teachers, and schools were already crowded (Chafe 1967, 99). The situation changed with the Second World War. The number of public schools with kindergartens in Winnipeg grew from four in 1943 to thirty-seven by 1948

(Chafe 1967, 99). By 1958, there were kindergartens in all schools in the Winnipeg School Division.

In both Vancouver and Victoria, kindergartens opened in a few public schools in 1944 as an intervention program for children from poor families, as well as a concern for the children of wage-earning mothers. In Victoria, kindergartens were originally planned for children of mothers employed in war work. The plan called for kindergartens to follow a day nursery schedule and to be open six days a week, from 7:15 a.m. to 5:30 p.m. The plan was abandoned when the province offered to finance kindergartens as an alternative to the federal wartime day nursery plan. One historian who studied the issue observed that the unusual plan showed "no real understanding or commitment to provision of preschool classes on the part of the Department of Education or the Boards themselves" (Weiss 1976, 49). The kindergartens continued after the war, but on their original limited basis, serving just 1 percent of eligible preschool children in British Columbia by 1948 (Weiss 1976, 52). Provincial and school board support for kindergartens continued to be debated on and off until 1972, when kindergarten classes were made available to all children in the province.

The wartime expansion of kindergartens in Western Canada resulted in their becoming a permanent part of schools in Winnipeg, Vancouver, and Victoria. However, they did not gain a lasting foothold in Alberta, and there were no kindergartens in the Atlantic provinces other than Nova Scotia. The words of the Edmonton superintendent of schools in an earlier time – "Kindergarten in Alberta has not caught on" (Superintendent 1919) – could be applied to many parts of Canada. In the 1950s, developments in public school kindergartens slowed once again. The Unified Kindergarten-Primary Movement and the takeover of kindergarten training by normal schools meant that the kindergarten curriculum was not always easy to distinguish from the first grade level. However, there were some developments in this period. An unusual initiative was the launching of "Kindergarten of the Air" on CBC Radio in 1947. The daily program was developed out of the CBC's "School of the Air," which was an experiment in distance education. The program was modelled on the radio kindergarten in Australia. It fit the general trend in the 1940s of ensuring access to elementary schooling for all children in Canada. The program consisted of songs, stories, and even a rest-time. In a report in *Saturday Night* magazine, Christobel Bendall (1948) described the "world's biggest kindergarten" as a boon to children and mothers. "When Mother turns off the vacuum cleaner and props the broom against the wall during the brief program and sits down at the radio beside Jimmie and Sally, her time is well spent as she grows closer to her children by sharing their program with them" (29). The radio kindergarten aimed to connect home and school via technology – a means that would be repeated using television in the years to come.

Other developments took place on the community level. In British Columbia, a number of small towns and cities opened kindergartens in the 1950s, including Vernon, Prince Rupert, Lake Cowichan, and Courtenay (Weiss 1976). In the Northwest Territories, two public school kindergartens opened in the mid-1950s (Olsen 1955, 48). In Quebec, a few kindergartens were established by the Catholic School Commission in Montreal in the 1950s. Although legislation had been in place in Quebec to establish *les écoles maternelles* since 1915, their widespread introduction into Catholic schools was delayed until the school reforms of the early 1960s (Audet 1971). Until then, most *maternelles* were private, a situation that restricted preschools to children from wealthier families.

Child Care in Canada

Many programs with an educational mandate provided child care to some degree. However, even in infant schools for poor children, it was not the primary role. The Edmonton School Trustees' reference to the child care function of the kindergarten was a call to arms for kindergarten promoters. In the 1890s, day nurseries were established in a few cities in Canada as supports for wage-earning mothers. However, this was not the only reason. At least one was started as a solution to the problem of overcrowding in a school – a move that resembled the creation of an infant school in Newfoundland earlier in the century. It was called the Crèche Nursing Institute (established in 1890), and it was the first day nursery in Toronto.

The desire for universal school attendance in Ontario in the 1880s resulted in the Truancy Act of 1891, which made attendance mandatory for all children aged eight to fourteen. Increased school attendance led to the perception that younger children were left unsupervised while their older siblings were in school. Thus, rescuing young children from the dangers of the streets was a goal of the Toronto kindergartens. The Toronto Board of Education equated the employment of mothers with child neglect, and used this as a rationale for providing kindergartens as a form of publicly supported child care. The inspector's report for 1895 noted that a kindergarten was opened in that year in the College Street School, for "the little ones whose mothers are occupied away from home in earning money, and who well neglect their children" (Toronto Board of Education 1895, 15). As the earlier discussion of kindergarten has shown, parents commonly sent children who were younger than the official age of enrolment to school. Houston and Prentice (1988) cited a nineteenth-century school inspector's report of a visit to an urban school in Ontario, which recorded that "not more than a dozen [children] were older than seven years of age and two-fifths ... were under six" (211). When kindergartens were formed, some of the youngest children in the first grade level moved down the hall into the kindergarten, joined by their even younger siblings. When Hester How was appointed principal of the Elizabeth Street School by Hughes (chief inspector for public schools in Toronto) in 1887, she found that a number of very young children attended the school. She responded by securing a room in the nearby Old Folk's Home as a nursery for the youngest children, which became the Crèche Nursing Institute. Although some sources maintain that the Toronto Board of Education provided funds for her venture, there is no record of support. Nonetheless, sponsoring a nursery was consistent with Hughes's other reform efforts.

Infant child care in English Canada had its origins in the Public Nursery in Toronto in 1857 (Prochner 1996a). In the late 1850s, day care for infants was a novel idea in North America. At mid-century, the day care idea, particularly in the case of infant day care, was as unfamiliar to wage-earning mothers as it was to philanthropists. Neither the Public Nursery nor its model, the Nursery for the Children of Poor Women in New York City (founded in 1854), survived for long in their original form. The Nursery for the Children of Poor Women is best known as the forerunner of a children's hospital. The Toronto Public Nursery was reoriented in the 1870s to become an orphanage for girls. Both the New York and Toronto institutions were originally inspired by the French crèche. In the United States, day care developed an identity that was distinct from other child welfare institutions (e.g., orphan care) earlier than in Canada. The Day Nursery of Philadelphia, founded in 1863, is generally regarded as the first child care centre in North America, after the false start in New York. Industrialization, immigration, and a concern over high infant mortality in cities in the Northeastern United States provided the conditions for the development of institutions similar to the one in Philadelphia. Day nurseries were part of a broad social reform movement – known historically as the Progressive Movement – aimed at improving the lives of children and their families, which included the establishment of settlement houses, charity kindergartens, and children's aid societies.

Day nurseries were a compromise between the nineteenth-century ideal of mothers nurturing children at home and institutional care in an orphanage. The increased popularity of nurseries in the 1880s may also have been linked to revival of the crèche in France. However, except for the occasional use of the term "crèche" in the names of institutions, the leaders of the Day Nursery Movement in North America largely disregarded their French counterparts. Instead, as the day nursery in North America was reconstructed to meet the needs of both its clients and its benefactors, it created its own history. Institutions that included "crèche" in their name, notably Edmonton Crèche, Vancouver Crèche, West End Crèche (Toronto), Victoria Crèche (Toronto), and Hamilton Crèche, could not even agree on its spelling or pronunciation. Crèche was variously written as "créche" or "creche" and was often unaccented. Its pronunciation was anglicized, and pronounced *crashe* or *creach*. Journalist Joseph Tinsley related the naming of the Hamilton Crèche in the 1890s: "'But we should give the undertaking a name,' remarked a lady. Many names were suggested – only one chosen. The Crèche appeared to be the favorite title. The news soon spread in the neighborhood that a crèche for children was coming. A crotchety old bachelor remarked: 'A good name, too. The kids will be screeching all day'" (Tinsley 1904).

By 1892, there were 90 day nurseries in the United States, located primarily in the industrialized Northeast, and by 1898 there were 175. The day nursery was sufficiently established as a charity that in 1892, a Conference of Day Nurseries was organized in New York City to discuss the future of the movement. At the second meeting, held in Boston in 1897, a decision was made to create a National Federation of Day Nurseries. In contrast, in English Canada there were three day nurseries by 1892, and only one more by the close of the century: Montreal Day Nursery (1887), Victoria Crèche (1890), East End Day Nursery (1892) in Toronto, and the Women's Christian Temperance Union Crèche (1895) in Hamilton. The delayed development of day nurseries in Canada had important implications for their future. Because of their small number and regional base, Canadian nurseries did not have a national organization to represent them. As a result, individual nurseries joined either the National Society for Day Nurseries in England or the National Federation of Day Nurseries in the United States. It was natural, therefore, that in the 1910s, when the managers of the West End Crèche in Toronto sought a model for their work, they looked to Detroit, Chicago, New York, and London, rather than to the few sister institutions in Canada. As a result, no particular Canadian approach to day nursery work existed (Prochner 1994).

There are several reasons for the slow growth of day nurseries in Canada in the nineteenth century. The most critical is that most cities in Canada did not have the correct combination of population and number of poor wage-earning mothers to provide the basis for a nursery. Day nurseries were an urban invention. A modest expansion of nurseries in Canada took place during the period from 1908 to 1912, as more cities approached or surpassed a population of 100,000. By 1912, six of the seven largest cities in Canada had at least one nursery. However, the need for a day nursery was not based solely on the presence of a large number of wage-earning mothers. In her study of women factory workers in Paris, Ontario, Parr

(1992) noted that child care was arranged privately between neighbours or relatives. Day nurseries were a response by philanthropists to the needs of poor families, which were made worse by city life. Despite its modest size, Halifax had a sufficiently large number of poorer citizens to warrant the Jost Mission's establishing a nursery on its premises in 1910. In some cities in Canada, other institutions provided day care, further inhibiting the growth of day nurseries. Even small cities and towns often had more than one orphanage, which provided short-term as well as permanent child care. And as we have seen, in the 1880s and 1890s, kindergartens met the need for child care for older children.

Child Care at the Turn of the Century

The Day Nursery and Industrial School in Montreal was the first institution in Canada to be established on the lines of the Progressive Era day nursery. The Montreal Day Nursery, as it was later named in its incorporation in 1899, opened in 1887. Originally affiliated with the Montreal Young Women's Christian Association, it provided temporary care for children aged three weeks to ten years. Temporary care, however, did not necessarily mean daily care. A limited number of children boarded by the week while their mothers were ill or employed as live-in servants. On its first day of operation, the nursery admitted only six children. Growth was slow and by 1899, it was still serving fewer than twenty children per day.

A feature of most nurseries in the late nineteenth century was that, unlike the orphan asylum or the religious *asile* in Montreal, they operated on a very small scale. In terms of meeting the needs of greater numbers of working mothers, *asiles* were far more successful. The first *asile* was established in Montreal in 1858. Four other *asiles* were established over the next thirty years, all in Montreal (Cross 1973; Dumont-Johnson 1980). They were popularly used by working-class francophone mothers. The largest cared for as many as 400 children each day from the 1860s to the 1880s. However, *asiles* accepted only children older than three. Wage-earning mothers of younger children had few options for temporary institutional care other than orphanages in nineteenth-century Montreal, and the Montreal Day Nursery played a unique role. It was typical of pre–First World War nurseries in North America. In its early years, it borrowed heavily from American ideas. In its combination of nursery and industrial school, it resembled the Troy Day Home in Troy, New York (the Day Home began as an industrial school and only later expanded to include day nursery work). It served a wide range of ages under one roof. Reasoning that it needed to serve both mothers and children, the nursery opened an employment bureau for charwomen. And as charity organization societies grew in influence in the early twentieth century, it came to see itself as part of the larger social welfare system. This uniformity of the day nursery was the result of what Neil Sutherland (1976) called the transnational nature of the Progressive Reform Movement.

Victoria Crèche in Toronto (the name given Crèche Nursing Institute when it incorporated in 1905) had a mission that was typical of the Progressive Era Day Nursery Movement: "To provide a home during the day for children whose mothers have to go out to work; to assist in securing day work for the mothers needing it; to encourage habits of thrift among the parents and children, and to enable Christian and charitably disposed women to come in touch with the home life of the mothers and children and take such action as may from time to time seem best to brighten their homes" (Victoria Crèche 1905, 1). By the late 1910s the rationale for the crèche had long since changed from easing the burden on public schools to the more familiar contention that wage-earning mothers frequently sacrificed their children's well-being. In the annual report for 1917, Lady Emily Moss, then president of the Crèche, suggested, "Many a mother, forced by necessity to become the wage earner of the family, would be obliged to choose between locking her little ones in a cheerless room, exposed to many dangers, or turning them into the street during her enforced absence, were it not for the Day Nursery" (Victoria Crèche 1917, 3).

The only competition for the Victoria Crèche in Toronto in the 1890s was the East End Day Nursery, founded in 1892. The East End Day Nursery originally shared quarters with the Sackville Street Mission. Its objectives, as outlined in annual reports, were word for word the same as those of the Crèche cited above. The East End Day Nursery also professed a role in preventing social problems. The 1905 annual report noted, "We come to the aid of people who, perhaps, might become paupers and possibly their children criminals" (East End Day Nursery 1905, 10). The East End Day Nursery was more heavily used than Victoria Crèche. In its first year, it cared for an average of forty-two children per day in a single room. In 1893, the nursery rented a house on Sackville Street and was locally known as the Sackville Street Crèche. In 1905, the managers purchased a house at 28 River Street (it was then called the River Street Crèche), which was the site of the nursery until it closed in 1959 to make room for a housing project for low-income families. The aim in providing a larger facility was "to turn no one away" (East End Day Nursery 1906, 10). The high number of children who attended the nursery indicates that this goal was achieved. Although its average daily admission was 80 in the 1910s, a record 146 children were cared for on a single day. The ever-increasing number of children in the nursery was referred to as "Development of the Work." The number of days of care increased from 13,062 in 1905 to 25,005 in 1909. A

East End Day Nursery playground, Toronto, 1909

two-storey addition was constructed in 1910 to make room for even more children. In 1912, the East End Day Nursery opened a second facility on Main Street near Danforth Avenue (Danforth Day Nursery).

A fourth nursery opened in Canada during the nineteenth century in Hamilton, Ontario, in 1895. The Crèche, as it was first called, was founded by A.M. Waters, a member of the Dominion Woman's Christian Temperance Union (WCTU) in Hamilton. The Crèche was administered by a board of twenty women who distinguished themselves by refusing to accept financial assistance from the province (they did not agree with the governing provincial party) or, later, from the Community Fund (they did not wish to be "guided entirely by its dictates" [Hunter 1933]). The Hamilton Crèche was unique at the time in that it was not associated directly with a particular religious denomination. Rather, it was part of the work of the WCTU. The WCTU was established in the United States in the early 1870s and grew throughout the 1880s and 1890s under the leadership of Frances Willard. While the WCTU was originally known for its crusade against drinking establishments, it later turned its attention to social programs. Willard's famous slogan, "Do Everything," inspired members to run a variety of programs for poor children and families. The WCTU shared the fear of institutions that was prevalent at the time and organized foster care for homeless children. It promoted kindergartens for poor children through the sponsorship of Free Kindergartens, the first of which was organized in San Francisco in 1880 (Bordin 1981). The early WCTU kindergartens offered full-day programs and thus resembled day nurseries for older children.

The Hamilton WCTU was formed in 1876 as part of the initial Union expansion. In the early 1890s, the Hamilton group was active in a number of social programs that targeted women and children, including visits to hospitals, jails, the House of Refuge, and the Industrial Home. The Hamilton Crèche was an extension of this work. It was jointly administered by the local branch and the provincial office of the WCTU. It initially cared for children from three weeks to six years old. It provided two unique services. One was the provision of rooms within the crèche for "poor, weak women to gain their strength, who have no friends and have just returned from the hospital," as the *Hamilton Spectator* put it, in an article entitled "In aid of needy mothers: A good work inaugurated by the Hamilton WCTU," 30 March 1896. The service was well used, and the Crèche provided 622 nights of shelter in 1904, which increased to 1,720 in 1905, or an average of five women each night. The second unusual feature, in contrast with Toronto day nurseries, was its flexible hours of operation. The Hamilton Crèche was open from 7 a.m. to 6 p.m., with longer hours available in the summer to permit mothers to work picking fruit in the nearby orchards (Tinsley 1904). The availability of lodging and meals for destitute women at the Hamilton crèche highlighted the desire of the early day nursery founders to provide a range of social programs in a single institution. Thus the nineteenth-century day nursery in Canada was a place for women and children to seek assistance in times of need, and was not created solely to provide temporary care for young children.

The Expansion of Day Nurseries

The second phase in child care development in Canada was marked by the opening of nurseries in cities not located in Ontario or Quebec. New immigrants and rural-to-urban migration placed tremendous strain on health and social services in the rapidly growing cities, where these services had been developed for much smaller numbers of poor and needy families. The same conditions that sparked the development of charity kindergartens in Winnipeg and public school kindergartens in Montreal and Toronto led to the opening of nurseries. In the early twentieth century, a day nursery was part of the usual repertoire of services offered by private charities. It was relatively inexpensive to operate, as opposed to an orphanage, for example. All it required was the rent or purchase of a building, which was usually inexpensive real estate. The furnishings were sparse, consisting mainly of donations or cast-offs from the homes of wealthy families. Staff expenses were minimal, with the key person being the matron, who often also served as cook, housekeeper, and caregiver. Some of the nurseries founded in this period were the Edmonton Crèche (1908); West End Crèche, Toronto (1909); Winnipeg Day Nursery (1909); the nursery in the Jost Mission in Halifax (1910); Ottawa Day Nursery (1911); and Vancouver Crèche (1912). The early years of some of these nurseries are described below.

In December 1908, the Local Council of Women in Edmonton opened a crèche for children of wage-earning mothers, with the ambitious aim of receiving "all neglected, ill-treated or homeless children brought to its door, as temporary or permanent residence, as need may be," as described by the *Edmonton Daily Bulletin,* 5 December 1908 (Lightfoot, Derksen, and Campbell 1997). The following year, Alberta established the Department for Neglected Children, which required every town with a population over 10,000 to have a children's shelter (Bosetti Piche 1990, 105). In Edmonton, as elsewhere in the province, women's clubs worked with local Children's Aid Societies to fill this requirement. Although little is known about this early crèche, the 1908 venture exemplifies the trend in the first decade of this century for women's clubs to make day nursery work a key component of their service to the community. The Edmonton Local Council of Women had only just reorganized in 1908, after being inactive for a number of years. Its members included prominent Alberta women such as Emily Murphy and, later, Nellie McClung. The honorary president of the Local Council of Women was the wife of the lieutenant governor of Alberta. One of its first efforts in community service was to create a sub-committee to study the need for a nursery. By 1914, the Edmonton Crèche and Children's Home had largely given up providing daily care.

In 1929, a new Edmonton Crèche and Day Nursery Society was organized by the Local Council of Women as a form of practical work in child welfare, under the leadership of Lady Rodney. By this time, the memory of the first crèche had completely faded, and Lady Rodney was credited with forming the first nursery in Edmonton. The Edmonton Crèche and Day Nursery, which opened in 1930, was, like the earlier crèche, notable for having support from the highest levels of Alberta's political and social élite. Lady Rodney and her husband, Lord Rodney, were wealthy British immigrants and ranchers in Alberta. Lady Rodney was well known for her support of children in the province and her leadership in the Girl Guide Movement. The honorary president of the crèche was the wife of a lieutenant governor of Alberta, and the honorary vice-presidents included the premier, the minister of health, the mayor, and the archbishop of Edmonton (Edmonton Crèche Society 1931).

The Edmonton Crèche and Day Nursery was established to fill the growing need for daytime care for children of wage-earning mothers. Unlike the original 1908 crèche, the new nursery focused on temporary care. Its aim was the following: "To keep intact the home where the mother is the only wage earner, or where the father's income is not sufficient to nourish and clothe the children ... To keep such families off relief, and help them to remain self respecting human beings, thus saving the taxpayers many hundreds of dollars annually" (Edmonton Crèche Society 1931, 4). Lady Rodney and the board of directors convinced city officials of the value of the crèche, and the city provided an operating grant and the use of a building. From its start in 1930 until its reorganization in 1966, the crèche was headed by a registered nurse. The first director was Edith World, who investigated each home prior to admitting a child. The nursery accepted children aged nine days to six and a half years, although they were occasionally older. It was open between the hours of 8:00 a.m. and 6:30 p.m. Throughout the 1930s, the attendance was stable, but there were rarely more than eighteen children per day. The crèche did not have an educational program until a kindergarten was started for the oldest children in the 1940s.

In Winnipeg, a day nursery was organized by the Mothers' Association of Winnipeg. The Association was formed in 1906 by a group of women interested in promoting issues related to families. They lobbied for Mother's Allowances in Manitoba and also played a role in the creation of a local playground association. The day nursery they sponsored opened on 12 March 1909, several months after the founding of the original

Mothers' Association Day Nursery (now known as Day Nursery Centre), Winnipeg, c. 1910

Edmonton Crèche; it was an extension of the group's practical work on behalf of women and children. The nursery moved several times before settling in a house at 378 Stella Avenue in 1911, where it remained until 1971, under the name Stella Day Nursery. It was located next door to the Methodist Stella Mission, which operated a charity kindergarten for many years. It still exists under the name the Day Nursery Center, which it assumed in 1953. As was the case with day nurseries in other cities, it opened in the midst of a tremendous growth in population. Services for the poor expanded rapidly to fill a range of educational, health, and social needs: the Winnipeg Children's Hospital, the Stella Avenue Mission, and the Juvenile Court all had their start in 1909. A survey by the Canadian Council on Child and Family Welfare concluded that by the 1930s, Winnipeg had the "heaviest comparative institutional provision" west of Montreal (Whitton 1934, 43).

The Ottawa Day Nursery also opened in 1909. It began as a service of a settlement house on Rideau Street, and became a separate institution in 1916; its development was typical of nurseries in the period. The managers quickly settled into the business of fund-raising, and the main issues centred on the cost of staff, sickness of children, and the number of children that could be accommodated. At the time the nursery separated from the settlement house, a trained kindergarten teacher was hired. Like the WCTU Crèche in Hamilton, the Ottawa nursery served as a temporary shelter for both mothers and their children, and offered long-term care for children in emergency circumstances. The nursery had substantial financial support from the Fleck family, and in 1932, the Andrew W. Fleck Memorial Building was opened on George Street, with a capacity of seventy-six children. The nursery never enrolled this number until the Second World War, when it reached a peak of seventy-seven children in 1943.

In Halifax, a nursery was established in 1910 as a service of the Jost Mission. The nursery was managed by the mission's Women's Committee. The committee operated an employment bureau for mothers and a nursery for their children, as well as a shelter for homeless children. The nursery accepted children aged three months to six years, with the majority under the age of two. It operated on a very small scale: in the fall of 1918, the daily attendance was generally four or five children. Low attendance was the rule rather than the exception, and the nursery rarely reached its capacity of forty children. In 1918, despite the small number of children served, the Women's Committee expanded the service to include a kindergarten in the afternoon, mothers meetings, and a girls club. The average daily attendance in the nursery increased to ten in 1919, and then to twenty by 1920. The kindergarten was generally well attended when it was in operation, but it was open sporadically, with periods of several months

Ottawa Day Nursery, c. 1920

passing when no teacher was available or when none was hired as a means of cutting costs. In the early 1930s, the managers expanded their services to include care for school-aged children during the lunch hour.

In 1910, a committee of the Associated Charities of Vancouver opened a day nursery, which became known as the Vancouver Crèche. According to Lilian Nelson, who was a city-employed social worker and superintendent of the crèche for many years, the original idea stemmed from a shortage of domestic labourers (British Columbia Preschool Teachers' Association 1974). The crèche's employment bureau was designed to fill this need. The Vancouver Crèche was similar to the Edmonton Crèche in having gained the support of the city. The Medical Health Officer for Vancouver, Dr. Underhill, was impressed with the fledgling crèche, and he was convinced that it could play a role in improving child health. According to Underhill, Vancouver had the highest rate of infant mortality in Canada. Infant mortality had recently received considerable attention in the United States, as the focus of the newly created Children's Bureau under the directorship of Julia Lathrop (Lindenmeyer 1995). As a progressive health reformer who shared this concern, Underhill successfully lobbied to have the City of Vancouver finance the construction of a building for the crèche on Haro Street. When it opened in late 1914, it was only the second nursery in Canada to be housed in a building constructed for the sole purpose of child care. The new West End Crèche of Toronto was the first, having opened in April of the same year. By 1916, a marked drop in attendance due to a shortage of employment for domestic workers led Dr. Underhill to recommend that the crèche be moved to

Vancouver Children's Hospital, formerly the Vancouver Crèche Building, Haro Street, 1919

make room for a children's hospital. The building was deemed "unnecessarily elaborate for [its] present purpose" (*Report on Infant's Hospital* n.d., 1), and it was taken over by the Vancouver General Hospital in February 1917. The crèche's new, more modest quarters were in the Relief Department, in space previously occupied by the Old People's Home.

Although the Vancouver Crèche is often portrayed as a model of progressive reform in child care in Canada (Schulz 1978), it benefited only for a brief time from the enthusiastic support of Dr. Underhill. Eventually, it became solidly entrenched as part of the City of Vancouver Relief Department. While it was always managed as a welfare service, when it was relocated, all new mothers using the crèche were required to have a needs assessment. Even the morning play group organized by Lilian Nelson in 1917 – known as the first preschool in British Columbia – was under the direction of a city-employed social worker. The Vancouver crèche closed in the early 1930s, when the economic depression made it difficult for women to find day work. This was a problem common in some other cities in Canada. The WCTU Crèche (Hamilton) and the Hamilton End Day Nursery also closed their doors. Fund-raising was difficult, and mothers used the nurseries only on a sporadic basis whenever work was available. By the time the WCTU Crèche closed in the early

1930s, it was caring for only three or four children a day (Hunter 1933). Attendance at the Vancouver Crèche decreased by over 50 percent from 1931 to 1932, and the Relief Department did not want to continue bearing the cost. The service was adopted as a project of the Graduate Nurses Association of Vancouver and transformed into a system of foster homes for the children of wage-earning mothers beginning in the summer of 1932. "Foster day care," the term used to describe supervised family home day care or child minding, was considered to be a more economical alternative to centre-based care. In addition, it was better suited to the changing ideas concerning out-of-home care for very young children.

Day Nurseries and the Second World War

The stagnant growth in the number of day nurseries in Canada in the 1930s was dramatically changed by the outbreak of the Second World War. In 1939, most day nurseries in Canada were operated by charities. In 1942, the federal government initiated a child care scheme as an incentive and support for mothers of young children to work in war-related industries (Prochner 1996b). The new demand for child care was created by the fivefold increase in the number of wage-earning women in Canada, from 200,000 in 1939 to 1,000,000 by 1944. The existing day nurseries soon filled to capacity and had long waiting lists. Moreover, their mandate was to serve children of poor wage-earning mothers. Social welfare councils and community groups called for a government-supported child care program. The most vocal and best-organized lobby was in Ontario, where the Welfare Council of Toronto and District sponsored needs assessments under the direction of its executive director, Bessie Touzel. Touzel interviewed 100 mothers on the waiting list of the West End Crèche in Toronto. She found that most families functioned with a patchwork system of child care, and that in some cases, children were left alone during the day in potentially dangerous situations. The government of Ontario responded in April 1942 by amending its Public Welfare Act to include support for day nurseries. In July of the same year, the Canadian government initiated a cost-sharing scheme with the provinces, called the Authorization of Agreements with Provinces for the Care of Children (Canada 1942). In the end, only Ontario and Quebec entered into the agreement. Wider participation was restricted by the requirement that a percentage of mothers who used the nurseries be employed in essential war work, as well as by a lack of interest by other provincial governments and, in some cases, weak support from community welfare councils.

Because the wartime nurseries were tied to labour recruitment, the program was administered by the Women's Division of the National Selective Service in the Ministry of Labour. At the provincial level, the nurseries

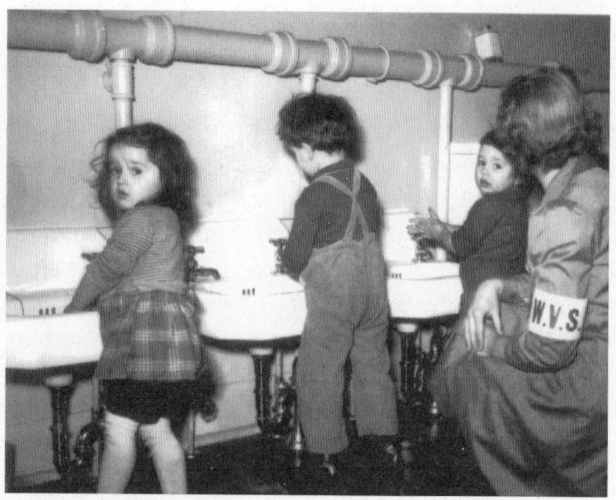

Children washing hands, Wartime Day Nurseries, Toronto, c. 1942

Teacher and child, Wartime Day Nurseries, Toronto, c. 1942

Children doing crafts, Wartime Day Nurseries, Toronto, c. 1942

Helen E. Armitage, Wartime Day Nurseries, Unit no. 13, Toronto, 1943

were managed by the Day Nurseries Branch in the Department of Public Welfare in Ontario, and by the Department of Day Nurseries in the Ministry of Health in Quebec, under the guidance of provincial committees made up of bureaucrats, community members, and local experts. The director of the Quebec nurseries was Elphège Lalonde, associate director of the Venereal Disease Division in the Ministry of Health. In Ontario, Dorothy Millichamp of the Institute of Child Study, University of Toronto, directed nurseries at the provincial level. Between 1942 and 1945, twenty-eight wartime nurseries were established in Ontario, and six in Quebec. The Quebec nurseries were controversial and mostly underused throughout the three years of their existence. At the end of the war, the newly elected government of Maurice Duplessis, which viewed the nurseries as a threat to families and Quebec nationalism, terminated the agreement with the Canadian government. All the Quebec nurseries closed in October 1945. In Ontario, community and consumer groups successfully lobbied to keep the nurseries open until June 1946. Twelve former wartime nurseries continued to operate after this time with joint municipal-provincial funding under the Ontario Day Nurseries Act (passed in March 1946).

The wartime nurseries served relatively few families. However, their influence on child care in Canada was considerable. For the first time, group child care was promoted as a normal support for families. "Share Their Care, Mrs. Warworker, with Your Able and Willing Helper, the Day Nursery," read a headline of the day (Ryan 1942). The National Film Board produced a film entitled *Before They Are Six,* which extolled the benefits of day nurseries for children and mothers: children would flourish under the guidance of well-trained teachers, and mothers could focus their full attention on their work, knowing their children were safe and happy. The film includes scenes of children at play in the training centre for Ontario wartime nurseries in Toronto. A newsletter produced by the Day Nursery Branch mused that mothers may even have sought employment in war industries in order to qualify for day nursery care for their children. The photographs on pages 52 and 53 were taken at the two Wartime Day Nurseries in Toronto. The teachers are wearing Women's Volunteer Services armbands in the two photographs.

Child Care in the 1950s

In wartime, the day nursery was not a charity service – a last resort for families in dire circumstances – but a day-long nursery school. Press reports added to this transformation by frequently calling the nurseries "wartime nursery schools." The infusion of nursery education principles into the day nursery meant that the service became oriented toward child rather than adult needs (Varga 1993). Although the wartime nurseries program did not start this process, it hastened its development and, in Ontario, entrenched it within public policy. The increased need for child care during wartime highlighted the ideological differences within the Day Nursery Movement, despite attempts to forge professional partnerships. Nursery educators saw wartime child care as an opportunity to promote their expertise and philosophy of early education on a national stage. Bessie Touzel believed that the "nursery school [movement] turned to day care to meet its goals" (23 March 1992, interview with author). On the other hand, the leadership of the major organizations representing day care in North America, the US-based National Association of Day Nurseries and, later, the Child Welfare League of America, strongly resisted the idea of child care as a service for wage-earning mothers. They argued that only careful social investigation by skilful technicians could determine whether child care was the appropriate option for a family. The insistence on a casework approach meant that the Child Welfare League of America, the most powerful group representing child care in the early 1940s, was at odds with the wartime function of nurseries as a service for mothers working in war industries. During the war years, the Child Welfare League of America adopted a marginally more conciliatory stance toward child care. After the war and the end of federal funding for wartime nurseries in Canada and the United States, child care settled back into its former social welfare orientation. However, the war experience and the absence of a strong advocacy movement in the 1950s had a profound impact on subsequent developments in child care. The old day nurseries run by private charities were open to new scrutiny. Some found a new mission, whereas others simply closed their doors. Those that did remain open witnessed the invasion of a new cadre of experts. Dozens of teachers and administrators of the former wartime nurseries – many of them nursery educators and child development experts – assumed leadership positions in research, teaching, and government. They proceeded to construct nursery schools within the walls of child care centres, calling them "full-day nursery schools." The client group of day nurseries also changed, as nursery educators and social workers moved to restrict child care to children over the age of two and a half or three.

The bias against very young children in day nurseries stemmed from the well-documented trend in psychiatry in the 1940s, which emphasized the importance of a child's secure relationship with his or her mother for healthy emotional development. Group child care was also thought to be overstimulating for young children. The recommended alternative to parental care for children under the age of two and a half or three was foster day care under the calm and gentle supervision of a "day-time mother." This was the model adopted by the Graduate Nurses Association when it took over the Vancouver Crèche in 1932. Critics did not make a distinction between the effects of different types of institutional care on human development. Orphanages and maternity hospitals, caring for hundreds of babies, were regarded in the same unsatisfactory light as small-scale, neighbourhood day nurseries. The central factors were the age of the children and the time they spent away from their mothers.

The reorientation of day nurseries was encouraged by the Child Welfare League of America, which participated in social surveys in a number of cities in Canada and the United States in the late 1940s and early 1950s. Study after study found that day nurseries were inefficient social agencies, with inadequately trained staff, and a lax approach to casework. Other surveys were conducted by local councils of social agencies or by national organizations such as the Canadian Council on Child and Family Welfare. Attempts to reform day nurseries into modern social service agencies were fraught with problems. The introduction of a social work orientation meant that mothers applying for child care were required to demonstrate a need beyond economic necessity. This moved day nurseries away from their traditional position of accepting all mothers who came to their door. For decades, the managers of the nurseries were volunteers who had been involved in the day-to-day operation of the nurseries. The transfer of management to professionals trained in social work or nursery education was a difficult process. Moreover, as day nurseries came to be seen as part of a network of social services for families, the nurseries needed to work cooperatively with other child welfare services – for example, mental health clinics, hospitals, and other day nurseries. For many private charities used to managing their own affairs, this was the most difficult task of all.

The managers of the West End Crèche in Toronto saw the problem as the "integration of state social services with private charity" (West End Crèche 1951, 3). After the war, the West End Crèche continued to make internal changes and by the early 1950s, offered several full-day nursery school programs. All the staff were highly trained, with even assistants having university degrees. In 1947, Margaret Lovatt, previously director of the Protestant Children's Home, was hired as the director of the West End Crèche. Under Lovatt, the crèche made several moves to provide therapeutically based care for children with special needs, in addition to its service for children of wage-earning mothers. Special-needs children included those with hearing and speech problems, cerebral palsy, childhood schizophrenia, and visual disabilities. Lovatt also worked with the Canadian National Institute for the Blind to arrange for the first blind child to be admitted in December 1949. On a number of occasions, doctors referred children to the crèche in the belief that they would benefit from the social experience of being with children in a normalized setting.

The managers of the West End Crèche saw these changes – the use of highly trained staff, the raising of the age of admission, and the inclusion of special-needs children – as a suitable response to push for the modernization of its services. However, by the mid-1950s enrolments had decreased and waiting lists had disappeared; the West End Crèche operated at 60 percent of its capacity. The problem was attributed to the existence of twelve other nurseries within a two-kilometre radius, and the managers realized that if the crèche did not specialize its service they would become redundant. In the end, the West End Crèche chose to undertake a day treatment program for children with childhood schizophrenia. The next summer the West End Crèche admitted on a trial basis a three-year-old girl who had been diagnosed with childhood schizophrenia. This initial experience evolved into a day treatment centre for emotionally disturbed children.

Unlike the West End Crèche, many nurseries in Canada continued to function in a custodial mode, despite the addition of nursery school and kindergarten programs. In hard times, professional teaching staff, who were more costly to employ, were laid off. In some cases, they were replaced by volunteers or untrained staff; in others, the kindergarten or nursery school was simply closed. The Edmonton Crèche exemplifies a day nursery that remained relatively unchanged from its start in 1930 to its restructuring in the 1960s. In 1955, the staff roster of the Edmonton Crèche included just one teacher. The remaining eight staff members were the matron, a cook, five nursemaids, and a laundress. The children's day consisted of long periods of unstructured play, and routines such as washing, eating, and sleeping. Considerable attention was paid to the health of the children, and regular inspections were conducted. The Edmonton Crèche continued to accept infants in the years following the Second World War, a practice that did not seem to be controversial. In 1955, the crèche cared for babies as young as two weeks. An ongoing problem, and an indication of the general neglect of the crèche, was the state of the city-owned building in which it was housed. The average daily attendance had risen from eighteen children in the early years to sixty in 1947, and seventy by 1950. As the numbers increased, the city undertook a series of renovations to ease overcrowding. As a result, the original building, which began life as a private residence, was surrounded by various additions, constructed in 1945, 1947, and 1949. Long before the problem of overcrowding, the building was known to be inadequate for use as a day nursery. In 1944, the city passed a motion to help the Crèche Society construct new quarters. No action was taken, however, and the building continued to deteriorate. Finally, in 1951 the fire marshall condemned the makeshift structure. At this time an Association of Crèche Parents was formed to

Edmonton Crèche exterior, 1951

protest against the demolition of the old crèche before plans were made for a move to better accommodation. The city appeared to respond to criticism, and an architect was commissioned to draw up plans. The superintendent of the Welfare Department recommended that the new crèche use the Ontario Day Nursery Act as a guide for construction. However, the city backed away from its promise, and in March 1952, the nursery moved into

Children doing crafts at the Edmonton Crèche, 1957

the city-owned Family Allowance Building on 102nd Avenue. Despite protests from some parents that the site was inconvenient, the number of children grew in the new quarters, to a daily average of 110 in 1959.

The move was followed by the withdrawal of support for day nursery work by the private charity that had governed the crèche for three decades. While the increase in families using the crèche clearly showed that there was a real need for the service, the board of directors interpreted it differently, and in April 1964, decided to close the crèche. The directors believed that it no longer served the original need of keeping families together and off the welfare rolls. Instead, it catered to mothers who worked by choice. They charged that "such a family is maintaining a higher standard of living at public expense," as reported by the *Edmonton Journal* in an article entitled "Crèche Board Explains Closure," 15 May 1964. Public protest did not convince the board to sustain the crèche. However, the city and the United Community Fund agreed to continue the service, and it reopened in June 1964 as the Community Day Nursery. The nursery had a new board, and the crèche was exposed to scrutiny by professionals in the fields of social welfare and early education. The federal Canada Assistance Plan of 1966 provided the impetus for a complete restructuring. Ironically, the new climate of support for child care as a preventive social service in the mid-1960s enabled the crèche to resume its original mission as a support for "needy families." The crèche was resurrected under a new name in 1966, with yet another new board of directors, under the overall direction of social worker Howard Clifford, who was employed by the City of Edmonton as the first director of Day Care Services.

The Mothers' Association Day Nursery in Winnipeg was also relatively isolated from trends in the day nursery field in the 1940s and 1950s, leading to the observation, "Day Nursery work in Winnipeg does not even compare favourably with Nursery Work of 15 years ago in the east ... There has never been in Winnipeg a Day Nursery as we know it in the east" (Mothers' Association Day Nursery 1953). Until 1917, and the opening of the Jeanne D'Arc Day Nursery by the Franciscan Sisters, the Mothers' Association Day Nursery was the only nursery in the city. In 1934, at the time of the survey of social services by the Canadian Council on Child and Family Welfare, these remained the only two nurseries (Whitton 1934). The job of modernizing the nursery was given to Gretta Brown. Brown, who was originally from Winnipeg, was one of the first graduates from the St. George's School for Child Study in Toronto. She briefly held the post of director of the nursery school program at the West End Crèche in Toronto, before being appointed director of the crèche, a position she held from 1931 to 1938. After returning to Winnipeg, she was involved in nursery school work as director of two schools located in local United Churches.

As a local expert, she was asked by the Welfare Planning Council to sit on a committee studying the nursery, and she ended up chairing the committee. In August 1953, she accepted the position of director of the reorganized day nursery, a position she held until her retirement in 1976. Brown organized the new nursery to operate on "Canadian nursery school standards," which were drawn from the Institute of Child Study (Varga 1997). Under Brown, the Mothers' Association Day Nursery offered an extended nursery school program in a day nursery setting, and it was the most influential and progressive child care centre in Western Canada for many years.

The Jost Mission nursery in Halifax continued to be what Simmons (1984) called an "arena for missionary effort" (19) well into the 1950s. Its growth away from the "tradition of 19th century women's Christian charity" (13) was limited by the lack of alternative models in Eastern Canada. In 1955, the Jost Mission nursery was the only one in the Atlantic provinces, and it was increasingly marginalized in relation to other social services in Halifax. The local council of social agencies was concerned that the reason for the low numbers was that the nursery turned mothers away in accordance with an overly strict admission policy. During the 1940s, the nursery did not experience the growth in the number of children that, for example, the Edmonton Crèche did. Rather, the enrolment declined markedly from the 1930s. In March 1943, the daily average was ten children. In May 1943, the nursery actually closed for two weeks when it was unable to find staff, who could find better paying work elsewhere. The program for the children was minimal, and one Halifax social agency called the nursery at the Mission a "sort of corral" for children (The Jost Mission 1959). Most mothers using the nursery from the late 1940s were divorced, single, new to the city, or their husbands were unemployed. Many were from areas outside Halifax, having arrived from Cape Breton or the South Shore of Nova Scotia to look for work. The experience of one family with the Jost Mission nursery, over a three-year period, highlights its role as a form of temporary relief. In November 1947, a man inquired about leaving his son at the nursery. His wife was looking for work in Halifax as a waitress. The boy was not admitted until the following March, when the father found work in a factory near the Mission. In June, the child was withdrawn. He was readmitted just before Christmas, while the mother, who was now pregnant, visited her husband in the hospital. In July 1950, the mother worked at the nursery for a short period, while her husband looked after the children at home. She later found employment as a domestic through the Jost Mission. This approach to day nursery work did not fit the new integrated model of day care as a social service that was promoted in the 1950s. The Halifax Council of Social Agencies believed that the Mission was "interested in the children, they want to do a good job, on the very limited scale they are pursuing to-day. [But] they do not see what a Day Nursery should be, what community responsibilities they have, or any responsibility for the future" (The Jost Mission 1959).

Conclusion

The 1950s saw the introduction of programs in new locations and of new types, in addition to reforms that took place in some of the established nurseries (see Chapter 6 for current types of child care). Child care and nursery school programs were opened for the first time in cities that had previously not had such provisions for preschool-aged children. In 1954, the first nursery school in Newfoundland was opened in St. David's Church Hall in St. John's (Sharp 1974, 64). Other programs were established to meet specialized needs, such as the Metro Toronto Association for the Mentally Retarded Nursery Schools and a nursery school for children with cerebral palsy sponsored by the Junior League in Toronto.

Similar programs were opened in communities across Canada, as the preschool field expanded its scope to include all children. Kindergarten education was rejuvenated in the 1960s, as attention was directed toward the role of schools as a force in reducing social inequities. The Montessori system was rediscovered and introduced into some kindergarten programs. Junior kindergartens were opened for children from "culturally disadvantaged" families; these kindergartens aimed to give children a head start on schooling. French immersion kindergartens were established in Montreal, Ottawa, and Toronto. Across Canada, kindergartens were influenced by the British Infant School and open education (Canadian Education Association 1965, 1972).

The gradual restructuring of child care as a social service, which began in the 1950s, was given a considerable boost by the introduction of federal funding in the form of the Canada Assistance Plan in 1966 (see Chapter 9). At this time, child care became a national concern, and provinces that previously had few or no child care services developed systems for training teachers and regulating a minimum standard of quality. The growth in child care coincided with an increase in the number of wage-earning women of preschool-aged children, and the rediscovery of early childhood education in North America. Yet as Patricia Schulz wrote in her history of child care in Canada in 1978, "when the government took on major responsibility for day care, it also took on traditional attitudes towards the service it was providing. Day care never outgrew the stigma of its charitable origins or its reputation as a low-status, inferior substitute for home care" (157). The Canada Assistance Plan was aimed at providing services for those "in need" or "likely to become in need" (Status of Women in

Canada 1986, 231). It entrenched a two-tier system of child care, which made working parents demonstrate their need for the service on a sliding scale. In a biting attack on this system, journalist Margaret Kesserling wrote about "Canada's backward thinking on day nurseries," for *Chatelaine* in 1966: "We applaud well-to-do parents who send their tots to 'enriching' nursery schools at top fees. Yet we let working mothers leave their children on the streets or in makeshift 'homes'" (41).

Considerable evidence exists that there has been a shift in the perception of child care over the three decades that have passed since the start of the Canada Assistance Plan. A greater integration of education, health, and social services has resulted in the rise of educare as an alternative model to the custodial programs of the past. An understanding of the way early experience can contribute to cognitive gains in young children has led to the use of child care and kindergarten environments as important sites for planned intervention, particularly with children judged to be at risk. A renewed call for the use of early education in the schools as a primary vehicle for social reform has made full-day kindergarten part of the new education and welfare policy of the government of Quebec. Junior kindergarten for even younger children is planned in communities with greater need. At present, kindergarten is available to most children in Canada as part of the public school system. This makes public school kindergartens in Canada virtually a national preschool program. The development of early education in Canada is clearly a topic of such breadth that a history on a national level can only hope to touch on themes and issues. One of the problems in writing the history is that local and regional initiatives often overshadow Canada-wide trends. Nonetheless, the evidence presented in this chapter indicates that services for young children have been a concern of Canadians for the past 200 years. An awareness of this legacy by early childhood professionals, policy makers, and parents may help us to arrive at creative solutions for the education and care of our children, today and in the future.

Note

The research for this chapter was supported by the Fond pour la Formation de Chercheurs et l'Aide à la Recherche and the Social Sciences and Humanities Research Council of Canada.

References

All People's Mission of the United Church of Canada. 1928. *Annual report.* Winnipeg: All People's Mission.

Audet, L.P. 1971. *Histoire de l'enseignement au Québec.* Montreal: Rinehart et Winston.

Beatty, B. 1995. *Preschool education in America: The culture of young children from the colonial era to the present.* New Haven, CT: Yale University Press.

Bendall, C. 1948. The world's biggest kindergarten class. *Saturday Night* 64 (December 18):28-9.

Bordin, R. 1981. *Woman and temperance: The quest for power and liberty, 1893-1900.* Philadelphia: Temple University Press.
Bosetti Piche, S. 1990. The interest of Edmonton club women in education, health and welfare, 1919-1939. Ph.D. diss., University of Alberta.
Braun, S.J., and E.P. Edwards. 1972. *History and theory of early childhood education.* Belmont, CA: Wadsworth.
British and Canadian Infant School Society. 1834. *Annual report of the British and Canadian Infant School Society.* Quebec: British and Canadian Infant School Society.
British Columbia Preschool Teachers' Association. 1974. *A brief history of the preschool movement in Vancouver.* Vancouver: British Columbia Preschool Teachers' Association.
Canada. 1942. Authorization of agreements with provinces for the care of children, Order in Council PC 6242. *Proclamations and Orders in Council Relating to the War,* vol. 8. Ottawa: King's Printer.
Canadian Education Association. 1965. *Survey of preschool education in Canada. Report no. 1.* Toronto: Canadian Education Association.
–. 1972. *Kindergartens in Canada: A survey of some pre-grade 1 programs in publicly-supported school systems.* Toronto: Canadian Education Association.
Chafe, J. 1967. *An apple for the teacher: A centennial history of the Winnipeg School Division.* Winnipeg: Winnipeg Board of Education.
Colvin, C. 1979. *Maria Edgeworth in France and Switzerland: Selections from the Edgeworth family letters.* Oxford: Clarendon.
Corbett, B.E. 1989. *A century of kindergarten education in Ontario.* Mississauga, ON: Froebel Foundation.
Cross, S. 1973. The neglected majority: The changing role of women in 19th century Montreal. *Histoire sociale/Social History* 6(11):201-23.
Desjardins, G. 1991. *Faire garder ses enfants au Québec.* Quebec: Gouvernement du Québec, Office des services de garde à l'enfance.
Dumont-Johnson, M. 1980. Des garderies au XIXe siècle: Les salles d'asile des Soeurs Grises à Montréal. *Revue d'histoire de l'Amérique française* 34(1):27-55.
East End Day Nursery. 1905, 1906, 1910, 1912, 1913. *Annual reports.* Toronto: East End Day Nursery.
Edmonton Crèche Society. 1931. *Annual report.* Edmonton: Edmonton Crèche Society.
Ferguson, R., A. Pence, and C. Denholm. 1987. The future of child care in Canada. In *Professional child and youth care: The Canadian perspective,* ed. C. Denholm, R. Ferguson, and A. Pence, 197-206. Vancouver: UBC Press.
Halifax Infant School Society. 1853, 1856. Petition. Halifax: Halifax Infant School Society.
Hawes, J.M., and N. Hiner, eds. 1991. *Children in historical and comparative perspective: An international handbook and research guide.* Westport, CT: Greenwood Press.
History of the kindergarten movement in the Southeastern States and Delaware, District of Columbia, New Jersey and Pennsylvania. 1939. Presented at the 46th annual convention of the Association for Childhood Education, Atlanta, GA.
History of the kindergarten movement in the Western States, Hawaii and Alaska. 1940. Presented at the 47th annual convention of the Association for Childhood Education, Milwaukee, WI.
History of the Winnipeg Free Kindergarten. 1910. Kindergarten Settlement Association Records. CSPCW, Box 663,664, Public Archives of Manitoba.
Houston, S., and A. Prentice. 1988. *Schooling and scholars in nineteenth-century Ontario.* Toronto: University of Toronto Press.
Hunter, R.M. 1933. A survey of child welfare agencies in the city of Hamilton. Master's thesis, McMaster University, Hamilton, ON.
The Jost Mission. 1959. Unpublished report of the Halifax Social Welfare Council. November. MG 20, vol. 408, No. 6.26-7, Provincial Archives of Nova Scotia.
Kesserling, M. 1966. Canada's backward thinking on day nurseries. *Chatelaine* 39(4):41, 68-75.
Kindergarten Settlement Association. 1921, 1926. *Annual reports.* Winnipeg: Kindergarten Settlement Association.

Lethbridge School District No. 51. 1985. *Lethbridge School District No. 51: The first 100 years, from cottage to composite, 1886-1986.* Lethbridge, AB: Lethbridge School District No. 51.
Lightfoot, A., E. Derksen, and S. Campbell. 1997. More history than you ever wanted to know about day care in Edmonton. Unpublished manuscript.
Lindenmeyer, K. 1995. The U.S. Children's Bureau and infant mortality in the Progressive Era. *Journal of Education* 177(3):57-69.
Madill, V. 1921. Vera M. Madill to the Edmonton Public School Board, 11 March. 84.1.560, 1912-21, Kindergarten, Edmonton Public Schools Archives.
Montessori, M. [1912] 1967. *The Montessori method.* Cambridge, MA: Robert Bentley.
Montreal Infant School Society. 1831. *First report of the Montreal Infant School Society, for 1830.* Montreal: Workman and Bowman.
Mothers' Association Day Nursery. 1953. Minutes of the Board of Directors Meeting, 17 November. P884. File: Minutes of the Board of Directors, 1953-5, Provincial Archives of Manitoba.
National Society for the Promotion of Education for the Poor [NSPEP]. 1843. *24th annual report of the state of the Madras School.* Saint John, NB: NSPEP.
Neely, B.R. 1946. The growth and development of the Regina education system from its beginnings to 1944. Master's thesis, University of Saskatchewan.
Olsen, M.I. 1955. The development of play schools and kindergartens and an analysis of a sampling of these institutions in Alberta. Master's thesis, University of Alberta.
Owen, R. [1857] 1967. *The life of Robert Owen written by himself with selections from his writings and correspondence,* vol. 1. New York: Augustus M. Kelley.
Parr. J. 1992. Rethinking work and kinship in a Canadian hosiery town, 1910-1950. In *Canadian family history,* ed. B. Bradbury, 220-40. Toronto: Copp Clark Pitman.
Paterson, Alice E. 1966. The development of kindergartens in Manitoba. Master's thesis, University of Manitoba.
Payzant, J.M. 1993. *Second to none: A history of public education in Dartmouth, Nova Scotia.* Dartmouth: Dartmouth Historical Association.
PBSCCM (Protestant Board of School Commissioners for the City of Montreal). 1877, 1899. *Report of the Protestant Board of School Commissioners for the City of Montreal.* Montreal: Montreal Herald.
–. 1886. *Special report for the India and colonial exhibition.* London: PBSCCM.
Phillips, C.E. 1957. *The development of education in Canada.* Toronto: Gage.
Prentice, A. 1977. *The school promoters: Education and social class in mid-nineteenth century Upper Canada.* Toronto: McClelland and Stewart.
Prentice, S. 1993. Militant mothers in domestic times: Toronto's postwar daycare struggle. Ph.D. diss., York University, Toronto.
Prochner, L. 1994. Themes in the history of day care: A case study of the West End Crèche, Toronto, 1909-1939. Ed.D. diss., University of Toronto.
–. 1996a. Quality of care in historical perspective. *Early Childhood Research Quarterly* 11(1):5-18.
–. 1996b. Share their care, Mrs. Warworker: Wartime day nurseries in Ontario and Quebec, 1942-1945. *Canadian Journal of Research in Early Childhood Education* 5(1):115-26.
–. 1997. The development of the Day Treatment Centre for emotionally disturbed children at the West End Crèche, Toronto. *Canadian Bulletin of Medical History* 14(2):215-39.
Report on Infant's Hospital. (n.d.) Series 101, 103-B-1, Infant Care 1912-20, City Archives, Vancouver.
Robins, S. 1872. Report of the inspector, Appendix XI. *Report of the Protestant Board of School Commissioners for the City of Montreal.* Montreal: PBSCCM.
Rooke, P. 1977. The child institutionalized in Canada, Britain, and the United States: A transatlantic perspective. *Journal of Educational Thought* 2:156-71.
Rooke, P.T., and R. Schnell. 1991. Canada. In *Children in historical and comparative perspective: An international handbook and research guide,* ed. J.M. Hawes and N.R. Hiner, 179-216. Westport, CT: Greenwood Press.
Ryan, K. 1942. Share their care, Mrs. War Worker, with your able and willing helper, the day nursery. *Canadian Home Journal* 39:16, 44-6.

Schulz, P. 1978. Day care in Canada: 1850-1962. In *Good day care: Fighting for it, getting it, keeping it,* ed. K. Gallagher Ross, 137-58. Toronto: Women's Press.
Schweinhart, L.J., and D.P. Weikart. 1997. The High/Scope preschool curriculum comparison study through age 23. *Early Childhood Research Quarterly* 12:117-43.
Seguin, J.J. 1977. Public policy planning in education: A case study of policy formation for the early childhood services program in Alberta. Ph.D. diss., University of Alberta.
Sharp, D. 1974. Early childhood programs: A study of provision for kindergarten and preschool programs in Newfoundland. Master's thesis, Memorial University of Newfoundland.
Simmons, C. 1984. Helping the poorer sisters: The women of the Jost Mission, Halifax, 1905-1945. *Acadiensis* 14(1):157-77.
Singer, E. 1992. *Child care and the development of psychology.* Trans. Ann Porcelijn. New York: Routledge.
Stamp, R. 1982. *The schools of Ontario, 1876-1976.* Toronto: University of Toronto Press.
Status of Women Canada. 1986. *Report of the task force on child care.* Ottawa: Status of Women Canada.
Steedman, C. 1990. *Childhood, culture and class in Britain: Margaret Macmillan, 1860-1931.* New Brunswick, NJ: Rutgers University Press.
Superintendent. 1919. Superintendent, Edmonton Public School Board, to Adella Whiting, 5 May. File 84.1.560, 1912-21, Kindergarten, Edmonton Public School Archives.
Support for Kindergartens. 1920. File 84.1.560, 1912-21, Kindergarten, Edmonton Public Schools Archives.
Sutherland, N. 1976. *Children in English-Canadian society: Framing the twentieth-century consensus.* Toronto: University of Toronto Press.
Talmud Torah Schools. 1937. Pamphlet. Jewish Library Archives, Montreal.
Tinsley, J. 1904. At the day nursery institution in which children are taken care of while their mothers are busy working – Its inception, progress, and prospects. *Hamilton Herald,* 30 April.
Toronto Board of Education. 1895. *Inspector's report.* Toronto: Toronto Board of Education.
Varga, D. 1993. From a service for mothers to the developmental management of children: Day nursery care in Canada, 1890-1960. In *Advances in early education and day care,* vol. 5, ed. S. Reifel, 115-44. Greenwich, CT: JAI Press.
–. 1997. *Constructing the child: A history of Canadian day care.* Toronto: Lorimer.
Victoria Crèche. 1905. *Declaration of incorporation of the Crèche.* Toronto: Victoria Day Care Services.
–. 1917. *Annual report.* Toronto: Victoria Crèche.
Weiss, G.M. 1976. The development of public school kindergartens in British Columbia. Master's thesis, University of British Columbia.
West End Crèche. 1951. *Annual report.* Toronto: West End Crèche.
Wheelock, L., and C.D. Aborn, eds. 1935. *The kindergarten in New England.* Presented at the Swampscott Convention of the Association for Childhood Education, 26-30 June.
Whitton, C. 1934. *Social welfare in Winnipeg.* Ottawa: Canadian Council on Child and Family Welfare.
Wilderspin, S. 1825. *Infant education: Remarks on the importance of educating the infant poor from the age of eighteen months to seven years.* London: J.S. Hodson.
Winnipeg Free Kindergarten Association. 1908, 1910. *Annual reports.* Winnipeg: Winnipeg Free Kindergarten Association.
Winsor, N. 1979. *A history of education in Greenspond, Newfoundland, 1816-1979.* Greenspond, NF: Heritage Academy.

2
A History of Early-Childhood-Teacher Education

Donna Varga

Teacher education for the early childhood years has historically followed two paths: one path has prepared teachers for the school system; the other has educated caregivers for day care programs. Choosing a particular path of education has more or less limited one's opportunities in the early childhood field. Those who have received teacher certification can work within the school system, in nursery schools and day care centres. But for those who have received caregiver education, options are limited mostly to nursery schools, day care centres, and related social service positions.

The history of teacher education is a complex matter, just as is the history of education in general. It is impossible, in one chapter, to adequately cover the entire scope of the history of teacher education for early childhood education and caregiving. The focus here is primarily on education, English Canada, Protestant schooling, and non-denominational caregiving. Teacher education carried out by religious orders, by private institutions, and for francophone students is not dealt with in the present chapter. Also omitted are differences across the country and in-depth details of government regulations. The author has preferred to highlight the history of institutions rather than the personal experiences of student-teachers. Even for the former, the reader will not find complete details of educational programs or a complete chronology of developments. Instead, the objective has been to outline broad philosophical and psychological influences on the institutions and practices of teacher and caregiver education for the early childhood years.

Teacher Education for Elementary Schooling

When contemporary education students recall their memories of elementary school, they depict images that have a marked similarity. They identify particular materials and equipment as having being present: the clock, blackboard, alphabet cards, individual student desks, and books. Most teachers are remembered as having been women, who spent much of their time standing or walking around the classroom. The school day is described as having been divided into different subject areas such as reading, arithmetic, and social studies. Students were grouped by age into separate classrooms and attended school from the fall through spring; advancement to a higher grade level usually took place at the beginning of each school year. The similarity of the recollections is not surprising to the students, since they take it for granted that their peers will have had experiences much like their own. What often does surprise them is to find out that their experiences have not always been similar and that teacher education has played a fundamental role in standardizing schooling practices.

Prior to the middle of the nineteenth century, school teachers learned their craft from having been common school students ("common schools" are now referred to as "public schools") and watching their own teachers at work. Secondary schools, including those of religious orders, provided educational qualifications for teaching but not specialized teacher education (Phillips 1957; Rowe 1964). Certificates of teaching were usually required before one could be hired as a teacher, and were obtained by passing an examination held by local school authorities. The examinations consisted of demonstrating some basic knowledge, such as spelling and arithmetic, but there was no consistency in requirements or examinations across, or even within, communities. The lack of training in methods of teaching meant that schools differed greatly in their form and content. Instead of students seated in rows of desks facing the front of a classroom, the preferences of the teacher and the availability of school furniture dictated the classroom arrangement: the students might have sat on chairs in a group surrounding the teacher or have stood while the teacher sat on the only available chair. Subjects taught, pace of learning, books used, and methods of examination could also differ greatly from school to school.

It is not necessarily true that before the availability of standardized teacher education, teachers lacked teaching skills or knowledge about school subjects. However, it was to the advantage of persons interested in government regulation of teachers to argue that differences in schooling were serious impediments to educational progress. Reports about the state of early schooling, made by supporters of government-regulated teaching, were filled with descriptions of teacher incompetence, abusive behaviour, and ignorance. In 1851, J. William Dawson, superintendent of education for Nova Scotia, reported the following to the provincial legislature: "The majority of the teachers were managing their schools on old and obsolete methods, and ... they often had a very imperfect acquaintance with the branches they professed to teach. Lessons in reading without any explanation or mental training, columns of unintelligible spellings, inability to explain the principles of arithmetic or the elements of English grammar, or to preserve order except by the harshest and most repulsive methods, formed the rule rather than the exception" (Nova Scotia Normal College 1955, 7). A similar assessment was made in 1854, by school inspector Charles Randall: "The state of the schools in our County is a matter of such notoriety that it seems almost superfluous to refer to it. The attendance is very irregular and in very small proportion to the number which should be under instruction. This is attributed to two causes – the one that parents generally attach but little value to education; the other, that teachers are in most cases so unqualified for their business that it admits of a question whether the benefit resulting from attending school is proportionate to the expense" (Nova Scotia Normal College 1955, 6).

Advocates of a standard form of common (public) schooling, whereby all teachers would conduct their classes in a virtually identical manner and in ways approved by the government, argued that it offered a "sound education of the masses" that would result in students having "habits, predispositions, loyalties, and sentiments" compliant with government authority (Curtis 1988, 102-3). In other words, systematic schooling was intended to develop students into good citizens.

Standardization of public schooling required that teachers be "normalized" – that is, that individual styles and behaviours of teaching were to be replaced with the government-approved model. All teachers would learn systems of educational processes (also called pedagogy), which would include their following a standardized curriculum of subject matter, grading and examinations; their developing a sameness of personality; their teaching in a similar fashion (Love 1978). This was the purpose of establishing normal schools (the historical term for teacher-education institutions). Standardized teacher education was to be the means for learning pedagogy and for forming a collective identity as "teacher." The following commentary in *The Globe*, 13 January 1847, in support of the establishment of the Toronto Normal School, illustrates a belief in the power of teacher education to obliterate what were considered deficient schools: "We think few can question the utility of such institutions. For until the qualifications of school teachers be raised, and their business take the rank of a regular well supported profession, we can hope for little radical improvement in our Common Schools. Give us religious, moral, well-trained School Masters or Mistresses, and the circulars, regulations, and reports of Superintendents will then require but little discussion, they will be of little practical importance."

Normal schools were established at different times across Canada (see Table 2.1) over a period ranging from 1847, when the Toronto Normal School was established, to 1921, when the Newfoundland Normal School opened. In Quebec, teacher training was divided in the same way as the province's division of schooling: into Roman Catholic and Protestant denominations, and within the Catholic denomination, into divisions according to English/French, male/female criteria. The training of women for Roman Catholic elementary schools was initially carried out by nuns of different orders, through convent boarding schools and later through scholasticates (Dumont 1990). Quebec's first Protestant normal school was established at McGill University by 1857. The first normal school for training male Catholic school teachers was the Jacques Cartier Normal School, which opened in Montreal in 1939, with separate English and French divisions (Henchey 1991).

Table 2.1

Establishment of selected Protestant and non-denominational normal schools

School	Founding date
Toronto Normal School, ON	1847
Fredericton Normal School, NB	1848
Saint John Normal School, NB	1849
Nova Scotia Normal School, Truro, NS	1855
Charlottetown Normal School, PEI	1856
McGill Normal School, QC*	1857
Ottawa Normal School, ON	1875
British Columbia Normal School, Vancouver, BC	1901
British Columbia Normal School, Victoria, BC	1915
Saskatoon Normal School, SK**	1912
Newfoundland Normal School, NF	1921

* In 1907, the elementary department was renamed School for Teachers and moved to Macdonald College at St. Anne de Bellevue. In 1955, it was renamed Institute of Education; in 1965 elementary training was moved back to McGill and incorporated into the newly organized Faculty of Education.

** In 1952, while the province still retained its normal schools, a four-year undergraduate program for elementary and secondary teachers was opened at the University of Saskatchewan.

Initially, normal school admission standards included a minimum age requirement (sometimes as young as fourteen, but generally sixteen years) and the successful passing of an entrance examination, rather than the completion of a particular level of prior schooling. A large proportion of the normal school curriculum was devoted to upgrading student knowledge in the subjects that they would be expected to teach, such as grammar, mathematics, geography, and science. In the early years of the Nova Scotia Normal School, its curriculum included a study of basic skills in reading, writing, grammar, geography, and arithmetic, at the beginning of each term (of ten to twelve weeks); only later in the term were students introduced to literature, mathematics, and philosophy (Nova Scotia Normal College 1955). Today teacher education is an advanced level of school undertaken after the successful completion of earlier levels, but in the nineteenth century it was commonly believed that normal schools were intended to provide educational upgrading for students who did not have basic schooling. In a letter to the Toronto Normal School, dated 10 December 1852, Peter Sammons expressed outrage that his son had been denied admission, stating that as far as he understood, the normal school was "for the education of young men, not for those that have their education finished" (Sammons 1852).

In addition to public school subjects, students took courses in school law, school organization and management, principles of teaching, the science of education, psychology, and the history of education. Normal school education was also about learning to take on the personality of a teacher. In Ontario, teachers with normal school training were all expected to have developed a physical appearance and manner so they would be able to use "looks, gestures, expressions and qualities of voice," rather than physical punishment, to govern the schoolroom (Curtis 1988, 104; see also Corrigan, Curtis, and Lanning 1987). Instead of sitting, teachers were to learn how to move about the room continuously so they could keep an eye on their students' behaviour. They were taught to memorize subject knowledge thoroughly, as a means of gaining their students' respect as schoolroom authorities. Another integral feature of normal schooling was practice teaching. Students planned lessons for a variety of subjects, and conducted them while being evaluated by normal school faculty and classroom teachers. It was especially during practice teaching sessions that students needed to demonstrate the personality and behavioural characteristics of the "good" teacher, as defined by the normal school (Hollihan 1997; Varga 1991a). The goals of teacher education to reconstruct the student into a teacher with a particular personality and behavioural characteristics has remained an important element of teacher education throughout the twentieth century (Sumara and Luce-Kapler 1996).

From their establishment, and for the first half of the twentieth century, the length of normal school programs ranged from a few weeks to ten months. Completing all requirements in such a short period of time was a rigorous process. During the early years of the Toronto Normal School, many students left before finishing their studies because of the physical and mental stress brought about by classes held six days a week from 6:30 a.m. into the late afternoon, followed by hours of study and practice teaching preparation. An alternative for many, up to the 1950s, was to work as teachers with lower level certificates during the school year, and complete the requirements for higher level certificates through normal school summer sessions.

For a time after the establishment of normal schools, public schools could hire teachers without normal school training, and teachers could earn certificates without going through a normal school. This was possible as long as decisions about appropriate teaching qualifications were made by local communities rather than by provincial governments. Through the early years of the twentieth century, most teachers continued to gain their certificates through means other than normal school training. In 1921, Nova Scotia had 3,089 teachers, but only 1,598 had attended normal school (Learned and Sills 1922). The number of normal school students throughout Canada for the period 1870-1900 has been estimated at 37,000, but the same number in Ontario alone were being trained as teachers through the model schools (Harrigan 1992). The model schools were elementary schools designated by provincial governments and local communities as teacher-training sites. Within these settings, student-teachers assisted the school teachers with classroom tasks and observed the teachers in action. The student-teachers were from fourteen to sixteen years of age and completed their training within a school year. The many model schools scattered throughout the provinces offered an inexpensive means of teacher training; they did not require special facilities or teaching staff, and the student-teachers were a cheap source of classroom labour. However, since model school training was based on the passing down of teaching behaviour and knowledge from teacher to student, it did not offer the systematic pedagogy desired by school reformers; nor was it designed to provide student-teachers with a higher level of academic knowledge than they had already received. Normal school attendance increased substantially after the first decade of the twentieth century, with 50 percent of teacher training taking place at such institutions from 1910 to 1950. After the Second World War, normal school training also became a significant source of elementary teachers for Quebec Catholic schools (Harrigan 1992). Although the dates vary widely across Canada, generally by the 1950s, a teaching certificate could only be obtained from a provincial department of education after the student had graduated from a normal school or from a university education program.

Initially, normal schools of mid-nineteenth-century Canada provided education for both elementary and secondary school teachers; the level of certificate received determined the level of schooling that a normal school graduate was qualified to teach. Certification for teaching in high schools required completing a longer program of study (from one to two years compared to the weeks or months of elementary school training) and one that included secondary school subjects. By the beginning of the twentieth century, education for secondary school teachers was completely separate from that for elementary teachers and was provided by different institutions. In 1885, Ontario secondary-teacher training was moved out of the normal schools to five training institutes at various locations throughout the province. In 1892, they were consolidated into the Ontario Normal College located in Hamilton. In 1897, secondary-teacher training was moved to the Ontario School of Pedagogy, located in Toronto, and in 1906, it was undertaken by the Faculty of Education at the University of Toronto. In Quebec, elementary school training for English-speaking Protestants was moved from the McGill Normal School in 1907 to Macdonald College at St. Anne de Bellevue; secondary school training remained at McGill.

One consequence of the division of teacher education into elementary and secondary institutions was an increased stratification in the types of certificates earned by men and women, and therefore a solidification of the feminized nature of the elementary school system (Danylewycz and Prentice 1984; Prentice 1975). During the early years of normal school training, almost equal numbers of women and men received elementary-teaching certificates. The proportion of women increased over the years, but with the creation of separate institutions for elementary- and secondary-teacher education, there was a dramatic change. Far fewer men attended the elementary-training institutions, and almost no women attended those preparing secondary teachers (Harrigan 1992; Heise 1987).

By the second half of the twentieth century, normal schools were being closed, and the different levels of teacher education were carried out through university faculties or departments of education. This took place in 1945 in Alberta, 1946 in Newfoundland, 1956 in British Columbia, 1964 in Saskatchewan, and 1965 in Manitoba (Sheehan and Wilson 1994). In addition to the transfer of programs from the normal schools to universities, was the expansion, from the 1950s, in the number of universities across the country providing teacher education. In Nova Scotia alone, Bachelor of Education programs were established by 1956 at Acadia, Dalhousie, St. Francis Xavier, and Mount Saint Vincent universities. By the mid-1970s, a university degree in education was necessary to receive teacher certification (Harrigan 1992). An exception was in Nova Scotia, where for 143 years, teacher certification could be obtained upon graduating from the Nova Scotia Normal School (later, the Nova Scotia Teachers College). Located in the city of Truro, it was closed by provincial government fiat, graduating its last class in April 1997.

When elementary-teacher education was moved to university institutions, advanced academic study (versus preparation only for elementary school subjects) was given the same emphasis as it had in the education of secondary school teachers since the early years of the twentieth century. This somewhat elevated the social prestige of elementary teaching, but it did not significantly increase the proportion of males who entered the elementary programs. As the twentieth century drew to a close, the number of women preparing for secondary school teaching significantly increased, but teacher education for the early childhood years remained primarily a female domain (see Chapter 8). While most students preparing for elementary teaching have been female, the faculty of normal schools and university elementary-education departments has mostly been male (Hallman 1998). Despite the inclusion of equity courses in teacher-preparation programs in the latter years of the twentieth century, many programs were not themselves transformed into gender-balanced sites.

The absorption of teacher-education programs for the elementary school years into universities has not been free of conflict. The practical nature of such programs has often been criticized by arts and science faculty as anti-intellectual. As teaching continues to be devalued within our society (evidenced by provincial cut-backs to education programs, based on the rationale of fiscal restraint), teacher education remains at risk of further marginalization. For example, in 1996, education departments were closed at Dalhousie and St. Mary's universities in Nova Scotia. Ontario's education regulations were revised in the late 1990s to allow specialists, such as persons in fine arts, business, and computer programming, to hold regular classroom teaching positions without having earned a degree in education. With fewer programs and increased years of study for an education degree (as of 1996 in Nova Scotia, a total of five to six years of full-time university study was required for teacher certification), the issue of accessibility for students with few economic resources is a concern. This scenario has implications for the future diversity of Canada's early-education teaching staff. Women make up the largest proportion of students in education programs for the early years of schooling and, as a group, they experience greater economic disadvantages than men; visible minority women suffer even greater economic inequalities as well as workforce discrimination. Financial costs for students rise when the number of years of education required for teaching certification increases. Rising tuition costs in response to government cut-backs to university funding, coupled with reductions in student loans and grants, mean that women, especially those from lower economic groups (which include women from visible minorities), will not have the same opportunity to complete education programs as persons from higher economic groups. As the availability of teaching positions declines, women who are members of visible minorities may have increasing difficulty finding employment within the school system as full-time regular teachers. The consequent potential lack of diversity in Canada's early-education teaching staff raises concerns over meeting the educational needs of Canada's diverse population of children (see, e.g., Robinson 1994).

Kindergarten-Teacher Education

In the history of teacher education for the early years of schooling, preparation for work in the kindergarten requires separate attention. As discussed in Chapter 1, kindergartens were established in Canada as private institutions, during the late 1800s. They were incorporated into the public school system at different times throughout Canada – in 1887 in Ontario, but only in the 1980s in New Brunswick. The term *kindergarten* now commonly refers to school-run programs for children who are four or five years old (in some provinces, school programs for this age group are referred to as primary classes). Therefore, where kindergartens are included in provincial education legislation, they are part of the public school system.

The kindergarten practices organized by Friedrich Froebel in Germany, in 1837, were the catalyst for a North American movement to provide educational experiences for young children that were different from the subject orientation of the school classroom (Weber 1984). It would be inaccurate to assert that contemporary kindergarten practices resemble the Froebelian kindergartens of the nineteenth century, since different ideas about the nature of childhood and the purpose of early education have eliminated most of the Froebelian elements. However, an examination of Froebelian kindergarten-teacher education provides a means for understanding the basis of contemporary practices (see also Chapter 7).

Kindergarten teaching in the nineteenth century (and still in the twentieth) was considered a natural expression of women's instinctive mothering nature. The purpose of training women for kindergarten work was to direct their "natural instincts" toward the understanding and application of Froebelian philosophical principles – namely, every child is born innocent, but as they grow older, they need to struggle against evil habits; and emotions and mental processes such as reason and perception are fully formed at birth and over time unfold according to a predetermined script. Originally, women in Canada who wished to receive training for the kindergarten worked as assistants in Froebelian kindergartens in the United States. Normal school provisions for educating teachers in kindergarten methods were established in Ontario by the end of the 1880s (Corbett 1968). In Nova Scotia, a Kindergarten Department was opened on the premises of the Normal School at Truro in 1891. It was a separate enterprise until 1907, when it came under the control of the Normal

School (Nova Scotia Normal College 1955). In Montreal, from 1892 to 1897, kindergarten-teacher training was available through the Protestant School Board. This was primarily an internship program, with candidates assisting in kindergartens and attending lectures on Froebelian philosophy and methods, psychology, history of Froebelian education, and school management. It was replaced by normal school training offered through McGill University from 1896, but only two or three students enrolled each year from 1899 to 1948 (Student Registers 1899-1949).

The 1890 syllabus for the Toronto and Ottawa normal school program for kindergarten assistants illustrates the type of knowledge expected of the women who undertook this work. The program was one year in length and required candidates to master an intimate knowledge of Froebelian philosophy and practices. Upon completing the course of study, candidates took an examination during which they had to explain the meaning and methods of the gifts, occupations, and mother plays. In explaining the gifts, candidates were to describe "their general objects as well as their specialities; how they are graded and why; their connection with other branches of Kindergarten work; also a full explanation of the general method of the Kindergarten, and how applied in exercises with the gifts [sic]. As the gifts have a mathematical foundation, a knowledge of the elements of geometry will be required" (Ontario 1890, 395).

For occupations, in addition to demonstrating the same type of knowledge as they had for the gifts, students were required to submit the occupation books that they had completed over their year of study. The occupation book for sewing needed to include "not less than sixty different figures, logically connected and illustrating the following lines and their combinations (a) vertical lines (b) horizontal lines (c) slanting lines of all orders (d) curves" (Ontario 1890, 398). Kindergarten Director certificates were earned by undertaking at least one year of work as an assistant in a kindergarten and then completing a normal school examination.

By 1902, in Ontario 247 women had received normal school kindergarten training, but by 1910, the numbers of women entering the training programs had significantly dwindled. This was likely caused by a number of factors. For many years, students could bypass the normal school programs by getting practical experience in a kindergarten classroom and then passing a Department of Education examination. Furthermore, the normal school program for assistant certification was not the same as the curriculum for training elementary school teachers. The kindergarten assistants, therefore, were not able to obtain certificates to teach in the grade-school classrooms. Kindergarten directors could assist in elementary classrooms, but could not be hired as elementary teachers. The one-year length of kindergarten-teacher education, the intensity of the program, and the limitation of working largely within kindergarten classrooms probably contributed to the decline in normal school enrolment as long as an alternative certificate route existed.

The Ontario Department of Education used two tactics to counter the decline. In 1914, it established a kindergarten-primary program that certified its graduates to work as teachers in the early grades. In addition, new provincial certification regulations abolished the alternative route and required all kindergarten assistants to complete a normal school program. The kindergarten-primary certification provided more occupational opportunities, but it also shifted the focus of the kindergarten away from the Froebelian emphasis on self-activity toward preparing the child behaviourally for the elementary classroom. Although some elements of the Froebelian self-activity approach were retained, they were now used for the purpose of training the child to become an "orderly and industrious pupil of the elementary school" (Ontario 1914, 150). To prepare teachers for this new role of the kindergarten classroom, the curriculum for kindergarten-teacher education was made similar to that of elementary-teacher education. It included courses in general methods of education, school organization and management, and child psychology. A similar pattern in the training of kindergarten teachers took place elsewhere in Canada. In Nova Scotia, a kindergarten-primary training program was established in 1950, replacing the previous kindergarten department. The new program enabled its graduates to teach kindergarten through grade 3 (Nova Scotia Normal College 1955).

Kindergarten-teacher education continued to change over the twentieth century in accordance with changing ideas about children and the purpose of the kindergarten year. Student-teachers spent less time learning about Froebelian activities and more on the progressive education philosophy of John Dewey. Developmental psychology gained an increasingly dominant position in education, first with the incorporation of the ideas of G. Stanley Hall, then Arnold Gesell, and by the 1970s, Jean Piaget. By the 1990s, developmental psychology had become the predominant theoretical focus in early childhood education (Silin 1987), combined with the principles of behaviour modification originating with John B. Watson and B.F. Skinner (Weber 1984). Along with these changes in the approach to educating the young child, kindergarten-primary–teacher education was expanded to include the early elementary school years beyond grade 1. This meant that teacher education became less specialized in terms of the earliest years of schooling. The incorporation of education for the kindergarten into the elementary program increased employment opportunities because teachers could be moved (voluntarily or involuntarily) across more grade levels. It also contributed to the raising of kindergarten teachers' salaries to the level of elementar The consolidation of elementary- and kindergarten-teacher ed presented problems. The tremendous differences in children's abilities and cognitive processes over the ages of five to eight years can be overshadowed by a general approach to teacher education. Furthermore, the elimination of differentiated teacher education for the early years has probably contributed to the increased subject orientation of kindergarten classrooms, a change that has been criticized as being more harmful than beneficial to children.

Education for Early Childhood Caregivers

In contrast to the long-standing history of teacher education for the elementary and kindergarten grades, education programs designed to train caregivers to work with young children are relatively recent. The term "early childhood caregiving" is used in this chapter to refer to the provision of centre-based day care programs. The work of early childhood caregiving requires a diversity of skills. It involves meeting the numerous needs of a wide age range of children over a long working day and over the entire year. It includes teaching children skills similar to those taught within the school system, such as numeracy and literacy, but additionally, it emphasizes the teaching of socialization and self-care skills – eating, toileting, and dressing. Despite the skills and knowledge needed, few regulations specify formal educational requirements for those who undertake this work. Unlike school teachers, who must hold provincial certificates in order to teach (or special dispensation, as during the late 1990s in Ontario), no such requirements existed for early childhood caregivers over the twentieth century in Canada.

In Canada, the first day care centres were established in the late 1800s, and until the 1960s, were referred to as day nurseries (Varga 1997). The earliest nurseries in English Canada were organized as philanthropic charitable services and were operated by groups of women, without any government provision. By offering employment services and child care, the nurseries enabled financially destitute mothers to engage in paid labour. Women of the wealthier classes contacted the nurseries when they wanted domestic help. Women of the working classes came to the nurseries to receive such employment, and their children were provided with care. The age of children cared for, until the 1930s, was from a few weeks old to twelve or fourteen years old, but most of the children in care were under six years old. The number cared for in individual nurseries varied greatly, reaching over 100 daily during periods of high employment.

The day-to-day operations and child care work of the nurseries were carried out by matrons. They were not expected to have any special training in child care work, and in any case, such training was not generally available. The primary criteria for hiring matrons were their experience and ability in managing a household (including the children of the household), reputation for honesty, skill in dealing with people, and tolerance for the hard work involved. They were expected to have the skills considered necessary at that time for meeting the needs of the children for whom they cared. The lack of adequate housing or state-provided medical care and the unreliability of vaccinations put financially destitute children at great risk of death from illness and disease. Therefore, the matrons' work included supervising the children's physical health so as to prevent the spread of illness. This meant overseeing the preparation and serving of meals for the children, ensuring that the children were bathed and dressed in nursery clothes each day upon their arrival, and dispensing tonics and medications. Matrons were also to keep the nursery children under control by providing direct or indirect instruction in industriousness, truthfulness, and temperance. In addition to their child care tasks, matrons were responsible for overseeing the work of nursery maids, cooks, and laundresses. They were also expected to engage in charitable activities directed toward the women and families who used the nurseries. In 1906, the Montreal Day Nursery matron needed to be able "to settle all kinds of difficulties for the women, to visit them in their homes when they were ill, to send properly prepared food to sick babies, and to help with money from the Poor Fund, for funeral and other pressing expenses" (Montreal Day Nursery 1906).

Until the 1930s, nurses were employed to care for the youngest children. The term "nurse" referred to persons (usually women) who had received formal health care training in a hospital setting. This was the case of Elizabeth Anderson, employed by the Ottawa Day Nursery from 1916 to 1918, who had been trained at the Royal Alexandra Hospital, in Fergus, Ontario. The Jost Mission Day Nursery employed graduate nurses for at least three years (Miss Grace Wilford in 1918 and 1919, and Miss E. Byron in 1921). "Nurse" was also used to refer to nursemaids – women who had received training in physical and hygienic care rather than specialized medical care, and whose status was thus equivalent to that of cooks or housekeepers. Nurse was also a general term of reference for women who worked with babies (Prochner 1996). Whatever their training or lack thereof, the main task of nursery nurses was caring for children a few weeks old up to about two years of age. They prepared formulas, gave feedings, administered medicines, and kept the children clean and dry.

Occasionally the nursery staff was supplemented by school teachers who provided lessons for the four- and five-year-olds following the Froebelian kindergarten curriculum. These were usually short-term arrangements dependent on voluntary teachers or on financial from a school board, rather than being a regular duty of nursery

Child Study Knowledge and Child Care

During the 1920s, growing importance was placed on caregivers having specialized education in child development and care (Prochner 1997; Varga 1993, 1997). The history of ideas about the child and scientific child study that is discussed here pertains primarily to English Canada. Marked differences existed in the time frame and philosophical approach to children in French Quebec (Turmel 1997a, 1997b). Arnold Gesell's systematic observations of children from birth to five years resulted in the first schedules defining the ages and stages of normal child development and an explanation of changes in development over time as being a result of genetic maturation. In addition to Gesell's child development theories, those of Sigmund Freud and Adolf Meyer influenced ideas about caregiver training. Both, in somewhat different ways, argued that childhood experiences determined adult personality characteristics (Cohen 1979). The features expected of the good child care provider were transformed in accordance with these changing ideas: from caring for the health and moral well-being of children to supervising and managing their genetic and personality development. Gesell, in the United States, and other child study experts, such as William Blatz in Canada, contended that persons who cared for children required knowledge of scientific child study and how to provide an environment that matched children's ages and stages of development as well as supported positive mental health development. As discussed in Chapter 3, during the 1920s, numerous child study research centres opened in North America. Their dual purpose was to provide education programs for parents and nursery school teachers. Such centres in the United States included Gesell's Yale-Psycho Clinic; the Institute of Child Welfare Research at Teachers College, Columbia University; and the University of Minnesota's Institute of Child Welfare.

The two centres that opened in Canada were the St. George's School for Child Study at the University of Toronto and the McGill University Nursery School and Child Laboratory. The McGill institution closed in 1930, and St. George's dominated education for child care in Canada until the 1960s. (In 1938, the St. George's School for Child Study was renamed the Institute of Child Study; the latter name will be used for the remainder of this chapter.) From its opening, the institute offered a master's degree in psychology and held special lectures for social service practitioners. Day nursery caregivers took courses in the graduate program, attended the professional lectures, and undertook practical work in the institute's nursery school under the supervision of institute faculty. In

1941, the institute established a two-year course for nursery school supervisors; this was Canada's first specialized course dedicated solely to nursery school training.

The director of the institute, William Blatz, and its other faculty members created a curriculum for child study and care distinct from programs in the United States, England, and Europe. The basis of the curriculum was maturationist child development theory and mental hygiene principles (Blatz, Millichamp, and Fletcher 1935). Institute students learned that for children to develop normally, caregivers needed to supervise and manage that development. To carry out this function, students were taught the behaviours typical of preschool children; how to observe children's development; and how to arrange a mentally healthy environment that included specialized arrangements of time, space, and human interactions. Within this approach, children's engagement in play activities was considered essential for normal development, with the caregivers needing to match toys and materials to the children's ages. For example, two-year-olds were to have play materials that both met and encouraged the development of two-year-old capabilities; five-year-olds required materials that demanded more complex skills and behaviours (Varga 1991b). During children's play, caregivers were neither to play with nor to lead children, the argument being that this would interfere with the children's natural developmental process. Instead, they were responsible for ensuring that the children played according to age-based abilities set out in the normative schedules.

Another component of the institute's child care curriculum was the management of children's development through routine activities. To understand why routines were considered so very important, it is necessary to comprehend the early-twentieth-century concept of "habit." From the maturationist perspective, habits were the internalization (habituation) of the child's external responses to demands of the environment, including those made by adults such as the ways to eat, wash, and toilet. Habits were considered essential for relieving the individual of having to think about the way regular daily activities were carried out, thereby reducing the "waste" of developmental energy sources. Correct habits were formed through experiencing regulated daily routines in a structured environment. They provided for mental health by reducing the emotional tension between adults and children caused by conflicts over the when and how of everyday activities. To instil in children habits of everyday living, institute students learned the importance of following a set timetable during the day when particular play and routine activities such as toileting, eating, dressing, and sleeping would take place. They were also taught to have children follow specific behavioural patterns when carrying out routines. For example, caregivers were to ensure that the washing-up procedure for three-years-olds was exactly followed: "Child turns on cold water; teacher puts some hot water into child's basin. Teacher carries basin to bench until child has proved he can carry it without spilling." In preparing for a nap, they had to supervise the children so that "child goes to his own cot, turns down his blankets, gets in and covers himself" (St. George's School for Child Study 1927). Such specific procedures included aspects of routine activities (but not play activities) that differed according to the degree of independence expected at different ages.

During the Second World War, the federal government funded the opening of day nurseries as an emergency measure to enable mothers with young children to enter the paid labour force, and thereby ease the shortage of workers created by the demands of war. Twenty-eight wartime nurseries operated in Ontario and six in Quebec, providing care for children between the ages of two and six. More training programs were needed to meet the heightened demand for caregivers, and they had to be completed more quickly. The institute shortened its two-year diploma course to nine months, and in 1942 provided a nine-week course for volunteers (Northway 1977). In October 1942, the government of Ontario established the Provincial Day Nursery Training Centre. Located in Toronto, the training centre was directed and staffed by graduates of the Institute of Child Study. According to the *Parent Education Bulletin* of 1943, it provided supervised practical work, with the intention of ensuring "that the programme in each nursery may incorporate the same principles of nursery education" (no. 24, p. 11). In 1945, the *Bulletin* revealed that the institute provided a shorter course for recent high school graduates to train as junior nursery assistants. Winona Lund travelled from Manitoba to take the institute's diploma course during the mid-1940s:

> It was a very thrilling experience because those people were so gifted and it was a professional school. A real eye opener for me and I learned a great deal ... This was '44 and '45 and they had trimmed it down to one year, made it more intensive. It should be a two year post graduate course. All the other girls had B.A.'s or were graduate nurses or teachers with certificates and I was just a grade 12 girl from Manitoba so I really had to work hard and I found it difficult but I did make it and got my diploma, of which I was very proud. It was such a privilege to be taught by these people. Dr. Blatz was a researcher, a clinician, a psychiatrist [actually a psychologist] and when we went to his classes I think we'd go if we had to crawl. It was such a treat to be in his seminars. We practiced in the nursery school ... We learned then about the playrooms of course and all the routines ... We learned all about children's food habits, and nutrition was

> on the course. We went right through the day with them, there was nothing left out at all. We had to do a research paper ourselves, of course, which was very difficult for me. I think mine was called *The incidence of ticks and emotional outbursts in children* ... Each of us had to do a thesis like this which was the end of our year and sent us forward into the world, diploma in our hand (Lund 1992).

At the end of the war, employed women faced intense social pressure to surrender their jobs to the returning men and to commit themselves to the traditional roles of wife and mother. The belief that a woman's proper domain was in the home and claims that out-of-home care was detrimental to children's well-being prompted the federal government to terminate funding for the wartime nurseries, resulting in their closure (Lind and Prentice 1991). With the loss of demand for caregivers, the Institute of Child Study discontinued its shortened courses and the Provincial Day Nursery Training Centre closed. Only the institute's master's program in psychology and the two-year diploma course remained.

The programs offered through the Institute of Child Study were the only specialized courses available for day nursery caregivers in Canada into the late 1950s. Even though graduates of the institute's courses took up positions of day nursery directors and staff, their training had focused on the half-day nursery school attended by a small number of children, who typically came from economically advantaged families. Even the program of the Provincial Day Nursery Training Centre, established during the war years, followed the Institute's nursery school curriculum, with little adaptation for the different needs of day nursery providers or for the children and families served. Only after the 1950s did the content of caregiver education correspond with the characteristics of day nurseries: ten- to twelve-hour days with large numbers of working-class children, and few staff.

From the 1950s, alumni and faculty of the Institute were influential in the establishment of numerous postsecondary child care training programs in Ontario and other Canadian provinces. These included, in 1959, a two-year course for nursery school teachers at Toronto's Ryerson Polytechnic Institute and, in 1968, a series of eighteen-week child care courses offered through the extension departments of the universities of Toronto, McMaster, Guelph, and Queen's. Gretta Brown, director of the Day Nursery Centre in Winnipeg, and an institute graduate, was the main proponent for the 1966 establishment of a two-year diploma program in Early Childhood Education at the Manitoba Institute of Technology (renamed Red River Community College).

In 1971, the Institute of Child Study was consolidated with the Ontario College of Education, and in 1973, the Ontario College of Education was itself absorbed into the Faculty of Education at the University of Toronto. While the Institute of Child Study continued to exist in name, it ceased to function as an independent entity and was charged only with educating school teachers for the kindergarten and elementary grades. Its diploma program for nursery school teachers and its master's program in psychology were discontinued. The institute's forced withdrawal from educating caregivers took place during the same historical period when other programs were being established across the country – a development for which institute graduates had campaigned for years. Their influence, together with an increasing public demand for centre-based, government-regulated day care, resulted in the mushrooming of university and community college programs. Brock, Concordia, Guelph, Manitoba, and Mount Saint Vincent universities each established three- and four-year child study degree programs. At Ontario colleges, such as Centennial, Seneca, and Mohawk, and at colleges in other provinces, one- and two-year early childhood education programs were created. A general pattern in Canada has been that once specialized educational opportunities have been available for caregivers, government regulations requiring formal education have been passed. Ontario was the first province to regulate caregiver qualifications, doing so in 1946. Manitoba enacted educational regulations for caregivers in 1982. In those and other provinces, such regulations were the outcome of advocacy by persons involved in caregiving and the establishment of educational programs for caregivers. However, the existence of the educational programs has not necessarily led to the introduction of regulations governing caregiver qualifications. Table 2.2 illustrates the differences throughout Canada. Whereas Ontario and Manitoba have detailed educational requirements, other jurisdictions have few to none.

Table 2.2

Selected educational regulations and programs for early childhood caregivers

Alberta	
1978	Legislation of day care standards through the Social Care Facilities Licensing Act, but no provision for training.
by 1993	All directors to hold a two-year early childhood education diploma; one in four workers to have a one-year college certificate or its equivalent (Roeher Institute 1993).
British Columbia	
1955-6	Training program for certification set out by Welfare Institutions Licensing Board.

▶

◂ *Table 2.2*

Selected educational regulations and programs for early childhood caregivers

1988	Basic certificate established, one year of full time study.
by 1993	Supervisors and one staff person with each group of children in a centre need to have one year of early childhood education training (Roeher Institute 1993).
Manitoba	
1966	Pilot child care program offered through the Manitoba Institute of Technology.
1970	University of Manitoba offers a four-year degree program in Family Studies in the Faculty of Home Economics.
1971	Two-year Child Care Services Diploma through Red River Community College (formerly, Manitoba Institute of Technology); University of Winnipeg offers three-year Bachelor of Arts degree with a major in Developmental Studies.
1982	Community Child Day Care Standards Act establishes educational requirements for child care workers; a certain proportion of child care staff must have specialized training; specific requirements similar to Ontario 1980 regulations set out.
1986	Provincial government introduces salary enhancement grants for trained child care workers.
New Brunswick	
1982	Community colleges offer one- and two-year Day Care Certificate Training programs.
1988	The only specialized requirement is first-aid training.
Newfoundland	
1986	Two-year diploma in Early Childhood Education through community colleges.
1988	Licensing Board requires day care centre directors or group supervisor to have one year of academic training or supervised experience.
Northwest Territories	
	No specialized training requirements.
Nova Scotia	
1968	First workshop for child care staff in Nova Scotia (held in Halifax): delegates form a steering committee to investigate training.
1969	Early childhood education summer school training available.
1970	Froebel Institute, Truro, establishes a two-year program in early childhood education.
1972	One-year training program offered through St. Joseph's Children's Centre.

▸

◄ *Table 2.2*

Selected educational regulations and programs for early childhood caregivers

1970s	Mount Saint Vincent University establishes a two-year diploma program in Early Childhood Education and a four-year degree program in child study.
1987	Minimum training standards require that by 1989 two-thirds of a centre's staff and all directors are to have specialized training.
Nunavut	
	No specialized training requirements.
Ontario	
1946	Ontario Day Nurseries Act requires that a supervisor must be "sympathetic to the welfare of children," have "specialized knowledge of and adequate experience in the pre-school methods of child guidance," and be "suitable in point of age, health and personality to occupy the position" (Regulations made under the Day Nursery Act, Regulation 33, 1950).
1980	A supervisor must hold an Early Childhood Education diploma or equivalent, and there must be one trained staff for each group of children (groups being determined on the basis of age and numbers, e.g., fifteen children aged two to four would be one group, sixteen children aged two to four would be another group).
Prince Edward Island	
1972	A two-year Early Childhood Education training program established at Holland College, Charlottetown.
1986	Amendment to the Child Care Facilities Act requires all supervisors in licensed child care facilities to have degree or diploma in Early Childhood Education or a related field.
1991	In centres with more than one staff person, a second person needs to have similar training or equivalent practical experience as required of supervisors.
Quebec	
1987	Regulations Respecting Day Care Centres require that one day care staff in three must have at least a college diploma in Early Childhood Education or related field.
Saskatchewan	
1970	Child Welfare Act requires that applicants for a day care licence be found "suitable."
1975	Provincial day care regulations require all day care centre staff to have completed a mandatory forty-two-hour in-service course.

►

…ational regulations and programs for early childhood

	Kelsey Institute in Saskatoon offers Child Care Worker Program. In 1983 this becomes Early Childhood Development, a one- and two-year program; not recognized in provincial regulations as a minimum level of training requirements for child care workers.
Yukon	
by 1980s	Early childhood education program available through Yukon College; no specialized education or training required.

Source: Unless otherwise noted, the information is from Pence (1992).

Provinces with the most stringent requirements have specified the proportion of staff in a day care centre that must have postsecondary education, but even then, regulations have not been rigorously enforced. Persons who have not earned a degree or diploma in early childhood education or care have been determined as having met educational requirements on the basis of their completing a combination of postsecondary courses in the social and human sciences. Because regulations have not required all caregiving staff within a centre to have a specific educational background, persons could be hired as caregivers without having had any specialized education. In some provinces, such as Manitoba, experience in child care work is deemed equivalent to specialized education. Despite the lack of government regulations, specialized education for caregivers has followed similar curricula across the country. Only from the 1980s were programs initiated with features different from those established initially by the Institute of Child Study, and modified by psychological and cultural theories of the 1960s.

Early Childhood Education and Care: The 1960s and Beyond

Originally the philosophies and practices of kindergarten and elementary education were significantly different from those of day care. From the 1960s, influences on both elementary schooling and day care were conflated, and the concept of early childhood education was born. Ideas originating in the United States were prominent in effecting this change. Most influential were the theories of Jerome Bruner, J. McVicker Hunt, and Benjamin Bloom, as well as translations and interpretations of the cognitive development theory of Jean Piaget. A synopsis of their ideas provides an understanding of the context for changes to the curriculum of educating both school teachers and caregivers from the 1960s.

Jerome Bruner made passionate arguments for new methods of teaching at the beginning of a period of general social unrest and fear among the American population that the United States was losing the race for military domination against the Soviet Union. Bruner maintained, "Any subject can be taught effectively in some intellectually honest form to any child at any stage of development" (Bruner 1960, 33). His assertion renewed interest in the abilities of young children to benefit intellectually from stimulating activities, and in assessing whether society could profit as a whole from children's early learning experiences. Bruner's ideas about learning capabilities were antithetical to Gesell's maturationist argument that learning, especially of formal school subjects, could occur only at certain points along the continuum of development. While Bruner's hypothesis did not displace the maturationist theory within the field of child study, it did result in the reconceptualization of development: from development as genetically determined, with the environment providing opportunities for its expression, to the concept that the environment has primary influence over the quality of development.

The Piagetian theoretical proposition that received the most attention in North America was that children's interactions with their environment resulted in structural transformations in their thinking processes (see, e.g., Piaget [1936] 1952). Piaget posited the child as a being who actively seeks out information about the world and whose thinking processes resulted from the continuous interplay between old and new experiences. It was the child's interaction with the environment that enabled cognitive development to occur in what Piaget considered to be an invariant and universal sequence of stages, or periods, of particular kinds of mental structures. Piaget's reference to ages when certain periods of development occurred differed from the maturationist concept of ages and stages: Piaget did not base *explanations* for developmental change on biological age, but used age as a marker to indicate the period of life when children typically had similar types of experiences. The popularization of Piaget's theories about children's cognitive abilities (how children think – as distinguished from intellectual capacity or what children know) stimulated a change in dominant ideas about the nature of child development, from being a passive outcome of maturation influenced by environmental stimuli to that of an active process, which, while biologically centred, could be determined by environmental factors.

During the same period of time that ideas about the nature of development were being reassessed, there arose in the United States and Canada a widespread concern about the continued existence of poverty and the realization that children from economically disadvantaged families failed in school more often than did children from economically privileged families. It was hypothesized that a lack of "cultural preparation" perpetuated of poverty. Children unfamiliar with typical features of middle-[illegible]ooling such as codes of behaviour, learning styles, and expecta-[illegible]e likely to fail in school. School failure led to underemployment or unemployment, which led to poverty, which led to the same culture of poverty that produced the next generation of culturally deprived children. J. McVicker Hunt was one of the most effective popularizers of ideas about child development and the culture of poverty thesis. He proposed that there are certain periods in a child's life when specific experiences are necessary for optimal development (critical or sensitive periods) (Hunt 1961). While he acknowledged that poverty was caused by socio-economic conditions, rather than personality deficiencies of the poor, he maintained that a lack of typical middle-class experiences had profound ramifications for the economically disadvantaged child's opportunities for cognitive development. His solution to the presumed effects of poverty on children was to supplement their early experiences with preschool programs (as opposed, for example, to transforming the economic structure of society) to compensate for so-called cultural deprivation. It was from his arguments that Head Start programs were initiated, first in the United States and later in Canada (see also Chapter 7).

In the 1960s, the focus on cognitive development and cultural deprivation was given further emphasis by Benjamin Bloom. Using longitudinal research to provide a statistical ratio of intellectual development, Bloom maintained that "culturally deprived" children had intelligence quotients (IQs) twenty points lower than those whom he labelled "culturally abundant" children (Bloom 1964). Bloom interpreted the IQ difference as proof that intellectual ability was permanently formed during the first four years of life, and that 50 percent of intellectual development was completed by the age of four. Bloom's theory of intellectual capacity, as popularly expounded during the 1960s and 1970s, symbolized childhood as a window of opportunity that was half closed by the age of four and offered minimal openings beyond the age of eight.

These new conceptual understandings of the child provided a continuity between the preschool, kindergarten, and the early elementary years that transcended settings of day care and school. In Canada, the new ideas about the child underlay demands that elementary schooling be radically transformed with a synthesis and continuity of learning experiences throughout the childhood years (see, for example, Hall and Dennis 1965). For child care providers, these theories provided the basis of arguments that infants and young children were able to gain intellectually and cognitively from specific types of adult-directed activities. In place of the previous belief that caregivers should manage children's development through supervision of the environment, they were now taught that they needed to actively *facilitate* children's interactions with the environmen For school teachers, there was an emphasis on helping young children use concrete materials to learn and a de-emphasis on direct teaching and rote learning. By the 1980s, this approach was referred to as the "developmentally appropriate curriculum."

The child-centred approach of the developmentally appropriate curriculum never became as pervasive within elementary schooling as its promoters had hoped and expected, for it was blended with the subject-orientation of teacher training. It did become the dominant perspective of educational programs for caregivers. In some cases, the new perspective resulted in a complete transformation of such programs. For example, the Ryerson Polytechnic early childhood education program was redeveloped from its earlier Institute of Child Study maturationist focus to the High/Scope early educational approach (see Chapters 4 and 7). The High/Scope program is based on Piaget's theory of cognitive development, which emphasizes the participation of children through a problem-solving approach to activities, and especially the active role of the early childhood teacher/caregiver in facilitating children's activities through intervention.

Changes in the education of caregivers and teachers continually took place in the latter years of the twentieth century. Increased numbers of mothers engaging in paid employment resulted in an expansion of full-time day care spaces. In response, caregiver education programs shifted away from a nursery school focus and toward teaching students how to provide for the needs of children from early morning to early evening. Demographic shifts in maternal employment also resulted in the creation of courses and practicum experiences pertaining to infants and school-age children. Closure of segregated programs for children who had special developmental needs, together with new beliefs about this population's developmental potential and human rights, resulted in more children with special needs attending regular schools and day care centres. In the late twentieth century, caregivers and teachers have also been challenged by the growing diversity of the children and families with whom they work and by research demonstrating how children benefit from environments that provide continuity between the culture of the home and early education settings. In response to the special-needs and culturally diverse populations attending day care centres and schools, the educational preparation of school teachers and caregivers was expanded to include material pertaining to the particular needs of both groups.

Since the 1980s, there has been a heightened emphasis on children learning marketable skills during their early years. Arguments have been made that the process orientation (learning by doing) of the developmentally ulum is not adequate preparation for workplace demands ry and should be replaced by a product-oriented curricu- ıd content of such an approach have included systematic en's knowledge, formal rote teaching of skills, and rigid ndards. These have found a place in both early education classrooms and day care centres, but to a lesser extent in education programs for teachers and caregivers.

Conclusion

Many of the changes in the education of early childhood teachers and caregivers have resulted in benefits for teachers, caregivers, children, and parents. The needs of children have been taken into account to a greater extent; caregivers and teachers with formal education in early childhood training have more resources to draw upon in dealing with the complexities of their tasks than do their untrained counterparts; and parents have some assurance that the quality of their children's education and care is improved when teachers and caregivers have specialized knowledge. For school teachers, increased educational qualifications have won them salaries and benefits that compensate for the work involved; unfortunately, this benefit has not been extended equally to caregivers. While acknowledging the positive aspects of teacher education, this chapter is not meant to be a laudatory history, but to provide readers with the material necessary for reflecting upon the way historical practices in teacher and caregiver education have been constructed.

As provincial departments of education undertook the regulation of teachers by establishing normal schools, communities lost their power to control schooling practices, and public schools were transformed from heterogeneous to homogeneous places: student groups divided by grade levels; the use of apparatus such as blackboards, maps, and globes; and teachers incessantly watching over students by standing and moving about the room. The overall success of government regulation and standardization of teacher education does not mean that everyone was pleased with this turn of events. Some teachers thought that normal schooling was an imposition on their individuality. Some parents disliked teachers with normal school training because their methods of teaching or the curriculum differed from what was favoured by the community (Curtis 1988; MacNaughton 1947; Prentice 1977). Early resistance to standardization included letters of protest to government authorities, refusals to send children to school, burning of school houses, and physical attacks on teachers trained in normal schools. Over the second half of the twentieth century, persons of First Nations descent have engaged in activities designed to resist the continued destruction of Aboriginal cultures and people by dominant schooling practices (Battiste and Barman 1995; Couture 1987). At the close of the twentieth century, critical examinations of normative developmental theories and the developmentally appropriate curriculum have stimulated a rethinking of the curriculum in the education of early childhood teachers and caregivers (Bernhard 1995; Bernhard et al. 1998; Lubeck 1996; Mallory and New 1994; Varga 1997). Criticism has been levelled at the claim that normative developmental schedules, constructed primarily from studies of white, middle-class males raised in Western societies, are universal in nature and can be applied toward all early childhood programs. The new hypothesis being raised is that even biological patterns of human development (not just behaviour) are outcomes of the social-cultural context (Newman and Holzman 1993; Nsamenang 1992).

There are acknowledged benefits of educating teachers and caregivers for their work with children – regardless of the theoretical and philosophical assumptions of such training. However, no standard requirements exist across Canada for early childhood caregivers to hold provincial certificates as demonstration of educational preparation for the work of child care. Unlike the case of school teachers, whereby provincial certification standards are virtually identical, regulations governing caregiver qualifications vary widely across the country (see Table 2.2). This can be partially explained by regional economic differences. Provinces or territories with fewer people, fewer urban areas, and higher levels of unemployment lack the taxation base and administrative infrastructure necessary to support education programs and enforce government regulations. Guidelines for standardizing caregiving practices nationwide have been developed (Canadian Child Day Care Federation 1990), but without federal funds to equalize economic differences, they are unlikely to be incorporated into government regulations.

While this economic explanation provides some understanding of differences across the country, it is incomplete. Caregiver educational provisions and regulations have been strongly resisted. And underlying much of this resistance has been the socio-biological ideology that child care is a natural instinct of women, with non-familial child care simply being an extension of women's domestic activities. From this perspective, specialized education in child care is a waste of money, because it is unnecessary (since women naturally have such skills). Even students in early education training programs have been found to believe that while academic knowledge about children and their care can be useful, child care is primarily a natural activity learned from one's own family experience (Field and Varga 1998; Varga and Lanning 1998). Another facet of the socio-biological argument is that instinctual and familial knowledge is naturally better than academic knowledge, and that the two forms of child care knowledge conflict with each other. The belief that child care is best learned through the experience of rearing children, rather than "from a book," and that the two ways cannot exist in harmony has often been the basis of caregiver resistance to new educational requirements.

Highly trained caregivers find that they receive little financial recognition for their schooling, not making it feasible for many to undertake advanced studies. The belief that educational qualifications for caregiving are unnecessary has limited the ability of publicly funded day care centres to receive monies to hire trained staff. This belief has also been the basis of the Ontario provincial government's attempts, in the 1990s, to reduce the educational qualifications required by law for staff of day care centres.

Resistance to academic knowledge for child care has had both benefits and drawbacks. Despite the similarity of educational programs for caregivers, variety has been maintained in the delivery of caregiving services. The needs of diverse families can therefore be taken into account – for example, through the establishment and funding of parent cooperative nurseries. Resisting dominant early childhood caregiving practices, the Mi'kmaq community of Nova Scotia has established a specialized program for caregivers, which has offered a combination of the normative child care curriculum and traditional native knowledge. In British Columbia, the University of Victoria School of Child and Youth Care and the Meadow Lake Tribal Council developed a joint educational program. Resistance by parents has resulted in their right to participate as board directors of day care centres, thereby having more direct authority over matters related to their children than is possible in most schools. Resistance has enabled individual practitioners to determine for themselves which aspects of the academic and the personal will be incorporated into their caregiving practices.

The past has not been created through a value-free evolutionary process, whereby educational practices have only become better with time. It is important to ask the following questions when one examines the history of education for early childhood teachers and caregivers: What practices and ideas have been lost? Are the needs of our diverse population met through standardized education in teaching and child care? Has more academic training resulted in teachers and caregivers having greater independence in their work, or in greater dependency on academics with a consequent lack of personal commitment (Depaepe 1997)? Should the future education of early childhood teachers and caregivers be more of the same or should it look very different? Asking such questions is a means of challenging the (comfortable) belief that educational programs for teachers and caregivers have reached the pinnacle of achievement.

References

Battiste, M., and J. Barman. 1995. *First Nations education in Canada: The circle unfolds.* Vancouver: UBC Press.

Bernhard, J.K. 1995. Child development, cultural diversity, and the professional training of early childhood educators. *Canadian Journal of Education* 20:415-36.

Bernhard, J., J. Gonzalez-Menza, H. Chang, N. O'Loughlin, C. Eggers-Piérola, G. Fiati, and P. Corson. 1998. Recognizing the centrality of cultural diversity and racial equity: Beginning a discussion and critical reflection on developmentally appropriate practice. *Canadian Journal of Research in Early Childhood Education* 7(1):81-90.

Blatz, W.E., D. Millichamp, and M. Fletcher. 1935. *Nursery education: Theory and practice.* New York: Morrow.

Bloom, B.S. 1964. *Stability and change in human characteristics.* New York: Wiley.

Bruner, J.S. 1960. *The process of education.* New York: Vintage.

Canadian Child Day Care Federation. 1990. *National statement on quality child care.* Ottawa: Canadian Child Day Care Federation.

Cohen, S. 1979. The mental hygiene movement, the Commonwealth Fund, and public education, 1921-1933. In *Private philanthropy and public elementary and secondary education,* ed. G. Benjamin, 33-46. Proceedings of the Rockefeller Archives Center Conference, June 8.

Corbett, B.E. 1968. The public school kindergarten in Ontario 1883 to 1967. Ph.D. diss., University of Toronto.

Corrigan, P., B. Curtis, and R. Lanning. 1987. The political space of schooling. In *The political economy of Canadian schooling,* ed. T. Wotherspoon, 21-43. Toronto: Methuen.

Couture, J. 1987. What is fundamental to Native education? Some thoughts on the relationship between thinking, feeling, and learning. In *Contemporary educational issues: The Canadian mosaic,* ed. L.S. Stewin and J. McCann, 178-91. Toronto: Copp Clark Pitman.

Curtis, B. 1988. *Building the educational state: Canada West, 1836-1871.* London, ON: Althouse.

Danylewycz, M., and A. Prentice. 1984. Teachers, gender and bureaucratizing school systems in nineteenth century Montreal and Toronto. *History of Education Quarterly* 24:75-100.

Depaepe, M. 1997. Demythologizing the educational past: An endless task in history of education. *Historical Studies in Education* 9:208-23.

Dumont, M. 1990. *Girls' schooling in Québec, 1639-1960.* The Canadian Historical Association Historical Booklet No. 49. Ottawa: Canadian Historical Association.

Field, H., and D. Varga. 1998. Canadian and Australian university students' attitudes toward maternal employment, mother care and child day care. In *Childhood and youth: A universal odyssey,* ed. A. Richardson, 387-98. Edmonton: Kanata Learning Company.

Hall, E.M., and L.A. Dennis. 1965. *Living and learning: The report of the provincial committee on aims and objectives of education in the schools of Ontario.* Toronto: Ontario Department of Education.

Hallman, D. 1998. Who teaches intending teachers? The case of disappearing women. Paper presented at the Canadian History of Education Association, Vancouver.

Harrigan, P.J. 1992. The development of a corps of public school teachers in Canada, 1870-1980. *History of Education Quarterly* 32:483-521.

Heise [Varga], D. 1987. Gender differentiated teacher training: The Toronto Normal School 1847-1902. Master's thesis, University of Toronto.

Henchey, N. 1991. St. Joseph Teachers College joins McGill: A view from the other side. In *Aspects of education,* ed. M. Gillett and A. Beer, 29-44. Montreal: Faculty of Education, McGill University.

Hollihan, K.A. 1997. "Willing to listen humbly": Practice teaching in Alberta normal schools, 1906-44. *Historical Studies in Education* 9:237-50.

Hunt, J.M. 1961. *Intelligence and experience.* New York: Ronald Press.

Learned, W.S., and K.C.M. Sills. 1922. *Education in the maritime provinces of Canada.* New York: Carnegie Foundation.

Lind, L., and S. Prentice. 1991. *Their rightful place: An essay on children, families and child care in Canada.* Toronto: Our Schools/Our Selves.

Love, J. 1978. The professionalization of teachers in mid-nineteenth-century Upper Canada. In *Egerton Ryerson and his times,* ed. N. McDonald and A. Chaiton, 109-28. Toronto: Macmillan.

Lubeck, S. 1996. Deconstructing "child development knowledge" and teacher preparation. *Early Childhood Research Quarterly* 11:147-67.

Lund, W. 1992. Manitoba Child Care Association oral history project. Provincial Archives of Manitoba.

MacNaughton, K.F.C. 1947. *The development of the theory and practice of education in New Brunswick 1784-1900.* Fredericton, NB: University of New Brunswick Historical Studies.

Mallory, B.L., and R.S. New, eds. 1994. *Diversity and developmentally appropriate practice: Challenges for early childhood education.* New York: Teachers College Press.

Montreal Day Nursery. 1906. *Annual Report.* Pat Schulz Collection, Baldwin Room, Metropolitan Toronto Reference Library.

Newman, F., and L. Holzman. 1993. *Lev Vygotsky: Revolutionary scientist.* New York: Routledge.

Northway, M.L. 1977. Tape-recorded interview. Pat Schulz Collection, Baldwin Room, Metropolitan Toronto Reference Library.

Nova Scotia Normal College. 1955. *One hundred years of teacher education.* Truro: Nova Scotia Normal College.

Nsamenang, A.B. 1992. *Human development in cultural context: A third world perspective.* New York: Sage.

Ontario. [1890] 1914. Department of Education. *Annual report of the Normal Model and Common Schools.* Toronto: Department of Education.

Pence, A.R., ed. 1992. *Canadian national child care study. Child care in context: Perspectives from the provinces and territories.* Ottawa: Statistics Canada and Health and Welfare Canada.

Phillips, C.E. 1957. *The development of education in Canada.* Toronto: Gage.

Piaget, J. [1936] 1952. *The origins of intelligence in children.* New York: International Universities Press.

Prentice, A. 1975. The feminization of teaching in British North America and Canada 1845-1975. *Histoire sociale / Social History* 8:5-20.

–. 1977. *The school promoters.* Toronto: McClelland and Stewart.

Prochner, L. 1996. Quality of care in historical perspective. *Early Childhood Research Quarterly* 11:5-17.

–. 1997. The psychiatrist in the day nursery: The development of day care as a clinical setting in Canada, 1930-1965. In *Canadian childhood in 1997,* ed. A. Richardson, 8-15. Edmonton: Kanata Learning Company.

Robinson, J.M. 1994. Reflective evaluation and development: Two Labradorians work toward a productive evaluation model for Aboriginal educators. *Canadian Journal of Education* 19:142-53.

Roeher Institute. 1993. *Right off the bat: A study of inclusive child care in Canada.* North York, ON: Roeher Institute.

Rowe, F.W. 1964. *The development of education in Newfoundland.* Toronto: Ryerson Press.

St. George's School for Child Study. 1927. *St. George's Annual Report, 1926/27.* Blatz manuscript collection, Rare Books and Special Collections, University of Toronto Libraries, Toronto.

Sammons, P. 1852. *Correspondence to Egerton Ryerson.* Archives of Ontario, RG 2 C-6-C.

Sheehan, N.M., and J.D. Wilson. 1994. From normal school to the university to the College of Teachers: Teacher education in British Columbia in the 20th century. *Journal of Education for Teaching* 20:23-37.

Silin, J.G. 1987. The early childhood educator's knowledge base: A reconsideration. In *Current topics in early childhood education,* ed. L.G. Katz, 17-31. Norwood, NJ: Ablex.

Student Registers. 1899-1949. Kindergarten class, McGill University, RG2, McGill University Archives.

Sumara, D.J., and R. Luce-Kapler. 1996. (Un)becoming a teacher: Negotiating identities while learning to teach. *Canadian Journal of Education* 21:65-83.

Turmel, A. 1997a. Historiography of children in Canada. *Paedagogica Historica* 23:509-20.

–. 1997b. The medical construction of childhood and family life. In *Canadian childhood in 1997,* ed. A. Richardson, 249-54. Edmonton: Kanata Learning Company.

Varga, D. 1991a. Neutral and timeless truths: A historical analysis of observation and evaluation in teacher training. *Journal of Educational Thought* 25:12-26.

–. 1991b. The historical ordering of children's play as a developmental task. *Play and Culture* 4:322-33.

–. 1993. From a service for mothers to the developmental management of children: Day nursery care in Canada, 1890-1960. In *Advances in Early Education and Day Care,* vol. 5, ed. S. Reifel, 113-41. Greenwood, CT: JAI.

–. 1997. *Constructing the child: A history of Canadian day care.* Toronto: Lorimer.

Varga, D., and R. Lanning. 1998. In support of working mothers? Students of early childhood education and issues of maternal employment. *Education and Society* 16:17-30.

Weber, E. 1984. *Ideas influencing early childhood education: A theoretical analysis.* New York: Teachers College Press.

3
Toronto's Institute of Child Study and the Teachings of W.E. Blatz

Mary J. Wright

The first Canadian laboratory preschools were established during the academic year 1925-6. They were part of the so-called Child Study Movement in North America. These laboratories were two university-based nursery schools – one at McGill University in Montreal and the other at the University of Toronto. The McGill nursery school had a very short history. In contrast, the Toronto school has a lengthy history. It has survived to the present as part of the Institute of Child Study. This chapter deals primarily with the founding and early history of the Institute of Child Study in Toronto and the work of its first director, Dr. William E. Blatz. It describes Blatz's theories about personality development and the educational practices growing out of the theories that he advocated.

Mental Health: The Goal

By the 1920s, Canada had been "invaded" by the Mental Hygiene Movement launched earlier in the United States by Clifford Beers. A Canadian Committee on Mental Hygiene, chaired by a dynamic psychiatrist named Clarence Hincks, had been established in Toronto. The goals of the movement had recently changed from the treatment and prevention of mental illness to the promotion of robust mental health. This had led to a recognition of the need for scientific knowledge about the way children develop and the conditions that support the attainment of mental health. The immediate objective therefore became the establishment of university-based nursery schools where the necessary research could be done.

Hincks persuaded McGill University in Montreal and the University of Toronto to permit the establishment of such an unusual thing as a nursery school on their campuses. The schools were to be fully financed by sources outside the universities, primarily by the Laura Spelman

Rockefeller Memorial Foundation in the United States. The initial grants from this foundation were for five years.

The McGill Nursery School

At McGill the nursery school was set up by the dean of the Faculty of Medicine. A paediatrician, Dr. A.B. Chandler, who seems to have had little interest in the project, was its director. Two teachers (Gwen Watkins and Sybil Howard) were imported from England. One had received Froebel training, and the other Montessori.

A psychologist, Katharine Banham-Bridges, was appointed to plan and implement the research. She first arrived in Canada from England in 1921 with a BS degree in psychology and physiology from the University of Manchester (1919) and a year of graduate study at Cambridge. She said (in personal correspondence) that she had completed the work for a degree at Cambridge, but the degree was not awarded. Cambridge degrees were not conferred on women at that time. However, she thinks that her work at Cambridge was what earned her a post as lecturer at the University of Toronto, where she taught from 1921 to 1924. While lecturing at the university, she also studied and in 1923 obtained an MA degree. Then in 1924 she married and joined her husband, J.W. Bridges, in Montreal. He was a member of the Department of Abnormal Psychology in the Faculty of Medicine at McGill. She worked with him on studies of juvenile delinquency until her appointment to the staff of the nursery school.

The McGill nursery school received no support from the Department of Psychology in the Faculty of Arts and Sciences. Some have suggested that this was due to rivalry between this department and the Department of Abnormal Psychology in the Faculty of Medicine and resentment that the Rockefeller Funds for psychological research, which included special grants in addition to the one for the nursery school, were invested in the Faculty of Medicine. Both departments had been established at about the same time, in 1924 (Ferguson 1982, 47). However, the Department of Psychology was small and its faculty was overworked, which may be a fairer and more accurate explanation for its lack of support for the nursery school. In any case, none of the faculty in psychology showed any interest in the nursery school, and no psychology students conducted any research there. Thus Banham-Bridges was on her own.

During her time in the nursery school, Banham-Bridges published a few minor papers on the preschool child and wrote a book on the social and emotional development of the preschool child (Banham-Bridges 1931). While doing this work, however, she became increasingly convinced that mental health problems had their origins in infancy rather than at the nursery school level, and she developed a genetic theory of emotions

(Banham-Bridges 1930). The research she completed at the nursery school was acceptable to the Rockefeller Foundation, but the fact that the school had not been used by the psychology or any other department in the university for teaching or research purposes was not acceptable. In 1930, the Rockefeller Foundation withdrew its support for the school. The stock market crash in 1929 may also have been a factor. The nursery school did not completely die, but it ceased to be associated with McGill or to be a research centre. Interested parents raised sufficient funds to maintain it as a private school and they renamed it (after the St. George's Nursery School in Toronto) the St. George's Nursery School of Montreal.

Banham-Bridges now found herself without a job but free to pursue her new research interests. She became a graduate student at the University of Montreal and turned in earnest to the study of the social and emotional development of infants. She conducted observational studies at the Montreal Children's Hospital, the Protestant Foundling Hospital, and the Crèche d'Youville and published her findings in a series of papers that appeared (in both French and English) in rapid succession (1932, 1933, 1934). This work earned her a PhD from the University of Montreal in 1934.

The University of Toronto Nursery School

The nursery school at the University of Toronto, known simply as the St. George's Nursery School (the street on which it was located) was a huge success. In 1938, it developed into the Institute of Child Study, one of the first of its kind on the North American continent, under the directorship of Dr. William E. Blatz. Blatz had a degree in medicine from Toronto, but also a PhD in psychology from the University of Chicago, where he had studied with J.R. Angell and H. Carr. The nursery school was sponsored by the Department of Psychology, but administered by a Management Committee that represented a number of other departments in the university that were interested in the project. Blatz, an extremely clever and highly motivated man, was the leader in the achievements that followed his appointment, but he had much support from within the university. The head of the Department of Psychology, Edward A. Bott, took an interest in the practical affairs of the school, chaired the staff meetings, and even designed and made equipment for the playground. Helen Bott, his wife, who was a talented person in her own right, also played a highly significant role in the school's research, scholarly efforts, and parent education programs during the early years. For example, she collaborated with Blatz in the writing of his first two books (Blatz and Bott 1929, 1930).

Running the nursery school was an immediate challenge. In the first year, Blatz hired a trained teacher, Miss Deadman, from the United States, but soon let her go. Instead he chose as teachers women who were not trained in nursery techniques, but were well educated, bright, and innovative. He collaborated with these women in planning and implementing an educational program. Blatz had the ability to inspire his teams of workers and arouse in them a remarkable degree of enthusiasm and dedication.

From its beginning, the Toronto Nursery School was part of a larger organization that had two divisions, each with its own supervisor: a Nursery School Division and a Parent Education Division. Both aimed to conduct research on child development and family relations and to provide instruction for teachers. Parents whose children were enrolled in the preschool were required to attend parent education classes.

Books were needed for instructional purposes and two, addressed mainly to parents, were produced in the first four years of the nursery school's operation: *Parents and the Preschool Child* (Blatz and Bott 1929) and *Management of Young Children* (Blatz and Bott 1930). Then came a book for teachers entitled *Nursery Education: Theory and Practice* (Blatz, Millichamp, and Fletcher 1935). Thus no time was lost in getting into print current knowledge about children, including the findings of Blatz and his staff, and the implications of that knowledge for practice. During this period an in-house journal, the *Parent Education Bulletin*, was also started and produced quarterly. Research papers produced in the first six years were published in scientific journals such as the *Genetic Psychology Monographs* and the *Journal of Genetic Psychology*, but in 1933, the University of Toronto Press established a special Child Development Series for this purpose.

Following the model of several other North American child study centres established in the 1920s, notably the one at Berkeley, California, Blatz immediately launched a longitudinal project. Parents registered their children for the nursery school before birth so that they could be observed in infancy as well as in the preschool. The children were then followed up at regular intervals until they were young adults, some up to the age of twenty-four. Furthermore, to obtain normative data, the researchers made systematic observations of the children's social, emotional, eating, sleeping, and toilet behaviours in the preschool.

By the 1930s, the productivity of Blatz and his team had won them recognition as significant contributors to the Child Study Movement in North America. Then an event occurred that brought them international fame. This was the birth, in 1934, of the Dionne quintuplets. As Pierre Berton put it, "To Blatz, the quintuplets, landing virtually on his doorstep, must have seemed sent from Heaven especially for his benefit. No social scientist had ever been faced with such a unique and intriguing challenge; here he had children who sprang from a totally different background (from those studied in Toronto) and not only that: there were five of them, all alike" (Berton 1977, 118).

The quints were born into a rural French Canadian family in Northern Ontario under primitive conditions and were not expected to survive. But they did live, and were made wards of the province and housed in a controlled environment away from their parents. For over two years Blatz was given the opportunity to study these children, and he made objective observations of all aspects of their behaviour. Others at the University of Toronto also studied the children. Among them was Norma Ford-Walker, who was interested in their genetics. Her research suggested that they were identical. Blatz's studies showed variability in the children, especially in their social development, suggesting that the environment and the interpersonal behaviour patterns of the children, rather than heredity, was the significant factor in this area (Blatz et al. 1937). In 1937, a conference was held in Toronto to report the findings of this work and was attended by many prominent North American psychologists. A special train was chartered to take them to Callander, in Northern Ontario, to view the children in their controlled environment. In 1937, a collection of these studies was published in the Child Development Series (Blatz et al. 1937). The following year a book about this work, *The Five Sisters,* was published (Blatz 1938).

The Institute of Child Study

It was the interdisciplinary nature of the research done with the quintuplets that led the University of Toronto to decide to turn Blatz's child study centre into the Institute of Child Study so that this type of research could be facilitated. In 1938, the Institute of Child Study was established as the first institute in the history of the University of Toronto. Thus, wrote President Sidney Smith, "an important area of study is removed from any rigid departmental or faculty pattern and is made the subject of a free and diverse approach." The institute was made an independent unit in the university, and its affairs became the responsibility of a committee of the Senate.

The Security Theory

From the start of his teaching career in Toronto, Blatz had been carving out his own theory of personality development, and this was the basis for his views on child rearing. Having been charged with the task of determining how to promote the development of mental health, he struggled to comprehend the psychological characteristics of the mentally robust and the conditions that facilitated the development of those characteristics. He finally proposed a concept and an operational definition of mental health. He called it security.

He postulated security as the primary goal of the human being, but conceptualized this not as safety – a static state that was always subject to crisis and hence an insecure state – but as a dynamic state. Security was for him a state of mind, characterized by serenity, which grew out of trust in one's ability to deal with the future. He said it was a state of mind that accompanies a willingness to accept the consequences of one's decisions, and he argued that security was acquired through early experience. Initially children needed to develop dependent security, a feeling of complete trust in their caretakers. This gave them the courage to be brave, accept insecurity, explore, learn, and develop trust in themselves (independent security). Blatz's plan for child guidance was aimed at emancipation and the development of responsibility. It emphasized the importance of gradually increasing the child's freedom to make decisions independently, to experience consequences – both successes and failures, and to acquire effective ways of coping with those consequences.

By the mid-1930s, Blatz was discussing his theory in his classes and capturing the interest of bright young graduate students such as Mary Salter (later Ainsworth), who went on to be a leading figure in the study of mother-child attachment. She wrote, "It was a theory of personality development, and that was what I had been waiting for! I was honoured when, having completed my Master's thesis (in 1937) Blatz proposed that I undertake my dissertation research within the framework of his security theory" (Ainsworth 1983, 203). So in 1937, research on the theory began in earnest. Salter's dissertation was devoted to the construction of self-report scales to assess the security of young adults. She studied the balance between security and insecurity (defensive behaviour) in certain major areas of life. One of the first statements of the security theory appeared in Salter's PhD thesis (Salter 1940). But that same year in *Hostages to Peace*, Blatz's first wartime book, the theory was described and interpreted in the context of the outbreak of war (Blatz 1940).

The Plan of Discipline

Blatz had a great deal to say about discipline. He defined it as a plan for guiding the development of children. Its aim was to help the child attain security, robust mental health, as he had defined it. Hence he advocated that children should be given as much freedom as possible to make their own decisions, discover the consequences of those decisions, and thus sharpen their knowledge about cause and effect relations through experience. Limits to their freedom were, however, necessary both to give them a sense of security and to protect them from catastrophic consequences with which they could not deal. But the limits were to be as few as possible and absolutely necessary either to facilitate essential learning or to ensure the safety of the child and others. Children were to be instructed about the requirements, which derived from the limits, in an objective, non-authoritarian way through the use of statements, never commands. Finally, of fundamental importance was the consistency of the caretakers with respect to the requirements. To promote the development of self-control, the caretakers were then to give the children the freedom to conform or not conform to the requirements and experience the consequences of both. Only then would they be in a position to make accurate predictions and in future select the behaviour that for them would produce the most desirable results. The kinds of consequences that the children were to experience if they chose not to conform were to be carefully planned. They were to be logical (related to the real reason for the requirement and, hence, instructive); consistent (hence predictable); and, if an adult had to be involved, objectively administered in a non-judgmental way with no reprimands or punishments. The latter was essential to prevent the child from blaming the adult for the outcome, thus avoiding responsibility and the opportunity to learn from the experience. Caretakers, Blatz said, must respect children as learners who inevitably make mistakes. The caretakers' role was not to save or protect the young from unhappy consequences, but to support them emotionally and help them see that making mistakes was not a disaster that could not be handled. As children gained in knowledge and ability, the limits to their freedom were to be systematically expanded until, eventually, they were managing all their own affairs and assuming full responsibility for the outcomes of all their actions.

Blatz was considered a prophet by some but a radical by others (Wright 1996). In Canada, he was one of the most controversial figures of his time. Today, many of his ideas may seem commonplace, but in the 1930s and 1940s they were shocking to many people. He vigorously attacked all the traditional ideas about child rearing. He spoke out against punishment of all kinds, such as shaming and spanking. He anticipated attribution theory and criticized the use of extrinsic rewards, such as stars or examination marks, and personal incentives, such as praise. He pointed out the dangers in using competition as a way of motivating children, and he vehemently attacked the schools, sports enthusiasts, and other do-gooders who made constant use of it. If the goal is to win, only one child can succeed. The others stop trying, and since the effort a child expends is the source of the joy in an activity, as the effort diminishes, so does the child's interest. Should children be trained to be strictly obedient? Blatz said no – the ability to think critically about authority was essential for survival in a democracy. His plan of discipline was aimed at putting the locus of control squarely on the child. This was the essence of his concept of independent security. Hence he taught that children should be given freedom to make choices and learn through experience. Making mistakes was, he pointed out, a more common experience than getting things right. And one's mental health depended on one's ability to cope with failures and turn them into learning experiences.

He even attacked love and motherhood. Don't worry about loving your child, he would say. If you do, you are probably feeling guilty, and guilt breeds "smother" love. Just be consistent and dependable, even to the point of being boring. This is what makes infants feel secure, and if they are bored they will reach out beyond you for excitement and will learn. In *Saturday Night,* there once appeared a hilarious parody entitled "I can't give you anything but consistency, baby" (Ross 1947), inspired by one of Blatz's public lectures on this subject. Moreover, because Blatz believed that consistency was what mattered, he maintained that fathers could raise children just as successfully as mothers. There seemed to be nothing he did not challenge: even honesty as an absolute virtue came under fire. Blatz said children had to learn how and when to lie, as well as when to tell the truth. To discourage their creativity in elaborating the facts was to make them dull companions indeed! Nor did he ignore the tabooed subject of sex. Sex, he said, was a basic appetite, and the child's first attitudes and feelings about it were generated in early childhood.

Blatz was controversial not only because of what he said, but because of how he said it. He applied his theories about the conditions that give rise to learning (Wright 1996, 206) in his approach to both the public and students. He deliberately shocked to arouse and alert. He induced cognitive dissonance to produce the affective energy and the motivation to think and to learn. He loved to say, for example, "No child in my school ever has to do anything he or she does not want to do." No wonder Blatz was so often misunderstood and the notions about his ideas so often extreme. There developed two schools of thought about the institute's plan of discipline. One contended that it was too permissive, and the other that it was too restrictive. Sometimes one heard that at the institute, the children were allowed to cut up the curtains and that Blatz's two sons were so out of control that they were the terror of the neighbourhood. This latter rumour was widely believed even though Blatz had no sons, only one very pleasant daughter. At other times one heard that the discipline at the institute was too rigid and destroyed the child's spontaneity. How did this idea develop? Certainly, Blatz's plan did include limits to ensure that the consequences of the children's decision making would not be beyond their coping capacity, and this plan was successful. The self-management that the institute program produced in its pupils was remarkable and beyond the comprehension of many who concluded that the control must have been authoritarian and imposed.

Educational Theory and Practice

Kohlberg (1968) argued that educational thought concerning the way children deal with the environment can be differentiated into three streams. The first stream regards children as active, the second as reactive, and the third as interactive. Blatz belongs in the last of these three streams, the cognitive developmental one, along with Dewey, Piaget, and Kohlberg. "Learning can never be mechanical," said Blatz, because of "the active conscious participation of the individual ... There is always a future reference in learning ... The past provides the means, the future reference determines the end" (Blatz 1944, 46-7). Blatz stressed the active role of the learner as a change agent, emphasizing the person's perception of a situation as the primary determinant of action. Thus a teacher who understood a child's motivation and past experience could create a learning situation for the child (i.e., set up conditions calculated to start adaptive, problem-solving striving), but could not make the child learn. It was the child, Blatz insisted, who must initiate the action, if real learning was to take place.

Thus Blatz was opposed to formal education and pointed out that direct instruction and authoritarian methods of control produced superficial and temporary change, but no real learning and development. His schools, at both the preschool and the primary grade levels, were therefore play-oriented – that is, organized around the interests of the child (Raymond 1991). He assumed that children were intrinsically motivated to be active and exploratory, and he postulated the appetite of change. The appetite of change "demands satisfaction in the form of new perceptual or ideational imaginative content of consciousness" (Blatz 1944, 100). Humans strive to induce as well as to reduce tension. The child seeks novelty and variety. No extrinsic rewards are needed to produce active learning, argued Blatz, and when used, these can be highly destructive. Blatz's overall goal was to help children "learn how to learn." He endeavoured to set the stage for children to become discoverers (curious, exploratory), constructive (goal-oriented, purposeful), creative (flexible, innovative problem solvers), and considered (reflective). His schools offered challenges that were hard enough to induce tension so the child would experience the thrill that came with the reduction of tension when the challenge was met. The challenges were, however, always self-selected by the children themselves. Hence the teachers' role was to set the stage for the child to find challenging, growth-producing activities in which to engage, but otherwise to maintain a low profile. Blatz's teachers even wore inconspicuous apparel (blue smocks) so that they would fade more effectively into the background.

Blatz's Influence Abroad

By 1939, Blatz's teachings were becoming well known both at home and abroad. In 1941, Blatz was invited, along with C.M. Hincks and Stuart Jaffrey of the Department of Social Work at the University of Toronto, to visit England to confer on the care of children during wartime and to determine what assistance Canada could give in providing suitable care. On their return, Hincks organized the Canadian Children's Service and, in 1942, sent three groups of workers to England: (a) elementary school teachers to help fill vacancies on the staffs of the London County Council schools; (b) social workers to work in the reception areas to which children had been evacuated; and (c) early childhood educators to train nursery school teachers. Blatz was in charge of this latter group.

Blatz established a training school for what were called Child Care Reservists in Birmingham. The reservists would help staff the many wartime day nurseries and additional nursery classes in infant schools that were being organized at this time. All able-bodied women in England had been mobilized into the workforce, and provision for the care of their children had become necessary. During Blatz's 1941 visit to England he had stressed the need for trained teachers to work with preschool-aged children and had offered to supplement the available resources for providing such training.

Early in 1942, Blatz visited Birmingham to make arrangements for the school. The site was chosen – an abandoned bomb-damaged school in the core area of the city – and alterations to the school were planned. In May, when the school was ready, he and five helpers went to England. "Garrison Lane Nursery Training School opened its doors on 1 July 1942, to forty-two children between the ages of two and five and forty student Child Care Reservists, much older" (Blatz 1944, ix). The training school included, for training purposes, a demonstration day nursery that provided services for working-class families in the area, who were living under extremely difficult conditions in bomb-damaged homes in the centre of this large industrial city.

Initially Blatz's five helpers included three senior members of the institute's staff: Dorothy Millichamp, the assistant director in charge of student training; Margaret Fletcher, the director of the nursery school; and Anne Harris (later Blatz). The other two were juniors: Mary McFarland (later Smith) and Mary Wright (the writer of this chapter). The full-day program in the day nursery was an adaptation of the shorter preschool program at the institute in Toronto, and the students were taught the institute's theory and methods. By the end of the first summer, the school was well established and Blatz and his three senior staff returned to Canada. However, Garrison Lane continued its work until the summer of 1944, with student training in the trembling hands of the writer, and the day nursery restaffed by a second contingent of teachers from Canada, who arrived in late August.

On the way home in 1942, Blatz decided to write another book on nursery school theory and practice for publication and use in England. It had not been possible to obtain a supply of the institute's publications for the Garrison Lane library, making the teaching of Blatz's system difficult. The book was started immediately and was completed during the summer of 1943 when Blatz returned to Birmingham. *Understanding the Young Child* (Blatz 1944) was published in England, in May 1944, too late to be much help at Garrison Lane. However, it was republished in Canada and served its purpose well there, where new training programs were being developed.

It is difficult to assess Blatz's impact on the thinking of early childhood educators in England, but there is reason to believe that it was substantial. His ideas were disseminated widely to those with influence in the early education field. At Garrison Lane, training programs were offered to school administrators as well as Child Care Reservists. These programs were a week in length and were fully enrolled. Furthermore, visits from important persons were an almost daily occurrence at the school. Beyond the school, Blatz was in much demand as a lecturer, and he often appeared on the platform with the most significant educators of the time, including Anna Freud who, as a refugee, was operating child care centres in the London area and disseminating her own ideas about child care. Although Blatz's style abroad was somewhat more constrained than it was at home, he did not fail to challenge conventional ideas or to express his views in his usual witty and forceful manner.

The informal early education offered in the English nursery classes and schools after the publication, in 1967, of the Plowden report, had much in common with the type of education Blatz promoted. In Lillian Weber's description of this early education system, Blatz's favourite terms (e.g., serenity) are prominent (Weber 1971). In a discussion of these informal programs, Evans points out that "there are many similarities, both philosophically and psychologically, between new infant school practice and the American progressive education of the 1939s" (Evans 1975, 322). Could Blatz have been one of the important sowers of the seeds of these ideas in Britain? It seems very likely.

Wartime Day Nurseries at Home

In the fall of 1942 when Blatz and his senior colleagues returned to Canada, they found that the need for wartime day nurseries at home had also been recognized. A survey conducted by the Welfare Council of

Toronto and District showed that many mothers who had been recruited for essential work in war-related industries were unable to provide adequate care for their children. The Welfare Council called on the provincial and federal governments to take steps to rectify this situation (Stapleford 1976). As a result, by July, a cost-sharing agreement had been worked out between Ontario and the federal government for the establishment and support of day care facilities. It is noteworthy that Ontario initiated this cost-sharing program and was the only Canadian province that took advantage of it on a large scale. Only a few wartime day nurseries were established elsewhere – in Quebec. Perhaps this was because only in Ontario were people sufficiently informed (by the institute) of the value of early education; or perhaps it was because only Ontario had the resources (the institute) to set up appropriate training facilities.

"The provincial government indicated its concern that the day care service provide a program of the highest standard aimed at the full development of the child" (Stapleford 1976, 2) and turned to the institute for direction. As a result, Millichamp was seconded to the Department of Public Welfare to direct its new Day Nurseries Branch, and she recruited several early trainees of the institute to help her. Thus the first public day nurseries in Ontario were placed in the province's most capable hands. These women pressed for an educational program for the children, rather than custodial care, and for teachers who were trained to implement such a program. Trained teachers were, however, in short supply, so emergency training programs had to be planned and launched. The early trainees at the institute were graduate students in psychology working on two-year MA programs. It was now clear that new shorter programs, which would emphasize teaching rather than research, must be offered. The first emergency training program was to run for eighteen months, but was cut to six, then to four, as needs in the field increased. In 1943, a one-year, post-BA diploma program was instituted, but the four-month program continued for the duration of the war and for some years later. Related as they were to the war effort, these programs attracted many well-educated and capable women, several of whom advanced far in the profession. The programs for the children in the day nurseries were modelled after the one developed at the institute. Thus a definable Ontario "traditional" early education program was established. It endured for more than two decades because it was soon legislated into law.

Ontario's First Day Nurseries Act

At the end of the war the federal government withdrew its support for the wartime day nurseries, but in Ontario they were not closed. This was mainly because of the hue and cry raised by mothers who had found them so helpful. The Ontario government developed a cost-sharing plan with interested municipalities and in this way continued its support. It decided, however, that if this was to be a permanently established program, it must be regulated. Hence in 1946, the first Ontario Day Nurseries Act was drafted and was passed into law. This law required that day nurseries and nursery schools meet specified standards and be licensed. Blatz and his colleagues were asked to set out the standards. Millichamp and Mary Northway described what then occurred. They said that because they were all so busy, meetings to deal with the Act were held at night. "We did fairly well on space and equipment, but when it came to programme, Dr. Blatz, who was very tired, said: 'Just tell them to do what we do at the Institute'" (Millichamp and Northway 1977, 14). And that is exactly what they did. The Act read, "Each procedure on the timetable shall conform to the standards currently accepted by the Institute of Child Study of the University of Toronto," and this statement appeared in every subsequent revision of the Act until 1968.

The 1946 Ontario Day Nurseries Act was one of the first of its kind in North America and the first in Canada. The standards it set were unequalled elsewhere. In fact, it provided a model for similar Acts passed in other jurisdictions for many years. The government also ensured that the requirements of the Act were implemented by hiring a well-qualified graduate of the institute to succeed Millichamp as director of the Day Nurseries Branch. This was Elsie M. Stapleford, who was a forceful child advocate. Stapleford had her MA and required only her thesis to obtain her PhD in psychology from the University of Toronto. She continued as director for some thirty years, until her retirement in the mid-1970s.

The Ontario Parent Education Program

Right after the Second World War there was a great upsurge of interest in parent education, and a province-wide parent education program was launched by the Ontario government. The Institute of Child Study played a major role in its implementation. Leaders for parent study groups were trained in great numbers in both large and small cities throughout the province. Frances Johnson, in charge of the Parent Education Division of the institute, was hired by the government to direct the program. Those of us who trained at the institute were recruited as instructors. The working materials employed for instruction were a series of outlines for parent education groups published by the institute in the early 1940s. (The outlines are included in a collection of the publications of the Institute of Child Study on deposit in the Thomas Fisher Rare Book Library at the University of Toronto.) They enunciated Blatz's philosophy and outlined his plan for guiding the development of young children. Blatz was indeed the Canadian Dr. Spock of his day, but he never gave parents a formula for managing behaviour. Instead, he challenged them to clarify their goals for their children and to consider the kind of guidance most likely to achieve those goals. He taught parents the principles to apply in guiding their children's development; these principles were based on an understanding of the child's developmental level, the problems the child faced, and the learning process.

Security Theory Research

After the war, research on the security theory was resumed. Blatz obtained grants from the Defence Research Board to support several graduate students, and he organized an enthusiastic research team. Salter, who returned to her academic post at Toronto in 1946, and Blatz co-directed the research program. During this period some changes in the theory were made. Blatz believed that in infancy and early childhood, children need to develop a secure dependence on their caretakers (immature dependent security). They need to feel safe at this stage in a predictable environment that can be trusted to meet their needs. This safety gives them the courage to brave the insecurity implicit in exploring the unfamiliar. And the predictability, which is in a sense boring, leads them to reach out for novelty and variety. Hence secure children are the ones most likely to be adventurous and to acquire the skills and knowledge that gradually enable them to depend on themselves (independent security). Blatz recognized, however, that as social beings, adults are of necessity dependent on others for the satisfaction of some of their basic needs and for the achievement of a variety of goals. He therefore saw immature dependent security as being gradually supplanted by mature dependent security, first on peers from a child's own age group and, later, on a heterosexual partner. In mature dependent relations the individuals have trust, faith, and confidence in each other; do not shirk responsibility but share it; and support one another in a reciprocal fashion.

In Blatz's original formulation of the security theory, independent security was emphasized as the ideal to be achieved even though it was not fully attainable. Insofar as a person could not make decisions or was unwilling to accept their consequences, that person was insecure. The individual could deal with his or her insecurity in constructive ways by accepting insecurity, learning needed skills, and, in areas where independence was not possible, develop mature dependent relations in which responsibility was shared. But insecurity was often dealt with in unproductive ways such as by finding a new agent to replace the parent as the decision maker (a return to immature dependent security) or by using what Blatz called deputy agents, which were pseudo devices similar to

Freudian defence mechanisms. These various forms of security and insecurity were described by Blatz as being expressed in four life areas: familial and extra-familial relations, vocation, avocation, and philosophy of life.

By the 1950s, the results of the security research suggested that the theory should be reformulated. It had been found that in young adults, independent security and mature dependent security were correlated and it seemed likely that they had a common origin (Ainsworth and Ainsworth 1958). It appeared that "(a) dependence was not cast off and replaced by independence, rather that the two grew in balance together; (b) that the form dependence took developed from a primitive to a complex sophisticated one, the extremes of this change being designated as 'immature' and 'mature' dependence, but the variations within the developmental pattern being much more subtle than a division into two types" (Northway 1959, 2). Had the notion of "attachment" been available at the time, this dilemma might have been more readily resolved, for attachments can be maintained throughout life even as children become independent of those to whom they are attached.

These conclusions generated greater interest in the development of mature dependent security and in the relationships that children formed with peers at different age levels (Ainsworth 1960). Northway's method of studying peer relations using sociometric techniques was now considered a promising approach, and she became part of the security research team. Northway's developmental sociometry used fictitious social situations (e.g., the "Birthday Test") to measure changes with age in the choice of adults or peers in situations that varied in the amount of help and support the child needed (Northway 1971). During this period, Dr. Michael Grapko, a member of the institute's staff, was working on the development of a method of measuring security in school-aged children, and he produced a test for nine- to twelve-year-olds called "The Story of Jimmy" and later one for six- to eight-year-olds called "The Story of Tommy" (Grapko 1956). In addition, Betty Flint developed a scale for measuring the mental health of infants (Flint 1959). It was a highly productive five years for research on security (Northway 1959; Ainsworth 1960).

The Move to 45 Walmer Road

In 1951 the Institute of Child Study celebrated its twenty-fifth birthday with a grand party and the presentation to Dr. Blatz of a magnificently bound copy of *Twenty-Five Years of Child Study* (Northway et al. 1951). Blatz was now fifty-six years old but he had yet to fulfil a major goal: to incorporate into the institute the private elementary school Windy Ridge Day School, of which he had been the director for many years. He wanted to study the growth of security longitudinally in the nine-to-twelve age group, a period when, he believed, moral and ethical principles were developed.

To achieve his goal, the institute needed a much larger building, one that could house classes up to grade 6 as well as an expanded teaching and research staff. Blatz had long been pressing the university for such a building, preferably located near the projected new Arts building on St. George Street. He even had architectural plans drawn up for it, but the university resisted. Finally, however, Blatz was offered the Leighton McCarthy mansion, which the university had inherited, at 45 Walmer Road (Millichamp and Northway 1977, 19-23). It was suitably renovated, and by the fall of 1953, Walmer Road was home to the staff and students of both the "old" institute and the former Windy Ridge school. This move ushered in a period plagued with administrative headaches. For two years, overcrowding and the noise and confusion of construction added to the tensions of integrating two formerly independent staffs, each with its own hierarchy of authority. In spite of the difficulties, significant progress was made, especially in research.

During the 1950s, the training and service demands made on the institute greatly increased. After 1954, the institute ceased to train master students in psychology, but the diploma programs were expanded. Mental health officers for the school system were trained, as well as a group of teachers from Thailand. Additional special courses were developed at the request of several different faculties such as graduate psychiatry, public health, social work, dentistry, food science, and education. For example, students training as primary specialists for the public school system did part of their work at the institute. Staff members, particularly in the Parent Education Division, were in constant demand as lecturers and consultants. In addition, clinical facilities were established. Blatz's institute had earned an enviable reputation and exercised a tremendous influence on the community. As the president of the University of Toronto put it, "The influence of the Institute of Child Study has not been confined to the University. Child study is not simply an affair of the classroom and the seminar. By its program of parent education, it has transformed the abstractions of research into wise counsels for home and school" (Northway et al. 1951, viii).

The End of the Blatzian Era

During the Christmas season of 1955, Dr. Blatz developed pneumonia, from which he never fully recovered. He resumed his duties in the fall of 1956, but lacked his former energy and drive. In 1960, he resigned as director of the institute and retired to an office in the Department of

Psychology. There he began work on his final book, *Human Security: Some Reflections,* which was published posthumously (Blatz 1966). William Blatz died on All Saints' Eve, 31 October 1964.

It is difficult to estimate Dr. Blatz's full impact on our society. Professor Bernhardt said: "His contributions to educational theory and practice, to child rearing and family life, to parent education and to an understanding of human development have had a profound influence on the life of his country and have extended beyond its boundaries to other parts of the world" (Bernhardt 1961, 2). As a psychologist, he was one of Canada's most innovative and challenging pioneers (Wright 1996).

The Institute after Blatz

The 1960s were full of uncertainties for the Institute of Child Study in Toronto. Fortunately, however, these did not include financial problems. Blatz had always been expected to procure the money required to fund all the institute's activities, but in 1958 the university decided to assume full financial responsibility for them. At this time, universities in Canada were becoming more affluent, but it is likely that Blatz's poor health was an important consideration in making this decision.

When Blatz retired in 1960, his successor as director was Dr. Karl S. Bernhardt. Bernhardt was a professor in the Department of Psychology who, for many years, had been closely associated with the institute and a regular participant in its programs. However, Bernhardt's health soon began to fail and he was forced to resign. The university then appointed a committee to find a new director and while the search went on, Grapko was made acting director.

The university's recruitment efforts for a new director were aimed at senior psychologists who were already eminent in the child development field. In the late 1960s, the competition for such people was extremely keen. In addition, the climate in psychology at the time favoured basic experimental rather than applied research. As a result, several recruitment attempts failed. At the same time, two of the institute's senior faculty, Northway and Millichamp, took early retirement. The university's officials became frustrated and discouraged, and suddenly the institute's very survival was in question. However, the cries of protest that arose at the thought of its demise led to a happier outcome.

In 1971, the institute was made part of the Ontario College of Education. With the gradual shift in focus from basic research to teacher training that occurred in the years following the Second World War, this seemed an appropriate arrangement. The diploma programs that had been developed during this period became two-year programs and, in 1977, one of them was recognized as a way to qualify for the Ontario Teachers

Certificate. Although educators were now a more influential presence at the institute, psychologists continued to play significant roles, especially on the academic and research side. In 1989, a psychologist, Dr. Carl Corter, was appointed director. With his appointment, Corter was given the mandate of renewing the scholarship of the Institute of Child Study.

In 1991, a million dollar endowment was secured to establish the Dr. R.G.N. Laidlaw Research Centre at the Institute of Child Study. The centre provides support for the renewed research efforts of institute faculty, laboratory school teachers, and collaborating scholars. Several new faculty members with internationally recognized research programs joined the institute in the 1990s.

In 1996, the Institute of Child Study, along with the Faculty of Education, was merged with the Ontario Institute for Studies in Education at the University of Toronto (OISE/UT). The two-year programs offered by the institute were then replaced by a new MA program in Child Study and Education, with the first admissions in the fall of 1997. This suggests that the educational goals of the institute have come full circle from its beginning. During its first two decades, it offered only graduate training in psychology. At present it offers the new MA program, which combines graduate study and pre-service teacher education. The institute also participates fully in other graduate programs offered through the Department of Human Development and Applied Psychology at OISE/UT.

The institute is still located at 45 Walmer Road in Toronto. It houses a laboratory school that includes an infant centre and classes for children aged three to twelve. Its merger with OISE/UT seems to have inspired renewed enthusiasm. Parents of its students have just completed a successful fund-raising campaign, with the funds being used for a new children's library and extensive renovations to the building. The new library will be named after the founding director of the institute, Dr. William E. Blatz (*University of Toronto Magazine* 1998).

References

Ainsworth, M.D. 1960. The significance of the five year research program at the Institute of Child Study. *Bulletin of the Institute of Child Study* 22(1):3-16.

–. 1983. Mary D. Salter Ainsworth. In *Models of achievement: Reflections of eminent women in psychology,* ed. A.N. O'Connell and N.F. Russo, 201-19. New York: Columbia University Press.

Ainsworth, M.D., and L.H. Ainsworth. 1958. *Measuring security in personal adjustment.* Toronto: University of Toronto Press.

Banham-Bridges, K.M. 1930. A genetic theory of the emotions. *Journal of Genetic Psychology* 37:514-27.

–. 1931. *The social and emotional development of the pre-school child.* London: Kegan Paul.

–. 1932. Emotional development in early infancy. *Child Development* 3:324-41.

–. 1933. A study of social development in early infancy. *Child Development* 4:36-49.

–. 1934. Measuring emotionality in infants. *Child Development* 5:36-40.

Bernhardt, K.S. 1961. Dr. Blatz and the Institute of Child Study. *Bulletin of the Institute of Child Study* 23(1):1-4.

Berton, P. 1977. *The Dionne years: A thirties melodrama.* Toronto: McClelland and Stewart.

Blatz, W.E. 1938. *The five sisters: A study of child psychology.* Toronto: McClelland and Stewart.

–. 1940. *Hostages to peace: Parents and the children of democracy.* New York: Morrow.

–. 1944. *Understanding the young child.* Toronto: Clarke, Irwin.

–. 1966. *Human security: Some reflections.* Toronto: University of Toronto Press.

Blatz, W.E., and H. Bott. 1929. *Parents and the preschool child.* New York: Morrow.

–. 1930. *The management of young children.* New York: Morrow.

Blatz, W.E., N. Chant, M.W. Charles, M.I. Fletcher, N.H.C. Ford, A.L. Harris, J.W. MacArthur, M. Mason, and D.A. Millichamp. 1937. *Collected studies on the Dionne quintuplets.* Child Development Series. Toronto: University of Toronto Press.

Blatz, W.E., D.A. Millichamp, and M. Fletcher. 1935. *Nursery education: Theory and practice.* New York: Morrow.

Evans, E.D. 1975. *Contemporary influences in early childhood education.* New York: Holt, Rinehart and Winston.

Ferguson, G.A. 1982. Psychology at McGill. In *History of academic psychology in Canada,* ed. M.J. Wright and C.R. Myers, 33-67. Toronto: C.J. Hogrefe.

Flint, B.M. 1959. *The security of infants.* Toronto: University of Toronto Press.

Grapko, M.F. 1956. The child and his development of security. *Canadian School Journal* 34:6.

Kohlberg, L. 1968. Early education: A cognitive-developmental view. *Child Development* 39:1013-62.

Millichamp, D., and M.L. Northway. 1977. *Conversations at Caledon: Some reminiscences of the Blatz Era.* Toronto: Brora Centre.

Northway, M.L. 1959. Studies of the growth of security. *Bulletin of the Institute of Child Study* 21:1-7, 17.

–. 1971. The sociometry of society: Some facts and fancies. *Canadian Journal of Behavioural Science* 3(1):18-36.

Northway, M.L., K.S. Bernhardt, M.I. Fletcher, F.L. Johnson, and D.A. Millichamp, eds. 1951. *Twenty-five years of child study.* Toronto: University of Toronto Press.

Raymond, J.M. 1991. *The nursery world of Dr. Blatz.* Toronto: University of Toronto Press.

Ross, M.L. 1947. I can't give you anything but consistency, baby. *Saturday Night,* 15 March, 10.

Salter, M.D. 1940. *An evaluation of adjustment based upon the concept of security.* University of Toronto Studies. Child Development Series, no. 9. Toronto: University of Toronto Press.

Stapleford, E.M. 1976. *History of the Day Nurseries Branch.* Toronto: Ontario Ministry of Community and Social Services.

University of Toronto Magazine. 1998. 26(1):C18.

Weber, L. 1971. *The English infant school and informal education.* Englewood Cliffs, NJ: Prentice-Hall.

Wright, M.J. 1996. William Emet Blatz: A Canadian pioneer. In *Portraits of pioneers in psychology,* ed. G.A. Kimble, C.A. Boneau, and M. Wertheimer, vol. 2, 198-211. Washington, DC: American Psychological Association and Mahwah, NJ: Lawrence Erlbaum Associates.

4

A History of Laboratory Schools

Kathleen Brophy

The history of university laboratory schools in Canada reflects the discipline basis from which they developed. The history of the McGill and University of Toronto laboratory schools, for example, derives from their psychology and medical traditions, which focused on the advancement of knowledge about child development and its relation to child-rearing practices. This research basis is reflective of later university-based laboratory schools such as the Institute of Child Study (discussed in the previous chapter) and the University of Western Ontario Laboratory School founded by Dr. Mary Wright (discussed in Chapter 7). Quite different histories are seen for those laboratory schools evolving out of the home economics and education traditions. The initial framework for the development of these programs was provided by the training of practitioners and the provision of practice-based learning opportunities specifically geared to student needs. Research was not initially a priority in these programs, in contrast to those in the psychology tradition. A historical trend in the development of home economics- and education-based laboratory schools is the gradual shift from teaching practice and demonstration to experimentation (McBride 1994).

As discussed in Chapter 2, the curriculum for the normal schools required practice teaching. This often took place in a local school where students "worked beside or with fully qualified professionals. The students, in this context, learn through observation and through being given opportunities to perform various tasks under the guidance of the field professional" (Ryan in Stuart et al. 1998, 305). To provide more of a directive role and guide the process of skill development in a systematic manner, laboratory schools were developed as training and observation facilities for students in education and home economics. The schools supplied a service context "that was designed to offer instruction in the practical and professional aspects" of the field and that was often referred to as a practicum (Ryan in Stuart et al. 1998, 305).

In such instances, the instructor within the laboratory context would design learning experiences to meet the needs of the university students. With the move of normal schools into university-based programs, laboratory schools housed within faculties of education trained students for positions in the school system. However, home economics provided the foundation for the development of training programs for early childhood care professionals. Programs such as those at the University of Manitoba and University of Guelph were originally designed to add a practical component to the early child development courses offered in home economics departments. Later, with the rise of nursery education and the growing need for child care professionals, such programs became training centres. Within both the education and the home economics traditions, the opportunity to provide systematic, high-quality practical experience for students guided the development of laboratory schools.

While many university-based laboratory schools developed out of the research or training needs of their various disciplines, they were not limited by these. It is quite clear that research-based programs offered training for early childhood professionals, and training-based programs often provided research opportunities for faculty. In 1981, Marion Barnett, director of the laboratory school at Carleton University, conducted a survey of child study centres in English language universities in Canada that were used for research or demonstration purposes. Of the twenty-two programs that responded to the survey, nine stated their faculty affiliation as education, five as psychology, one as medicine, and one as family studies. All programs identified the development of quality programs for children and families as one of their primary goals. Eleven also included training and/or research as primary goals (Barnett 1981).

What follows is a description of seven laboratory programs currently operating in conjunction with university programs in five provinces in Canada. Six are organized in relation to their roots in one of three disciplines that inform early education: home economics, education, and psychology. The final program is provided as an example of a hybrid – combining the needs of working parents with those of training students. These seven programs were chosen because they reflect, in their own histories, the different traditions of university laboratory schools in Canada. They also incorporate mandates for both teaching and research. Finally, all but one of these seven programs are still in existence, having survived financial restraints and restructuring processes. Although they have taken different directions, they continue to fulfil their commitment to research and training. The chapter ends by considering the future of laboratory schools through an examination of recent developments at the University of Guelph that evolved from the sometimes conflicting interests of a number of stakeholders.

The Home Economics Tradition

The Child Development Centre, University of Manitoba

The Child Development Centre at the University of Manitoba originated in 1910 with the Department of Home Economics, whose aim was the practical application of science "to the duties of the home." Duties included "care of the expectant mother," "care of the infant," the "diet of infants and young children," and "the making of infant garments" (Manitoba Agricultural College 1912-3, 75). Brockman described the evolution of the centre:

> The first mention of actual care of children was in 1929 when, under the supervision of Florence McLaughlin, two children ... were cared for by students in Household Management. The laboratory requirement for this course was to "live in the management home" for a period of three weeks. At about this same time a special course in child care with a weekly lab was introduced in the fourth year of the degree program. Care of one to three foster children, often an infant, by students in the "home management family" continued until the late 1940s (Brockman 1989, 8-9).

The aim was to simulate conditions of a home for home economics students by including a child. This aspect of the program continued until the 1950s. At this time, changes in thinking about child welfare led authorities to favour foster care for the children rather than care in the laboratory by a shifting cadre of students of "home management and child care" (other aspects of their laboratory work included sewing, laundry, cooking, and ironing). A 70 percent increase in student enrolment in Home Economics in a decade resulted in insufficient laboratory space for Household Management. The University of Manitoba responded in 1939 with the construction of a new Home Management House. In 1943, the Department of Child Development and Household Management was created. With the new facilities and new department came a proposal for the development of a nursery school. The purpose of the nursery school was to provide opportunities for students to observe groups of children. In 1943, four preschool children came to the Home Management House. With the return of veterans of the Second World War and their families, playroom space was needed for children of student families living on campus. In 1945, a nursery school was opened in the basement of the new Home Management House two afternoons a week for the children of the veterans.

With a move to the current Home Economics Building in 1950, a full-time nursery school with an observation booth opened and functioned as a laboratory for university students enrolled in Home Economics. The nursery school served the children of faculty and staff of the university. "In 1960, 14 children between 2 1/2 and 4 years of age attended every weekday morning" (Brockman 1989, 9). The nursery school became an integral part of the course work for students enrolled in child development courses. In the first two years of their program, students observed the children. In their third and fourth years, students were required to complete a student placement in the nursery school under the supervision of a qualified nursery school teacher.

In 1970, with the establishment of a Faculty of Home Economics, child development became part of the new Department of Family Studies. Two additional staff were hired and the program in the nursery school was expanded to include an infant room and individual testing rooms with observation facilities. In 1973, the infant group program was opened, and in 1978, infant and preschool children with special needs were included in the group program; a course named Exceptional Development of the Infant and Young Child was offered.

In 1979, a series of video programs for teaching child development were produced. Research in child development was also encouraged. The nursery school and infant program were licensed as a part-time child care centre in 1985 and became known as the Child Development Centre. The centre, which draws its population from the broad community, is structured to allow students taking child development courses to observe and work with children from four months to four years. The centre supports the functions of teaching, research, and service. The teaching function relates to student learners and the children attending the centre. Research focuses on basic research in the areas of child development and family functioning as well as on applied research – for example, program planning and policy. Service includes parents, children with special needs, training for child care professionals, and consultation with the provincial government, to name a few functions.

In 1990, a minor in Child Studies was introduced with three areas of specialization (Infant Development and Care, Special Needs Children, Child Centre Management). Students graduating with a minor in Child Studies and an area of specialization are eligible for Early Childhood Education III classification from the provincial Department of Family Services. In 1991, a Master of Applied Child Studies was implemented. The Child Development Centre is used for the teaching of two graduate assessment courses – namely, "Developmental Assessment of the Infant and Toddler" and "Social-Emotional Assessment of the Preschool Child."

The Ryerson Early Learning Centre, Ryerson Polytechnic University

In September 1963, the Department of Home Economics at Ryerson Polytechnic Institute opened the Ryerson Nursery School to serve as a training program for students specializing in preschool education. The melding of theory and practice was a driving force behind the program from its inception. In 1963, the Home Economics program was expanded from two to three years with a preschool major as an option in the second year of study. Students observed in the nursery school for the first two weeks and then engaged in actual practice teaching later in the year (Fortney 1994). Initially, the nursery school enrolled twenty-five children in a half-day program, expanding to an afternoon program in 1968. The afternoon program was developed to serve children with special needs who had been referred from the Neighbourhood Workers Association (Fortney 1994). Skilled teaching on a one-to-one basis was desirable for this group of children, and ten children were initially enrolled in this program. The nursery school at Ryerson was modelled on that of the Institute of Child Study, and faculty from the institute lectured at Ryerson.

In 1972, the School of Early Childhood Education separated from the Department of Home Economics, and a separate four-year degree program began in September 1972. With the demand in the 1970s for more child care rather than nursery school facilities, there was a growing requirement for early childhood teachers. Increasing enrolment of students in the program resulted in the need for additional field placements. Consequently, the School of Early Childhood Education submitted a proposal to operate the Ryerson Day Care Centre. It was felt that the day care centre would offer a laboratory training program for students, be a service to the Ryerson community, and provide leadership in the development of child care centres in Canada. By May 1974, approval was given for the opening of a small day care centre serving fifteen children of faculty, students, and staff of Ryerson. The nursery school was still offered as a service to families in the Toronto community. By 1978, the nursery school was phased out and full-day care services were offered to meet the increasing demand. A second centre was added, the Infant and Toddler Centre, providing child care for children from the age of six months to two and a half years, while the original centre changed its name to the Early Learning Centre and served children from the age of two and a half to six years.

In 1975, the Ryerson Day Care Centre adopted the High/Scope curriculum after faculty attended a conference offered by the High/Scope Foundation. By 1979, the integration of children with special needs into the centre was planned. In 1982, the Gerrard Resource Centre was opened as a third site to complement the Infant and Toddler Centre and the Early Learning Centre as a drop-in centre to serve the local community. In addition, it provided resources for educators working with families and children with special needs. It also served as a general resource for the early childhood education community, and students had the option of a placement there. In 1995, the Infant and Toddler Centre and the Early Learning Centre were integrated into one centre with multi-age groupings (children from six months to five years being grouped together). Research is currently being undertaken by faculty and staff to explore the factors that are essential to the provision of high-quality programming in multi-age groupings.

With Ryerson becoming a university and expanding its research role, the centres of the School of Early Childhood Education have responded by supporting research opportunities within their various programs and continuing their commitment to teacher training. The relationship between research and practice is highly valued. Fortney (1994) sees the vision for the laboratory schools as embedded in the principles of leadership to the community, and the integration of theory and practice.

The Education Tradition

The Child Study Centre, University of British Columbia

The Child Study Centre at the University of British Columbia was established in 1961 by Dr. N. Scarfe, dean of the Faculty of Education (Dixon 1992). The centre was originally designed as an early childhood research and laboratory facility to serve the needs of the university community. In the 1960s, the centre served as "a model preschool for three- and four-year-olds, where research was carried out by postgraduate students and their supervising professors" (Dixon 1992, 53). At that time, nursery school and child care facilities were growing rapidly in Western Canada, and the Child Study Centre served as a demonstration site for early childhood professionals. By the 1970s, the role of and the need for the centre as a model of good practice declined as the practitioners in the field of early childhood became more skilled. With financial cuts to the operating funds of the University of British Columbia in the 1980s, the value of the centre came into question. Its survival depended on its role as an active research facility, and to this end, Dr. Glen Dixon was hired in 1982 as director with the mandate to revitalize the centre as a research facility.

The restructuring of the centre took place in three phases. First, the entry age for the children's program was lowered to two years, and a kindergarten program for five-year-olds was offered in cooperation with the Vancouver School Board. Staff qualifications were raised and head teachers were required to hold a master's degree. Second, a major research initiative in the area of early literacy (ANCHOR Project) was launched to attract external funding; four faculty members and several graduate students were involved. Concurrently, the Child Study Centre Research Advisory Committee was struck to develop ethical and advisory procedures and to supervise and encourage research. Lastly, to re-establish itself as a major presence in the early childhood field both provincially and nationally, the centre instituted an annual lecture series, developed video materials to be distributed to colleges and universities across Canada, and participated in national and international conferences.

Despite the increasing use of the centre as a research facility and as an observation site for university students, the development of a lecture series open to students and teachers in the field, its links with parents and the professional early childhood community, and its involved and dedicated staff, the Child Study Centre at the University of British Columbia closed on 30 June 1997 mainly as a result of budgetary constraints. Prior to its closing, there were approximately 140 children enrolled annually in the centre, with 30 children involved in a summer program. The facility had two components: first, the children's program, which operated as a model school for teaching and curriculum development; second, the research facility with staff involved in on-site research, as well as participating in other research in diverse settings. "In this way, it has become clear that the Centre is now widely regarded as the home for early childhood research and development in our province, and is the administrative head-quarters for several research projects being carried out further afield" (Dixon 1992, 57).

Even before it closed, Dixon questioned whether the Child Study Centre was seen as vital to the university. "In spite of its recognition as a model program and a productive research facility it is still not yet viewed as a basic element in the teaching program of the Faculty of Education" (Dixon 1992, 58). The location of the centre at a distance from the Faculty of Education could have been one negative factor. Dixon further reflects that early childhood education in Canada was, at that time, not as "worthy" an object of study as later education, despite public awareness and growing interest in early education and development. "Early childhood programs such as ours tend to be critically underfunded" (Dixon 1992, 59).

University Elementary School, University of Calgary and Calgary Public School Board

The University Elementary School (UES) opened on 8 March 1968 as a cooperative venture between the Calgary Public School Board and the University of Calgary. At the time, it was seen as a demonstration facility where students and visitors could observe high-quality innovative educational practice. The terms of reference, which were agreed upon by the two institutions, specified four major areas of activity for the school: the teaching function, the demonstration function, the resource function, and the research function. The physical design reflected the open plan concept in vogue in the 1960s. Movable walls allowed teachers to change the configuration of the classrooms from an open area concept to a more self-contained arrangement, to meet the instructional needs of the program. It was clear that this facility was to be utilized for observation purposes since multiple observation galleries commanded views of the main floor teaching area.

An Advisory Committee was struck to deal with the entire educational policy. The committee comprised four representatives from the Calgary School Board administration staff, four from the Faculty of Education, one from the Alberta Teachers' Association, and the principal of the school. There were twenty professional staff with a student population of approximately 500 from kindergarten to grade 6. Students lived within walking distance of the university, although children with special needs were drawn from the larger community. The UES was funded by the province of Alberta, the Calgary Board of Education, and the University of Calgary.

At the start, the objective of the school was to facilitate the "fullest development of each child as an individual being and as a social being" (S. Mutch, personal communication, July 1997). Cooperative teaching and planning were employed extensively, in particular, in the areas of reading, arithmetic, and social studies. The Faculty of Education used the UES extensively for observation. In the first five months of operation, the staff provided 234 hours of demonstration teaching. At that time, no practice teaching was done by university students. The role of the UES was that of a training school for pre-service teachers, with the role of the two cooperative founding partners being that of, "encouraging innovative practice, opportunities for collaborative inquiry, and active research" (S. Mutch, personal communication, July 1997).

By 1996, the school had been organized into three collaborative teaching units: two of them housing 125 students from grades 1 to 6, and the other with 156 children from kindergarten to grade 6. Twenty-two children with learning disabilities, forty-four English-as-a-second-language students, and many gifted children were included with the 370 regular students. Individual program plans are developed for all students in need (University Elementary School 1996-7). On 27 September 1996, the UES and the University of Calgary signed a contract to further strengthen ties with the Faculty of Education. As part of this new collaborative relationship, several UES teachers have taken on teaching roles for university courses. This allows for a blending of theory and practice. Research opportunities are actively supported by graduate students and faculty. The mission statement of the school outlines its commitment to excellence in education. "UES is an interdependent community of students, staff, parents and University of

Calgary partners interconnected through a shared commitment to building a strong foundation of knowledge, inspiring a passion for learning, challenging perceived boundaries, designing active research and the continuous improvement of safe, open learning environments" (Mutch 1996, 6).

In 1995, the UES established practicum placements for pre-service teachers. Education students are exposed to a multi-aged learning environment that encourages instruction, teamwork, and cooperative learning. "Faculty of Education instructors are involved with children and teachers in the planning, observing, teaching, and evaluating results of work" (Mutch 1996, 7). Children, too, are active in the feedback process. The teachers at the UES are selected for their skill in "high quality principled practice" and belief in communities of learners and teachers. Volunteer parent and support staff are part of the teaching and learning teams.

The Psychology Tradition

Early Childhood Education Centre, University of Waterloo

The Early Childhood Education Centre (ECEC) was founded in 1974 under the leadership of Dr. Ken Rubin, a faculty member of the Department of Psychology at the University of Waterloo. The ECEC was originally established for the threefold purpose of providing preschool for high-risk and nursery school-aged children; training for students in the Bachelor of Arts, Psychology, and Early Childhood Education Honours program; and a research facility for undergraduate and graduate students and faculty (Gillen, personal communication, July 1997). From its inception, the ECEC preschool provided a program for children judged to be at risk developmentally, and in fact half the children enrolled were considered high risk. A University of Waterloo bus provided transportation for these children. The parents of the high-risk children paid no fees, but arrangements were made for them to participate in the actual preschool program and the accompanying toy-lending library. Three teachers were hired to implement a Piagetian-based program focusing on academic skills. Between 1977 and 1979, the Ontario government shifted its funding for programs serving children at developmental risk and, as a result, many of the participants went to other day care centres. The change in the nature of the child population at the ECEC resulted in a change in curriculum to focus on social relationships and socio-emotional development, rather than academic skills.

Since 1974, student training had been a core aspect of the ECEC program. In 1989, with funding cutbacks, the Psychology Department discontinued the Bachelor of Arts, Early Childhood Education (ECE) degree program. The ECEC remained, however, and continues to provide a preschool program for seventy-two children, aged two and a half to six, from the Kitchener-Waterloo area. Student training continues at the ECEC with Conestoga College students in the ECE diploma program completing field placements and University of Waterloo Psychology students fulfilling practica. It also maintains a research role in projects in the study of child development conducted by members of the Department of Psychology.

Meeting the Needs of Parents First

In the 1970s, as child care developed as a support for wage-earning mothers of young children, child care centres were established on university campuses across North America. Many were experimental with regard to their curriculum, approach to teaching, or administration. Some, such as the Campus Co-op Day Care at the University of Toronto, became well known in Canada for child care activism. Some campus child care centres that developed in this period combined a service for parents with the traditional laboratory function of preschools described earlier – for example, the Child Study Centre at Mount Saint Vincent University, in Nova Scotia. Provision of child care for students attending Mount Saint Vincent University was the mandate of the Day Care Committee appointed in January 1971 by the president of Mount Saint Vincent University. After reviewing the available literature and visiting centres in Halifax, the committee supported the development of a day care centre, and the program was opened in 1973. Known as Gingerbread House, the centre was developed to serve twenty-five to thirty children aged two to five, who were children of faculty and staff of the university. When the Child Study Centre opened in 1977, Gingerbread House was closed (Mount Saint Vincent University 1985).

The Child Study Centre was developed to serve the observation and training needs of students enrolled in the two-year Child Development Certificate Program and the four-year Bachelor of Child Study program offered at Mount Saint Vincent University. Both programs required field placements and the Child Study Centre provided the opportunity. The centre was also used for research by the broader university community. The centre opened on 17 January 1977, and operated on a trial basis. For the first months of operation the centre operated only in the morning, and only served children from the former Gingerbread House program.

In February 1977, the Board of Governors of the university was granted a licence, by the Minister of Social Services, to operate a day care centre under the name Mount Saint Vincent University Child Study Centre (CSC). A faculty member of the Child Study Program served as the centre's director. In 1979, when full-day child care was offered in addition to the existing part-day child care program, early childhood teachers were employed at the CSC. A faculty member of the Child Study Program continued to serve as director until 1980, when a full-time director was hired to serve as administrator of the CSC and as supervisor of the teaching staff. Students continued to complete early childhood practica at the CSC, with the CSC staff serving as cooperating teachers and a faculty member of the Child Study Program serving as the practicum supervisor.

The CSC currently has eleven full-time spaces for children of single-parent students that are subsidized by the provincial government; an additional two spaces are subsidized by the university, and two bursaries are given for part-time care. The centre provides a program for children with special needs, with additional funding from the provincial government. In 1997, a revised mission statement for the Child Study Centre was approved. The objectives of the Child Study Centre are the following:

- to provide children (aged two to five) with an environment conducive to their individual needs and the development of their abilities
- to provide resources and support to the families of the Mount Saint Vincent University and the external community, including families with special needs (e.g., single-parent families and families with children with special needs)
- to operate an effective education facility by providing students of the Bachelor of Applied Arts (Child and Youth Study) programs with the opportunity to participate in early childhood practical experiences supervised by trained professionals (Child Study Centre 1997).

The Future of Laboratory Schools

With Canadian universities facing financial cutbacks and restructuring, the continued existence of laboratory schools is uncertain. All existing programs described in this chapter are committed to providing the training and research needs of the students and faculty of the departments with which they are connected. In addition, these programs are leading the way in designing quality programs to serve children and families. The history of these programs contains some common features. First, preschool programs are seen as a way to support the social development of children rather than the teaching of academic skills. Second, infant and toddler programs and full-day child care programs as a service for working parents have replaced many of the traditional part-time nursery school programs. Third, a priority of many programs is to include children with special needs. These changes have meant a reorientation of traditional research interests to include such topics as factors affecting the quality of child care.

The laboratory schools have been at the forefront in confronting issues for professionals and students in the field. Shrinking budgets have, however, made it necessary to develop new and innovative ways to continue their work. Collaborative partnerships with existing on-campus child care programs or with agencies such as boards of education may be a way to provide continuing support for these programs (Barbour and Bersani 1991; Stuart et al. 1998).

The laboratory schools at the University of Guelph exemplify the collaborative model at work. The Family Studies Laboratory Schools (FSLS) housed within the former Department of Family Studies had a long history in training students. The laboratory preschool developed out of the home economics tradition. Since 1903, the Macdonald Institute has offered studies in home economics, which focus on quality of home life for families (Macdonald Institute Director 1960). Dr. Margaret S. McCready, principal of the Macdonald Institute from 1949 to 1969, recognized the need to provide some practical experience for students enrolled in the program. In 1959, both a one-year diploma course and a four-year Bachelor of Household Science degree were offered at the Macdonald Institute. The opening of the Macdonald Institute Nursery School (MINS, as it was called), on 8 September 1959, was the realization of McCready's vision to provide students with opportunities to relate theory and practice. The first mention of the Macdonald Institute Nursery School can be found in the course calendar for 1959-60, which stated, "Beginning in September, 1959, a Nursery School, for a limited number of children between the ages of two and a half and five years opened at Macdonald Institute." (Macdonald Institute 1959-60, 42). The nursery school was developed as a laboratory to provide observation opportunities for students in both the degree and the diploma programs. A course entitled "Child Development" was listed (but not offered) as an elective in the 1960-1 calendar. This course was for third- and fourth-year students and was meant to provide "opportunity to discuss children after having observed their behaviour in the nursery school situation" (Macdonald Institute 1960-1, 33). The course name was changed the following year to "Child and Family Studies." In addition, by 1962, students in a Survey of Research course could complete research projects in MINS. At the time of opening in 1959, sixteen children attended the half-day program operating Monday to Friday. Families from the surrounding community were encouraged to apply. In the 1962 brochure for MINS, the program was described as being play-based, with a maximum capacity of twenty-five children. Objectives for the program focused on helping children make the transition from home to school, and learning to cooperate as part of a group. Parents were supported in their interactions with other parents and in increasing their understanding of child development. Objectives for the students were the following:

- to provide an opportunity for all students in courses related to Child and Family Studies to have supervised observations of preschool children in a nursery school setting
- to provide an opportunity for a few students to assist and to participate, under supervision, in the school program
- to provide an opportunity for practice teaching for students selecting the Preschool Education option in the Child and Family Studies program
- to provide an opportunity for students and staff members to carry on research projects in areas related to Child and Family Studies and Home Economics (Macdonald Institute Director 1962).

In 1970, when the name changed from Macdonald Institute to the College of Family and Consumer Studies, the nursery school's name was changed to the Family Studies Laboratory School. In 1974, the toddler program was opened, requiring "School" in the name to be pluralized. The toddler program was first housed in what is now the Macdonald-Stewart Art Gallery.

The building had been designed as an elementary school and when the Board of Education stopped using it as a school, the department leased it for a year. The Family Studies Toddler Program offered fifteen children aged two and a half years, a group experience for two half-days a week.

By the 1990s, the FSLS were offering two half-day, licensed child care programs operated by the Department of Family Studies. The Family Studies Preschool was licensed for thirty children aged two and a half to five years, and the Family Studies Toddler Program was licensed for sixteen children, aged fifteen to thirty months. The FSLS enrolled approximately 100 children per semester, who attended half-day programs twice a week. Although not physically accessible for children in wheelchairs, since the 1970s the FSLS had accommodated children with special needs and worked with local health and social service agencies (Stuart et al. 1998).

The mandate of FSLS was to meet the teaching and research needs of the university community. In particular, students who were enrolled in the Child Studies major of the Department of Family Studies were required to complete their third-year practicum in the schools. The objective of the practicum was to provide direct experience with children so students could apply theory to practice and demonstrate communication skills, self-evaluation, skills in developmental programming, and team work. Twenty-five to thirty students per semester received practicum training in FSLS. Students at other levels in the Child Studies major used the laboratory schools for observation purposes and field placements. In addition, faculty and graduate students from the Department of Family Studies and elsewhere conducted research projects there.

While the programs for children and families were of high quality, the mandate of FSLS was very much directed at student practica for those enrolled in the Child Studies area of the department. The University of Guelph Child Care Centre (UCCC) opened in 1990 and had as its primary mandate to provide care and education to children while their parents worked or studied. It was "developed as a result of efforts of a group of highly committed staff, faculty, and students of the University who wanted to promote educational equity for student parents and identified the need for additional child care at the campus in 1982" (Stuart et al. 1998, 301)

In 1991, the director of Child Care Services responsible for the operation of UCCC and the director of FSLS were asked by the university administration to look at the possibility of merging their two distinct programs. The challenge that arose was the development of a collaborative model that focused equally on student training and quality programming for children and families. At an initial glance, this did not seem to be an impossible task. FSLS had always provided quality programs for children and families, and its lengthy waiting list attested to its high regard in the local community. UCCC had provided field placement experiences for students in the fourth year of the Child Studies program and for community college students enrolled in diploma courses. In addition, there were a number of factors that facilitated the process (Stuart et al. 1998). From its conception, it was hoped that the UCCC would be used for research and observation. Faculty from the Department of Family Studies had been involved in the planning and designing of the centre and had served as members of the UCCC Advisory Board. The director of UCCC was a graduate of the Family Studies Department graduate program and had served as a practicum instructor at FSLS. Many of the teachers at UCCC were graduates of the Child Studies program and had themselves been students at the FSLS. So while FSLS and UCCC were two separate entities, there was much communication and a shared history.

It took four years for faculty and university administrators to develop and approve a plan to merge the facilities of FSLS and the services of UCCC. During this time, six trials of the student practicum course offered by the Child Studies program were conducted at the UCCC. A working group composed of faculty of the department and staff of the child care centre was given the task of planning how the partnership might operate.

Three guiding principles emerged as discussions progressed, and it is in the implementation of these principles that challenges have arisen in the development of the collaborative model. The first guiding principle states that the new model must "support the goals of the child care centre by contributing to the quality of care provided for children and families by the child care centre staff" (Stuart et al. 1998, 304).

Initially there had been some concern that the families using the child care facility would question how this new collaborative model would affect their children and the quality of care they received. From a philosophical perspective, the two original programs were very compatible; both articulated a child-centred, play-based approach to learning and development. However, the increased number of adults in the centre was of some concern. Twenty-four students, per semester, from the Child Studies program would each be spending eight hours a week Monday through Thursday in the children's programs. In addition, there was a concern that contact with the child's teacher would be reduced. An evaluation conducted by Livingston and Positano (1998), however, has shown that parents are very positive about the quality of programming their children receive. In fact, parents report that students bring new ideas and energy to the program, thereby enriching their child's day. Staff report, in the same study, that children receive more attention, especially during transition times. So the principle of quality care is maintained, largely through a common philosophical commitment to this principle by staff, parents, and the faculty involved.

The second guiding principle is that the model must "ensure the integrity and quality of students' learning experience in a manner agreeable to Child Studies faculty" (Stuart et al. 1998, 304). The implementation of this principle was faced in the six trials of the practicum and, despite full implementation in September 1996, continues to be a challenge. Moving from a half-day nursery program to a full-day child care program necessitated changes in the students' schedules. In addition, routine tasks such as diapering, feeding, and transition activities occupied much more of the students' time than the half-day FSLS program had required. Expectations, roles, and responsibilities of the practicum students needed to be clearly defined, not only for the students but for all the staff at the centre. While the staff at the original FSLS were specifically hired to train students, staff at the child care centre were hired to plan programs and care for children. Faculty from the department would still supervise the practicum, but child care staff were now needed to observe, give feedback, and become involved in the process of student learning. In addition, the implementation of a practicum required that faculty be more involved in the curriculum decisions of the staff and the daily functioning of the centre. Developing the lines of communication became vital. An evaluation by Bauld and Coulman (1996) identified the need for role clarification and improved communication. The mechanics of scheduling times for feedback, seminars, and meeting as a team; negotiating for space; and developing materials must all be considered. These issues are very much embedded, however, in the new and additional responsibilities of the staff and the addition of a new service group – the students from child studies in the practicum course – to the mandate of the centre. Formerly, students were not the staff's responsibility, nor were faculty members as conspicuous in the centre. These new responsibilities thus created the need for clarification of staff roles.

From the students' perspective, the practicum could be offered; however, from the staff's perspective, the viability of the practicum hinged on the implementation of the third guiding principle: "The new centre and its operation must build on and reflect a strong commitment to the development of an integrative collaborative model of student training and ongoing staff development which would be supported by both the UCCC and the Department of Family Studies" (Stuart et al. 1998, 305). The need to train staff at the centre so that they, in turn, could support student training was clearly identified in Bauld and Coulman's evaluation (1996). Skills in observing students, providing feedback, and using modelling techniques became vital. Not all staff needed or wanted to be involved in student practica. A combination of self-selection and director-support brought one group of staff into these positions; however, an unanticipated result was the creation of two "solitudes" (Livingston and Positano 1998), with one staff group having practicum responsibilities and the other not. The challenge was for staff to maintain a team focus with regard to working with children, families, and each other when members of staff had quite different and, at times, conflicting responsibilities. In addition, staff who supervised students had to let go of "their" children's program to give students opportunities to learn and take ownership. Perhaps because this is a transition period, this letting go was hard for staff who were hired as teachers for children and had worked in this capacity for, in some cases, eight years.

In order to develop a collaborative model, the needs of staff, children, and students must all be taken care of, and in some instances, the policies and procedures necessary for quality for one group conflict with those required for another. When laboratory schools move away from the academic mandate of having student training as their primary concern, priorities must be juggled. Whose needs are paramount? Some laboratory schools have made choices: Mount Saint Vincent provides quality programming for children, and students receive more of a field-placement experience; University of Waterloo had to let go of its research mandate. At Guelph, the difficult question has not yet been asked. Whether or not the needs of all groups – children, staff, students, and faculty – can be met is a question still unanswered.

Even as early as 1981 (Barnett 1981), research and training were often joint mandates of university laboratory schools regardless of their discipline base. The usefulness of such a distinction was probably beginning to blur even at that time. Currently, programs that are solely research-based are struggling amid funding cutbacks. In addition, the question is being raised whether research conducted in laboratory school programs truly reflects the real experience of children, families, and staff in the broader community. For programs with a training focus, there is a move to develop partnerships with boards of education and community child care services. Collaborative models are increasing, as mentioned earlier, but whether the quality of training can be maintained and whether training institutions will be able to provide the resources, particularly financial, necessary to support a training mandate are questions still to be answered. The collaborative nature of a partnership requires choosing options; and these will shape the direction that laboratory schools will take and will determine whether they will continue as places for demonstrating excellence in teaching and research.

Note

Kathleen Brophy would like to thank the following individuals for kindly providing information for this chapter: Lois Brockman, University of Manitoba; Glen Dixon, University of British Columbia; Ann Marie Gillen, University of Waterloo; Mary Lyon, Mount Saint Vincent University; Sylvia Mutch, Calgary Board of Education; June Pollard, Ryerson Polytechnic University; and Barbara Stuart, University of Guelph.

References

Bauld, S. and L. Coulman. 1996. Evaluation of the Child Studies Practicum at the University of Guelph Child Care Centre. Unpublished report for the University of Guelph Child Care and Learning Centre, Guelph, ON.

Barbour, N.B., and C.U. Bersani. 1991. The campus child care centre as a professional development school. *Early Childhood Research Quarterly* 6:43-9.

Barnett, M. 1981. Starting young: A survey of child study centres in Canadian anglophone universities. Paper presented at the annual meeting of the Canadian Society of the Study of Education, Halifax.

Brockman, L. 1989. Kids for a classroom. *University of Manitoba Alumni Journal* 49:8-10.

Child Study Centre. 1997. *Mission Statement.* Department of Child and Youth Study, Mount Saint Vincent University, Halifax.

Dixon, G. 1992. The Child Study Centre at the University of British Columbia. In *The logics of education,* ed. Bernhard Möller, vol. 4, 53-61. Oldenburg, Germany: Bibliotheks und Informationssystem der Universität Oldenburg.

Fortney, J.K. 1994. The Ryerson Early Learning Centre: A historical survey of events and relationships. Unpublished manuscript, Ryerson Polytechnic University, Toronto.

Livingston, S., and K. Positano. 1998. An evaluation of the Child Studies practicum at the University of Guelph Child Care and Learning Centre: Staff and parents' views. Unpublished report for the University of Guelph Child Care and Learning Centre, Guelph, ON.

McBride, R. 1994. *University-based child development laboratory programs: Emerging issues and challenges.* ERIC document no. ED 372 842.

Macdonald Institute. 1959-60. *Calendar.* Guelph: Ontario Agricultural College. Special Collections, University of Guelph Library, Guelph, ON.

–. 1960-1. *Calendar.* Guelph: Ontario Agricultural College. Special Collections, University of Guelph Library, Guelph, ON.

Macdonald Institute Director. 1960. Memo for MINS, 7 February 1960. 1949-1969: McCready. Special Collections, University of Guelph Library, Guelph, ON.

–. 1962. Macdonald Institute Nursery School. 1949-1969: McCready. Special Collections, University of Guelph Library, Guelph, ON.

Manitoba Agricultural College. 1912-3. *Calendar.* Winnipeg: Agricultural College, University of Manitoba Archives (19??-1923), UPC-Gen.18.23.

Mount Saint Vincent University, Department of Education. 1985. *History of Mount Saint Vincent University Child Care.* Halifax, NS: Mount Saint Vincent University.

Mutch, S. 1996. Quality principled children. *Quality Focus* 12: 6-7.

Stuart, B., K.B. Brophy, D. Lero, J. Callahan, and A. deVoy. 1998. The development of a collaborative model of child care and student learning at the University of Guelph. *Canadian Journal of Research in Early Childhood Education* 6(4):299-312.

University Elementary School. 1996-7. Brochure. Calgary Board of Education, Calgary, Alberta.

5

Child Care Research in Canada, 1965-99

Alan R. Pence and Allison Benner

This chapter narrates the evolving story of Canadian child care research during the period from the mid-1960s to the end of the century. The mid-1960s saw the emergence of a continuing body of early childhood research literature that was specific to the caregiving needs of children of working parents. Although organized, work-related child care has a history in Canada that extends back to the Infant Schools of the 1820s, it is only since the 1960s that a continuing body of research literature and continuing policy discussions have existed. Using the perspective of three decades of research, 1965-75, 1976-85, and 1986-95 (plus a 1996-9 postscript), we see the emergence of certain key issues and themes during each period. These resulted from the changing public perception of the need for child care services, the government response to those needs and perceptions, and the gradual construction of a research base for the country as a whole as well as for specific regions of the country. As the country enters the fourth decade of having child care as an important public policy issue, significant gaps remain – in the Canadian child care research and knowledge base as well as in the infrastructure required to fill those gaps.

The Context for Canadian Child Care Research

From the 1960s through to the 1990s, child care has assumed an increasingly important place in the lives of families and communities. Changes in family structure, the labour market, and the economy have dramatically increased the demand for child care. In 1951, approximately 24 percent of all adult women participated in the paid labour force. By 1971, that figure had grown to 40 percent. In the twenty-five years that followed, the participation rate of women in the labour market grew to nearly 60 percent. Women with children have constituted the fastest growing portion of the labour market throughout this period. The most recent available census figures (1996) indicate that more than two-thirds of women with children under the age of six participate in the labour force. Family structures have also changed significantly during this period. The prevalence of divorce and changes in attitudes toward single parenthood have contributed to a dramatic increase in single-parent families, which now account for approximately 22 percent of all families in Canada, compared with 9 percent in 1971 (Statistics Canada 1998). A minority of families now fit the traditional pattern of male breadwinner and stay-at-home mother; in 1995, in more than 60 percent of all husband-wife families, both spouses were employed – almost double the figure in 1967, when just 33 percent of families had both spouses employed (Statistics Canada 1997).

Changes in the nature of work and the multicultural make-up of the Canadian population have occurred alongside the increased participation of women in the labour market. The working days of many Canadians are very different from what they were thirty years ago, and these changing circumstances not only affect the demand for child care generally, but create demands for new kinds of child care: one size does not fit all (as can be seen in Chapter 6). For example, the Canadian National Child Care Study showed that although 55 percent of parents with children under the age of thirteen worked a standard work week (Monday to Friday, 8 a.m. to 6 p.m.), about 25 percent of working parents with primary responsibility for child care worked at least one weekend day, and about 10 percent worked a fixed late day or night shift (Lero et al. 1992). Over time, the population has become increasingly diverse. Approximately 11 percent of Canadians belong to a visible minority, and more than 16 percent have a first language other than English or French (Statistics Canada 1998). In some cities, such as Vancouver, the majority of children under the age of six speak English as a second language. There has also been a growing need to respond to the needs of Aboriginal people, who make up about 5 percent of the population, as well as to children requiring additional support.

Despite the growing need for child care, the public attitude toward child care has been slow to change. During the 1950s, in the period of economic prosperity that followed the Second World War, Canadians embraced an ideal of the father working outside the home while the mother stayed at home to look after the children and maintain the private haven of the home. Notwithstanding the fact that this model does not reflect the economic division of labour throughout history, it continues to this day to be Canadians' image of the traditional family.

This attitude has profoundly affected the way Canadians view child care and, in turn, the way governments have responded to the need for child care. There has been an overriding tendency to view the need for child care as a problem, rather than an opportunity for communities to support families in providing for the physical, social, emotional, and intellectual development of their children. Economic and social changes that occurred in the 1960s increased the demand for child care, without significantly changing attitudes toward child care. The introduction of the Canada Assistance Plan (CAP) in 1966 reflected the government's and society's view of child care as a welfare service, designed to provide financial assistance to those families in need or likely to become in need of assistance (see Chapters 9 and 10). The perception of child care as a problem, as an inferior form of care for children, may be of no small significance in answering the question why a comprehensive system of care has not been established over the past thirty years, despite the steady increase in the need for child care.

Yet over the past three decades, in spite of the profound conflict between belief and reality, families, communities, and governments have responded to the need for child care with a range of services. These services include non-profit and commercial child care; centre-based and family-based care; licensed and unlicensed child care; and child care for infants and toddlers, for preschoolers, and for school-aged children (see Chapter 6). The provinces and territories exhibit great diversity in the distribution of such forms of care, as well as in child care funding mechanisms, policies, standards, and regulations (see Chapter 9). The sum total of this diversity is a patchwork quilt of dissimilar policies and programs – essentially, a "non-system" of child care (Pence 1993). As Canadians move forward into the twenty-first century, this non-system will serve as the foundation for future developments.

The Status of Child Care Research in Canadian Child Care Literature

Despite, or perhaps because of, the non-system of child care that has developed in Canada over the last thirty years, growth in the discussion and debate about child care in this country has been remarkable. Previous reviews of the child care literature reveal a dramatic increase in this literature, particularly in the volume of government and advocacy-related documents. In 1985, and again in 1989, reviews of Canadian child care literature were conducted (Pence 1985; Pence and Greenwood-Church 1989). In total, approximately 2,150 references were collected, from sources such as the Social Sciences and Humanities Research Council, Health and Welfare Canada, and Laidlaw Foundation Reports; theses and dissertations; academic journals, books, conference presentations, association newsletters, and government documents; ERIC (Educational Resources Information Center); and psychology, sociology, and social work abstracts. In general, newspapers and popular publications were not included in the review – had they been, the bibliographies might have gone to several volumes.

Examination of the references found in the 1989 bibliographic update revealed a weakness in Canadian child care research. Government works vastly outnumbered experimental or quasi-experimental research reports. For example, of the 1,631 references collected between 1985 and 1989, the vast majority were government works: research reports were outnumbered 73:1. Of course, government works during this period were inflated because of the social and political attention child care gained as a result of the Task Force on Child Care, the Special Committee on Child Care, and Bill C-144. However, even excluding the written submissions and responses to the above, experimental or quasi-experimental research reports were still outnumbered 16:1. Similarly, such reports were still in a minority, 7:1, when compared with other reports, surveys, and needs assessments. In brief, the reviews of the bibliographies revealed that "the Canadian research base for informing public opinion was decidedly thin. The image that came to mind was that of an inverted pyramid, with a bulk of position statements, policy discussion papers and government reports precariously balanced atop a small tip of research. Even within the small core of research, the bulk of studies reported were survey in nature" (Church and Pence, 1989).

While a full bibliography of Canadian child care literature covering the period 1989-96 has yet to be funded, preliminary analyses support the earlier finding that research continues to make up a small portion of Canadian child care literature. At least part of the reason for this is that child care research remains a low priority in the allocation of Canadian child care funding, even when the stated intentions are otherwise.

Consider, for example, the Child Care Initiatives Fund (CCIF), introduced in 1988 as part of the National Child Care Strategy. CCIF was established to encourage innovation and to enhance the development of child care approaches and services across Canada. The CCIF funded three types of child care projects:

- Demonstration/pilot projects: New or innovative approaches to child care services; for example, the integration of special-needs children into a normal child care setting
- Development: Educational materials and activities, including conference workshops, audio-visual materials and publications
- Applied research: Child care surveys, field experimental studies and exploratory investigations.

During the seven years that CCIF was in operation, it constituted the major source of funding for innovative child care research projects in Canada. An evaluation of the CCIF program revealed, however, that few research projects were funded. Of the 519 projects funded through CCIF, a mere 26, or 5 percent, were research-oriented. The total CCIF investment in child care research was $7,166,857, or 9.3 percent of the total funding of

$86 million (Norpark Research Consultants 1995). Moreover, the majority of the research conducted was in the area of needs assessments and feasibility studies. CCIF staff who participated in the evaluation commented, "These studies provided a clear picture of what was needed and have been valuable, but there is no more need for them. Other areas of research were neglected." (Norpark Research Consultants 1995, 86) Certainly it appears, then, that as child care research in Canada progresses, many areas are in need of development. The current research base in Canada provides, at best, a partial foundation on which to build.

Overview of Canadian Child Care Research, 1965-95

As a basis for the present analysis of Canadian child care research, a bibliography of 662 child care research–related references spanning the period from 1965 to 1995 has been compiled. This bibliography includes published journal articles, books, book chapters, monographs, conference proceedings, and unpublished manuscripts. While funds were not available to conduct an exhaustive search, the bibliography broadly represents the child care research literature over the past thirty years. (By "child care research," the authors refer to research that focuses specifically on nonparental care of children primarily for employment-related purposes; as such, research on broader issues pertaining to children and families that might have an influence on child care research has not been included.) For the period 1965 to 1989, previous bibliographies compiled in 1985 and 1989 (Pence 1985; Pence and Greenwood-Church 1989) were consulted. For the period 1990 to 1995, academic journals, books, conference presentations, ERIC, and unpublished work contained in the Research Resource at the Unit for Child Care Research, University of Victoria, were searched. An attempt was made to restrict the bibliography to works that were research-oriented, as opposed to those which were primarily policy- or advocacy-related. Research-oriented material included published and unpublished work that explored various aspects of child care in relation to children, families, caregivers, communities, and economics of care (either survey-type or quasi-experimental research), as well as work that discussed and/or contextualized the existing Canadian research base from an academic or social policy perspective. As such, articles from popular publications were generally not included, nor were policy and training manuals, or government and community-based discussion and position papers, except when these were research-oriented, as defined above.

Drawing the line between policy and advocacy literature, on the one hand, and what is here designated research-oriented literature, on the other, is not always easy. To some extent, policy and advocacy literature is based on research, but is often selective in its use of relevant data. The exclusion of policy and advocacy documents from this collection does not, therefore, reflect the lack of importance of these documents within child care literature. Over the past fifteen to twenty years, Canada has developed strong provincial and national child care advocacy organizations. These organizations have played a critical role in advancing the child care agenda in Canada. Their exclusion from this analysis reflects a desire to broadly portray the course of child care research over the past thirty years, rather than reflecting a view that places policy and advocacy documents lower in a hierarchy of child care literature.

In order to identify general trends in Canadian child care research literature, the references have been classified according to decade (1965-75, 1976-85, and 1986-95), and have been grouped into eighteen major theme areas (plus "other"), as depicted in Table 5.1. (It is recognized that these themes are not mutually exclusive and that a given research project may touch upon more than one theme; in these instances, a choice was made to group the research according to its primary focus, as judged by the authors.) The literature has also been analyzed according to type of research – namely, survey/needs assessment, quasi-experimental, and other (see Table 5.2). "Other" includes research-related work such as literature reviews, annotated bibliographies, qualitative studies, and child care history. Quasi-experimental studies include "most so-called field experiments, operational research, and even the more sophisticated forms of action research which attempt to get at causal factors in real life settings where only partial control is possible; e.g., an investigation of the effectiveness of any method or treatment condition where random assignment of subjects to methods or conditions is not possible" (Isaac and Michael 1977, 15). Further, the literature has been analyzed according to the type of publication and format – that is, whether it is published by government or by a journal, whether it is published in a book (or another) form, or whether it is unpublished (see Table 5.3). The analysis, like the bibliography on which it is based, represents the first step in an attempt to determine the overall shape of child care research in Canada for the period 1965-95. As such, it is useful for identifying general trends, and should be considered as work-in-progress. Further attempts to build on this work will involve compiling a more comprehensive bibliography and developing more rigorous classification schemes and methods of analysis.

Reviewing the literature decade by decade makes clear that the volume of child care research has steadily increased over the past thirty years, with the number of references more than doubling each decade. Grouping the references by theme and decade reveals how the focus of child care research has both changed and expanded. A shift from primarily government-

Table 5.1

Research themes by decade, 1965-95

	1965-75	1976-85	1986-95	Total
Family and child care policy in Canada	26	45	39	110
Economics of child care	4	11	6	21
Effects of child care on children	8	36	2	67
Parental child care needs and preferences	17	18	29	64
Quality	1	3	32	36
Auspice	–	3	8	11
Health and safety/the physical environment	3	16	6	25
Human resources	–	18	36	54
Child care support services	3	3	8	14
Family day care	6	13	13	32
Infant/toddler child care	2	4	4	10
School-age child care	1	5	20	26
Rural child care	–	1	13	14
Work-related child care	2	22	24	48
Flexible child care	–	–	17	17
Aboriginal child care	–	–	42	42
Multicultural child care	–	4	11	15
Special-needs child care	3	4	20	27
Other	–	16	13	29
Total	76	222	343	662

Note: Research themes are not mutually exclusive. Each cited work has been classified into one theme area, according to the primary focus of the work, but may touch on one or more of the other themes.

Table 5.2

Research type by decade, 1965-95

	1965-75 (%)	1976-85 (%)	1986-95 (%)	1965-95 (%)
Survey/needs asssessment	54	23	39	35
Quasi-experimental	20	28	29	28
Other	26	49	32	37

Table 5.3

Publication type by decade, 1965-95

	1965-75 (%)	1976-85 (%)	1986-95 (%)	1965-95 (%)
Government	55	37	14	27
Book chapter, monograph, conference proceedings	11	19	33	36
Journal	12	22	21	20
Unpublished	22	22	32	27

conducted studies and needs assessments in the 1960s toward more academic- and professionally based research is also clear over this period.

The First Decade: 1965-75

The decade from 1965 to 1975 marked a growing recognition by governments and communities of the necessity of child care services. At the outset of this period, little was known about the services available, who was using these services, and child care needs and outcomes for children and families. During this period, the bulk of child care research in Canada was undertaken by various levels of government (see Table 5.3), who were attempting to get a picture of child care and the need for child care. Hence, most of the research undertaken, 54 percent (see Table 5.2), was survey and/or needs assessment in nature and focused on creating a basis for formulating family and child care policy. In the mid- to late 1960s, several municipal governments launched child care studies and needs assessments (Calgary 1967; Hamilton 1967; Montreal Council of Social Agencies 1969; Toronto 1966; Vancouver Community Chest 1965). There were also some attempts to gain a nation-wide perspective of child care services (Canadian Welfare Council 1968; Clifford 1969). There were virtually no experimental research studies conducted on child care in the mid- to late 1960s, but there were some preliminary attempts to view child care as an integral part of Canadian family and social policy (Clifford 1969; Mayer 1965).

Generally speaking, however, it was not until the early 1970s that child care developed a strong presence on national and provincial public agendas. In 1970, the *Royal Commission on Women Report* was released (Royal Commission on the Status of Women 1970). For the first time, a major government document noted the shifting structure and economic base of families and called for enhanced government involvement in the provision of child care. The royal commission report noted: "The time is past when society can refuse to provide community child care services in the hope of dissuading mothers from leaving their children and going to work" (Cooke et al. 1986). In the wake of this report, the federal government took a number of important steps to respond to the growing importance of child care in Canadian social and economic life. In 1971, the federal Department of Health and Welfare, in cooperation with the Canadian Council on Social Development (CCSD), co-sponsored the First National Child Care Conference in Winnipeg, Manitoba. Recommendations from the Winnipeg conference called for the establishment of a federal Day Care Information Office. In 1972, the federal Day Care Information Office was established within the Department of Health and Welfare, and in 1973, the first annual *Status of Day Care in Canada* was issued. This report marked the earliest effort of the federal government to document the status of day care services across the provinces and territories.

Child care research in the early 1970s experienced a slight growth over the mid- to late 1960s. The number of child care surveys and needs assessments continued to grow (Canada 1972a; Hamilton 1971; Stevenson and Strawbridge 1974; University Women's Club of Regina 1975), but in some cases became more focused on specific aspects or types of child care than they had been earlier. For example, for the first time, there were needs assessments focused on employer-supported care (Macrae 1974), surveys on the child care needs of university and college students (McLeod 1975), surveys on the child care of children with special needs (Robinson and McDermick 1973), studies into the child care needs of school-aged children (Toronto 1971), surveys on the prevalence of latchkey children (Hamilton 1971), and surveys on unsupervised child care (Toronto 1975). These studies all reflected a growing recognition of the complexity of Canadians' child care needs.

The early 1970s also signalled a move toward research and study focusing on ways of creating child care services, and the beginnings of quasi-experimental child care research in Canada. There were a number of efforts to analyze child care funding models (Calgary 1974; Citizens Day Care Action Committee 1972; Montreal Council of Social Agencies 1971; Vancouver 1973), to analyze the regulation and legislation of child care (Canadian Council on Social Development 1973; Canadian Pediatric Society 1973; Hamilton 1973; Canada 1972b; Stevenson and Fitzgerald 1971), and to examine prototypical child care service models (Family Bureau of Greater Winnipeg 1973; Fowler and Khan 1974, 1975; O'Kiely and Alban 1973). Very little quasi-experimental research was conducted in Canada up to 1975, and very little of that was published. Most research focused on the effects of different types of programs on children, as measured by language or other developmental criteria (Brouwer 1971; Fowler 1975; Haffenden 1972; Shaefer 1975; University of Western Ontario 1975).

The Second Decade: 1976-85

In general, the profile of child care research, along with the profile of child care itself, rose only slowly in the 1970s, awaiting the 1980s for more dramatic actions and activities. Only during the period 1976-85 (and particularly the period 1982-5) did child care advocacy in Canada truly come of age and Canadian child care research begin to develop a more specific identity. This was a time of rapid expansion in the volume of research and debate about child care.

During the mid- to late 1970s, the small proportion of quasi-experimental child care research (see Table 5.2) continued to focus on the developmental effects of child care on children (Adler 1978; Doyle 1976a; Doyle and Somers 1978; Fowler 1978; Fowler and Khan 1976; Fowler and Swenson 1977; Taylor 1976; University of Western Ontario 1976a, 1976b). These studies and related research into the health and safety of child care environments (Bellemare 1978; Campbell and Dell 1980; Doyle 1976b; Garner 1979; Hepworth 1976; Massing 1980), as well as studies of the value of child care as a compensatory program for disadvantaged children (Bérubé 1981; Shell and James 1977; Wright 1980, 1981, 1983) laid the foundations for later discussion and research into quality child care.

Increasingly, communities, governments, and researchers were coming to see child care as a complex issue: the experiences of children and families, as reflected in the existing research base, demonstrated that child care could not be viewed as a single variable in assessing developmental outcomes for children. Many other variables, such as the child care setting, family situation, attitudes and training of child care providers, and community support for child care and caregivers (to name but a few variables), emerged as critical in assessing the effects of child care on children. Hence, in the early 1980s community advocates and researchers alike began to frame their discussions of child care with a multiplicity of factors in mind. Encouraged by the work of Urie Bronfenbrenner (1979), Canada joined the United States in a new wave of ecologically sensitive child care studies (Pence and Goelman 1982).

Surveys and needs assessments, so prevalent in the previous decade, continued to occupy a significant proportion of child care research from 1976 to 1985 (Hamilton 1977; University of Regina 1978a, 1978b, 1980; Vancouver Council of Women 1980; Prince Edward Island 1983). However, increasingly, surveys and needs assessments focused on gaining a picture of particular categories and sub-categories within the child care system. For example, a number of studies of family day care were undertaken (McNaughton 1985; PMA Consulting Group 1983; Saskatchewan 1978), as well as of particular aspects of family day care, such as care for infants and toddlers (Better Home Day Care Association 1979); unlicensed, registered family day care (Bouchard 1982); unsupervised, informal child care (Longwoods Research Group 1982; Toronto 1978); and family day care for children with additional support needs (Albert, Wihak, and Woolner 1981). Similarly, a number of survey-type studies of work-related child care were conducted (Friendly and Johnson 1981; Toronto 1982; Grant, Sai-Chew, and Natarelli 1982), including specific aspects of work-related child care, such as municipal child care (Toronto 1981), union involvement in child care (Canadian Union of Public Employees 1979; Kerans 1982), child care in the civil service (Ontario 1983), child care in the education system (Canadian Education Association 1983; Canadian Teachers Federation 1979), hospital-based child care (Mayfield 1985), and company-supported child care (Erickson and Veit 1985; Ontario 1984). In addition, comparisons of non-profit versus commercial child care operations were conducted (Buroker and Sort 1983; Regroupement des garderies du Montréal Métropolitain 1982).

Along with a growing recognition of the complexity of child care in Canada came a renewed focus on parents. Earlier parent surveys had centred on identifying parents' needs; in the late 1970s and early 1980s, parent surveys were now broadened to include analyses of parental child care preferences, including factors influencing child care choices such as affordability, availability, accessibility, and quality of child care (Lero 1981; Regroupement des garderies de la région 6C 1981; University of Regina 1980).

For the first time, too, child care researchers and policy makers began to focus on child care providers – their knowledge, training, wages, working conditions, and motivation for providing child care (Gould 1977; Johnson 1978; Middleton 1982; Pence and Goelman 1982; Polowy 1978; Schom-Moffatt 1984) – as well as ways to support and train caregivers to improve child care environments for children (Biemiller, Avis, and Lindsay 1976; Canning 1985; Dimidjian 1982; Rimstad 1985; University of Guelph 1978). The development of the Early Childhood Environment Rating Scale, or ECERS (Harms and Clifford 1980) and the Day Care Home Environment Rating Scale, or DCHERS (Harms and Clifford 1982) provided new opportunities to assess quality in a range of child care settings (Goelman and Pence 1984; Stuart and Pepper 1985). The ECERS and DCHERS also allowed researchers to consider the interrelationships between the quality of child care settings, family circumstances, caregiver characteristics and developmental outcomes for children, contributing to an understanding of the complex ecology of child care in Canada (Pence and Goelman 1982; Goelman and Pence 1985).

In the early 1980s, the growing appreciation of the complexity of child care, combined with the increased demand for care, fuelled interest in child care policy and research at a national level. Many believed that Canada was facing a child care crisis (Johnson and Dineen 1981); at the very least, child care advocates, policy makers and researchers needed to join forces to create a vision of child care for the future – and they did.

In 1982, the federal government and the Canadian Council on Social Development co-sponsored the second National Day Care Conference. The second national conference, held in Winnipeg, has been viewed by many as key to bringing child care to the forefront of the public agenda in Canada. Following the second national conference, two national child care organizations were formed: the Canadian Day Care Advocacy Association (now called the Canadian Child Care Advocacy Association, or CCCAA), an active day care lobbying association committed to a comprehensive system of universally accessible, publicly funded, high-quality child care services; and the Canadian Child Day Care Federation (now called the Canadian Child Care Federation, or CCCF), an organization committed to improving the quality of child care services by providing information and support services to the child care community.

In 1984, the federal government appointed the Task Force on Child Care, led by Dr. Katie Cooke, a sociologist and researcher. The task force undertook an extensive research and review process that culminated in the 1986 release of the task force's final report, which recommended the development of "complementary systems of child care and parental leave that are as comprehensive, accessible, and competent as our systems of health care and education" (Cooke et al. 1986, 281). Much of the important research relating to child care policy in the period 1976-85 was commissioned by the task force, as reflected in the significant volume of government research during this period (see Table 5.3). This comprehensive research included reports on child care funding (Blain 1985; DPA Group 1984; Power and Brown 1984; Rose-Lizee 1985; Stotsky 1985; Status of Women 1985a, 1985b; Townson 1985); child care standards (Blais Bates 1984; Thomson 1985); the effects of child care on children (Esbensen 1985); components of quality child care (Lero and Kyle 1985; Status of Women 1985c); wages and working conditions of centre-based caregivers (Schom-Moffatt 1984); the informal child care market (Miller-Chenier 1985); parental child care needs, preferences and concerns (Lero, Pence, Brockman, and Charlesworth 1986); work-related child care (Rothman Beach Associates 1985); the child care needs of immigrants (Downie 1985); the existing Canadian child care research base (Pence 1985); and the history of health and education services in Canada (Domina Group 1985).

The Third Decade: 1986-95

From 1986 to 1995, the volume of child care research–related literature nearly doubled over the previous decade, suggesting a period of continued growth and expansion in child care research. Yet in many ways, this decade lacked the excitement and momentum of the previous one. Whereas the period from 1976 to 1985 marked a time of mounting crisis in child care, followed by a gathering of strength, energy, and activity that culminated in the release of the task force report (Cooke et al. 1986), the period from 1986 to 1995 marked a long, slow, and frustrating *dénouement*. During the previous decade, child care research benefited from the combined efforts of child care advocates, policy makers, and researchers working toward the development of a shared vision for child care in Canada. In the wake of the Cooke task force report, with no substantial federal commitment to a national system of child care, the various parties lost a sense of collective purpose. Generally speaking, child care advocates continued to press for a universal, publicly funded system of non-profit child care; policy makers developed a range of programs and initiatives intended as compromise solutions to meeting Canadians' child care needs; and researchers strove to build on the foundation they had created in the previous decade, although perhaps with little sense that the most significant of their findings would inform public policy. Notwithstanding this unpromising context, many important developments took place in child care research from 1986 to 1995.

In general, Canadian child care research in this period reflected a growing recognition of the complex ecology of child care, largely driven by efforts to identify the components of quality child care – the dominant theme in most quasi-experimental research of this decade (see Chapter 6). The pre-1980s period of research on the effects of child care on children (Brouwer 1971; Doyle and Somers 1978; Fowler 1975, 1978; Haffenden 1972; Shaefer 1975; University of Western Ontario 1975) was based on a desire to answer the question whether child care was harmful or beneficial to children's development. The results of these studies were inconclusive, suggesting that the effects of child care on children were largely dependent on the quality of child care they received (Esbensen 1985; Doherty 1991a, 1991b, 1991c). This overall finding generated a number of questions that permeated the research agenda in the 1980s and 1990s, such as: What is quality? How can it be defined and put into practice? What circumstances enhance or inhibit the quality of child care?

These questions provided the basis for much of the quasi-experimental research conducted in the late 1980s and throughout the 1990s. Indeed, much of the research classified under the following themes might easily have been included under the theme of quality (see Table 5.1): effects of child care on children (Goelman and Pence 1988), auspice (DeGagné and DeGagné 1988; Friesen 1995; SPR Associates 1986), health and safety/the physical environment (Esbensen 1987), human resources (Collins, Gabor, and Ing 1987; LaGrange and Read 1990a), family day care (Pepper and Stuart 1992), infant/toddler child care (McKim, Stuart, and O'Connor 1994), school-age child care (Betsalel-Presser et al. 1995), multicultural child care (Bernhard et al. 1995), and special-needs child care (Brophy 1995; Crawford 1993). Moreover, many of the references included under the theme of family policy and child care in Canada also concerned the issue of quality (LaGrange and Read 1990b; Friendly 1993; Howe and Jacobs 1995).

Just as in the early 1980s, when child care came to be seen as a complex entity, hardly to be contained within two words, in the late 1980s and throughout the 1990s, quality was similarly hard to pin down. The development of the ECERS (Harms and Clifford 1980) and the DCHERS (Harms and Clifford 1982) in the early 1980s provided researchers with useful instruments to assess the quality of child care environments as it was then understood (Lyon and Canning 1995; Pence and Goelman 1987a, 1987b; Pepper and Stuart 1992). Similar instruments were later developed to measure global aspects of quality child care for specific types of child care, such as infant/toddler child care (Harms, Cryer, and Clifford 1990) and child care for school-aged children (Harms, Vineberg-Jacobs, and Romano-White 1996). As useful as these instruments were (and are) in furnishing a general sense of the quality of a child care environment and in helping child care regulators and caregivers to provide quality care (Hunter 1995), a number of researchers became increasingly concerned about their inherent limitations. These measures were devised by child care professionals and may, therefore, reflect professional biases about quality child care. In addition, they provide little insight into how external factors, such as socio-economic status and family situation, might affect children's experiences of child care or the likelihood of their being placed in high-quality child care environments. Some studies attempted, therefore, to measure quality in relation to variables such as auspice (Lyon and Canning 1995), caregiver training and attitudes (Pence and Goelman 1991), and family situation (Pence and Goelman 1987a). In the 1990s, some Canadian researchers, drawing on international discussions on quality child care (often grounded in feminist, postcolonial and/or postmodernist critical perspectives), as well as Canadian experiences in cross-cultural child care, began to suggest that the presence or absence of "stakeholder" inclusion in the definition and negotiation of quality is itself a critical component of quality child care (Pence and Moss 1994; Hunter and Pence 1995; Bernhard et al. 1995).

The many child care needs assessments and surveys conducted in the late 1980s and early to mid-1990s (see Table 5.2) are best seen in the contexts of both the research into quality and the efforts to develop an ecological perspective on child care. For example, the wages and working conditions of centre-based child care workers (Ferguson 1990; Schom-Moffatt 1992) and family settings (Independent Child Caregivers Association 1990) were often discussed in relation to the possible impact of these conditions on quality (Doherty 1991a, 1991b; Lyon and Canning 1995). Studies of parents' child care arrangements, such as the Canadian National Child Care Study (Lero et al. 1992), were conducted with a view to linking child care with interrelated factors such as parental work patterns and workplace benefits and flexibility, all of which might affect child care choices and, in turn, quality.

Similarly, the budding interest in meeting the child care needs of diverse populations during this period can be seen in the light of issues related to the quality and ecology of child care. From 1986 to 1995, numerous surveys and needs assessments were conducted on flexible child care (Barnhart 1990; Friendly 1989; Galloway 1992), rural child care (Abramovitch 1987; Brophy and Sugarman 1988; Federated Women's Institutes of Canada 1990; Quiring 1991), multicultural child care (Mock 1986, 1988), and Aboriginal child care (Assembly of First Nations 1989; Native Council of Canada 1990; Ontario Metis Aboriginal Association 1990). In the preceding decades, very little research had been conducted on the child care needs of these populations. In some ways, these surveys and needs assessments were an extension of earlier efforts to acknowledge and respond to the complexity of Canadians' child care needs. In this sense, they might be comparable to surveys conducted in the 1970s on the child care needs of school-aged children or the parental child care needs of university and college students with family responsibilities. In other words, in the late 1980s and early 1990s, Canadians had simply recognized additional groups of people who needed child care. Yet this third generation of needs assessments took place in a very different context; some reflected a nascent understanding that quality child care might mean something very different to an Aboriginal person on a reserve, an urban shift worker, a farm worker, or a family whose primary language was not English. Some of these surveys and needs assessments therefore reflected the principle that people must be involved in the articulation and definition of their needs and choices. This principle formed the basis of a number of quasi-experimental studies on the development of community-based child care services and training programs for rural and/or Aboriginal populations, such as the Nain Daycare Project in Labrador (Canning 1986) and the Meadow Lake Tribal Council Indian Child Care Program (Pence et al. 1993; Pence and McCallum 1994).

Reflections on Child Care Research, 1965-95

The above discussion provides a broad overview of the main themes and trends of Canadian child care research from 1965 to 1995. As already noted, this research has evolved considerably over the past thirty years, exhibiting a growth in volume and complexity that shows strong potential for the future. The diversity of the Canadian population, the multiplicity of child care arrangements open to families in our nation's non-system of care, and the broad continuum of themes pursued by Canadian child care researchers provide nearly unlimited opportunities for creative enquiry and experimentation in the future.

Notwithstanding the significant accomplishments of the past three decades and the strong potential for future study, Canadian child care research is still in its infancy. Despite a steady increase in the proportion of quasi-experimental research relative to surveys, needs assessments, and other research-related literature, this type of research still represents a small portion of child care research in Canada. While nearly 30 percent of the references compiled from 1965 to 1995 related to quasi-experimental research (see Table 5.2), it is important to keep in mind that in many cases, a single study generated numerous references. For example, four major studies conducted between 1982 and 1995 (Pence and Goelman's Victoria Day Care Research Project; Mayfield's study of employer-supported child care; Pepper and Stuart's study of licensed and unlicensed family day care; and the school-age child care study by Betsalel-Presser et al.) accounted for forty-four references over this period. By contrast, surveys and needs assessments seldom generated more than one reference each. Thus the proportion of quasi-experimental research, while still small, may appear inflated in the current analysis. Although there is no shortage of information on the child care needs and preferences of Canadians, there is still very little research on the effects of different types of child care on children's development. While it is important to know family and community child care preferences in developing child care policy, it is equally important to have an adequate research base on how child care can enhance or inhibit the physical, emotional, social, and intellectual development of children. In this regard, there are still large gaps in knowledge in the Canadian research base. By way of illustration, the annotated bibliography *Factors Related to Quality in Child Care* (Doherty 1991b) discusses forty-nine international child care studies bearing on the issue of quality – an issue of critical importance to the well-being of children, families, and communities. Of the forty-nine studies described, only nine are Canadian. Of the nine Canadian studies, only three are published (Goelman and Pence 1988; Peterson and Peterson 1986; Stuart and Pepper 1988), and the remaining six are either unpublished or unrefereed (Biemiller, Avis, and Lindsay 1976; Pence and Goelman n.d.; Pepper and Stuart 1989; SPR Associates 1986; Schom-Moffatt 1984; West 1988). Furthermore, two references are based on one study (Stuart and Pepper 1988, 1989); one study discusses quality only in relation to licensing standards (West 1988), a limited indicator of quality; and another study (Schom-Moffatt 1984) does not bear directly on the issue of quality. These facts lead one to conclude that the Canadian research base on quality needs to be strengthened.

It is also significant that only 31 percent of the quasi-experimental research results considered in this chapter were published in academic journals (see Table 5.4). In turn, only 15 percent of these articles were published in journals circulated outside Canada. The lack of an international research presence may be a reflection of the quality of research in Canada; more significantly, the relative absence of Canadian researchers from internationally known journals and publications limits opportunities to benefit from the exchange of perspectives and knowledge that could strengthen child care research in Canada. The gaps in child care research have been noted in other research reviews (Pence and Greenwood-Church 1989; LaGrange and Read 1990b) and figured prominently in the evaluation of the Child Care Initiatives Fund: "CCIF staff said there is a need to do more evaluation of the current services, programs and practices – whether they are appropriate and cost-effective and whether they meet the need. Research needs to be done in the determinants of quality care, standards of care, quality of child care services in disadvantaged areas, school-based care, and in special groups such as infant/toddler care." The authors of the report also noted the need for research on "employer practices, leave, family/work balance, self-employment, non-traditional hours and the impact they will have on child rearing and what services can meet those non-traditional needs. More knowledge is needed regarding comprehensive services and there is a need to know how commercial child care compares with non-profit. According to provincial government officials, the provinces, the principal area in which more knowledge is needed was said to be 'quality'" (Norpark Research Consultants 1995, vi).

Table 5.4

Quasi-experimental research by publication type, 1965-95

	Percentage
Government	7
Book chapter, monograph, conference proceedings	25
Journal	31
Unpublished	37

Conclusion

There are many opportunities for Canadian child care advocates, practitioners, policy makers, and researchers to work together in building on the knowledge base that currently exists in Canada, with a view to enriching our understanding of child care in the lives of children, families and communities, and most important, with a view to improving the quality, accessibility, affordability, and availability of child care in this country. For example, the federal government, through the recently created funding program, Child Care Visions, could take active steps to make child care research a priority in its funding decisions, thereby responding to one of the key recommendations that flowed from the evaluation of CCIF – namely, "A new program should be more proactive and more focused on research" (Norpark Research Consultants 1995, iv). Federal and provincial governments alike could respond to the need for infrastructure that supports innovative, high-quality child care research. At present, no such infrastructure exists: there is no graduate-level program at a Canadian university that focuses exclusively on child care research; nor is there a single funded, dedicated chair at a Canadian university to advance excellence in child care research. Remedying these situations would represent steps in the right direction for Canadian child care research and, ultimately, for the well-being of children, families, and communities.

Postscript

The time between book preparation and book publication is fraught with challenges. The extension of that time for this publication allowed the authors the opportunity to glance back at the opening years of a fourth decade of Canadian child care research. This period reveals both continuity in certain established directions in child care research and the emergence of a number of new themes and directions.

Continuity is represented in work such as the "You Bet We Care" project (Doherty et al. 1997), which builds on two earlier studies on caregiver wages and working conditions (Schom-Moffatt 1984, 1992), but expands to include family day care. The theme of better understanding the nature of employment in early childhood care and education was also carried forward in the large-scale sector study funded by Human Resources Development Canada. The result of that study, *Our Child Care Workforce* (Beach, Bertrand, and Cleveland 1998), represents an important benchmark in the development of the child care profession. In addition, some teams of researchers are in the process of extending their earlier work. *The National School-Age Child Care Quality Assurance Study* (Jacobs, White, and Baillargeon 1996) builds on these researchers' earlier school-age studies, while Phase 3 data collection for the Victoria Day Care Research project (Pence and Goelman 1996) will provide additional longitudinal data on children who participated in various centre- and family-based child care settings in the early 1980s.

A theme with an episodic history going back to the mid-1980s (Krashinsky 1984; Townson 1985) is the economics of child care. Emerging partially from this history, but also stimulated by new players and forces in Canadian child care, cost-benefit analyses of child care are achieving levels of visibility that are unprecedented in Canadian child care literature. The work of Cleveland and colleagues (for example, Cleveland and Krashinsky 1998) has led the way in opening up this aspect of child care research in Canada. This attention to the economics of good-quality care has been driven in part by the emergence of new advocacy and research groups in Canada. These groups, largely inspired by American work such as the Perry Preschool Project in Michigan (Schweinhart, Barnes, and Weikart 1993), the Carnegie Task Force Report on meeting the needs of young children (Carnegie Task Force 1994), and the public awareness successes of the "I Am Your Child" campaign, have become powerful new forces influencing the child care field. The message of these new groups is much broader than child care – for example, emphasizing the overall importance of the early years – but their success in creating enhanced governmental and public support for children's issues, and their identification and creation of noteworthy research has the potential to profoundly affect established child care teams and themes.

Central to the emergence of this new dynamic is the work of Dr. Fraser Mustard, longstanding president of the Canadian Institute for Advanced Research (CIAR) and now with the CIAR-related Founders Network. In the early 1990s, Mustard created a Human Development group within the broad research structure of CIAR, bringing together some fifteen outstanding North American researchers from a broad range of backgrounds in the health and social sciences. Members of this group were instrumental in promoting the development of the *National Longitudinal Study of Children and Youth* (NLSCY 1993); beginning to explore that database for child care–related issues (NLSCY 1998); and opening up new and important lines of research, such as the relationship between early care and later patterns of aggression (Tremblay et al. 1994). CIAR's efforts, along with those of national action groups such as the National Children's Agenda Caucus Committee and related provincial groups, promise to keep children's issues, and with them child care issues, active for most of the fourth decade of child care research.

As the child care research stage fills with more actors, several key issues emerge. A critical concern is the ability of the traditional child care structures and players to liaise and communicate with those from different backgrounds who may be driven by somewhat different agendas and understandings. One element of this diversity is associated with the broader children's agenda, but adding to the complexity is a growing postmodernist critique of the positivist positions that have tended to dominate early childhood care and education literature and discussions of the children's agenda (Bernhard et al. 1998; Dahlberg, Moss, and Pence 1999). An awareness of social constructionism can also be found in recent Canadian historical work, notably Varga's (1997) publication *Constructing the Child: A History of Canadian Day Care*. There is a growing need for these diverse communities to both inform and learn from one another.

Related to these concerns is the need for child care researchers and those in the child care field not to lose sight of the progress that has been made in creating a dialogue between them. The Canadian Child Care Federation's hosting of a large-scale conference on research and practice, in Banff in October 1998, provided evidence of how far the two fields have travelled together in trying to better inform each other.

And finally, as children's issues are given prominence, it is critical that the popular media not succumb to the dictum "that for every complex question there is a simple answer ..." In fact, those who have worked in this field for many years have come to appreciate the complexity of child care and child development – and understand the concluding point of the dictum, "... and it is wrong!" Truly, there are no simple answers, and many of our questions are equally problematic. The great challenge of the fourth decade of child care research will be to remain open to unforeseen possibilities in the New – and in the Known.

References

Abramovitch, R. 1987. *An overview of rural child care needs and preferences*. Toronto: Ontario Ministry of Community and Social Services, Child Care Branch.

Adler, B. 1978. Egocentrism and interactive style related to differential peer experience in daycare, nursery school and home-reared children. Master's thesis, Concordia University, Montreal.

Albert, J., C. Wihak, and S. Woolner. 1981. *Supervised family day care and the special needs child*. Ottawa: Carleton University, School of Social Work.

Assembly of First Nations. 1989. *Report of the national inquiry into First Nations child care*. Ottawa: Assembly of First Nations.

Barnhart, K. 1990. Addressing a need: Quality, affordable care for sick children. Unpublished report. Red Deer Child Care Society, Red Deer, AB.

Beach, J., J. Bertrand, and G. Cleveland. 1998. *Our child care workforce: From recognition to remuneration*. Ottawa: Human Resources Development Canada.

Bellemare, A.D. 1978. Correlates of physical activity in day care centres. Master's thesis, Dalhousie University, Halifax.

Bernhard, J., G. Chud, M.L. Lefebvre, and R. Lange. 1995. *Cultural, linguistic and racial diversity in Canadian early childhood education: Executive summary*. Toronto: Ryerson Polytechnic Institute.

Bernhard, J., J. Gonzalez-Menza, H. Chang, N. O'Loughlin, C. Eggers-Piérola, G. Fiati, and P. Corson. 1998. Recognizing the centrality of cultural diversity and racial equity: Beginning a discussion and critical reflection on developmentally appropriate practice. *Canadian Journal of Research in Early Childhood Education* 7(1):81-90.

Bérubé, S.R. 1981. Expérience de prévention de l'inadaptation scolaire à la maternelle.

Thèse, Université de Montréal, Montreal.
Betsalel-Presser, R., D.R. White, M. Baillargeon, and E.V. Jacobs. 1995. *Services de garde et maternelle: Sélection, qualité et continuité.* Final Report, Project No.: 4774-5-91/9 (688), Child Care Initiatives Fund, Canada.
Better Home Day Care Association. 1979. *At home: A report on infant family day care.* Halifax: Better Home Day Care Association.
Biemiller, A., C. Avis, and A. Lindsay. 1976. Competence supporting aspects of day care environments. Paper presented at the Canadian Psychological Association Convention, Toronto, June 1976. Available from the University of Toronto, Childcare Resource and Research Unit.
Blain, C. 1985. *Government spending on child care in Canada.* Report prepared for the Task Force on Child Care, Ottawa.
Blais Bates, H. 1984. *Day care standards in Canada.* Report prepared for the Task Force on Child Care, Ottawa.
Bouchard, S. 1982. *Garder chez soi les enfants des autres: Profil des gardiennes reconnues par les agences de services de garde en milieu familial au Québec en 1982.* Collection Études et recherches, vol. 2. Québec: Québec, Office des services de garde à l'enfance.
Bronfenbrenner, U. 1979. *The ecology of human development: Experiments by nature and design.* Cambridge, MA: Harvard University Press.
Brophy, K. 1995. Components of successful integration in child care centres: An Ontario study. *Early Child Development and Care* 112:53-63.
Brophy, K., and R. Sugarman. 1988. Who's looking after our children: A study of child care needs in rural Ontario. *Canadian Journal of Research in Early Childhood Education* 2(2):141-8.
Brouwer, A. 1971. *Developmental needs of children in day care.* Calgary: University of Calgary, School of Social Welfare.
Buroker, T., and V.C. Sort. 1983. *Private and board operated day care centres in British Columbia: A report on funding.* Victoria, BC: Vancouver Island Early Childhood Centre Operators Association.
Calgary. 1967. Social Planning Council. *Day care needs in Calgary.* Calgary: Social Planning Council.
–. 1974. Community Services Committee of City Council. *A review of subsidized day care programs with a consideration of alternative funding and long term planning.* Calgary: City of Calgary.
Campbell, S.D., and N. Dell. 1980. *The effects of a change in spatial density on children's behaviour in a daycare setting.* ERIC Information Retrieval #P.S. 012 265. Edmonton: University of Alberta, Department of Elementary Education.
Canada. 1972a. Health and Welfare. *Canadian day care survey.* Ottawa: Health and Welfare Canada.
–. 1972b. Health and Welfare. *Day care legislation in Canada.* Ottawa: Health and Welfare Canada.
Canadian Council on Social Development. 1973. *Day care: Growing, learning, caring. National guidelines for the development of day care services for children.* Ottawa: Canadian Council on Social Development.
Canadian Education Association. 1983. *Day care and the Canadian school system: A CEA survey of child care services in schools.* Toronto: Canadian Education Association.
Canadian Pediatric Society. 1973. Day Care Centres Committee. *Standards for child development programs including day care centres and family day care homes.* Toronto: Canadian Pediatric Society.
Canadian Teachers Federation. 1979. *Working paper for the quality and innovations in education committee: Study on child care in the public sector, 1978-79.* Ottawa: Canadian Teachers Federation.
Canadian Union of Public Employees. 1979. *Brief regarding daycare centre budgetary needs.* Ottawa: Canadian Union of Public Employees.
Canadian Welfare Council. 1968. Research Branch. *The day care of children in Canada.* Research report No. 1, June. Ottawa: Canadian Welfare Council.

Canning, P. 1985. An interdisciplinary approach to training teachers and other child care personnel. *Canadian Journal of Research in Early Childhood Education* 3(2):91-4.
–. 1986. The Nain Daycare Project. *Canadian Journal of Education* 11(1):1-8.
Carnegie Task Force. 1994. *Starting points: Meeting the needs of our youngest children.* New York: Carnegie Foundation.
Church, M., and A. Pence. 1989. Canadian day care research in review. *Network News* (February):4-7.
Citizens Day Care Action Committee. 1972. *Day care services in Nova Scotia: A cost analysis.* Halifax: Citizens Day Care Action Committee.
Cleveland, G., and M. Krashinsky. 1998. *The benefits and costs of good child care: The economic rationale for public investment in young children.* Toronto: Childcare Research and Resource Unit.
Clifford, H. 1969. An overview of Canadian day care services. In *Day care: A resource for the contemporary family,* 56-62. Ottawa: Health and Welfare Canada.
Collins, D., P. Gabor, and C. Ing. 1987. Communication skill training in child care: The effects of preservice and inservice training. *Child and Youth Care Quarterly* 16(2):106-15.
Cooke, K., J. London, R. Edwards, and R. Rose-Lizee. 1986. *Report of the Task Force on Child Care.* Ottawa: Supply and Services Canada.
Crawford, C. 1993. *Right off the bat: A study of inclusive child care in Canada.* Toronto: York University.
Dahlberg, G., P. Moss, and A. Pence. 1999. *Beyond quality in early childhood education and care: Postmodern perspectives on the problem with quality.* London, UK: Falmer Press.
DeGagné, C., and M.P. DeGagné. 1988. *Garderies à but lucratif et garderies sans but lucratif subventionées vers une évaluation de la qualité.* Montreal: Gouvernement du Québec, Office des services de garde à l'enfance.
Dimidjian, V.J. 1982. Understanding and combating stress in family day care. *Journal of Child Care* 1(2):47-58.
Doherty, G. 1991a. *Factors related to quality in child care: A review of the literature.* Toronto: Ontario Ministry of Community and Social Services, Child Care Branch.
–. 1991b. *Factors related to quality in child care: Annotated bibliography.* Prepared for the Ontario Ministry of Community and Social Services, Child Care Branch. Toronto: Queen's Printer for Ontario.
–. 1991c. *Quality matters in child care.* Huntsville, ON: Jesmond Publishing.
Doherty, G., H. Goelman, A. LaGrange, and J. Tougas. 1997. *Caring for a living, part two.* Proposal submitted to Child Care Visions, Human Resources Development Canada.
Domina Group. 1984. Principal researcher: N. Miller-Chenier; research assistant: D. LaBarge. *Toward universality: An historical overview of the evolution of education, health care, day care and maternity leave.* Prepared for the Task Force on Child Care, Ottawa.
Downie, P.T.H. 1985. *Child care needs of immigrants.* Prepared for the Task Force on Child Care, Ottawa.
Doyle, A.B. 1976a. *Relationship between maternal employment and development of nursery school children.* Montreal: Concordia University, Department of Psychology.
–. 1976b. Incidence of illness in early group and family day care. *Pediatrics* 58(4):607-13.
Doyle, A.B., and K. Somers. 1978. The effects of group and family daycare on infant attachment behaviours. *Canadian Journal of Behavioural Science* 10:38-45.
DPA Group. 1984. *National day care costing model.* Prepared for the Task Force on Child Care, Ottawa.
Erickson, D., and S. Veit. 1985. *Caring for children: Child care needs associated with hydrocarbon development in the Beaufort Region.* Victoria, BC: Erickson Associates.
Esbensen, S.B. 1985. *The effects of day care on children, families and communities: A review of the research findings.* Prepared for the Task Force on Child Care, Ottawa.
–. 1987. *Outdoor classroom: Early childhood playground.* Ypsilanti, MI: High/Scope.
Family Bureau of Greater Winnipeg. 1973. *Family day care homefinding service project.* Winnipeg: Family Bureau of Greater Winnipeg.
Federated Women's Institutes of Canada. 1990. *Rural child care: Survey project, 1988-1991.* Ottawa: Federated Women's Institutes of Canada.

Ferguson, E. 1990. *Where we work: Nova Scotia child care centres as workplaces.* Halifax: Child Care Connection – NS.

Fowler, W. 1975. How adult/child ratios influence infant development. *Interchange* 6(1):17-31.

–. 1978. *Daycare and its effects on early development: A study of group and home care in multi-ethnic working class families.* Toronto: Ontario Institute for Studies in Education.

Fowler, W., and N. Khan. 1974. *The development of a prototype infant and child day care centre in Metropolitan Toronto: Year III progress report.* Toronto: Ontario Institute for Studies in Education.

–. 1975. *The development of a prototype infant and child day care centre in Metropolitan Toronto: Year IV progress report.* Toronto: Ontario Institute for Studies in Education.

–. 1976. *The comparative effects of group and home day care on early development.* Toronto: Ontario Institute for Studies in Education.

Fowler, W., and A. Swenson. 1977. The influence of early language stimulation development: Four studies. Unpublished paper, Ontario Institute for Studies in Education, Toronto.

Friendly, M. 1989. *Flexible child care in Canada: A report on child care for evenings, overnight and weekends, emergencies and ill children and in rural areas.* Toronto: University of Toronto, Centre for Urban and Community Studies, Childcare Resource and Research Unit.

–. 1993. Moving toward quality child care: Reflections on child care policy in Canada. *Canadian Journal of Research in Early Childhood Education* 3(2):123-32.

Friendly, M., and L. Johnson. 1981. *Perspectives on work-related day care.* Child in the city report no. 11. Toronto: University of Toronto, Centre for Urban and Community Studies.

Friesen, B. 1995. *A sociological examination of the child care auspice debate.* Occasional paper no. 6. Toronto: University of Toronto, Centre for Urban and Community Studies, Childcare Resource and Research Unit.

Galloway, S. 1992. *Shift worker child care project: A needs assessment for shift workers in the city of Kingston.* Kingston, ON: Dawn House Women's Shelter.

Garner, J. 1979. Child care citizen: Report on deficiencies in Canada in child care. *Canadian Medical Association Journal* 120(3):351-4.

Goelman, H., and A.R. Pence. 1984. Cognitive language and social development in three day care environments. Paper presented at the Annual Conference of American Educational Research Association, April, New Orleans.

–. 1985. Toward an ecology of day care in Canada: A research agenda for the 1980s. *Canadian Journal of Education* 19(2):323-44.

–. 1988. Children in three types of child care experiences: Quality of care and developmental outcomes. *Early Childhood Development and Care* 33:67-76.

Gould, D.E. 1977. A survey of day care teachers nutrition knowledge, opinion and reporting use of food. Master's thesis, University of Guelph, Guelph, Ontario.

Grant, L., P. Sai-Chew, and F. Natarelli. 1982. *Work-related day care: An inventory of work-related day care in Canada.* Child in the city report. Toronto: Toronto Social Planning Council.

Haffenden, E. 1972. *The effects of day care programs on levels of intellectual functioning.* Calgary: Alberta Guidance Clinic.

Hamilton. 1967. Social Planning and Research Council. *Report on the provision of day nursery care in Hamilton.* Hamilton, ON: Hamilton Social Planning and Research Council.

–. 1971. Committee on Day Care for Children. *Day care needs of children in Hamilton and district.* Hamilton, ON: Hamilton Social Planning and Research Council.

–. 1973. Social Planning and Research Council. *Hamilton consultation on day care standards.* Hamilton, ON: Hamilton Social Planning and Research Council.

–. 1977. Social Planning and Research Council. *Day care: A study of users.* Hamilton, ON: Hamilton Social Planning and Research Council.

Harms, T., and R.M. Clifford. 1980. *The Early Childhood Environment Rating Scale.* New York: Teachers College Press.

–. 1982. *The Day Care Home Environment Scale.* New York: Teachers College Press.

Harms, T., D. Cryer, and R.M. Clifford. 1990. *The Infant/Toddler Environment Rating Scale.* New York: Teachers College Press.

Harms, T., E. Vineberg-Jacobs, and D.R. Romano-White. 1996. *The School Age Environment Rating Scale.* New York: Teachers College Press.

Hepworth, H.P. 1976. *Canadian day care standards, 1976: Better day care, slowly but surely.* Ottawa: Canadian Council on Social Development.

Howe, N., and E. Jacobs. 1995. Child care research: A case for national standards. *Canadian Psychology* 36:131-48.

Hunter, T. 1995. *Quality assessment of early childhood programs demonstration project.* Victoria, BC: Unit for Child Care Research.

Hunter, T., and A.R. Pence. 1995. Supporting quality in early childhood programs. *Interaction* (Fall):30-4.

Independent Child Caregivers Association. 1990. *Who cares: A study on home-based caregivers in Ontario.* Ottawa: Independent Child Caregivers Association.

Isaac, S., and W. Michael. 1977. *Handbook in research and evaluation.* San Diego, CA: Edits Publishers.

Jacobs, E., D. White, and M. Baillargeon. 1996. *The national school-age child care quality assurance study.* Proposal submitted to Child Care Visions, Human Resources Development Canada.

Johnson, L.C. 1978. *Taking care: A report of the Project Child Care caregiver survey.* Toronto: Toronto Social Planning Council.

Johnson, L.C., and J. Dineen. 1981. *The kin trade: The day care crisis in Canada.* Toronto: University of Toronto Press.

Kerans, D. 1982. *Trade union initiatives and day care: A report to Ontario Ministry of Community and Social Services.* Ottawa: Carleton University, Centre for Social Welfare Studies.

Krashinsky, M. 1984. Day care policy in Canada in the 1980s. Presentation to the Colloquium on the Economic Status of Women in the Labour Market, November, Montreal.

LaGrange, A., and M. Read. 1990a. *Those who care: A report on child caregivers in Alberta daycare centres.* Red Deer, AB: Child Care Matters.

–. 1990b. *Towards a research agenda on child care in Alberta.* Red Deer, AB: Child Care Matters.

Lero, D.S. 1981. *Factors influencing parents' preference for and use of alternative child care arrangements for preschool age children: Final report.* Ottawa: Health and Welfare Canada.

Lero, D.S., H. Goelman, A. Pence, L. Brockman, and S. Nuttall. 1992. *Parental work patterns and child care needs.* Report from the Canadian National Child Care Study. Ottawa: Statistics Canada; Health and Welfare Canada.

Lero, D.S., and I. Kyle. 1985. *Day care quality: Its definition and implementation.* Prepared for the Task Force on Child Care, Ottawa.

Lero, D.S., A. Pence, L. Brockman, and M. Charlesworth. 1986. *Parents' needs, preferences, and concerns about child care: Case studies of 336 families.* Prepared for the Task Force on Child Care. Ottawa: Status of Women Canada.

Longwoods Research Group. 1982. *Informal daycare in Ontario.* Consultant's report. Toronto: W.P. Wittman.

Lyon, M., and P.M. Canning. 1995. *The Atlantic day care study.* Ottawa: Human Resources Development Canada.

McKim, M.K., B. Stuart, and D. O'Connor. 1994. Infant Care: Evaluation of pre-care differences hypotheses. Unpublished manuscript, Queen's University.

McLeod, E.M. 1975. *A study of child care services at Canadian universities.* Ottawa: Association of Universities and Colleges of Canada.

McNaughton, K. 1985. *Family day care in Saskatchewan.* Saskatoon: Ministry of Social Services.

Macrae, H.W. 1974. *Manufacturers Life Insurance Company day care study.* Toronto: Manulife Head Office.

Massing, C.A. 1980. Children's use and perception of space in a day care play room. Master's thesis, University of Alberta, Edmonton.

Mayer, A.B. 1965. *Daycare as a social instrument.* Toronto: Toronto, Social Planning Council.

Mayfield, M.I. 1985. Employer-supported child care in Canada: A descriptive analysis. *Canadian Journal of Research in Early Childhood Education* 1(1):3-17.

Middleton, M.A. 1982. *Early childhood education: A survey of practitioners.* Victoria, BC: British Columbia Ministry of Education.

Miller-Chenier, N. 1985. *The informal child care market: Public policy for private homes.* Prepared for the Task Force on Child Care, based on research by Hélène Blais Bates. Ottawa.

Mock, K. 1986. *Multicultural early childhood education in Canada: A cross-Canada survey.* Ottawa: Secretary of State.

–. 1988. Child care needs of cultural and racial minorities. *Canadian Journal of Research in Early Childhood Education* 2(1):11-26.

Montreal Council of Social Agencies. 1969. *A survey of day care facilities for children of Metropolitan Montreal.* Montreal: Council of Social Agencies, Research Department.

–. 1971. *Study of cost analysis for the provision of day care services for children in day nursery settings.* Montreal: Montreal Council of Social Agencies.

Native Council of Canada. 1990. *Native child care: The circle of care.* Ottawa: Native Council of Canada.

NLSCY. 1993. Project Team. *National longitudinal study of children: Overview.* Ottawa: Health and Welfare Canada; Statistics Canada.

–. 1998. Project Team. *Proceedings: Investing in children: A national research Conference.* Ottawa: Human Resources Development Canada.

Norpark Research Consultants. 1995. *Evaluation of the Child Care Initiatives Fund.* Ottawa: Human Resources Development Canada.

O'Kiely, E., and C. Alban. 1973. Family day care within a comprehensive day care service. *Viewpoint* 7:3.

Ontario. 1983. Ministry of Labour. *Ontario civil service child care survey.* Toronto: Ontario Ministry of Labour.

–. 1984. Employer-funded daycare provisions at Canadian Fabricated Products Ltd. Memorandum to the members of the Standing Committee on Social Development, Toronto.

Ontario Métis Aboriginal Association. 1990. *Native child care and its cultural components.* Sault Ste. Marie, ON: Ontario Métis Aboriginal Association.

Pence, A.R. 1985. *A bibliography of Canadian day care research.* Prepared for the Task Force on Child Care. Ottawa: Minister of Supply and Services.

–. 1993. Canada. In *International handbook of child care policies and programs,* ed. M. Cochran, 57-81. Westport, CT: Greenwood Press.

Pence, A.R., and H. Goelman. n.d. Can you see the difference? Regulation, training, and quality of care in family day care. Unpublished manuscript, University of Victoria, Victoria, BC.

–. 1982. Day care in Canada: Developing an ecological perspective. Unpublished manuscript, University of Victoria, School of Child Care, Victoria, BC.

–. 1987a. Silent partners: Parents of children in three types of day care. *Early Childhood Research Quarterly* 2:103-18.

–. 1987b. Who cares for the child in day care? Characteristics of caregivers in three types of care. *Early Childhood Research Quarterly* 2:315-34.

–. 1991. The relationship of regulation, training, and motivation to quality of care in family day care. *Child and Youth Care Forum* 20(2):83-101.

–. 1996. *Victoria's children at 18: A proposed longitudinal study.* Proposal submitted to Child Care Visions, Human Resources Development Canada.

Pence, A.R., and M. Greenwood-Church. 1989. *The 1989 update of: A bibliography of Canadian day care research, 1985.* Ottawa: Minister of Supply and Services.

Pence, A.R., V. Kuehne, M. Greenwood-Church, and M.R. Opekokew. 1993. Generative curriculum: A model of university and First Nations co-operative post-secondary education. *International Journal of Educational Development* 13(3):39-49.

Pence, A.R., and M. McCallum. 1994. Developing cross-cultural partnerships: Implications for child care quality research and practice. In *Valuing quality in early childhood services,* ed. P. Moss and A. Pence, 108-22. London, UK: Paul Chapman Publishing.

Pence, A.R., and P. Moss. 1994. Towards an inclusionary approach in defining quality. In *Valuing quality in early childhood services,* ed. P. Moss and A. Pence, 172-9. London, UK: Paul Chapman Publishing.

Pepper, S., and B. Stuart. 1989. Quality in family day care. Paper presented at the annual meeting of the Canadian Psychological Association, Halifax. Available through Dr. Pepper at the University of Western Ontario.

–. 1992. Quality of family day care in licensed and unlicensed homes. *Canadian Journal of Research in Early Childhood Education* 3(2):109-18.

Peterson, C., and R. Peterson. 1986. Parent-child interaction and day care: Does quality of day care matter? *Journal of Applied Developmental Psychology* 7:1-15.

PMA Consulting Group. 1983. *A survey of private-home day care in Ontario.* Toronto: Ontario Ministry of Community and Social Services.

Power, D.J., and M.G. Brown. 1984. *Child care and taxation in Canada, who pays?* Prepared for the Task Force on Child Care, Ottawa.

Polowy, H. 1978. Day care supervisors' interaction with three and four year old children perceived as behaviourally different in a natural day care setting. Ph.D. diss., University of British Columbia, Vancouver.

Prince Edward Island. 1983. Department of Health and Social Services. Special Services Division. *Study of child care services on Prince Edward Island.* Charlottetown: Department of Health and Social Services.

Quiring, S. 1991. Rural Saskatchewan childcare development: A report on child care needs. Unpublished report. Lakeland Preschool Cooperative.

Regroupement des garderies de la région 6C. 1981. *Travailler juste pour payer la garderie: Une étude sur la capacité financière des parents et le choix d'un mode de garde, rapport de recherche.* Montreal: Regroupement des garderies de la région 6C.

Regroupement des garderies du Montréal Métropolitain. 1982. *Enquête sur la situation du logement des garderies sans but lucratif de Montréal.* Montreal: Regroupement des garderies du Montréal Métropolitain.

Rimstad, B.L. 1985. *Staff training and development in a child welfare setting.* Winnipeg: University of Manitoba.

Robinson, C.C., and P.A. McDermick. 1973. Report on the survey of the day care child with special needs. Unpublished manuscript. Children's Hospital, Diagnostic Centre, Vancouver.

Rose-Lizee, R. 1985. *A proposal to cost-share operating and start-up grants to day care centres: Ten-year estimate of the impact on day-care spaces, percentage of need met, salaries, user fees, employment, and federal expenditures.* Prepared for the Task Force on Child Care, Ottawa.

Rothman Beach Associates. 1985. *A study of work-related day care in Canada.* Prepared for the Task Force on Child Care, Ottawa.

Royal Commission on the Status of Women. 1970. *Report.* Ottawa: Government of Canada.

Saskatchewan. 1978. Social Services, Day Care Division. *Family day care providers survey results.* Regina, SK: Saskatchewan Social Services

Schom-Moffatt, P. 1984. *The bottom line: Wages and working conditions of workers in the formal day care market.* Prepared for the Task Force on Child Care. Ottawa: Status of Women Canada.

–. 1992. *Caring for a living.* Ottawa: Canadian Child Care Federation.

Schweinhart, L., H. Barnes, and D. Weikart. 1993. *Significant benefits.* Ypsilanti, MI: High/Scope.

Shaefer, W.A. 1975. The effect of day care centre attendance upon teachers' ratings of some aspects of children's adjustment in kindergarten. Master's thesis, University of Windsor.

Shell, N.J., and S. James. 1977. Day care workers in the prevention process: A study of their orientation to children and implications for day care training. *Canadian Counselor* 11(3):131-3.

SPR Associates. 1986. *An exploratory review of selected issues in for-profit versus not-for-profit child care.* Prepared for the Special Committee on Child Care, Ottawa.

Statistics Canada. 1997. *Characteristics of dual-earner families.* Catalogue no. 13-215-XPB. Ottawa: Ministry of Industry.

–. 1998. *Population, 15 years and over by age groups and marital status, showing labour force activity and sex for Canada, Provinces, Territories, 1981-1996 Censuses.* Catalogue No. 93FOO27XDB96001. Ottawa: Ministry of Industry.

Status of Women. 1985a. *Series 1, Financing child care: Current arrangements.* Prepared for the report of the Task Force on Child Care. Ottawa: Ministry of Supply and Services Canada.

–. 1985b. *Series 2, Financing child care: Future arrangements.* Prepared for the report of the Task Force on Child Care. Ottawa: Ministry of Supply and Services Canada.

–. 1985c. *Series 3, Child care: Standards and quality.* Prepared for the report of the Task Force on Child Care. Ottawa, ON: Ministry of Supply and Services.

Stevenson, J.A., and E.E. Strawbridge. 1974. *Newfoundland and Labrador day care needs survey.* St. John's: Memorial University, Early Childhood Development Association and Extension Service.

Stevenson, M.B., and H.E. Fitzgerald. 1971. *Standards for infant day care in the United States and Canada.* Lansing, MI: Michigan State University.

Stotsky, K. 1985. *An overview of some federal-provincial fiscal arrangements and proposed options for financing a system of child care in Canada.* Prepared for the Task Force on Child Care, Ottawa.

Stuart, B., and S. Pepper. 1985. Private home day care providers: A study of their personal and psychological characteristics. Unpublished manuscript, University of Guelph, Department of Family Studies.

–. 1988. The contribution of caregiver's personality and vocational interests to quality in licensed family day care. *Canadian Journal of Research in Early Childhood Education* 2(2):99-109.

Taylor, L.J. 1976. Outcome and process evaluation of a day care centre. *Canadian Journal of Behavioural Science* 8:410-3.

Thomson, T.L. 1985. *Enforcement of provincial day care standards.* Prepared for the Task Force on Child Care, Ottawa.

Toronto. 1966. Social Planning Council. *Meeting day care needs in North York Township.* Toronto: Toronto Social Planning Council.

–. 1971. Social Planning Council. *Report on the special study committee on day care needs of school age children.* Toronto: Toronto Social Planning Council.

–. 1975. Social Planning Council of Metropolitan Toronto and Community Day Care Coalition. *Private arrangements: A study of unsupervised child care in Metro Toronto.* Toronto: Toronto Social Planning Council.

–. 1978. Social Planning Council. *A study of unsupervised day care in Metropolitan Toronto.* Toronto: Toronto Social Planning Council.

–. 1981. Bureau of Municipal Research. *Work-related day care: Helping to close the gap.* Toronto: Toronto Bureau of Municipal Research.

–. 1982. Social Planning Council. *Report of the social planning task force on work-related day care.* Toronto: Toronto Social Planning Council.

Townson, M. 1985. *Financing child care through the Canada Assistance Plan.* Prepared for the Task Force on Child Care, Ottawa.

Tremblay, R., R. Pahl, F. Vitaro, and P. Dobkin. 1994. Predicting early onset of male antisocial behavior from preschool behavior. *American Psychiatry* 31:732-9.

University of Guelph. 1978. Department of Family Studies. *An experimental analysis of the impact of an early childhood consultant on family day care providers.* Guelph, ON: University of Guelph.

University of Regina. 1978a. *Day care users survey.* Regina, SK: Saskatchewan Department of Social Services.

–. 1978b. Sample Survey and Data Bank Unit. *Final report: Day care needs and demands in Saskatchewan 1978.* Regina, SK: Saskatchewan Department of Social Service, Planning and Evaluation Branch.

–. 1980. Sample Survey and Data Bank Unit. *Survey of child care preferences.* Regina, SK: Saskatchewan Department of Social Services, Planning and Evaluation Branch.
University of Western Ontario. 1975. *Competence in preschool children: Two years in the laboratory preschool.* London, ON: University of Western Ontario, Department of Psychology.
–. 1976a. *The laboratory preschool: Program development in the first three years.* London, ON: Ontario Ministry of Community and Social Services.
–. 1976b. *The effects of preschool experience on the adaptive abilities of disadvantaged and advantaged children.* London, ON: University of Western Ontario, Department of Psychology.
University Women's Club of Regina. 1975. *Working mothers in Regina and their child care arrangements: A study.* Regina, SK: University Women's Club of Regina.
Vancouver. 1973. United Community Services. *The economics of day care.* Vancouver: Vancouver United Community Services.
Vancouver Community Chest. 1965. *Report on day care needs: The report of the committee to assess the day care needs in Greater Vancouver.* Vancouver: Vancouver Community Chest.
Vancouver Council of Women. 1980. *Vancouver Council of Women study on day care and nursery school needs and services in Vancouver city.* Vancouver: Vancouver Council of Women.
Varga, D. 1997. *Constructing the child: A history of Canadian day care.* Toronto: Lorimer.
West, S. 1988. *A study on compliance with the Day Nurseries Act at full-day child care centres in Metropolitan Toronto.* Toronto: Ministry of Community and Social Services.
Wright, M. 1980. Compensatory education for preschoolers. A non-technical report on the University of Western Ontario. *Canadian Journal of Early Childhood Education* 1:3-15.
–. 1981. Compensatory education for preschoolers: More on the University of Western Ontario preschool project. *Canadian Journal of Early Childhood Education* 1(2):15-21.
–. 1983. *Compensatory education in the preschool: A Canadian approach.* The University of Western Ontario preschool project. Ypsilanti, MI: High/Scope.

Part 2
Current Contexts

6
A National Picture of Child Care Options

Ellen Jacobs

Child care may be defined as care provided for a child that is "other than parental" care; historically, this has taken many forms. The history of child care in Canada dates back to the 1800s in provinces such as Quebec, Nova Scotia, and Prince Edward Island (see Chapter 1). Women who joined the labour force in Montreal, Halifax, and Charlottetown and had young children requiring care were able to leave their children in group settings that resembled the infant schools of Scotland and England (Pence 1986). These types of programs were funded by religious and charitable organizations to care for the children primarily of working parents – for example, in Montreal the religious orders established *les salles d'asiles* for this purpose. The establishment of other child care programs followed in major urban centres. From these beginnings, other child care programs developed, some to support the Second World War effort, others to offer support to needy families; the nature of the programs differed in accordance with the purpose for establishing the particular child care program.

There was a lull in the development of child care programs between the end of the Second World War and the 1960s. During this period many women stayed at home and raised their children while men entered the workforce as the sole provider for the family. However, many aspects of life changed when the children reared during this period (baby boomers) became adults. Their new ideas about work, education, child rearing, family structure and lifestyle all had an impact upon societal structures, and the resulting changes significantly affected social programs in general, and child care in particular. (For a presentation of the individual, social, or economic issues that have spurred the demand for child care, see Chapter 9.)

As this group of mothers of young children began to join the workforce in record numbers, the demand for care for children of all ages, from birth to thirteen, increased substantially (Hoffman 1989; Lero, Goelman, et al. 1992). This need for child care has increased unabated as the numbers of

Canadian mothers employed outside the home has risen from approximately 1.4 million in 1971 to approximately 3.3 million in 1991. As a result, the variety of care arrangements available in Canada in the 1990s has grown. Canadian child care options have expanded from two basic offerings – in-home care (relative or sitter) and group care (centre care) – to include several types of arrangements with different auspices (for-profit or non-profit) and hosts (YMCA, schools, religious groups).

The purpose of this chapter is to describe the various types of child care arrangements currently available to Canadian families living in rural and urban areas across the country. Descriptions of the five most prevalent forms of child care will be presented: (a) non-relative sitter care, (b) relative care, (c) family day care home, (d) centre care, and (e) school-age care. There are variations of these five basic types of care, and employer-sponsored on-site child care is one that warrants special consideration, given its reported impact on families (Mayfield 1990). Each province and territory has legislation relating to specific child care options. The legislation deals with various aspects of child care programs such as licensing, monitoring, and the enforcement of regulations. These regulations have been designed to control elements of care such as caregiver-to-child ratios, group size, caregiver training, physical environments, hours of operation, as well as administrative and fee structures. Given the importance of these regulations to the functioning of the various day care options, a description of the regulations will be provided for each type of child care arrangement. As the purpose of child care regulations is to offer families good-quality non-parental care, the issue of quality in child care arrangements will be introduced in the following section and elaborated in each of the sections describing the five types of child care options. In addition, the potential advantages and disadvantages of each type of care option will be discussed, and relevant research findings reviewed.

Quality of Care

"Quality of care refers to the extent to which the care environment supports and promotes age-appropriate social, emotional, physical, and intellectual development and at the same time provides the family with a sense of security regarding the child's out-of-home care" (Jacobs et al. 1995, 222).

Over the course of the past twenty years, countless debates and discussions have been held about the relationship between child care and children's development. Initially, studies focused on whether group child care as compared with maternal care would be detrimental to a child's development (Hoffman 1974, 1979; Belsky and Steinberg 1978; Etaugh 1980). When these studies illustrated that the quality of care varied significantly within and between the various types of child care, researchers began to study quality issues in child care to determine how differences in quality might be related to different child outcomes (Clarke-Stewart 1989; Pence 1989; Scarr, Phillips, and McCartney 1989). Current research into child care outcomes has expanded to include other variables, such as family and child characteristics. With the increased complexity of the questions being posed and sophistication of the studies and analyses being conducted, many important issues about the relationship between child care and child development have been examined for specific portions of the child care population. One of the more significant and consistent findings is that the quality of care the child receives is an important factor in children's social competence, and language and cognitive development, regardless of the other factors. With this in mind, researchers have included a wide variety of factors and used various instruments in their studies to measure several aspects of the quality of care.

Quality in a child care environment is a composite of many factors such as structural features, global measures, and human factors. Structural features are sometimes referred to as regulatable variables because they can be observed and measured and, as such, can be regulated by government agencies. Group size, centre size, caregiver training, and caregiver-to-child ratios are regulatable features of any type of child care arrangement (Scarr, Phillips, and McCartney 1989). The most effective ranges for these factors have been established through research with children of different age groups in specific types of care (Holloway and Reichhart-Erikson 1988; Phillips and Howes 1987; Smith and Connolly 1986; Vandell and Powers 1983; Whitebook, Howes, and Phillips 1990). On the basis of these research findings, the Canadian Child Day Care Federation (Friendly 1994) has recommended caregiver-to-child ratios of 1:3 for infants; 1:3 or 1:4 for toddlers; 1:4 to 1:6 for two-year-olds; 1:5 to 1:7 for three-year-olds; and 1:8 to 1:9 for four-, five-, and six-year-olds. The recommended maximum group sizes are six children for infant and toddler classes; eight to ten children for two-year-olds; ten to fourteen for three-year-olds; sixteen to eighteen for four-, five-, and six-year-olds; and twenty to twenty-four youngsters for six- to nine-year-olds.

In addition to the structural dimensions of quality, there is a global dimension to quality that refers to the total child care environment (i.e., equipment, activities, atmosphere, routines, provisions for adult needs, and health and safety practices and policies). Although these global features are more difficult to quantify and measure, several instruments have been designed to facilitate this task, and these will be presented in the appropriate section for each type of care arrangement – for example, the Early Childhood Environment Rating Scale – Revised (Harms, Clifford, and Cryer 1998).

As well as measuring global and structural variables as determinants of child care quality, one must consider the human factors, otherwise known as the process variables (Howes, Phillips, and Whitebook 1992) or interactive behaviour (Zaslow 1991). These factors refer to the caregiver's interactions with children (warmth, harshness, attachment), but should also include the centre director's support for the staff since these variables are interrelated. For example, by providing opportunities for in-service training, the director can increase a caregiver's awareness of child development issues, thereby giving her or him better insight into a young child's needs and increasing the likelihood that the caregiver will be more responsive to the children. A caregiver who is well educated and well paid, and who receives support from the director is less likely to suffer from burnout and more likely to provide children with warm, supportive care. The most important issue associated with the quality of child care is its influence on children's development with respect to language skills, social competence, and task-oriented behaviour.

To sum up, creating a high-quality child care environment for any of the five types of care that are described below requires the fulfilment of many conditions. Well-trained caregivers who have an undergraduate early childhood education degree along with a number of child development courses are an essential aspect of high-quality care (Whitebook, Howes, and Phillips 1990). They must be able to interact with the children in a warm, sensitive, and responsive manner. They should be able to provide developmentally appropriate activities that stimulate language and cognitive development and give the children opportunities to enhance their physical and social skills. For this to happen, administrators of programs must ensure that caregivers are well paid, have good benefits, are offered in-service programs to improve their expertise, and have a physical environment that allows for relaxation. They should also have the opportunity to meet parents in a private setting. At the very minimum, caregiver-to-child ratios and group sizes should meet government regulations.

The program should consist of developmentally appropriate fine and gross motor activities, both indoors and outdoors, with sufficient equipment that is in good repair. There should be a good mix of creative activities, as well as those that are designed specifically for the development of language and other cognitive skills. The program should respond to children's curiosity about the concrete and abstract aspects of life, and materials should be available to support the children's interests. It should also encourage and support children's attempts to become independent individuals.

The physical environment should at least meet government regulations, and as these are minimal, it should surpass the minimum requirements regarding space per child (2.32 square metres), maintenance and repairs, and outdoor space. Furnishings should support independent activity on the part of the children – that is, materials should be safe for children's use and easily accessible. Health and safety policies and practices should adhere to the known best practices, particularly with respect to sanitation (e.g., hand washing between the diapering of each child and prior to eating). The environment should be designed to support these practices (e.g., appropriately sized toilets, diapering tables close to a water supply).

Much of the research on child care quality is very specific to certain types of care; therefore, the quality issues associated with each type of care will be discussed at the end of each section.

Non-Relative Sitter Care

Description

Non-relative sitter care is defined as non-parental care of a child in the child's own home or the sitter's home by an individual who is not related to the family. The number of children cared for at the same time depends upon the size of the child's own family or the arrangements the parent has made with the sitter. Usually the sitter is hired to tend to one family's child(ren) from the time the parents leave for work in the morning until they return at the end of the work day. The label "sitter" most often refers to caregivers who work in the family's home but who live elsewhere; on the other hand, a person who is hired to look after a child and lives in the family's home is usually referred to as a "nanny." Many parents prefer sitter care, in one form or another, to group care. Their reasons range from convenience to the individualized attention that they believe their child will receive.

For many years this was the most frequently used form of child care for working mothers because other child care options were quite limited. Using figures from the 1988 Canadian census, the Canadian National Child Care Study reported that 6 percent of six- to nine-year-olds, 8 percent of three- to five-year-olds, 10.5 percent of toddlers (eighteen to thirty-five months), and 9.3 percent of infants (birth to seventeen months) were in sitter care in their own homes (Pence 1992). A province-by-province analysis of the use of non-relative sitter care is presented in Table 6.1. Currently, this is not a popular form of child care for families in Canada. One of the reasons may be the high cost of individual care; it becomes less expensive than group day care only when there are two or more siblings requiring child care.

No legislation exists in any of the provinces or territories concerning non-relative sitter care. The only regulation that must be adhered to in

Table 6.1

Percentage of children in each age group using non-relative sitter care, by province and territory, 1988

Age groups	AB	BC	MB	NB	NF	NT	NS	ON	PE	QC	SK	YT
Infants and toddlers 0-35 months	6.5	10.6	n/a	n/a	15.4*	n/a	15.1	10.0	10.3*	10.4	n/a	n/a
Preschoolers 3-5 years	n/a	11.1	n/a	15.6		n/a	13.0	6.8		9.3	n/a	n/a
School age 6-9 years 10-12 years	n/a	5.7	n/a	6.7	n/a	n/a	6.3	4.3	n/a	5.3	3.6	n/a

Table 6.2

Percentage of children in each age group using relative care, by province and territory, 1988

Age groups	AB	BC	MB	NB	NF	NT	NS	ON	PE	QC	SK	YT
Infants and toddlers 0-35 months	18.1	19.5	19.6	26.2	30.5*	n/a	27.4	21.2	21.1*	23.9	20.0	n/a
Preschoolers 3-5 years	12.0	15.6	n/a	22.3		n/a	14.8	17.1		14.3	15.0	n/a
School age 6-9 years 10-12 years	7.4	12.5	9.0	16.3	20.5	n/a	16.3	10.5	11.0	9.6	8.1	n/a

*Includes preschool-aged children (0-5 years).

Source: All information derived from Pence (1992).

some provinces is that no one younger than twelve years old can be hired as a sitter.

Measuring Quality in Non-relative Sitter Care

No specific instruments have been developed to assess the quality of care that the child is receiving from a sitter. The parent must be an astute evaluator of the child's social and emotional behaviour, and physical and cognitive skill development. This can be accomplished by knowing what to look for and by spending time with the child in different settings, observing the child's actions and discussing various issues. In the case of an infant, the most obvious indicator of positive or negative caregiving may be the physical state of the child (i.e., cleanliness, rashes), whereas emotional well-being, which is more difficult to detect, must be determined through reactions to situations (i.e., distress at separation). One of the most important aspects of non-parental care is the warmth displayed by the caregiver toward the child. The Arnett Caregiver Interaction Scale is an observational instrument that a parent might use as a guide to assess sitter warmth in interactions with the child. Items on the Arnett scale direct the observer to examine the extent to which the caregiver encourages the children to try new experiences, the caregiver's level of enthusiasm about the child's work and efforts, the level of warmth and affection the caregiver displays toward the child, and the degree of harshness the caregiver exhibits when scolding the child (Arnett 1989).

Relative Care

Description

In this type of care arrangement, the adult caring for the child(ren) is a relative of the family, who provides the care either in his or her own home or in the child's home. Frequently, the relative looking after the child is a grandparent. Parents tend to turn to their own parents for help with child care, particularly for infants, if the grandparent is not employed and is healthy enough to provide the necessary care on a daily basis. The thinking behind this arrangement is that the child's grandparent would be the best-qualified adult to raise the child because she or he raised the child's parent.

In 1988, the statistics regarding child care in Canada indicated that 24.7 percent of infants (birth to seventeen months), 19.3 percent of toddlers (eighteen to thirty-five months), 15.8 percent of preschool-aged children (three to five years), 12.4 percent of school-aged children (six to nine years), and 8.1 percent of ten- to twelve-year-olds were cared for by relatives in or out of the home (Pence 1992). It is evident from these data that relative care was used for a larger percentage of younger children (infants and toddlers) than for older children (preschoolers and school-age children). The reason for this may be that parents place greater trust in the ability of relatives to provide care for their very young children, whereas they recognize the need for their older children to be in group settings where they can interact with peers. The provincial figures are presented in Table 6.2.

Provincial/Territorial Regulations

In Canada, no specific regulations exist regarding relative care other than that the caregiver must be older than twelve. Measuring the quality of relative care would have to be conducted in much the same manner recommended for non-relative sitter care. The child's reaction to the relative and the care setting would be the most salient indicators of the quality of the child's experiences.

Research Findings

A study of children in family child care and relative care conducted in the United States yielded interesting results (Galinsky et al. 1994). Fifty-five percent of parents whose children were in relative care stated that they preferred to use family members, and 14 percent said that they selected this type of care because they trusted their relative with their child and that their relative was reliable. The same study indicated that regulated family child care providers (i.e., those licensed by the state or municipality) were more sensitive and responsive to the children than non-regulated or relative caregivers. Given that sensitive and responsive care is valued by parents, the results of this study require further explanation. In this study, 60 percent of the relative caregivers provided this service because they wanted to help their relatives; however, only 25 percent indicated that child care was their chosen profession. This may be interpreted as meaning that relatives provided caregiving out of a sense of obligation rather than commitment (Galinsky et al. 1994). A second and important factor was that 65 percent of the caregivers who were relatives were living in stressful, poverty-stricken situations. A combination of life stresses and lack of commitment to providing care may result in children's not receiving the warm and sensitive caregiving that parents desire and believe they will be able to attain by leaving the child with a relative. Given that there is no agency to monitor the care provided and advise parents of the results, individuals using this form of care cannot be assured of the quality of care their children are receiving.

Family (Home) Day Care

Description

Family day care is child care offered in the home of a caregiver who is not related to the children. The hours of operation may differ from one home to another; on average, providers offer ten hours of care per day. In most provinces and territories, the regulations established for family day care make it possible for providers to care for a maximum number of children of various ages, including their own children. (The maximum varies from five to nine across the country.) This means that provision must be made to support the physical, cognitive, emotional, social, and creative needs of several children from infancy to school age for up to ten hours per day. As the caregiver's home is the site for the provision of care, the caregiver must make appropriate adjustments to the home to guarantee the safety of all the children in the setting and provide them with age-appropriate stimulation to meet their needs. Most provinces and territories have established regulations that govern the essential aspects of family day care, yet both regulated and unregulated family day care homes do operate in most urban and rural areas.

Provincial/Territorial Regulations

To be part of a regulated family day care system, the home must be sanctioned by a government official who has determined that it meets minimum standards of health, safety, and program quality (Lero, Pence, et al. 1992). Passing the screening procedure is just one part of the process. In many cities, family day care providers attend in-service training programs offered by community agencies and participate in a monitoring system whereby their homes are assessed on a regular basis.

Provincial regulations for family day care homes vary widely. Family day care is individually licensed in New Brunswick, Prince Edward Island, Manitoba, Saskatchewan, British Columbia, Northwest Territories, and the Yukon. This means that these family day care homes are inspected by provincial government staff. In Nova Scotia, Quebec, and Ontario, family day care homes are supervised by licensed agencies that send their officials out to monitor these homes. Alberta operates differently in that it hires approved family day care agencies, which in turn contract with caregivers. Some family day care homes are licensed under the Alberta Day Care regulation, and these homes operate independently of the Family Day Care Agencies (Friendly 1994).

The elements of care that are regulated include provider qualifications, maximum group size, age ranges of children, and health and safety issues such as the amount of usable space, nutritional value of meals and snacks, and the proper storage of materials that may pose a threat to children's health. Tables 6.3 and 6.4 list the provincial and territorial requirements for maximum group size, permissible adult-to-child ratios, and provider qualifications as examples of the family day care regulations applied in Canada in 1995.

Table 6.3

Maximum group size in family day care

Province/ territory	Ratio of caregiver to children	Group size
AB	1:6	Maximum of six children under eleven years including provider's own children with a maximum of three children under three years and no more than two children under two years.
BC	1:7	Up to seven children under twelve years including provider's own children; no more than five preschoolers and two school-age, no more than three under three years and no more than one under one year.
MB	1:8 2:12	Maximum of eight children under twelve years including provider's own children under twelve years; no more than five children under six years and no more than three children under two years. With two caregivers, maximum of twelve children including provider's own children under twelve years of age; maximum of three under two years of age.
NB	1:3 (infants) 1:5 (2-5 years) 1:9 (6 years+) 1:6 (mixed ages)	Three infants or five children two to five years of age or nine children six years and older. When all age groups are combined, a maximum of six children.
NF	No regulated family day care	
NT	1:8	Maximum of eight children under twelve years including provider's own children; maximum of six may be five years or less; maximum of three may be three years or less; and maximum of two may be two years or less.

►

◄ *Table 6.3*

Maximum group size in family day care

Province/ territory	Ratio of caregiver to children	Group size
NS	1:6 (mixed ages) 1:8 (school-age)	No more than six children of mixed ages including provider's own children; no more than eight school-age children including provider's own children.
ON	1:5 (0-12 years)	Maximum of five children from birth to twelve years of age; maximum of two under two years; no more than three under three years including provider's own children under six years.
PE	1:7	No more than seven children including provider's own children under twelve years; maximum of three children under two years.
QC	1:6 (0-12 years) 2:9	Maximum of six children including the provider's own children under twelve years of age; no more than two children under eighteen months. With two adults, maximum is nine children including the provider's own children, with no more than four under eighteen months.
SK	1:8	Up to eight children between six weeks and twelve years, including the provider's own children under thirteen years; maximum of five younger than six years; maximum of two younger than thirty months.
YT	1:8 2:12	Up to eight children including provider's own preschool children (but not school-aged); maximum of three infants if there are also three preschoolers or school-aged children. With an additional caregiver, four additional school-aged children.

Table 6.4

Provider qualification requirements for regulated family day care

Province/ territory	Provider qualification requirements
AB	No training qualifications are specified.
BC	Provider must be at least nineteen years of age and have a first-aid certificate. No early childhood training requirements.
MB	Provider must be at least eighteen years of age and have a first-aid certificate. No training requirements are specified. Suitability of providers to provide care is assessed.
NB	Provider must be at least nineteen years old and have first-aid training. No early childhood education training or experience required.
NF	No regulated family day care.
NT	Provider must be at least nineteen years of age and have a first-aid certificate. No early childhood training requirements.
NS	Provider must be at least eighteen years old, not on child abuse registry, and have no criminal record. No early childhood education training or experience required.
ON	Provider must be older than eighteen years. No training qualifications are specified.
PE	Provider must participate in a thirty-hour training program, have two letters of reference and current first-aid certificate.
QC	Provider must complete a twenty-four-hour training program focused on child development, health, diet, organization, and leadership. Provider must also have a first-aid certificate.
SK	Provider must be at least eighteen years of age. Must complete an orientation course and have first-aid training.
YT	Provider must be eighteen years of age and have a first-aid certificate. Must complete a sixty-hour introductory early childhood development course, a specific family day home course or the equivalent within the first year that care is provided for children.

Note that among all the provinces and territories only Prince Edward Island, Saskatchewan, Quebec, and the Yukon have requirements specifically for the training of providers (see Table 6.4). Of the eight provinces and territories that specify a minimum age requirement for providers, eighteen years of age is deemed acceptable in Manitoba, Nova Scotia, Ontario, Saskatchewan, and the Yukon, whereas nineteen years of age is the minimum for British Columbia, New Brunswick, and the Northwest Territories (see Table 6.4). Given that most of the regulations regarding provider qualifications are minimal, one might question the rationale for drafting regulations of this nature.

By establishing regulations and licensing homes, the governments are ensuring at least a minimum level of care for children in family day care homes. Being identified on a formal list of licensed family day care homes gives providers a sense of professionalism regardless of their level of qualifications. In addition, licensed providers are usually given in-service training sessions that afford them the opportunity to meet other providers, exchange ideas, and discuss problems that are relevant to this form of care.

Newfoundland does not have regulated family day care. In an unregulated family day care home, no agency is watching over the home or the caregiver. The rules that a caregiver must adhere to are those associated with running a small business, but the quality of the operation is not regulated. No government official makes spot checks or unannounced visits to observe the caregiver and the children in the family day care environment. No one reviews the daily programs planned by the caregiver for the children.

Using the 1988 data, the Canadian National Child Care Study reported that 26.3 percent of infants, 27.8 percent of toddlers, 20.4 percent of preschoolers, and 13.5 percent of school-aged children in a child care arrangement were in family day care homes (Pence 1992). The province-by-province statistics are presented in Table 6.5.

Measuring Quality in Family Day Care

The instrument that is currently used most frequently to measure quality of care in family day care is the Family Day Care Environment Rating Scale (Harms and Clifford 1989). It is composed of several items that deal with the issue of children of different ages being cared for in a small group by one caregiver. These items include the arrangement of indoor space for a broad age range, and managing mealtimes and naps or rests with infants, toddlers, and preschoolers. As family day care is located in a home, all the safety problems usually associated with being in a home are considered. The variety and extent of stimulating materials available for comprehension, use of language, and development of reasoning skills for a wide age

Table 6.5

Percentage of children in each age group using family day care, by province and territory, 1988

Age groups	AB	BC	MB	NB	NF	NT
Infants and toddlers 0-35 months	24.8	25.8	18.1	26.7	11.0*	n/a
Preschoolers 3-5 years	15.6	16.8	18.2	22.1		n/a
School age 6-9 years 10-12 years	7.8	8.4	6.3	12.1	n/a	n/a
	NS	**ON**	**PE**	**QC**	**SK**	**YT**
Infants and toddlers 0-35 months	20.3	33.9	20.3*	25.4	27.2	n/a
Preschoolers 3-5 years	12.4	22.8		21.6	25.6	n/a
School age 6-9 years 10-12 years	8.9	10.6	8.5	10.4	9.6	n/a

*Includes preschool-aged children (0-5 years).
Source: All information derived from Pence (1992).

range are examined and rated. One of the items deals with an activity that is particularly relevant to home care – the use of television during the day; another item that considers adult needs looks at the balancing of personal and caregiving activities.

Research Findings Related to Family Day Care Homes

Families tend to select caregivers who are similar to themselves in terms of income and ethnic background, and use family day care and relative care most frequently for children two years of age and younger (Galinsky et al. 1994). Family day care homes that are operated by individuals who have had formal training, who belong to child care associations, and who are committed to providing care tend to offer higher quality care than homes of care providers lacking these factors (Goelman 1990). The language scores of children are positively correlated with the quality of these family day care homes (Goelman 1990).

Group size in family day care cannot exceed a total of eight children in most provinces in Canada; however, in the United States some family day care homes have groups as large as thirteen. Clarke-Stewart's (1987) study of family day care homes in the United States found that children in a group of five or more displayed poorer social competence with unfamiliar peers than did those in groups of two to four children. Howes and Rubenstein (1985) indicated that children in smaller groups displayed less crying behaviour and more play and communication with their peers than children in larger groups. These findings are very interesting in the light of the results of the study by Galinsky et al. (1994), which indicated that caregivers with somewhat larger groups were likely to be more sensitive in their caregiving and that those with somewhat larger than average groups (3.98 was average) and higher ratios (1:3.3 was average) were more likely to offer higher quality care than those with lower numbers and lower ratios. The researchers suggest that the factors at work in this situation are intentionality and an understanding of the way to provide care. They maintain that caregivers who have a somewhat larger than average enrolment are more likely to have more formal training and experience and, therefore, accept more children knowing that they are well equipped to offer good-quality care. In addition, some research indicates that children fare better in family day care when there are slightly larger groups (more than two) and higher ratios (Dunn 1993). The reasons cited for this relate to the stimulation provided by the other children and the fact that when there are more children in a group, the caregiver is more likely to plan activities for the children.

Centre-Based Group Care

Description

Centre-based group care or community day care is defined as group care for children ranging in age from infancy through the preschool years. This care is provided in a facility other than a private home (Lero, Pence, et al. 1992). The two main factors that differentiate centre-based group care from other types of child care are the physical environment in which the care is provided and the size of the population. Centre care is usually offered in an environment that can accommodate thirty or more children. Some of the buildings used have been designed specifically for child care purposes, but more often they are structures that required renovation to conform to municipal regulations and building codes. These regulations focus on health-related issues such as proper ventilation, natural lighting, and a specific number of square metres per child, and on safety factors such as sprinklers, fire escapes, accessible exits, and fencing around playgrounds. Both health and safety factors must be adequate for the operation of a centre-based child care program.

In centre-based care, the enrolment is usually sufficient to create several groups of children organized by age; and each age-group may be cared for by one or more caregivers. The number of adults assigned to a group is determined by the provincial regulations concerning adult-to-child ratios. In most provinces, the ratio rises in accordance with the ages of the children in the group, as set out in Table 6.6. The total number of children permitted to be enrolled in a centre depends upon the calculation of usable square metres in the centre. This is based upon the amount of space with natural lighting minus the amount of space occupied by furnishings (tables, chairs, shelves).

Most child care centres operate on a ten- or eleven-hour day. Children may attend day care on a full- or part-time basis, and this is determined by parental needs and availability of full- or part-time spaces in the centre. Throughout the day, the group of children and their caregivers engage in a wide variety of indoor and outdoor activities. The daily schedule for each group is supposed to be designed to meet the needs, interests, and capabilities of that specific age group. The routine for preschoolers (three to five years of age) may include free play, circle time, gross motor activities, fine arts, story time, sociodramatic play, snack, rest, lunch time, and field trips, to name just a few activities usually offered preschoolers. The curriculum should correspond to the centre's philosophy of child development and preschool education. Currently, many centres subscribe to the curriculum based upon the developmentally appropriate practice model proposed by the National Association for the Education of Young Children, which is a US-based organization that has as its mandate high-quality care and education for young children. There are, however, centres that also incorporate particular educational approaches such as the Montessori style, the constructivist approach, or the Reggio Emilia philosophy (see Chapter 7). Parents living in large urban areas may be able to select a centre on the basis of the curriculum, in addition to the usual set of priorities that parents use when choosing a day care centre (White et al. 1992).

Employer-Sponsored Child Care

Centre care may be provided in the child's community or it may be close to the parent's workplace or even on the parent's work site. The involvement of the employer in the provision of child care for employees can take many forms and is called employer-sponsored child care. For example, the employer may offer families subsidies for child care regardless of where the family chooses to register the child; or it may support families in the search for appropriate care by paying the fees of a child care consulting firm. The employer may also provide a list of qualified sitters ready to step in when the child is ill and unable to attend the child care centre.

However, the most visible form of sponsored care is the workplace child care centre. This type of centre is located on the work site and is subsidized by the employer. Since the care centre is thus subsidized, it may be able to allocate more of the parents' fees toward higher wages for the caregivers, making it possible to attract highly qualified, well-trained caregivers.

Provincial and Territorial Regulations

Provincial regulations regarding adult-to-child ratios, maximum group size, and caregiver training requirements vary enormously among provinces and territories. Table 6.6 lists the ratios and group sizes required for selected age groups in each province and territory. Caregiver-to-child ratios for two-year-olds range from 1:4 in British Columbia to 1:8 in Quebec. For four-year-olds, the range is from 1:7 in Nova Scotia to 1:10 in Prince Edward Island, New Brunswick, and Saskatchewan (Friendly 1994). Maximum group sizes in child care centres for two-year-olds range from ten in New Brunswick to thirty in Quebec. For four-year-olds, the maximum group size is sixteen in Alberta and Ontario, and rises to thirty in Quebec.

Table 6.7 outlines provincial regulations regarding caregiver qualifications

Table 6.6

Regulated staff-to-child ratios in full-day centre-based child care, selected age groups, 1995

Province/ territory	Two years (maximum group size)	Four years (maximum group size)	Six years (maximum group size)
AB	1:6 (12)	1:8 (16)	1:10* (20)
BC	1:4 (25)	1:8 (25)	1:8 (25)
MB	1:6 (12)	1:9 (18)	1:15 (30)
NB	1:5 (10)	1:10 (20)	1:15 (30)
NF	1:6 (25)	1:8 (25)	1:8 (25)
NT	1:6 (12)	1:9 (18)	1:10 (20)
NS	1:7 (ns)**	1:7 (ns)	1:15 (ns)
ON	1:5 (15)	1:8 (16)	1:15 (30)
PE	1:5 (ns)	1:10 (ns)	1:12 (ns)
QC	1:8 (30)	1:8 (30)	1:15 (30)
SK	1:5 (20)	1:10 (20)	1:15 (30)
YT	1:6 (ns)	1:8 (ns)	1:12 (ns)

Note: In some provinces, an age may fall into more than one age group. For example, a two-year-old may be categorized as zero to two or two to three years. The ratios in this table represent the older age range in these cases.

* The Alberta legislation covers children up to six years. Therefore, this ratio is for a five-to-six-year age group.

** not specified in regulations

Source: Friendly (1997).

Table 6.7

Staff qualification requirements in centre care

Province/ territory	Staff qualification requirements
AB	Program directors are required to have training equivalent to a two-year public college diploma in early childhood education.
	One in four staff in each centre is required to have training equivalent to a one-year public college early childhood education certificate.
	All other child care staff are required to have a fifty-hour orientation course or equivalent course work.
BC	There are three categories of training:
	Early childhood educator: Basic (at least ten months) early childhood training program offered by an approved institution and 500 hours of supervised work experience.
	Infant/toddler educator: Basic early childhood education program plus specialized training related to infant/toddler care and education.
	Special needs educator: Basic early childhood education program plus specialized training related to children with special needs.
	For the purposes of defining staffing requirements in child care programs, people who are currently enrolled in basic early childhood education training are called assistant early childhood educators.
	Group day care, children under thirty-six months: each group of five to eight children requires one infant/toddler educator and one early childhood educator. Each group of nine to twelve children requires one early childhood educator and one assistant.
	Group day care, children thirty months to school-age: each group requires one early childhood educator plus assistants.
	Out-of-school and child-minding: staff must be older than nineteen years and have taken a course on the care of young children or have relevant work experience.
	Special needs facilities (group care facilities where at least 25 percent

►

◄ *Table 6.7*

Staff qualification requirements in centre care

Province/ territory	Staff qualification requirements
	of the children have special needs) require one special needs educator for every group of four or fewer children. Larger groups require one special needs educator plus early childhood educators.
MB	Manitoba has the following three qualification levels: CCW (Child Care Worker) I: Complete secondary education (grade 12 or equivalent), or any certificate, diploma, or graduate/postgraduate degree unrelated to child care; or one postsecondary level accredited course in child care. CCW II: Child Day Care Competency-Based Assessment (CBA) Program, or an approved diploma in child care services from a recognized community college. CCW III: An approved CCW II program and a recognized certificate program, or an approved degree program from a recognized university. All staff must be eighteen years of age and have first-aid training. Two-thirds of a full-time centre's preschool staff must have a CCW II or III. One-half of staff employed in school-age centres and nursery schools must have completed early childhood education training. Supervisors are required to be qualified as a CCW III and to have one year's experience.
NB	No early childhood education training or experience is required. Staff must be at least sixteen years old. Staff sixteen to nineteen years old are required to be supervised by a primary staff member who must be at least nineteen years old. All staff must have first-aid training.
NF	Centre supervisors must have either a one-year certificate in early childhood education and one year's experience in a licensed centre, or a two-year diploma with no specifications regarding experience. A related degree with one year's experience in a licensed centre is considered a comparable qualification. Supervisors approved before 1989 are not required to have these qualifications. If more than twenty-five children are enrolled in a centre, the Day Care and Homemaker Services Licensing Board recommends, but does not require, that a second person with supervisor qualifications be present.

►

◄ *Table 6.7*

Staff qualification requirements in centre care

Province/ territory	Staff qualification requirements
NT	Must be at least nineteen years and have a first-aid certificate. There are no early childhood training requirements.
NS	Centre director and two-thirds of the staff must have either a one- or two-year early childhood education certificate or diploma or two years' experience, one course and a thirty-five-hour workshop on child development and curriculum. All staff must have first-aid training.
ON	Centre supervisors must have a two-year diploma in early childhood education from an approved College of Applied Arts and Technology (CAAT) or the equivalent, and at least two years' experience working in a day nursery with children who are of the same age and developmental level as the children in the day nursery where the supervisor is employed. A ministry director has the authority to waive the educational requirements for directors and other staff in a specific program.
	One staff person with each group of children must have a two-year early childhood education diploma (CAAT) or equivalent.
	A resource teacher must hold a diploma in early childhood education or academic equivalent and have completed a postsecondary school program related to the needs of children with disabilities. If working with children who have multiple disabilities, the resource teacher must also have a current standard certificate in first aid. There are no training or experience requirements for staff other than resource teachers who are working with children who have special needs.
PE	Centre supervisors and one full-time staff member in each program must have at least a one- or two-year childhood development diploma or university child study degree.
	Thirty hours of in-service training every three years are required for all staff.
QC	One-third of staff must have a college diploma or university degree in early childhood education (ECE) or three years' experience plus a college attestation degree or certificate in ECE.
SK	Centre supervisors must have a one-year certificate in child care or equivalent.

►

◄ *Table 6.7*

Staff qualification requirements in centre care

Province/ territory	Staff qualification requirements
	Every staff member must take a 130-hour child care orientation course or equivalent, provided through regional community colleges, unless the person has a one-year certificate in child care or equivalent.
	One staff member in each centre must have completed a first-aid course.
	Staff working with children who have special needs must have additional training.
YT	In centre-based care, each group of children must be under the supervision of at least one caregiver who is certified in a first-aid course approved by the director.
	By September 1997, 50 percent of the regular staff in a program must meet or exceed the CCW I qualifications. By 1999, an additional 30 percent of the staff must meet or exceed the CCW II qualifications. By 2000, an additional 20 percent of staff must meet or exceed the CCW III qualifications.
	CCW I: successfully complete a sixty-hour introduction to early childhood development course or equivalent.
	CCW II: successfully complete one year of training in early childhood development or equivalent.
	CCW III: successfully complete two or more years of training in early childhood development or equivalent.

and reveals the differing requirements. For example, only in Ontario is each group of children required to have one ECE-trained staff member (i.e., having a two-year ECE diploma). In the other provinces where training is required, a percentage of the staff members in the centre must have ECE training. The rationale for requiring only some of the caregivers to have specific training could be a matter of finances. Caregiver wages are based upon training and experience, and whether the centre functions as a non-profit or for-profit centre (see Chapter 10).

Using the 1988 Canadian census figures, the National Child Care Survey reported that 5.4 percent of Canadian infants, 12.5 percent of toddlers, 13.9 percent of preschoolers, and 1.6 percent of school-aged children were enrolled in child care centres. A province-by-province analysis of the use of

Table 6.8

Percentage of children in each age group using centre care, by province and territory, 1988

Age groups	AB	MB	ON	PE	QC	SK
Infants and toddlers 0-35 months	14.8*	n/a	5.7	8.0*	16.4	n/a
Preschoolers 3-5 years	18.7	20.1	11.5		25.1	8.2
School age 6-9 years 10-12 years	3.1	4.2	2.8	n/a	7.7	n/a

Note: Figures not available for British Columbia, New Brunswick, Newfoundland, Nova Scotia, the Northwest Territories, and the Yukon.

* Includes preschool-aged children (0-5 years).

Source: All information derived from Pence (1992).

centre-based group care is presented in Table 6.8. It is evident that in 1988, centre-based care did not draw as large a proportion of the child care population as did family day care, particularly in the case of infants (see above, as well as Table 6.5). One reason for this, however, might have been that there were not many spaces for infants in child care centres. See Table 6.9 for spaces available. The regulations regarding adult-to-child ratios for infants make it very expensive for centres to provide child care for this age group. Another reason may be that parents prefer to have their infants with a small group of children in an environment that resembles a home setting. Interestingly, in some provinces the adult-to-child ratios required in licensed child care settings are lower than in family day care. However, the total number of infants in the group may be larger than in family day care settings.

Measuring Quality in Centre Care

The structural variables of centre care can be measured by caregiver-to-child ratios, centre size, group size, and caregiver training. However, assessing the global quality of a centre requires a measurement instrument that takes all elements of the care environment into account and permits evaluators to arrive at a total score. The Early Childhood Environment Rating Scale – Revised can be used to produce a score for the global dimensions for preschoolers in centre care (Harms, Clifford, and Cryer 1998). The items measured are space and furnishings, personal care routines, language and reasoning, activities, interactions, program structure, and provisions for parents and staff. In centres where infants and toddlers are

Table 6.9

Regulated child care spaces in Canada, 1995

Province/ territory	Centre-based full- and part-day child care[a]	School-age child care	Regulated family care	Total regulated spaces	Percentage of children 0-12 for whom there is a regulated child care space
AB	43,262	0	7,826	51,088	9.6
BC	31,462	13,360	14,972	59,794	9.6
MB	12,480	3,255	3,111	18,856	9.5
NB	7,838	n/a	114	7,952	6.3
NF	3,705	497	0	4,202	4.3
NT	1,182	n/a	104	1,286	n/a
NS	10,476	n/a	169	10,645	6.8
ON	128,955	n/a	18,898	147,853	7.7
PE	3,292	568	28	3,888	15.5
QC	52,911	40,670[b]	17,871	11,452[c]	9.4[d]
SK	3,727	926	2,613	7,266	3.8
YT	649	189	222	1,060	n/a
Total	299,939	59,465	65,928	25,332[e]	8.3[f]

a This category comprises both full-day and part-day spaces because a number of provinces cannot provide a breakdown.

b School-age child care in Quebec is not regulated by *l'Office des services de garde à l'enfance* but is operated by school boards. These spaces are included here.

c This figure includes the school board-operated school-age child care spaces that are not regulated by *l'Office*. Therefore, the total given in this table will not match the total number of regulated spaces given in the Quebec provincial literature, where the school-age spaces have been listed separately.

d This percentage has been calculated including the school board-operated unregulated school-age child care spaces.

e Will not equal the sum of all types of services as given in the table. Some facilities offer more than one service and the licensed capacity for a particular facility does not always equal the sum of spaces by service. Total includes school board-operated unregulated school-age child care spaces for Quebec.

f Figures for the number of children 0-12 years in the territories were unavailable. Therefore the territorial figures for regulated child care spaces have been excluded from the calculation of this percentage. It has been calculated including school board-operated unregulated school-age child care spaces for Quebec.

Source: Friendly (1997).

present the Infant/Toddler Environment Rating Scale (Harms, Cryer, and Clifford 1990) should be used. It examines furnishings and display for children, personal care routines, listening and talking, learning activities, interactions, program structure, and provisions for adult needs. The National Association for the Education of Young Children has developed a scale that assesses the quality of the child care environment and serves as the basis for its accreditation system (NAEYC 1991).

Research Findings on Centre Care

The research findings referred to in this section are from studies that either examined factors associated with centre care in comparison with other forms of child care or simply included factors that arose from child care environments (e.g., caregiver warmth, children's peer interactions). Since the body of research into this type of care is so enormous and the findings so important, reference should be made to most of these findings; the research findings are divided here into three different segments. Debates persist about various issues associated with for-profit versus non-profit centre care. The results of these comparative studies have important implications, which are presented in Chapter 10.

Caregiver Factors

Caregivers who have some early childhood training or have taken child development courses display more positive behaviours toward the children than those caregivers who have only high school credentials (Arnett 1989; Ruopp et al. 1979). The caregivers with training are more responsive to the children, prepare more developmentally appropriate activities, and provide the children with higher levels of language stimulation than caregivers with only secondary school certificates. Similarly, caregivers with an undergraduate degree in early childhood education behaved more appropriately with the children than did caregivers with early childhood training from a vocational program (Whitebook, Howes, and Phillips 1990). Thus the training related to child care beyond secondary or vocational school has been found to be very important.

Caregiver factors mentioned above have been shown to be essential to the healthy growth and development of young children attending child care centres. High rates of caregiver turnover have been associated with less responsive caregiver behaviour (Phillips and Howes 1987). Children who experienced a high rate of caregiver turnover showed less mature play with age-mates than children in a more stable caregiving situation (Howes and Stewart 1987). In addition, children in centres with high caregiver turnover exhibited more aimless wandering, spent less time interacting with peers, and scored lower on language measures than children receiving more stable care (Whitebook, Howes, and Phillips 1990). Another American study found that children who experienced frequent losses of their primary caregivers became more aggressive than those who did not have frequent changes of caregivers (Howes 1983). In contrast, children who experienced high levels of positive caregiver interaction exhibited more exploratory behaviour than children who had lower levels of interaction with their caregivers (Anderson et al. 1981; Kontos and Wilcox-Herzog 1997). There were also long-term consequences of these levels of positive caregiver-to-child interactions. Howes (1990) found that kindergarten children who had experienced more positive interactions with their caregivers exhibited better social skills, were less distracted, less hostile, and more task-oriented than those who had lower levels of involvement with their caregivers.

Appropriate caregiving in child care centres has been found to be positively related to the level of appropriate play with peers and of language development (Howes, Phillips, and Whitebook 1992; Whitebook, Howes, and Phillips 1990). The responsiveness of caregivers to children's questions, bids for attention, and moods are positively related to children's cognitive development, verbal skills, and social competence (Melhuish et al. 1990; Rubenstein and Howes 1983; Whitebook, Howes, and Phillips 1990). Children in centres with adults who react positively to them by encouraging their initiatives and showing interest in their activities tend to exhibit more emotional security and more advanced language and cognitive development than children whose caregivers exhibit lower levels of positive responses (Anderson et al. 1981; Carew 1980; Howes 1990; Whitebook, Howes, and Phillips 1990). Moreover, the amount and type of verbal interactions the child has with the caregiver can predict the child's language development (Carew 1980; McCartney 1984). Verbal exchanges, explanations, and encouragement have a positive impact on the child's language development.

Two types of negative caregiver behaviour have been studied in terms of their association with child development. Caregiver harshness is related to aimless wandering within the classroom setting and lower levels of attachment to the caregiver (Whitebook, Howes, and Phillips 1990). Caregiver detachment is also related to increased levels of aimless wandering, along with poor language development, immature forms of play with age-mates, and an unwillingness to cooperate with peers (Ruopp et al. 1979; Whitebook, Howes, and Phillips 1990). It is evident from these findings that many of the caregiver's skills and behaviours play a vital role in a child's development. However, other research has shown that the caregiver is not the only factor at the day care centre that influences the child's development.

Centre-Based Factors
Group size, centre size, organization of space, adult-to-child ratios, health and safety policies and practices, materials and equipment, and density have all been demonstrated to have an effect on the behaviour and development of children who attend centre care; these factors also individually influence the types of interactions caregivers have with the children (Howes, Phillips, and Whitebook 1992; Love 1993).

One study that compared the health of children in child care centres to that of children who were home-reared found that children in centre care were more likely to experience bouts of serious diarrhea than those reared at home (Hayes, Palmer, and Zaslow 1990). The link between the occurrence of diarrhea and the number of young children in a child care centre who were not yet toilet-trained has been clearly documented (Ekanem et al. 1983; Hadler et al. 1982; Pickering, Bartlett, and Woodward 1986). The size of the centre also appears to be associated with health risks. The larger the centre, the greater the risk of infectious diseases, particularly in centres with fifty or more children (Hadler et al. 1982; Pickering and Woodward 1982; Silva 1980). Group size also influences caregiver behaviour. Ruopp et al. (1979) found that with three- to five-year-olds in groups of twelve children or fewer, caregivers were more communicative than with groups of twenty-four or more, even when caregiver-to-child ratios were adjusted for the larger group size. For the toddler age group, studies have shown that larger groups result in caregivers being more restrictive, more negative, less involved, and less responsive than caregivers with smaller groups (Howes 1983; Howes and Rubenstein 1985; Kontos and Fiene 1987).

The manner in which the space is organized in the child care centre is reported to affect the way children play within that space. When a large play space in a child care centre was divided into smaller play spaces, the three- and four-year-olds displayed more frequent peer interactions, more fantasy play, and more cooperative play than those who played in the same space when it was not partitioned (Field 1980). Other studies have shown that there is a relationship between well-organized play spaces, which are supplied with appropriate materials, and children's performance on tests of social and cognitive performance (Clarke-Stewart and Gruber 1984).

Although the issue of caregiver-to-child ratios has been discussed elsewhere in this chapter, it is important to reiterate that ratios have a significant impact on caregiver behaviour and attitude (Bruner 1980; Clarke-Stewart and Gruber 1984; Cummings and Beagle-Ross 1983; Howes 1983; Howes and Rubenstein 1985; Ruopp et al. 1979), which in turn affect the quality of care provided and thus children's social, cognitive, and language skills (Galluzzo et al. 1988).

Quality Factors
Results of research projects that have examined the relationship between quality of care and child outcomes have provided the child care community with invaluable information. This information has had an influence on caregiver training; parental expectations; supervisory evaluations; and licensing, policies, and procedures in many centres. In a study of children aged three to five and a half enrolled in centre care, Phillips and Howes (1987) found that high-quality care was associated with higher ratings of children's task orientation, social skills, considerate behaviour, and language development levels. In one American study that included regulatable variables as indicators of quality, Vandell and Powers (1983) found that children attending low-quality centres displayed more solitary behaviour and more negative behaviour with peers than did children in high-quality centres. Their findings also indicated that children in higher-quality centres exhibited more positive behaviour with adults. In a second American study using regulatable variables to determine quality of care, Howes and Olenick (1986) found that children in high-quality centres were more compliant with adult requests to adhere to rules than were children in lower-quality centres. Another American study used both structural and global quality factors to find that children aged fourteen months to four and a half years in high-quality child care centres were more likely to be in classrooms that were rated higher in both caregiving and activities. In this type of classroom, children were more likely to be securely attached to their caregivers and more competent with their peers than were children in lower-quality centres (Howes, Phillips, and Whitebook 1992).

The findings for cognitive development have been mixed. Wright (1983) reported that a high-quality cognitively based preschool program facilitated IQ gains, whereas Kontos and Fiene (1987) did not find this association when child care quality and family background were taken into account. However, several longitudinal studies indicated that the quality of care children received at the preschool level carried over to the elementary school setting. Children who had attended high-quality care were more socially skilled and better adjusted in elementary school than those who had attended low-quality child care as preschoolers (Howes 1990; Jacobs and White 1994; Vandell, Henderson, and Wilson 1988).

In several Canadian studies, auspice has been shown to be related to certain indicators of child care quality such as caregiver turnover, staff training, job satisfaction, ratio, and group size (Ross, Altmaier, and Russell 1989; Friesen 1992; Krashinsky 1986; LaGrange and Read 1990).

Although all the studies and types of care reviewed to this point focus on preschool and younger children, there are also school-aged children who require care. Enrolment in elementary school does not eliminate the need for child care, because most parents' work hours do not correspond to the short school day. Consequently, many parents need care for their children during the out-of-school periods of the day; this form of child care is known as school-age care.

School-Age Care

Description

School-age care is defined as child care for children who have reached elementary school age and require supervision, care, and support before the school day begins, at lunch time, and after school. It is important to note that 1991 statistics indicated that there were close to two million children aged between six and twelve whose mothers were in the labour force, and there were only 59,465 regulated child care spaces for this age group as of 1995 (Friendly 1997). In the past, parents customarily put together a patchwork of arrangements to get their school-aged children through the day. In response to this growing need for supplemental care for the elementary school-aged child, schools, community centres, religious groups, child care centres, and recreational organizations have developed different types of school-age care programs.

The philosophy of the school-age program determines the type of activities available for the children. Some centres offer purely recreational activities, whereas others focus on the fine arts or have an academic bent. There is a continuing debate over the content of school-age care programs among parents, child care staff, and school teachers. Many parents would like their children to complete their homework before returning home for the evening, whereas others want their children to unwind after school and participate in activities that are not offered in the school curriculum (White 1990). Many teachers want the school-age care staff to refrain from academic activities for fear that the caregivers will duplicate the elementary school program (Betsalel-Presser et al. 1993). As there are no regulations regarding school-age care curricula, the program content varies; and this may well be a positive factor. Parents and children living in urban areas that may offer many different types of programs can select the most appropriate one for the child. In areas where options do not exist, children have to manage with the curriculum of the available program. Although the largest proportion of children attending school-age care is in the five- to nine-year-old age range, the curriculum must respond to the needs of ten- to twelve-year-olds as well. The latter age group presents a formidable challenge to caregivers because the programs and activities must be stimulating, engaging, and enjoyable, yet offer the opportunity for relaxation, independence, and privacy, which children of these ages seek.

The organization of the school-age child's day is a concern, since excessive fragmentation can be a problem. In the course of one school day these children may have to adjust to the rules and styles of interaction of several different adults, in addition to their complement of teachers. Most parents try to arrange as seamless a day as possible, wherein the caregiving is provided in one location with as few changes as possible.

School-age programs may be located on school premises, in family day care homes, in day care centres, on sites belonging to non-profit organizations, or in municipal recreation facilities. School-age programs that operate off school premises require the children to travel to the centre. Some programs provide a school bus service whereas others have escorts who pick up the children at their classrooms and walk them to the centre where the program is held. The hours of operation of most school-age programs are fragmented, reflecting the periods of the day when the care is needed. An early morning drop-off arrangement is usually available and most centres stay open until 6 o'clock in the evening. In many cases, the school-age program operates at lunchtime as well.

Provincial/Territorial Regulations

The agencies responsible for licensing school-age programs in Canada differ across the country. In some cases, licensing falls under the purview of the provincial/territorial Ministry of Health, whereas in others, the Department of Education licenses the programs. Within provinces/territories some school-age programs must be licensed, whereas those sponsored by the schools are exempted. Regulations regarding adult-to-child ratios and maximum group size vary considerably from one province/territory to another, and in many cases ratios differ according to the ages of the children, as shown in Table 6.10. Training requirements for staff in school-age care centres also vary across the country. The training requirements for family child care providers offering care for school-age children is as limited as for preschool children. Beside the paucity of training requirements, what is required may not meet the needs of individuals who work with pre-adolescents. An early childhood education diploma or degree usually would not cover relevant developmental or curricular issues for older school-age children. Table 6.11 indicates that most of the provinces listing training requirements for school-age staff specify early childhood education diplomas or degrees. Given the few requirements, one might ask whether training programs exist for school-age providers. Stand-alone programs are relatively scarce, but more community colleges than ever before are offering special programs for school-age staff (e.g., Durham College, ON). Interestingly, many individuals working in school-age programs are well qualified. An Ontario study indicated that 72 percent of the school-age staff had postsecondary training in subject areas related to child care and 32 percent had early childhood education diplomas or degrees (Park 1992).

Table 6.10

Regulations regarding adult-to-child ratios and group size in school-age centre care

Province/ territory	Age group	Adult:child ratio	Maximum group size
AB			
Calgary	6-12 years	1:14	28
Edmonton	6-12 years	1:12	36
St. Albert	6-12 years	1:15	30
BC	< grade 2	1:10	20
	> grade 2	1:15	25
MB	Separate age groupings		
	5-6 years	1:10	20
	6-12 years	1:15	30
	Mixed age groupings		
	2-6 years	1:8	16
	6-12 years	1:15	30
NB	5-6 years	1:12	24
	6-12 years	1:15	30
NF	7-12 years	1:15	25
NT	5-11 years	1:10	20
NS	5-12 years	1:15	25
ON	5-6 years	1:12	24
	6-12 years	1:15	30
PE	5-7 years	1:12	Centre size 50
	7-12 years	1:15	Centre size 50
QC	5-12 years	1:20	Guideline states 30
SK	6-12 years	1:15	30 (except before 9 a.m., nap, meals, last hour of operation, special activities)
	Field trips	1:10	–
YT	6-12 years	1:12	24

Source: All information derived from government documents listed in Jacobs et al. (1998, Appendix B).

Table 6.11

Staff qualification requirements for school-age centre care

Province/ territory	Employment requirements
AB	
Calgary	At least one of the following: • a two-year diploma or a minimum of two years' training in a child-related area from an accredited institution plus eight hours of orientation for Out-of-School Care from City of Calgary Community and Social Development • one-year certificate in school-age care recognized as an accredited institution and completion of the eight-hour orientation program • one-year certificate I ECE from an accredited institution and completion of the eight-hour orientation program.
Edmonton	• At least one person must have a Level A certification, which consists of at least a two-year diploma in ECE or the equivalent, plus completion of the Out-of-School course (Grant McEwan College) within one year of employment. • Level B certification requires one year of an ECE program plus Out-of-School course within one year of employment. Can only work with children when Level A person on premises. • Police security clearance. • Valid first-aid certificate.
St. Albert	• Assistant must have Level 1 certificate plus courses and work experience in recreation, teaching, or child development. • Valid first-aid certificate.
BC	Individuals must meet the criteria for "Responsible Adult," including • having a good character • ability to provide mature guidance • completion of a course on caring for young children or relevant work experience • satisfactory criminal record check.
MB	• ECE I: completed secondary education. May have begun but not completed further training. • ECE II: completed two-year diploma in ECE. • ECE III: B.HEc. or B.A. Developmental Studies or Diploma plus 240 credit hours post-diploma specialization (e.g., special needs, child care management, aboriginal child care).

►

◄ *Table 6.11*

Staff qualification requirements for school-age centre care

Province/ territory	Employment requirements
	• Half of all school-age centre staff must meet requirement of ECE II or III.
NB	• Ability to understand children. • Willingness to participate in training programs and workshops recommended by the Ministry. • Awareness of community resources. • Ability to maintain working relationship with community-based professionals and parents of children attending the centre. • Acceptable first-aid training.
NF	• None except when there are more than twenty-five children; then must have one person with ECE certificate plus one year's experience in licensed day care or related degree.
NT	• Ability to communicate with children. • Awareness of ECE developmental theory. • First aid and CPR. • Certificate of medical examination. • Satisfactory criminal record check. • Awareness of multiculturalism.
NS	• Two-thirds of staff must have completed training in ECE or the equivalent. • Grandfather clause applied.
ON	• Academic qualification equivalent to diploma or ECE diploma. • One staff member with ECE diploma must be present in centre at all times. • First-aid training. • Satisfactory criminal record check.
PE	• Postsecondary training: university degree or training in a community college. • If degree, diploma, or courses are not related to early childhood development, two to four extension courses are required (i.e., a one-semester, approved university course in early childhood development, a community college course, 30 hours of training in other programs, or any combination of courses or seminars approved by Board).

►

◄ *Table 6.11*

Staff qualification requirements for school-age centre care

Province/ territory	Employment requirements
QC	• Proof of secondary IV (Grade 11) level of education or a recognized diploma or proof of studies that is recognized by an appropriate authority. • Two years of pertinent experience allowing for the development of skills in psychology and human relations. • Capacity to express oneself clearly. • Relevant work experience.
SK	• Orientation course within first six months of employment. • At least one person on the premises must have completed a first-aid course.
YT	• CCW I level: must have sixty hours of introduction to child development. • CCW II level: must have one year of training in child care. • CCW III level: must have two or more years of training in child care. • Of total staff 50 percent must meet CCW I level, 30 percent CCW II level, and 20 percent CCW III level.

Source: All information derived from government documents listed in Jacobs et al. (1998, Appendix B).

Research Findings Associated with School-Age Care

There has not been a great deal of research on school-age care per se; however, a few studies have examined the related issue of self-care and the lack of adult supervision associated with this type of after-school arrangement. The literature is filled with dire predictions for children of elementary school-age who are in self-care situations (Genser and Baden 1980). However, when Rodman, Pratto, and Nelson (1985) compared children in grades 4 and 7 who were in self-care with the same age group in adult care, there were no differences between the two groups in issues associated with self-esteem or in social and interpersonal competence. A number of researchers wondered if the Rodman et al. study had been sufficiently rigorous in its exploration of the types of self-care that are possible (Steinberg 1986). Thus a study was designed to examine the relationship between the range of self-care possibilities and susceptibility to

Table 6.12

Percentage of children using self or sibling care, by province and territory, 1988

	AB	BC	MB	NB	NF	NT
School age 6-12 years	22.9	20.4	23.4	17.8	16.2	n/a
	NS	**ON**	**PE**	**QC**	**SK**	**YT**
School age 6-12 years	16.3	19.4	20.0	25.7	25.4	n/a

Note: Does not apply to younger children
Source: All information derived from Pence (1992).

peer pressure. Steinberg (1986) found that children who reported home after school and contacted their parents were not significantly different from those who were supervised by an adult after school. However, the adolescents who were more removed from adult supervision were found to be more susceptible to peer pressure and to engage in antisocial activity. The adolescents who were home alone were less susceptible to peer pressure than those at a friend's home. Interestingly, those at a friend's house were less susceptible to negative peer pressure than those who "hung out." It was also noted that adolescents who were reared in an authoritative manner and whose parents knew of their whereabouts were less susceptible to peer pressure than their peers. This is interesting, given the percentage of Canadian children of elementary school age who are in self-care after school (see Table 6.12).

The largest proportion of children enrolled in school-age programs is usually the kindergarten group, which is followed by those in grades 1 to 3; there is a significant drop in registration beyond grade 3. Studies of school-age care programs have found that although there may be a wide age range of children attending school-age care programs, in many cases, all those registered in the school-age program were treated as one developmental group (Cloutier 1990). When children were interviewed about the school-age care programs, the older children indicated that the activities were more appropriate for younger children and that this was a deterrent to enrolling or staying in the program (Betsalel-Presser et al. 1995; Proulx 1991). Lalonde-Graton (1992) discovered that in 75 percent of the programs, the caregivers did not have different curriculum plans specifically for the nine- to twelve-year-olds, particularly when there were fewer than ten children of this age registered in the program. This seemed to be sufficiently problematic for this age group and was a factor in their choice of self-care as an after-school arrangement. However, the proponents of mixed-age grouping stress that it is a natural arrangement that mirrors what normally occurs outside the school; it also allows older children to assume leadership positions and provides younger children with models that they can imitate (Alexander 1986; Albrecht and Plantz 1991).

A few studies examined what transpired when children did enrol in school-age programs and remained as active participants. Posner and Vandell (1994) found that attending a formal school-age program was associated with better academic achievement and social adjustment in comparison with other types of after-school arrangements. The children in formal programs spent more time in academic activities and enrichment lessons and less time watching television and playing outdoors unsupervised by adults than did other children. They also spent more time engaged in activities with peers and adults and less time with siblings than did other children.

A Montreal and Quebec City study of children attending school-age care programs found that the children in school-age care were more outgoing and willing to participate in classroom activities, but at the same time were more aggressive than home care children; however, their aggression scores were within a normal range (Betsalel-Presser et al. 1995). When the social skills of these children were examined, the children in school-age care appeared to be more efficient in their ability to enter a group of children who were already playing than the home care children. Those who did experience some difficulty being accepted by the group were more persistent than the home care children.

As children in school-age programs move between two settings, the transition from one setting to another is not always smooth. Betsalel-Presser et al. (1995) explored the issue of teacher and caregiver communication and found that there was little communication between teachers and caregivers. Caregivers reported a great deal of competition between themselves and the teachers concerning the curriculum. This tended to strain the relationship and affect the children's behaviour.

Measuring the Quality of School-Age Care

A number of instruments have been designed to assess the quality of school-age care such as the Assessing School-Age Child Care Quality, or ASQ (O'Connor 1991), the Assessment Profile for Early Childhood Programs (Abbott-Shim and Sibley 1987), the School-Age Care Environment Rating Scale, or SACERS (Harms, Vineberg-Jacobs, and Romano-White 1996), and Quality Criteria for School-Age Child Care Programs (Albrecht and Plantz 1991). All these instruments examine basic issues associated with good-quality care and have incorporated certain factors that are specific to school-age care. For instance, in the SACERS, the room arrangement is rated in terms of provision of space for children to do their homework. The activities considered in this scale reflect the fact that older children attend these programs at the end of the school day, thus recreational activities are examined as well. In addition, interactions between program staff and teachers are rated, and access to host facilities is examined.

Parental Selection of Child Care and Levels of Satisfaction

As the survey of the five types of child care has indicated, many kinds of child care options are available to families. How parents decide upon the care arrangement that is best suited to their family is an interesting process and has been examined by a number of researchers.

Selection of Type of Care Arrangement

There has not been a great deal of investigation into the way parents select a particular type of care for their children and the quality of care their children receive (Bogat and Gensheimer 1986; Bradbard and Endsley 1980; White et al. 1992). In studies conducted with middle class populations, the two most commonly cited selection factors were convenience (Atkinson 1987) and caregiver qualities (Bogat and Gensheimer 1986). These findings were the result of categorizing selection factors into (a) logistical considerations (fees, hours of operation, and location) and (b) program considerations (safety issues and child-rearing values) (Fuqua and Labensohn 1986), (c) parental needs (reliability of care and communication with caregivers), and (d) child needs (caregiver sensitivity to children, quantity of toys, and supervision by caregivers) (Atkinson 1987). Although these findings were associated with the selection of centre care, a study of relative and family day care found that mothers using family day care and relative care cited caregiver qualities as the major reason for selecting their children's care arrangement. Cost and convenience were secondary reasons for selecting the caregiving situation (Galinsky et al. 1994).

Quality of Care and Selection

The relationship between the quality of the child care centre selected and parental selection factors was examined by White et al. (1992). The researchers examined logistical and program considerations along with parental and child needs for low socioeconomic status (SES) families using high- and low-quality care, and high SES families using high-quality care. The results indicated that all families made program-oriented choices (e.g., experienced and qualified caregivers, good child supervision, cleanliness, caregiver warmth), all cited employment as the major reason for looking for child care, and all reported using the same procedures to find child care: phoning centres and visiting. In rating the effort necessary to find child care, all indicated that getting information and finding a child care centre was a difficult and frustrating process. However, parents who used low-quality care indicated that they had more practical concerns than parents using high-quality care; that is, the parents whose children were in low-quality care had less time to search for care and selected centres that did not have a waiting list. In addition, they indicated that child care fees were an important factor and that they selected centres that offered more hours of care.

The fact that all parents were concerned about program factors indicates that parents have a good sense of what is important to look for in terms of good-quality care. Given that some parents were unable to enrol their children in good-quality care when they needed it, choice of care is often influenced by other constraints such as hours of operation of the centre, as well as the cost and availability of good-quality care. This finding was replicated in a study of family child care and relative care (Galinsky et al. 1994). Mothers at different income levels agreed on the five most important items in the provision of good-quality care for their children: children's safety, communication with caregivers, cleanliness, attention given to the children, and caregiver warmth.

Satisfaction with Care

Although parents know what the important aspects of quality care are, even when these aspects of quality are not evident in their children's care settings, parents tend to report high levels of satisfaction with the care provided (Ferland 1997; Galinsky et al. 1994; Shinn, Galinsky, and Gulcur 1990). In the Galinsky et al. (1994) study of family day care, relative care, and sitter care, parental satisfaction with quality was not related to the quality of care observed by the researchers; the same results were obtained in a large study of centre care (Shinn et al. 1990). The reason for this may be that parents do not know how these aspects of quality translate into actions or it may be associated with their knowledge that existing options are not satisfactory. In the Galinsky et al. study, of the 62 percent of parents who looked for alternatives before finally settling on their child's care arrangement, 65 percent indicated that they could find no acceptable options to the care they were currently using.

Searching for Care

Parents are reported to use a number of different processes in their search for care. In some cases, they knew the caregiver prior to needing child care; in other cases, they were referred by friends. Some perused newspaper ads and the phone book, whereas others turned to child care resource and referral agencies and/or community services (Galinsky et al. 1994;

Kaiser and Rasminsky 1991; Powell and Eisenstadt 1980). In three studies that explored the difficulty parents encountered finding a care arrangement, between 15 percent and 100 percent of the parents indicated difficulty and frustration in their search for care (Galinsky et al. 1994; Powell and Eisenstadt 1980; White et al. 1992). In the Galinsky et al. (1994) study, mothers who used non-relative care found it twice as difficult to find care as those using relative care.

We can conclude from these studies that finding good day care is an arduous and frustrating process. Even when parents can identify factors that make for good-quality care, they cannot always procure it for their children. Parents searching for good quality care need the luxury of time to find the perfect match. Once that match is found, more time may be required for the child to move from a waiting list to actual enrolment. Unfortunately, not every parent has time to wait for the desired placement.

Issues for Further Consideration

Among the many issues that have been raised in this chapter, four should be discussed in greater depth; these include (a) insufficient care options; (b) weak regulations, specifically with reference to caregiver training requirements; (c) fragmented and uncoordinated child care services; and (d) inappropriate programs for school-aged children.

Insufficient Care Options

Given the various options for care presented in this chapter, the child care needs of Canadian families should presumably be met by one of these arrangements. However, this is not the case. Many individuals have working hours that extend beyond or begin after most day care programs have closed. For example, shift workers (doctors, nurses, technicians, line workers) have schedules that do not correspond to the hours of operation of most day care programs. Thus these individuals are hard pressed to find care arrangements for their children. If we are to meet the child care needs of all Canadian workers, evening and weekend care must be included in the list of options. Although group care might not answer the needs of evening workers, some form of child care is required. Possible arrangements might be sitter care in the child's home or, if this is too costly, a family day care arrangement that would provide overnight facilities might be preferable. Perhaps on-site child care with the caregiving staff working the same shift hours as the firm's other employees would be viable.

Weak Regulations

If, as research shows, caregiver training is a vitally important component of quality care, then one must question why training requirements are so lax and/or limited across the country. In particular, the training requirements for family day care providers are abysmal, as are those for school-age caregivers. Given that family day care is a frequently used form of care for young children, one would expect governments to be more stringent about training requirements for family day care providers. If young children are to have a good-quality, developmentally appropriate experience in their early years, the person with whom they spend most of their waking hours should be well schooled in child development and early childhood education. If the only real requirement for family caregivers is a minimum age of eighteen or nineteen years, the system is failing to provide young children with caregivers who have the qualifications correlated with providing high-quality care (Goelman 1990).

If only a fraction of the caregivers in day care centres in many provinces in Canada must have early childhood training or child development courses, then the individuals who drafted the regulations for caregivers' employment requirements in child care centres have not taken into account the research findings regarding the importance of caregiver training. As mentioned earlier, there is a relationship between early childhood training or child development courses and caregiver display of positive behaviours toward children (Arnett 1989; Ruopp et al. 1979). These positive interactions have been shown to have an impact on children's development of good social skills and task-oriented behaviours (Howes 1990). By requiring only a proportion of caregivers to be adequately trained, government regulations are not supporting children's best interests, which is precisely the reason for drafting these regulations in the first place. The solution to this problem is obviously to alter the regulations and make training in child development and/or early childhood education mandatory for *all* caregivers.

The training requirements for caregivers of school-aged children are minimal at best. Half of the provinces and territories do not require any training for staff of school-age programs. The reason for this is difficult to ascertain. Even if one surmises that those responsible for drafting regulations view school-age programs as purely recreational in nature, staff should still have formal training that relates to the care of the school-aged child. Moreover, as many programs stress homework completion, it is essential for staff to be able to provide academic support in order to help children with their homework. The training requirements should reflect these issues.

Fragmented and Uncoordinated Services

In the best of all worlds, child care services would be well coordinated within communities so that the specific type of care required by families living in the community could be readily available and accessible. In many of the provinces and territories, separate government departments license and monitor family day care homes, child care centres, and school-age programs. This perpetuates a lack of coordination among care arrangements. Currently, Quebec is attempting to coordinate the provision of child care and make it universally accessible to all families regardless of socio-economic status. Family day care homes are to be linked to child care centres and the fee for all forms of care is $5 a day for all children. Parents are not required to be employed outside the home in order to register their children in a child care arrangement. Thus the program makes day care in Quebec universally accessible and available. This initiative is experiencing start-up problems, but the basis for the program is a well-intentioned philosophy of child care for all who want it.

If this plan becomes a functioning reality, it will be possible for children who would benefit from one type of care arrangement over another to be placed in the most appropriate form of care. As the child's or family's needs change, the child would be able to shift to another form of care and still remain within the home community. For instance, with the family day care homes linked to centre child care, it would be possible for an infant to have a space in a family day care home and as soon as the child is old enough to benefit from centre care, the move could be made easily within the community's system. This would also apply to school-aged children whose specific needs could be assessed and the most appropriate form of after-school care determined. Options might include a small group in a family day care home, a larger group of young children in a child care centre, or a large group of mixed-age children on the school site or in a recreation centre.

Currently, child care arrangements in most provinces and territories are too fragmented, and this is strikingly so for school-aged children who may have to be in several different care settings during the day in order to provide the family with the coverage needed when out-of-school time does not correspond to the parents' work hours.

Inappropriate School-Age Programs

In addition to the problem of fragmentation, many school-age programs are simply inappropriate for the older school-age group (nine to twelve years of age). The solution to this problem, which causes many school-age children to drop out of supervised care, may be the creation of programs that operate more like clubs and afford the nine- to twelve-year-olds the level of independence that they desire. In an attempt to meet the particular needs of this age group, a few provinces have incorporated into their regulations two special forms of supervision for mature and responsible nine- to twelve-year-olds. Distal supervision allows the child to leave the school-age care site if the parents and the child have signed a contract regarding the whereabouts of the child and the amount of time that can be spent off site. Intermittent supervision allows the child to participate in school-based activities that are on the school site but are not under the direct supervision of the school-age caregiver. The time away from the school-age program is specified, and the activity that the child will be attending is noted. Any breach of the conditions in the contract has consequences that are specified in the contract. Although these arrangements may meet the needs of some children, it may not be appropriate for all; some children may simply want to be free to go home alone. Coordinators or directors of school-age programs for nine- to twelve-year-olds must give some thought to the issue of independence and consider how to train children to function independently and responsibly when they are on their own. It is neither realistic nor wise to think that children should always be in a child care arrangement during their out-of-school time. Therefore, it is best to plan school-age programs that will prepare them to function independently, by teaching them how to make wise decisions and cope with the wide variety of problems they may encounter when on their own.

Conclusion

Child care is a highly emotionally charged issue that draws upon all levels of a province's resources. It depends upon the willingness of politicians to support the concept of day care by lobbying for funds to run departments that draft regulations and then license, monitor, and enforce the regulations. It also depends upon the resources of universities and colleges to provide training programs for caregivers. It is essential to have individuals who are motivated to acquire the necessary training to work with children on a full-day basis for a very modest salary. In addition, there must be parental interest in this form of care and a willingness to be a member of child care boards that make decisions regarding the functioning of individual centres. It is evident that good-quality child care is expensive in terms of time, effort and money, but the alternative is even more expensive if we consider the consequences of poor-quality care.

References

Abbott-Shim, M., and A. Sibley. (1987). *Assessment profile for early childhood program: Preschool, infant and school-age*. Atlanta, GA: Quality Assist.

Albrecht, K.M., and M.C. Plantz, 1991. *Developmentally appropriate school-age care programs*. Alexandria, VA: American Home Economics Association.

Alexander, N. 1986. School-age child care: Concerns and challenges. *Young Children* 42:3-12.

Anderson, C.W., R.J. Nagle, W.A. Roberts, and J.W. Smith. 1981. Attachment to substitute caregivers as a function of center quality and caregiver involvement. *Child Development* 52:53-61.

Arnett, J. 1989. Caregivers in day-care centers: Does training matter? *Journal of Applied Developmental Psychology* 10:541-52.

Atkinson, A.M. 1987. A comparison of mothers' and providers' preferences and evaluations of day care center services. *Child and Youth Care Quarterly* 16:35-47.

Belsky, J., and L. Steinberg. 1978. The effects of day care: A critical review. *Child Development* 49:929-49.

Betsalel-Presser, R., D.R. White, M. Baillargeon, and E.V. Jacobs. 1993. *Evaluation of children in two environments: Kindergarten and school-based child care.* Final report for the Child Care Initiatives Fund, Health and Welfare Canada. No. 477-5-88.

–. 1995. *Services de garde et maternelle: Sélection, qualité, et continuité.* Final report for Canadian Child Care Initiatives Fund, Human Resources Development Canada. No. 4774-5-91/9 (688).

Bogat, G.A., and L.K. Gensheimer. 1986. Discrepancies between the attitudes and actions of parents choosing day care. *Child Care Quarterly* 15:159-69.

Bradbard, M., and R. Endsley. 1980. The importance of educating parents to be discriminating day care consumers. In *Advances in early education and day care,* vol. 1, ed. S. Kilmer, 187-201. Greenwich, CT: JAI Press.

Bruner, J. 1980. *Under five in Britain.* Ypsilanti, MI: High/Scope.

Carew, J. 1980. *Experience and the development of intelligence in young children at home and in day care.* Monographs of the Society for Research in Child Development 45, serial no. 187.

Childcare Resource and Research Unit. 1997. *Child care in Canada: Provinces and territories 1995.* Toronto: University of Toronto, Centre for Urban and Community Studies, Childcare Resource and Research Unit.

Clarke-Stewart, K.A. 1987. In search of consistencies in child care research. In *Quality in child care: What does research tell us?* ed. D. Phillips, 105-20. Washington, DC: National Association for the Education of Young Children.

–. 1989. Infant care: Maligned or malignant? *American Psychologist* 44:266-73.

Clarke-Stewart, K.A., and C.P. Gruber. 1984. Day care forms and features. In *The child and the day care setting: Qualitative variations and development,* ed. R. C. Ainslie, 35-62. New York: Praeger.

Cloutier, R. 1990. *Exposé sur la problématique de la garde des enfants de 9 à 12 ans.* Proceedings of the fourth conference on school-based child care. Longueuil, QC: Bibliothèque Nationale du Québec.

Cummings, E.M., and J. Beagles-Ross. 1983. Towards a model of infant daycare: Studies of factors influencing responding to separation in day care. In *The child and the day care setting: Qualitative variations and development,* ed. R.C. Ainslie, 159-82. New York: Praeger.

Dunn, L. 1993. Ratio and group size in day care programs. *Child and Youth Care Forum* 22:193-226.

Ekanem, E.E., H.L. DuPont, L.K. Pickering, B.J. Selwyn, and C.M. Hawkins. 1983. Transmission dynamics of enteric bacteria in day care centers. *American Journal of Epidemiology* 118:562-72.

Etaugh, C. 1980. Effects of nonmaternal care on children: Research evidence and popular views. *American Psychologist* 35:309-19.

Ferland, M. 1997. L'influence de la directrice sur la qualité générale de la garderie et la satisfaction des parents. Master's thesis, Concordia University, Montreal.

Field, T. 1980. Preschool play: Effects of teacher-child ratio and organization of classroom space. *Child Study Journal* 10:191-205.

Friendly, M. 1994. *Child care policy in Canada*: Putting the pieces together. Don Mills, ON: Addison-Wesley.

–. 1997. *Child care policy in Canada: Provinces and territories 1995.* Toronto: University of Toronto, Centre for Urban and Community Studies, Childcare Resource and Research Unit.

Friesen, B.K. 1992. A sociological examination of the effects of auspice on day care quality. *Dissertation Abstracts International,* 54, 3239A-3616A. University Microfilms No. DANN83145.

Fuqua R.W., and D. Labensohn. 1986. Parents as consumers of child care. *Journal of Applied Family and Child Studies* 35:295-303.

Galinsky, E., C. Howes, D. Kontos, and M. Shinn. 1994. *The study of children in family child care and relative care.* New York: Families and Work Institute.

Galluzzo, D.C., C.C. Matheson, J.A. Moore, and C. Howes. 1988. Social orientation to adults and peers in infant child care. *Early Childhood Research Quarterly* 3:417-26.

Genser, A., and C. Baden. 1980. *School-age child care: Programs and issues.* Urbana, IL: University of Illinois, College of Education. ERIC document no. ED 196543.

Goelman, H. 1990. The Vancouver day care research project. Paper presented at Child Care in the Early Years Conference, Sept., Lausanne, Switzerland.

Goelman, H., A. Pence, D. Lero, L. Brockman, N. Glick, and J. Berkowitz. 1993. *Where are the children? An overview of the child care arrangements in Canada.* Ottawa: Health and Welfare Canada.

Hadler, S.C., J.J. Erben, D.P. Francis, H.M. Webster, and J.E. Maynard. 1982. Risk factors for Hepatitis A in day-care centers. *Journal of Infectious Diseases* 145:255-61.

Harms, T., and R.M. Clifford. 1989. *The Family Day Care Environment Rating Scale.* New York: Teachers College Press.

Harms, T., R.M. Clifford, and D. Cryer. 1998. *Early Childhood Environment Rating Scale (Revised).* New York: Teachers College Press.

Harms, T., D. Cryer, and R.M. Clifford. 1990. *Infant/Toddler Environment Rating Scale.* New York: Teachers College Press.

Harms, T., E. Vineberg-Jacobs, and D. Romano-White. 1996. *School-Age Care Environment Rating Scale.* New York: Teachers College Press.

Hayes, C.D., J.L. Palmer, and M.J. Zaslow. 1990. *Who cares for America's children: Child care policy for the 1990s.* Washington, DC: National Research Council and National Academy Press.

Hoffman, L.W. 1974. Effects of maternal employment on the child: A review of the research. *Developmental Psychology* 10:204-28.

–. 1979. Maternal employment: 1979. *American Psychologist* 34:859-65.

–. 1989. Effects of maternal employment in the two-parent family: A review of research. *American Psychologist* 44:283-92.

Holloway, S.D., and M. Reichhart-Erikson. 1988. The relationship of day care quality to children's free play behaviors and social problem solving skills. *Early Childhood Research Quarterly* 3:39-56.

Howes, C. 1983. Caregiver behavior in center and in family day care. *Journal of Applied Developmental Psychology* 4:99-107.

–. 1990. Can the age of entry into child care and the quality of child care predict adjustment in kindergarten? *Developmental Psychology* 26:292-303.

Howes, C., and M. Olenick. 1986. Family and child care influences on toddler's compliance. *Child Development* 57:202-16.

Howes, C., D.A. Phillips, and M. Whitebook. 1992. Thresholds of quality: Implications for the social development of children in center-based child care. *Child Development* 63:449-60.

Howes, C., and J. Rubenstein. 1985. Determinants of toddlers' experience in day care: Age of entry and quality of setting. *Child Care Quarterly* 14:140-51.

Howes, C., and P. Stewart. 1987. Child's play with adults, toys and peers: An examination of family and child care influences. *Developmental Psychology* 23:423-30.

Jacobs, E., D. Mill, H. Gage, I. Maheux, and J. Beaumont. 1998. *Directions for further research in Canadian school-age child care.* A study commissioned by Child Care Visions, Human Resources Development Canada.

Jacobs, E.V., and D.R. White. 1994. The relationship of child care quality and play to social behaviour in the kindergarten. In *Children's play in child care settings,* ed. H. Goelman and E.V. Jacobs, 85-101. New York: State University Press.

Jacobs, E.V., D.R. White, M. Baillargeon, and R. Betsalel-Presser. 1995. Peer relations among children attending school-age care programs. In *Readings in child development: A Canadian perspective,* ed. K. Covell, 209-34. Toronto: Nelson.

Kaiser, B., and J.S. Rasminsky. 1991. *The daycare handbook.* Boston: Little, Brown.

Kontos, S., and R. Fiene. 1987. Child care quality: Compliance with regulations and children's development: The Pennsylvania study. In *Quality in child care: What does research tell us?* ed. D. Phillips, 57-79. Washington, DC: National Association for the Education of Young Children.

Kontos, S., and A. Wilcox-Herzog. 1997. Teachers' interactions with children: Why are they so important? *Young Children* 1:4-12.

Krashinsky, M. 1986. Educational vouchers and economics: A rejoinder. *Teachers College Record* 88(2):163-7.

LaGrange, A., and M. Read. 1990. *Those who care. A report on child caregivers in Alberta daycare centres.* Red Deer, AB: Child Care Matters.

Lalonde-Graton, M. 1992. *La réalité des jeunes de 9 à 12 ans dans les services de garde en milieu scolaire du Québec.* Rapport de recherche, Ministère de l'Éducation du Québec en relation avec l'Office des services de garde à l'enfance, à l'Association des services de garde en milieu scolaire, Gouvernement du Québec.

Lero, D., H. Goelman, A. Pence, L. Brockman, and S. Nuttall. 1992. *Canadian national child care study: Parental work patterns and child care needs.* Ottawa: Statistics Canada and Health and Welfare Canada.

Lero, D., A. Pence, M. Shields, L. Brockman, and H. Goelman. 1992. *Canadian national child care study: Introductory reports.* Ottawa: Statistics Canada and Health and Welfare Canada.

Love, J.M. 1993. Does child behavior reflect day care classroom quality? Paper presented at the meeting of the Society for Research in Child Development, March, New Orleans, LA.

McCartney, K. 1984. Effect of quality of day care environment on children's language development. *Developmental Psychology* 20:244-60.

Mayfield, M. 1990. *Work-related child care in Canada.* Ottawa: Women's Bureau, Labour Canada.

Melhuish, E., A. Money, S. Martin, E. Lloyd. 1990. Type of child care at 18 months: Differences in interactional experience. *Journal of Child Psychology and Psychiatry and Allied Disciplines* 31:849-59.

NAEYC. 1991. *Guide to accreditation,* revised edition. Washington, DC: National Association for the Education of Young Children.

O'Connor, S. 1991. Assessing school-age child care quality. Unpublished manuscript, Wellesley College, School-Age Child Care Project, Wellesley, MA.

Park, N. 1992. *A comparative study of school-aged child care programs.* Toronto: Ministry of Education.

Pence, A.R. 1986. Infant schools in North America, 1825-1840. In *Advances in early education and day care,* vol. 4, ed. S. Kilmer, 1-26. Greenwich, CT: JAI Press.

–. 1989. In the shadow of mother-care: Contexts for an understanding of child day care in North America. *Canadian Psychology* 30:140-7.

Pence, A.R., ed. 1992. *Canadian child care in context: Perspectives from the provinces and territories.* Vols. 1 and 2. Canadian national child care study. Ottawa, ON: Statistics Canada and Health and Welfare Canada.

Phillips, D., and C. Howes. 1987. Indicators of quality in child care: Review of research. In *Quality in child care: What does research tell us?* ed. D. Phillips, 1-19. Washington, DC: National Association for the Education of Young Children.

Pickering, L.K., A.V. Bartlett, and W.E. Woodward. 1986. Acute infectious diarrhea among children in day care: Epidemiology and control. In *Infectious diseases in child care: Management and prevention,* ed. M.T. Osterholm, J.A. Klein, S. Aronson, and L.K. Pickering, 27-35. Chicago: University of Chicago Press.

Pickering, L.K., and W.E. Woodward. 1982. Diarrhea in day care centers. *Pediatric Infectious Diseases* 1:47-52.

Posner, J.K., and D.L. Vandell. 1994. Low-income children's after-school care: Are there beneficial effects of after school programs? *Child Development* 65:440-56.

Powell, D.R., and J.W. Eisenstadt. 1980. *Finding child care: A study of parents' search processes.* Ford Foundation Report 780-0372. Washington, DC.

Proulx, M. 1991. Perceptions et attentes des 9-12 ans. Mémoire de maîtrise, Faculté des études supérieures, Université de Montréal, Montreal.

Rodman, H., D. Pratto, and R. Nelson. 1985. Child care arrangements and children's functioning: A comparison of self care and adult care. *Developmental Psychology* 21:413-8.

Ross, R.R., E.M. Altmaier, and D.W. Russell. 1989. Job stress, social support, and burnout among counseling center staff. *Journal of Counseling Psychology* 36(4):464-70.

Rubenstein, J., and C. Howes. 1983. Adaptation to infant care. In *Advances in early education and day care,* vol. 3, ed. S. Kilmer, 13-45. Greenwich, CT: JAI Press.

Ruopp, R.R., J. Travers, F. Glantz, and C. Coelen. 1979. *Children at the center: Summary findings and their implications.* Final report of the National Day Care Study. Vol. 1. Cambridge, MA: Abt Associates.

Scarr, S., D. Phillips, and K. McCartney. 1989. Working mothers and their families. *American Psychologist* 44:1402-9.

Shinn, M., E. Galinsky, and L. Gulcur. 1990. *The role of child care centers in the lives of parents.* New York: Families and Work Institute.

Shinn, M., D. Phillips, C. Howes, M. Whitebook, and E. Galinsky. 1990. *Correspondence between mothers' perceptions and observer ratings of quality in child care centers.* New York: Families and Work Institute.

Silva, R.J. 1980. Hepatitis and the need for adequate standards in federally supported day care. *Child Welfare* 59:387-400.

Smith, P.K., and K.J. Connolly. 1986. Experimental studies of the preschool environment: The Sheffield project. In *Advances in early education and day care,* vol. 4, ed. S. Kilmer, 27-67. Greenwich, CT: JAI Press.

Steinberg, L. 1986. Latchkey children and susceptibility to peer pressure: An ecological analysis. *Developmental Psychology* 22:433-9.

Vandell, D.L., V. Henderson, and K. Wilson. 1988. A longitudinal study of children with day care experiences of varying quality. *Child Development* 59:1286-92.

Vandell, D.L, and C.P. Powers. 1983. Day care quality and children's free play activities. *American Journal of Orthopsychiatry* 53:493-500.

White, D.R. 1990. After school care: A service for children? Paper presented to the Canadian Society for the Study of Education, June, Victoria, BC.

White, D.R., M. Parent, H. Chang, and J. Spindler. 1992. Parental selection of quality child care. *Canadian Journal of Research in Early Childhood Education* 3:101-8.

Whitebook, M., C. Howes, and D. Phillips. 1990. *Who cares? Child care teachers and the quality of care in America.* Final report of the national child care staffing study. Oakland, CA: Child Care Employee Project.

Wright, M. 1983. *Compensatory education in the preschool: A Canadian approach.* Ypsilanti, MI: High/Scope.

Zaslow, M. 1991. Variation in child care quality and its implications for children. *Journal of Social Issues* 47:125-38.

7

The Curriculum

Nina Howe, Ellen Jacobs, and Lisa M. Fiorentino

Early childhood education has been an important part of the educational system only in the present century, although the idea that young children should receive some kind of education goes back to Greek philosophers such as Plato and Aristotle. However, we can turn to the nineteenth century for the more modern roots of contemporary ideas regarding curriculum for early childhood education. By "curriculum" we mean the approach to education that is employed in the classroom, specifically the theoretical orientation and goals of the program, which domains of development are emphasized, the degree of structure in the program, the kinds of materials used, and the roles of the teacher and the learner. Over the past 200 years different aspects of the curriculum have been emphasized (Weber 1984) – for example, social or intellectual skills and the degree of teacher-directed and child-oriented learning strategies. Nevertheless, one theme running through the history of curriculum models is that many programs and approaches have been designed as a means to help poor children overcome social problems. Thus early childhood education has often been viewed as a means of alleviating major societal problems (e.g., poverty, crime). This view is evident in nineteenth-century ideas (e.g., those of Pestalozzi, Froebel, Montessori) as well as in more recent US programs (e.g., Head Start) and current Canadian programs (e.g., Better Beginnings in Ontario, pre-kindergarten programs in Quebec).

To understand current practice and theory in early childhood education, we need to discuss the roots and history of particular ideas. This chapter is designed to provide an overview of approaches to curriculum in the past 200 years and the way they have been adapted to the Canadian context. We thus start with two early figures, Pestalozzi and Froebel, who believed in child-centred education. We then present the influential ideas and practices advocated by Maria Montessori and John Dewey, and follow this with a discussion of the constructivist approaches to early childhood education (Piaget, Weikart, Vygotsky, Reggio Emilia, Wright) and the Developmentally Appropriate Practice model. We consider how US Head Start programs have influenced Canadian approaches to developing early intervention programs for children from low socio-economic families. In each section, we discuss the way these philosophical approaches have been applied and adapted to the Canadian context. We also discuss how researchers have assessed the recent effectiveness of various curriculum approaches on children's development and directions for the future. To conclude the history, we trace the process whereby earlier views influenced later curriculum models, which, in turn, were sometimes modified. Finally, we consider future directions in Canadian efforts to create new and unique curriculum models. Thus, the history of curriculum tells the tale of a changing, dynamic process that reflects the efforts made to provide the best possible education for young children in Canada and elsewhere.

As the reader will note, European and US developments in early childhood curriculum have dominated the field in Canada. Except for models designed by Blatz (see Chapter 3) and Wright, and recent generative curriculum models (both described in the current chapter), there are few uniquely Canadian contributions to preschool curriculum. Nevertheless, a wide range of curriculum models have been employed in Canadian early childhood settings, and we discuss how these models have been adapted to and modified for the Canadian milieu.

Nineteenth-Century Pioneers: The Influence of Pestalozzi and Froebel on the Canadian Kindergarten Movement

In the nineteenth century, two European educators had a major influence on the development of early childhood curriculum: Johann Heinrich Pestalozzi (1746-1827) and Friedrich Froebel (1782-1852). Pestalozzi, a Swiss educator, developed and implemented a radical new child-centred approach to education in response to the very rigid, authoritarian, and teacher-centred methods of the time (e.g., memorization and rote reciting of prescribed material). Pestalozzi believed that children should learn about the world through direct sensory experiences and interactions with peers. His curriculum emphasized intellectual, moral, and physical education, which was implemented through hands-on activities that (a) were designed to move from a very simple to a more complex level, (b) began with concrete materials and later introduced more abstract materials, and (c) focused on the child's immediate world and gradually moved to the unfamiliar. Pestalozzi also argued that activities should be developmentally appropriate for the particular age and ability of each child, and should only be introduced when the child was ready to learn particular activities (Heafford 1967; Weber 1984). Today Pestalozzi's ideas and methods have been so thoroughly incorporated into current curriculum models, such as the Developmentally Appropriate Practice model, that we have some difficulty understanding that they were once viewed as radical. In addition, Pestalozzi's ideas that children learn best through active interaction with the sensory and physical environment in a self-directed way – when they are ready to do so – clearly influenced later writers such as Dewey and Piaget.

Pestalozzi opened several schools in Switzerland and was particularly interested in providing education and training for poor children. Thus he had an opportunity to implement, as well as write about, his educational ideas (Morrison 1997). Pestalozzi's ideas were read by many educators in this period; additionally, many influential people visited his schools, and his ideas were implemented across Europe and North America (Munroe [1907] 1969). The Canadian Egerton Ryerson (1803-82), founder of the public school system in Ontario, was strongly influenced by Pestalozzi's ideas (Munroe [1907] 1969) and advocated incorporating these ideas into Ontario classrooms. In addition, Pestalozzian methods were employed in teacher-training programs in some Normal Schools (see Chapter 2). Thus we believe some Canadian children attended school programs based on Pestalozzi's model of early education.

Froebel, a German innovator who visited Pestalozzi's schools, is known as the founder of the kindergarten movement (Weber 1984). "Kindergarten" is the German word for "garden of children," which exemplifies Froebel's spiritual view of children; he thought of them as little plants that required nurturing and protecting before starting more formal schooling (Evans 1975). He thus emphasized the need for harmonious relationships between teachers and children. His curriculum was heavily child-centred with a focus on play, spiritual feelings, and self-directed activities, which created a pleasant environment for children.

Froebel's curriculum included three forms of knowledge: (a) life (e.g., gardening, animal care, domestic tasks), (b) mathematics (e.g., geometry, pattern recognition), and (c) beauty (e.g., colour, musical harmony). To implement instruction in these forms of knowledge, Froebel designed two types of pedagogical tools: gifts and occupations. Gifts were concrete play materials, such as wooden cubes to build houses or geometric patterns, that Froebel believed would awaken the child's mental and spiritual powers. He classified occupations into four groups of media: solids, surfaces, lines, and points. Each of these employed malleable materials. Children handled clay and wood, for example, to explore solids, paper and paint to engage surfaces, and beads to investigate points. Drawing and weaving allowed children to explore lines. All were introduced in a sequence and as specific, teacher-directed activities (such as weaving a mat with strips of paper). Although Froebel believed that children learned best by playing with the gifts and occupations, he had a very detailed and prescriptive approach to the way children should handle the materials in order to derive the desired concepts. This prescriptive approach eventually led to a very rigid and structured implementation of Froebel's ideas in the late nineteenth century in Canada.

Froebel's writings and school received much attention, and his ideas were implemented across Europe and North America. In Canada, Ontario was the leader in introducing kindergarten programs and by 1887, officially supported programs for four- and five-year-olds in many public schools (Corbett 1989). By the turn of the century, however, Froebelian ideas had become rather distorted and were implemented in a rigid, formalized way by poorly trained teachers (Weber 1984). A reform movement began, influenced by a number of educators such as Maria Montessori and John Dewey. In Toronto, Ada Marian Hughes was a leading advocate of reform for Canadian programs. By the Second World War, the beginnings of change were apparent in kindergarten practice in Ontario; these were based on the new ideas of Dewey and Montessori, the free play movement (Corbett 1989), and new approaches developed at the Institute of Child Study at the University of Toronto (described in Chapter 3). However, as Prochner argues, in Chapter 1, real reform did not occur until the 1960s. In sum, Froebel's ideas and pedagogical materials certainly did not disappear, but the kindergarten curriculum became more flexible and encouraged more self-directed, free-play activities by the children. Froebel's long-term influence on early childhood education is seen in the use of concrete materials and in the notions that children learn through play and active involvement in a warm, happy atmosphere; that the developmental stage of the child should be taken into account; and finally, that kindergarten is the bridge between home and formal schooling. These ideas have become the foundation for Canadian kindergartens, as well as for the establishment of junior kindergartens for four-year-olds.

Ontario first introduced junior kindergarten programs in the mid-1940s and, over the years, many classes were established to prepare inner-city children from low socio-economic homes for more formal schooling (Corbett 1989). Kindergarten programs were also established in many rural Ontario localities by the 1960s. Other provinces have developed both kindergarten and junior kindergarten programs, although for the most part these programs are still not mandatory. Most recently (1998), Quebec created a universal program of junior and full-day kindergarten aimed initially at the children of low-income families, although the plan is to create opportunities for all Quebec children to attend both these programs.

Again, the emphasis on the role of early childhood education in preparing all children, but particularly low-SES (socio-economic status) children, for formal schooling is apparent in the Quebec mandate.

Montessori's Approach

Maria Montessori (1870-1952) was an Italian educator whose ideas have also had a long-term impact on the early childhood field both in Europe and North America. She worked with mentally disabled and poor children at the turn of the century and, in 1907, opened the Casa dei Bambini (Children's House) in the slums of Rome to provide early educational experiences for preschoolers. Montessori developed her educational system to foster children's optimal development. She viewed children as unique individuals capable of independent and self-directed learning, and active explorers of their environment. She believed that young children had the ability to learn naturally and independently without formal instruction from an adult (Orem 1974). Thus the role of the teacher was to guide and prepare the environment for learning.

In her writings, Montessori ([1912] 1964, 1965) identified three major areas of child development and designed specific activities and materials to promote each area. The first domain of development was practical life, for which the activities focused on developing skills in (a) personal care such as washing and dressing, (b) care of the environment such as sweeping and wiping, (c) social relations and behaviour such as rules of courtesy and politeness, and (d) analysis and control of movement such as walking and balancing. The second area was sensory development – for example, the promotion of visual discrimination skills such as identifying differences in width, height, or size. The third area was the cognitive or intellectual area of development, for which Montessori was particularly interested in creating activities that promoted language and early writing and reading skills.

A major part of the curriculum was the proper preparation of the physical environment (Montessori [1912] 1964). For example, Montessori developed child-sized and functional furniture, neat and orderly classrooms, and activities and materials that promoted development and were easily accessible (e.g., materials were located on low shelves for children to reach). Moreover, she believed that the environment should promote independent and self-directed learning by allowing the children to make their own choices. The activities were broken down into small, sequential steps and involved concrete, hands-on types of learning and materials that supported this philosophy. Montessori is well known for the didactic or teaching materials that she created – for example, the self-correcting cognitive toys such as the cylinder blocks of varying sizes or diameters that could only be assembled correctly in one way. The teacher's role was to guide the children's learning and to prepare the environment; to facilitate curriculum planning, the teacher needed to spend considerable time observing the children in his or her care. There was little emphasis on group or teacher-led activities.

Many of Montessori's ideas have been successfully adopted into current educational practice in Canadian classrooms: specifically, the focus on active, concrete, individualized, and independent learning; the integrated curriculum; the interest in cognitive and sensory development; and an awareness of what constitutes developmentally appropriate practice (Lillard 1972; Morrison 1997). Certainly the current physical environment of Canadian early childhood classrooms has been influenced by Montessori's ideas, as seen in the size of furniture and the accessibility and types of materials. While Montessori education was very popular in the early part of this century in both Europe and North America, by 1920 interest had declined sharply – although there was renewed interest in the 1960s. In Canada, the Montessori approach has been used in intervention programs with inner-city children (Reich 1971) and, currently, Montessori preschools are very popular in Canada, particularly with middle-class parents. To ensure proper implementation of the Montessori curriculum, certification programs to train Montessori teachers have been developed (Orem 1974). However, little information is available about how the curriculum might be adapted to meet the needs of the current Canadian multicultural context; moreover, there is some concern about how well Montessori's original ideas have been implemented. The Montessori approach has been criticized for the heavy emphasis on structured, closed-ended materials (with only one right answer) focusing primarily on cognitive and sensory concepts (Hunt 1964; Knudsen-Lindauer 1993) with little attention on creative development (e.g., art and music), emotional expression through pretend play, or opportunities for social interaction. Nevertheless, Humphryes (1988) argued that the Montessori curriculum is in fact developmentally appropriate and sensitive to the needs of the whole child. Research assessing the impact of this curriculum on children's development is discussed in a later section.

John Dewey and Progressive Education in Canada

The American educator and philosopher John Dewey (1859-1952) has had an enduring influence on notions regarding child-centred education in North America. In the late nineteenth century, the prevailing traditional view of North American educators was that there was a fixed body of knowledge (i.e., subjects such as history, math) to be taught by the teacher and learned (i.e., memorized) by the children (Carmichael 1956).

In addition, by the turn of the twentieth century, the kindergarten movement had become very teacher-centred, because of the rigid, formal presentation of Froebel's gifts and occupations. In response, Dewey developed a radical new approach, called Progressive Education, which became the foundation for child-centred approaches. He argued that the curriculum should be derived from the child's experiences and interests, and should be activity-based, and that the school should be part of, not separate from, the community. As we see later in the chapter, both Piaget and Vygotsky espoused similar ideas. Dewey viewed schools as a way to improve the lives of children, by including a concern for health, family, and vocational aspects of children's lives, and by adapting the curriculum to meet the needs of individual children (Dewey [1902 and 1915] 1956).

According to Dewey, children have four expressive impulses that form the basis for the curriculum: (a) social impulses to communicate with others, (b) constructive impulses to make or build things within a play context, (c) investigative impulses to explore the environment, and (d) expressive or creative impulses. The child's growth depends on the ability to use and exercise these four impulses; thus the role of the teacher is to design a curriculum to allow for this kind of development. To test his ideas about education, Dewey designed a laboratory school at the University of Chicago (1896-1904).

The curriculum and philosophical foundation of the Dewey School has been described by two former teachers (Mayhew and Edwards [1936] 1965), so we have a good idea of the way Dewey's ideas were implemented. Children (aged four to fourteen) were grouped according to age, with each group focusing on particular kinds of activities or "occupations." The themes of these occupations started with the household, for the very youngest children, and expanded to include the study of the neighbourhood, larger community, society, and world history, for the older children. Daily activities included many hands-on, concrete experiences that fostered real-life skills (e.g., cooking, gardening) within a meaningful and thematic context, and that developed a strong sense of community within the children. Dewey promoted the notion of an integrated curriculum that enabled children to learn about a particular theme (e.g., winter) across all aspects of the curriculum (e.g., art, music, social studies, math). Free play was also a critical part of the curriculum, as was make-believe play. Most basic to the progressive view was the notion that the child was the centre of the curriculum and that the interests of the child should dictate the direction of the learning and the developmentally appropriate activities designed by the teacher. Dewey believed that discipline should not be rigid or authoritarian, but that the structure built into the daily schedule, the use of space, and the curriculum would lead to child-initiated responsibility and self-discipline.

The Dewey School did not function as a model to train teachers, although the curriculum had a major impact on North American education. No systematic or objective evaluations were conducted on the school's success; nevertheless, Dewey's progressive educational ideas had popular appeal and were carried on by other educators. In the United States, Lucy Sprague Mitchell (1878-1967) developed the Bank Street Approach, an early childhood education program that is still in operation today. Based on Dewey's ideas, the primary goal of this child-centred approach was to foster children's competence and meaningful learning (Zimilies 1993). Originally designed for middle-class children, the Bank Street Approach was adapted as one of the many Head Start programs for inner-city children in the 1960s (research assessing its success is discussed later).

In conclusion, Dewey's ideas about education have left an important legacy for Canadian early childhood education. The major influences have been outlined as (a) broadening the curriculum to include a wide range of domains such as home, health, and community; (b) the integrated curriculum; (c) a more flexible view of classroom and self-discipline; (d) relating school subjects to real-life applications; (e) focusing on the process and not the end-product of learning; and (f) the view that teachers should receive intensive and pedagogically appropriate training (Greene 1965; Hendley 1986). Dewey's ideas are reflected in the philosophy and pedagogy of the nursery school movement, which has had a long history in Canada. Recent Canadian textbooks designed for training programs for early childhood teachers frequently advocate a child-centred approach (e.g., Blaxall et al. 1996). Moreover, the emerging literacy approach to teaching reading and writing in the early years of schooling is based on a child-centred foundation (Shapiro 1987). This approach, favoured by many Canadian early childhood educators and school boards, emphasizes the links between reading and writing in the process of becoming literate. The social aspects of communication and the notion that literacy should be encouraged within a context that is personally relevant to the child reflect the child-centred approach. In fact, the pedagogical link between child care and home settings, with reference to language issues, has been raised in the context of our present multicultural Canadian society (Bernhard et al. 1996).

Head Start as a Model for Canadian Early Intervention Programs

The US Head Start program, initiated in the mid-1960s, is a large-scale program funded by the federal government and continues to the present day. The Head Start Movement was designed to create a variety of early childhood education programs to help disadvantaged, inner-city, African American children, as well as children living in impoverished rural communities. The main goal of this early intervention model was to help children overcome the influence of "culturally and economically impoverished" homes (Clarke-Stewart and Fein 1983). A wide range of early education programs have been funded through Head Start, including many with a Montessori curriculum, as well as the child-centred Bank Street approach described earlier. We discuss below an influential program, DISTAR, which is based on learning principles, and in a later section, we look at the High/Scope model, which is based on Piagetian approaches. Finally, we consider the influence of the Head Start movement on Canadian approaches to early intervention.

It is important to note that in the 1960s, many of these US early childhood education intervention programs were designed using white, middle-class values, attitudes, and home environments as the standard or model without regard for the values and attitudes of the particular families that the programs were designed to help. This criticism has been successfully resolved in more recent Head Start programs; however, it should be kept in mind as we discuss the DISTAR program.

DISTAR

The DISTAR (Direct Instruction System for Teaching Arithmetic and Reading) program was designed to help "culturally and linguistically deprived" children overcome the impact of their early experiences and achieve success in school (Bereiter and Engelmann 1966). By the age of four, argued Bereiter and Engelmann (1966), poor children were already at least a year behind middle-class children in academic performance; therefore, a program should help them catch up by the time they were five years old. Otherwise, it was likely that these children would do poorly in school (e.g., fail grades, be tracked into special education classes, fail to graduate from high school). Bereiter and Engelmann (1966) advocated an intensive, academically oriented, and teacher-directed program of direct instruction.

The DISTAR curriculum focused heavily on academic skills training (language, reading, arithmetic) and employed a very didactic or teacher-directed approach. Fifteen goals were developed, and the curriculum was organized to provide direct instruction in these specific skills. The goals included naming the basic colours, naming vowels and consonants, and skill in using both affirmative and negative statements in answering the question "What is this?" "This is a truck. This is not a book." This language-intensive program relied on two main teaching techniques: (a) verbal bombardment, where the teacher spoke in a fast-paced and intensive way, and

(b) pattern drill, where the teacher asked questions or demonstrated skills repeatedly during a lesson. Clearly, the curriculum was very much teacher-directed. Behaviour-modification techniques were employed to motivate the children – specifically, children were given cookies or verbal praise to reinforce correct responses to the teacher's questions.

The DISTAR program has been condemned on a number of grounds (we discuss the effectiveness of this curriculum in a later section). The basic assumption that Black English used by poor US children was somehow inferior to the language of middle-class white children has been criticized as inaccurate and as reflecting a culturally biased view (Evans 1975). Moreover, the pressure-cooker pace of the lessons, the use of teacher-directed pattern drill, and the requirement that children answer in full sentences have been rebuked as developmentally inappropriate. The program devoted little attention to individual differences in children's learning styles, and did not emphasize social development, play, or creative and divergent thinking skills. The single focus on academic skills, isolated from other areas of children's development and aspects of their environment (e.g., home, neighbourhood), seemed too narrow an approach to early education (Crittenden 1970). Moreover, it did not fit well with more recent constructivist approaches (e.g., those of Vygotsky and Reggio Emilia). Nevertheless, DISTAR has not disappeared from the Canadian scene. In 1993, the Canadian Psychological Association and the Canadian Association of School Psychologists proposed a Canadian version of Head Start called CANSTART (Simner 1997). One goal of this initiative was the publication of a monograph series aimed at providing research-based practical ideas for teachers to implement. The first monograph provided ideas for teachers working with preschoolers who are at risk for early school failure, and it included a section on early reading skills (Canadian Psychological Association 1996); specifically, it advocated the use of a structured sequential format for teaching early reading skills, and DISTAR was included as one example of this approach. Simner (1998) argued that some components of DISTAR have been successfully integrated into current phonemic awareness programs for use with at-risk children, although the approach has been criticized (Bobrow and Hellstrom 1998; Simner 1998).

Canadian Versions of Head Start

A number of Canadian programs are based on the premise that the key to later social and academic success is to provide a head start for poor children who may be at risk for school failure. One well-researched Head Start program conducted in Quebec City was called *Apprenti-Sage* (Wise Beginnings). Designed to take care of the needs of children from at-risk families, this longitudinal intervention program followed children from infancy to school age (Piché, Roy, and Couture 1992). Starting in infancy, for four years children attended an intervention program aimed at facilitating all aspects of development (e.g., cognitive, social, emotional, language, motor), while their parents also took part in parenting classes that provided information on child development and practical parenting techniques. Results indicated that children who attended the intervention program achieved greater cognitive and intellectual gains compared with control children not involved in the program.

In 1993, the Ontario provincial government began an ambitious project to assess the longitudinal effects of a program called Better Beginnings (Peters and Russell 1996). The program focuses on children (from birth to eight years of age) and their families in low socio-economic neighbourhoods. The three main goals of this program are (a) the prevention of serious social, emotional, behavioural, physical, and cognitive problems in young children; (b) the promotion of all aspects of children's development; and (3) the enhancement of the lives of socio-economically disadvantaged families and communities. The program stresses a shared responsibility; seven urban neighbourhoods and five First Nations communities are involved. The project will follow the children, their families, and their communities until the children reach their mid-20s. An extensive evaluation of the project includes baseline measures, parent interviews, child measures, and program participation patterns. This long and in-depth process will undoubtedly provide insight into the applicability of this Head Start program to a Canadian context.

Municipalities such as Moncton, New Brunswick, have developed other Canadian Head Start programs (One way to build better families, *Globe and Mail,* 29 September 1998, A1 and A6). This particular program is aimed at helping disadvantaged and abused children through an active parent-education component, which includes counselling, support, literacy classes, cooking lessons, and parenting classes. The philosophy of the program is that the most effective approach to helping at-risk children is to provide a high-quality preschool program involving entire families. The basic premise of this philosophy is that when steps are taken to work with the entire family and help parents escape the poverty cycle, children will also benefit. In October 1998, the Canadian federal government announced that a program called Aboriginal Head Start (which originated in 1995) will expand existing programs for Aboriginal children who live in urban areas and large northern communities (Budgell 1998; Aid for poor Aboriginal kids, Montreal Gazette, October 1998, A10). A community-oriented approach has been taken and consists of a variety of initiatives such as high-quality preschool programs, as well as programs in health and nutrition, social support, education, culture, and language. These programs are designed to meet the needs of the various Aboriginal communities through giving these local communities responsibility for devising the programs and curriculum. In fact, the intervention model of early childhood education exists now in many Aboriginal communities, both on and off reserves. Approaches to curriculum development have varied in these programs. Some communities have modified Western approaches by adding on aspects of Aboriginal culture (Budgell 1998), whereas others have adopted a community-specific or generative curriculum (Pence et al. 1993; Pence 1998; Pence and McCallum 1994). In the latter case, the curriculum emanates directly from Aboriginal values and notions concerning children's development, the role of families, spirituality, social structures, language, and culture. It may thus be more sensitive to the needs of the community. In sum, the Head Start model of early intervention has great appeal and has clearly influenced Canadian approaches to early childhood education. Nevertheless, research assessing the effectiveness of these programs is limited.

Constructivist Approaches to Curriculum and Their Influence on Canadian Models

There have been several constructivist approaches to curriculum, most of which can trace their historical roots to a Piagetian understanding of child development. In the following sections we discuss Piaget and the High/Scope curriculum, Vygotsky's contributions, the Reggio Emilia approach, and how these have been applied to the Canadian context. Finally, we discuss a uniquely Canadian curriculum designed by Mary J. Wright.

Piaget and Cognitive Curriculum

Jean Piaget was a Swiss epistemologist whose theory of cognitive development has significantly influenced our understanding of children's acquisition of knowledge. His works have also influenced our understanding of child development, as well as the ways that adults can instruct children (Pellegrini 1991). Piaget theorized that children develop their thinking as a result of their experiences with other human beings and their encounters with unfamiliar physical environments. This is a constructivist approach to intellectual development – that is, children construct knowledge by virtue of experiences that expand their knowledge beyond concepts with which they are familiar. These experiences make children reorganize their previous ways of thinking and force them to reconstruct their existing ideas. Piaget postulated that cognitive development proceeds through a sequence of four stages, which every child experiences in the same order. A description of these stages can be found in many other books, but it is important to remember that children's thinking in each stage is a unified whole – that is, it makes sense to the child and forms the basis of his or her intellectual development. Piaget's constructivist approach was applied to curriculum with the aim of making education both instruct and provide a milieu for facilitating the child's intellectual, affective, and moral development (DeVries and Kohlberg 1987). In this type of learning environment, children play an active role in their own cognitive development, and teachers develop methods that appeal to children's spontaneous activity and that offer them opportunities to become deeply engaged in activities that promote questioning and thinking. Several programs base their curriculum on Piaget's ideas. The basic principles of the programs are articulated below in the description of the best-known curriculum, the High/Scope program. Originally designed as a Head Start intervention model in the 1960s, the High/Scope program is still in place today in both the United States and Canada.

High/Scope

The High/Scope program, developed by David Weikart and others (Weikart et al. 1971; Hohmann and Weikart 1995), includes five central principles: (a) active learning, (b) positive adult-child interactions, (c) a child-friendly learning environment, (d) a consistent daily routine, and (e) team-based daily assessment. First, through active learning, young children have immediate and concrete experiences from which they construct knowledge and make sense of the world. By taking initiative, exploring the environment, asking questions about things they do not understand or are curious about, and developing new strategies to solve problems, children have key experiences "that promote their mental, emotional, social and physical growth" (Hohmann and Weikart 1995, 5). Second, adult-child interactions should be supportive during ongoing conversations and during play, by focusing on the child's strengths and social problem-solving skills. This gives children the sense that their thoughts and feelings are valued and can be expressed freely; children can thus experience a true partnership in their dialogues with adults. Third, the physical design of the classrooms and the materials selected should offer children the opportunity to experience various materials and equipment (e.g., sand, water, blocks). Placing the child-accessible materials on low shelves gives children the opportunity to make choices and decisions. Thus preschoolers can decide on the purpose of their play, the materials to use, where they will play, and with whom they will interact. Here we can see examples of Montessori's and Dewey's influence on classroom design and pedagogical approach. Fourth, the daily routine is organized by teachers to support active learning in free play and in small and large groups. The routine forms the framework for the children's day by allowing them to anticipate each period, consider what they will do within the time frame, and develop a sense of autonomy. Finally, the assessment process is conducted daily using a team approach. Anecdotal observations of the children are recorded on the Child Observation Record (COR) and shared with all the adults in the program. These CORs form the basis for information regarding each child's interests and strengths and are used to determine daily programming.

Critics have focused on several points of the High/Scope program. (The effectiveness of the program is discussed in a later section.) Social-emotional objectives are given less emphasis than cognitive ones and neither are well integrated in the curriculum. In the early version of the program, there was a concerted effort to encourage thinking skills more characteristic of school-aged than preschool-aged children. However, the program has been modified to be more developmentally appropriate (Kamii and DeVries 1973). Teachers in High/Scope programs have also been criticized for not being accepting of children's incorrect answers and for interfering too frequently in the children's play, thus perhaps being intrusive rather than unobtrusive.

As noted in Chapter 4, the High/Scope curriculum has been implemented in some Canadian laboratory nursery schools – for example, at Ryerson Polytechnic University and the University of Waterloo. The degree to which the High/Scope model was adapted in these university preschools to meet the needs of the milieu (frequently middle-class children) is hard to assess. More recently, Quebec has introduced a universal program of $5 per day child care for all preschool-aged children, and the High/Scope curriculum has been recommended as the official curriculum, now called *Jouer, c'est magique* (Quebec 1998). Similar to the original curriculum, the principles of the Quebec program stress that each child is a unique, important facilitator in her or his development. Moreover, the child's development is a global and integrated process that includes the collaboration of educators and parents. The Quebec curriculum program also encourages child exploration, reflection, and problem-solving skills, while stressing language development and conditions for an ideal learning environment. It is too early to determine how effectively the *Jouer, c'est magique* curriculum, which was only officially recommended in 1998, will be implemented in Quebec child care centres or how closely the government will monitor its implementation. Although the official curriculum guide maintains that the High/Scope curriculum has been adapted to the Quebec milieu, a survey of the guide indicates the changes are rather superficial. For example, French songs and rhymes have been substituted for American favourites; however, the philosophy, explanation of key experiences, and activities follow the original High/Scope curriculum (Hohmann and Weikert 1995) very closely. Without extensive teacher training, there is a risk that this program will be implemented in a haphazard manner in Quebec and may not achieve the desired goals. Since it is only a recommended curriculum, teachers have the option of implementing the program or not, or merely adapting it to best suit the needs of their present program. This last option, adapting *Jouer, c'est magique* to the present curriculum, seems to have been taken by a number of the child care centres (Hanlon-Ledoux, personal communication 1998).

Vygotsky and Sociocultural Theory

Lev Vygotsky was a Soviet psychologist (1896-1934) and a contemporary of Piaget. Vygotsky postulated that learning plays a leading role in development; growth and change are a result of the child's interactions with more competent individuals, who provide guidance within the child's zone of proximal development. Specifically, adult-child interactions offer children the support they need to solve problems and learn cognitive and social concepts, a process labelled "teaching within the child's zone of proximal development" (Vygotsky 1978; Wertsch 1979). By "zone of proximal development," Vygotsky meant the difference between what the child could do independently and the problems he or she could solve with some adult help. By providing the necessary support for effective teaching/learning interactions within the zone of proximal development, the more knowledgeable teacher helps the child construct his or her own learning through a process called scaffolding. Two important components of scaffolding are joint problem-solving and intersubjectivity. Joint problem-solving is defined as the kind of cues, strategies, hints, leading questions, and demonstrations that the adult uses to help the child solve a problem (Brown, Collins, and Duguid 1989; Lave and Wenger 1991). Intersubjectivity refers to adjusting to the perspectives of one another. For example, a child and an adult engaged in a task may think about the task in very different ways, and to work collaboratively, they must arrive at a shared understanding regarding the task. Learning and development are, therefore, the outcomes of an active child in a social environment collaborating with others.

For Vygotsky, cognition was a deeply social phenomenon, because social experiences shape the way children think and interpret their immediate world. Language forms a link between the child's sociocultural world and his or her mental functioning (van der Veer and Valsiner 1991). Thus language is the main cultural tool that individuals use to mediate activities, restructure and develop higher order thinking, and regulate their own behaviour (Berk and Winsler 1995). Vygotsky maintained that higher mental activity had its roots in the individual's social, cultural, and societal context. Since all cultures are different, children's cognition is contextualized – that is, thinking is the result of and derives meaning from particular activities and social experiences that are important in the child's culture (Perret-Clermont, Perret, and Bell 1991). In particular, Vygotsky identified pretend play as an important context for children's sociocultural learning because they manipulate language symbolically ("Let's pretend..."). A number of Canadian educators have described how teachers can support children's problem solving and play from a Vygotskian perspective (e.g., Reynolds 1996). Additionally, Meyer (1997) explained how pretend play can promote opportunities for children to learn about different cultural traditions and customs – an important factor in our multicultural Canadian society. Moreover, the position statement of the Canadian Association for Young Children, *Young Children Have the Right to Learn through Play,* advocates that play opportunities create a context for the development of representational thought, as argued by Vygotsky. Many Canadian educators argue that educational curriculum, pedagogy, and teachers must be very sensitive to young children's cultural background and way of understanding the world (Bernhard 1995).

It is important to note that while Vygotsky's ideas have been incorporated into some programs (e.g., Reggio Emilia), to date there is no specific Vygotskian curriculum. However, Vygotskian notions have been applied to whole-language methods of teaching reading (Goodman and Goodman 1990) and the development of scientific concepts (Panofsky, John-Steiner, and Blackwell 1990).

Reggio Emilia

Reggio Emilia is a town in northern Italy that has developed an interesting approach to early childhood education. The program founded by Loris Malaguzzi draws its inspiration from a number of different educational philosophies, in particular, Dewey, Piaget, and Vygotsky. Since the program is community-based, parents and others become involved and are invested in all aspects of education. Dewey's influence is seen in the focus of each child in relation to other children, family, teachers, community, and the wider society. Parent participation is essential and takes place in many different ways and on many levels – for example, daily interactions when parents assist in the schools; special meetings to discuss educational and psychological issues; involvement in special events, field trips, and seasonal, cultural, and religious celebrations.

The town has infant/toddler centres for children (aged four months to three years) and preschools for children aged three to six, where children are grouped according to age. The physical environment of each school is unique, and the layout encourages social interactions, communication, and relationships by allowing for individual exchanges with the teacher or another child, small and large group interactions, as well as opportunities for children to be alone. The design of the environment supports Vygotskian notions of the way children learn from peer and adult interactions.

Teachers act as partners in the children's learning. They observe the children closely, have weekly meetings to discuss their observations, and plan future programs based upon the children's questions and interests. Although programs may be planned, teachers follow the children's interests by listening, asking questions of the youngsters, and adjusting their plans accordingly. In sum, the curriculum emerges as the children and teachers engage in each activity or project, many of which are team projects. Clearly, this approach has its roots in Dewey's ideas about child-centred education. Group work is reinforced because the Reggio Emilia program is based on the belief that children cannot develop a good sense of self if they are isolated from others, which follows from Vygotsky's ideas. Thus children spend time moving back and forth between small groups and larger classes and are encouraged to share and debate ideas, resolve problems among themselves, learn how to communicate important concepts, negotiate, acquire information, and provide support for one another. Children gain a level of autonomy that can only come from experiencing success in social settings.

This program has received very positive feedback from European and North American educators, although, at present, it is so new that it has not yet been subject to rigorous scientific study. The lack of rigorous evaluation means that the long-term effectiveness of this curriculum for children's development is not yet known. However, it has generated a great deal of recent interest in the ECE field. The journal *Canadian Children* included an invitational article (New 1997) that contains some interesting and thoughtful points for those in the early childhood field. A Canadian, Carol Anne Wien (1997), paints a vivid picture of her visit to Reggio Emilia and provides some thought-provoking comparisons with Canadian approaches to early education. Sue Bredekamp (1993) from the United States raised similar questions about whether educators have set their sights too low in the quest for high-quality early childhood education.

Recent attempts to translate the Reggio Emilia approach into the Canadian milieu are now evident. As a case in point, Loyalist College in Brockville, Ontario, has implemented the Reggio Emilia approach in its child care centre, which is used as a model teaching laboratory for its early childhood education teacher-training program. The centre has adopted a number of Reggio Emilia principles concerning the physical environment – for example, creating a home-like atmosphere using natural materials (e.g., low wooden and not plastic tables, table cloths at mealtimes), providing spaces for large and small group activities, and paying attention to the aesthetic aspects of the environment. The emergent curriculum is based on the children's interests and aspects of the immediate, natural, rural setting and the local milieu (e.g., airport). Project work is emphasized and there are ample opportunities for exploration of the classroom environment. Teachers work collaboratively and devote much attention to documenting what children have discovered about their worlds, rather than evaluating their strengths and weaknesses. The shift in the role of the classroom teacher toward a collaborator and researcher takes much reflection and analysis. Fyfe (1998) outlined the kinds of questions that teachers need to consider if they wish to adopt a Reggio Emilia approach; in many ways, it means adjusting our ideas about the role of the classroom teacher, a process that takes time to learn. Given the flexibility inherent in the Reggio Emilia approach and the interest in the emergent curriculum that allows teachers to focus on the defining characteristics of the children in their care, we may see greater integration of this model in Canadian early childhood education in the future.

University of Western Ontario Pre-school Project

Initiated in 1973 by Mary J. Wright, this program was a uniquely Canadian experiment designed to assess the impact of compensatory education on low-SES children. Wright (1983) developed a curriculum in the constructivist tradition that employed a cognitive-developmental approach but also emphasized social-emotional development, which derived from Dewey and the Canadian William Blatz (1944, 1966) (see Chapter 3). The curriculum was partly derived from the High/Scope model, specifically the emphasis on an active-discovery approach to learning and on particular aspects of cognitive development (e.g., number, classification, spatial relations). However, the curriculum also focused on the development of social competence (getting along with peers), self-management skills, self-esteem, and the promotion of an inner locus of control – that is, helping the child to take responsibility for his or her learning and decision making. These goals were achieved by the careful structuring of (a) the physical environment, (b) the daily schedule, and (c) the employment of teachers. The organization allowed for active discovery, experimentation, and child-initiated activity within the context of free play. In addition, there were teacher-guided circle times and small-group activities focusing on specific skills. However, the emphasis was always on the process of learning and not on an end-product. Detailed Assessment and Curriculum Guides were developed to help the teachers implement the cognitive program and were included in the description of the University of Western Ontario (UWO) Pre-school Project (Wright 1983). The teacher's role was to be a participant-observer, highly responsive to the needs of individual children, and to use the teachable moment to help children solve their cognitive and social problems independently. By "teachable moment," Wright meant the critical point in the child's play when he or she could solve a particular problem or benefit from some new knowledge. The teacher's goal was to facilitate this process by asking questions or probing. This process is similar to Vygotskian ideas regarding the zone of proximal development and scaffolding.

Two groups of children from economically disadvantaged families attended the UWO Pre-school for either one or two years. Their intellectual, cognitive, and social development was compared with that of middle-class children also attending the preschool. Furthermore, the low-SES children were followed-up during the first four years of primary school (kindergarten to grade 3) and compared with a control group of low-SES children without preschool experience. Low-SES children who attended the UWO Pre-school for two years demonstrated greater intellectual, cognitive, and self-management skills than low-SES children who attended for only one year. Moreover, after two years some low-SES children (of average rather than low intellectual ability) performed at the same level as the middle-class children also attending the UWO Pre-school. Over the long-term (to grade 3), both groups of children with UWO Pre-school experience generally maintained superior intellectual, cognitive, and academic achievement compared with a control group of low-SES children without prior preschool experience. However, the children with two years of preschool experience were rated by their elementary school teachers as more academically competent, demonstrating more appropriate and independent classroom behaviour, and more self-reliance compared with children with only one year of preschool. Finally, both groups of UWO children were more likely by grade 3 to be at grade level (82 percent) compared with only 58 percent of control children, of whom 10 percent were two or more grades behind. Moreover, two control children had been placed in special education classes, whereas no UWO children had been by the end of the project. Overall, the findings of the UWO Pre-school Project supported the idea that compensatory education can have long-term beneficial outcomes for low-SES children, particularly if the preschool experience is two years in length. A word of caution is in order: the study was based on a very small number of subjects, and it is difficult to generalize the findings.

Research on the Effectiveness of Early Childhood Curricula

One inevitable question that arises after a survey of the different curriculum models is whether one or two approaches are more effective in facilitating optimal child development than others. Proponents of particular curricular approaches to early childhood education have long argued, on the basis of philosophical grounds, that their specific method was best suited for children; however, it is only recently that researchers have examined this question. Much of this research is based in the United States and emanates from the Head Start era when investigators were interested in whether early childhood intervention programs would provide children with a head start on the educational process. As one part of this larger question, a variety of curriculum models were compared to determine if one approach was superior to others. Generally the children studied were considered to be at risk for later school failure, because they came from poor, African American families with few economic, educational, or social advantages. Much of this research literature has problems that must be taken into consideration – for example, the training of teachers was often not consistent across programs, and there were few checks on how well the specific curricula were implemented. We have limited the following discussion to studies that have compared at least three different curriculum models, thus providing us with a broader picture. However, our review is by no means exhaustive. Aside from the studies by Piché, Roy, and Couture (1992) and Wright (1983) already discussed, to date few Canadian studies have investigated this question, although we expect that the Better Beginnings Project in Ontario will produce some pertinent information in the near future.

One longitudinal study followed poor, African American inner-city children from the time they attended one of four preschool programs (Montessori, DISTAR, DARCEE, traditional nursery school) to grades 9 and 10 (Miller and Bizzell 1984). Initially, the children attending the DISTAR preschool program demonstrated the largest gains in IQ; however, a dramatic drop was evident in kindergarten (Miller and Dyer 1975). Between grades 1 and 9 or 10 children demonstrated consistent patterns in IQ and school achievement. Specifically, boys who had attended a Montessori preschool program demonstrated the highest math and reading achievement scores and IQs, whereas girls who had attended the DARCEE program (i.e., a language-achievement motivation curriculum) had the most effective preschool experience. Another longitudinal project compared the academic and social achievements of children attending a DISTAR, High/Scope, or traditional nursery school program to children who had no preschool experience (Schweinhart, Weikart, and Larner 1986; Schweinhart, Barnes, and Weikart 1993). At age ten, there were no significant curricular effects on children's academic performance; however, by age fifteen, children who had attended the DISTAR program showed evidence of poorer social adjustment compared with other children. Specifically, they were more likely to engage in delinquent acts, have poorer family relationships, and be less involved in school activities and sports, and they were less likely to seek help for personal problems. The irony of these findings is that the Bereiter-Engelmann program was designed to improve children's poor academic skills, yet the lack of focus on interpersonal and social skills appears to have had a more significant long-term effect. Other studies have suggested that children attending constructivist or child-centred programs were more academically successful and socially competent than children attending more teacher-directed and academically oriented programs (Rawl and O'Tuel 1982; Marcon 1992). Perhaps giving children opportunities to make decisions about and direct their own learning sets an early pattern of responsibility and the need for challenge. Nevertheless, none of these studies provide information about which specific aspects of the curriculum were significant (e.g., degree of structure, types of activities, focus on specific aspects of development, teacher-child ratio, quality of the environment, or parent involvement). Thus we cannot pinpoint the factors that may have led to children's higher academic or social skills.

Finally, the question whether middle-class children benefit more from particular curriculum models has generally been ignored in the literature, although one Canadian study found no differences in academic, social, or physical skills in middle-class elementary school–aged children who had Montessori, traditional nursery school, or no preschool experience (McKinnon, Flieger, and Patterson 1982).

Where Do We Go from Here? How Do We Develop Canadian Curriculum Models?

Given the research on the effectiveness of the various programs, the question arises as to what curriculum Canadian early childhood programs should follow. Clearly, there is no single best program or curriculum. Research has, however, helped us delineate optimal and poor teaching practices. This kind of information has been compiled for teachers of early childhood programs by the National Association for the Education of Young Children (NAEYC), the largest professional organization of early childhood educators in North America. NAEYC has published several position statements on its recommendations regarding programs for young children. These position statements do not offer recipes for a program nor do they issue a prescription as to which program should be followed. Rather, a coherent philosophy is presented regarding program content, teacher-child interactions, teacher education, cultural content, and parental and community involvement in a book entitled *Developmentally Appropriate Practice in Early Childhood Education* (Bredekamp and Copple 1997). We believe these ideas can be integrated easily into the Canadian milieu.

The philosophy presented in the book is based on the idea that "programs designed for young children must be based upon what is known about young children" and must "reflect a commitment regarding the rights of young children to respectful and supportive learning environments as well as to an education that will prepare them for participation in a free and democratic society" (Bredekamp and Copple 1997, v). This concept of developmentally appropriate practice (DAP) reflects and incorporates current knowledge about child development and learning, social and cultural contexts in which children live, and adaptation for and responsiveness to individual variation in children's strength, interests, and needs. Suggestions regarding the construction of a developmentally appropriate curriculum are as follows:

- The curriculum should include physical, social, emotional, linguistic, aesthetic, and cognitive areas of development.
- The curriculum should include content from all disciplines and be socially relevant, intellectually challenging, and personally meaningful.
- The curriculum should build on the children's prior knowledge so they can consolidate their learning and facilitate the acquisition of new skills and concepts.
- The curriculum should cross traditional disciplines so children can make meaningful connections and enrich their conceptual development.
- The curriculum should facilitate the development of understanding, knowledge, skills, processes, and the motivation to learn.
- The curriculum should have a strong intellectual foundation and include key concepts and tools of enquiry in ways that are accessible and appropriate for young children (e.g., scientific experiments, writing, performing, solving math problems, collecting, and analyzing data).
- The curriculum should recognize and support children's home culture and language while encouraging involvement in the shared culture of the program and community.
- Children in the age range of the class should be able to achieve most of the curriculum goals.
- Technology should be accessible and philosophically integrated into the curriculum.

All nine guidelines are based on current knowledge about educational practice that is likely to have optimal results for the children. However, the implementation of these recommendations depends upon the skills of the teachers and educators (see Chapter 2 for a critique of teacher training and DAP). The collaborators who drafted the DAP guidelines have also presented seven recommendations regarding teacher/educator practice. Although only the main points are outlined below, the NAEYC position statement provides teachers and educators with concrete suggestions as to how they might put these recommendations into practice. The influence of the theorists and curriculum models presented in this chapter can be identified in the following recommendations:

- Respect, value, and accept children and treat them with dignity at all times.
- Make it a priority to know each child well.
- Create an intellectually engaging, responsive environment to promote each child's learning and development.
- Make plans to enable children to attain key curriculum goals across various disciplines.
- Foster children's collaboration with peers on interesting and important enterprises.
- Develop, refine, and use a wide repertoire of teaching strategies to enhance children's learning and development.
- Facilitate the development of responsibility and self-regulation in children (Bredekamp and Copple 1997, 17-9).

It should be evident that there is no single best program and that programs must reflect the developmental levels of the children enrolled, the culture and values of their families and the community, and address the individual children's needs, interests, and strengths. The DAP model has recently been criticized for its failure to fully recognize the centrality of cultural diversity and racial equality issues (Bernhard 1998). Nevertheless, we argue that accepting the basic DAP principles implies that not all programs can or should offer the same curriculum.

The next question that arises must logically be "Who should decide upon the curriculum for the particular program and the children enrolled?" We would argue, on the basis of all that has been presented in this chapter, that the children, teachers, and parents should be involved in setting the program. Some teachers may disagree with this position because the parents are not usually in the classroom observing the children, listening to their ideas, and following their lead. However, since parents should be supporting their children's learning, we can expect them to do so only if they agree with what is being presented and understand where it might lead. One might then consider the children and the teachers and educators to be the initial decision makers regarding what will be explored and learned. Interestingly, the quality of the experience that the children will have depends upon the teacher and also upon the peers in the classroom. The way the teacher handles children's explorations, questions, and suggestions will determine much of what is presented to the children as a curriculum. However, there is a great deal of intellectual activity and stimulation that comes from a child's peer group. For instance, children in a classroom with an accomplished pretend player will have extensive experiences with pretend play that they might not have had if that child had not been in the classroom. Furthermore, a curious young scientist might stimulate the teachers and his or her peers to explore concepts that others in the class had not thought about. Thus the community of peers can play a definitive role in the creation of a classroom curriculum if the teacher allows this to happen. This takes us back to the teacher and his or her training and in-service experiences. Much of what happens in the classroom depends upon the latitude that the teacher is willing to offer the children and how much time and effort he or she is willing to invest to research unfamiliar material. It also depends on the willingness of the teacher to call upon the expertise of others in the children's community to broaden their horizons and stimulate their interests. This willingness to be a guide and facilitator rather than the leader in the classroom in turn depends upon the teacher's own childhood educational experiences and upon his or her experiences in a teacher-training program.

Should a teacher set some curriculum goals for the class or should he or she let the curriculum roam from one topic to another without a rudder or an anchor? Most professionals in the field would recommend goals to guide the activities in the class. These goals might include the promotion and development of social and interpersonal skills; self-help skills; self-esteem; academic skills that include fine and gross motor skills, literacy, cognitive and learning skills; and offering many opportunities for the children to learn about their world through play and self-guided activity. Clearly, the development of goals should reflect the context in which children live and grow.

While these may be rather lofty goals, flexible, knowledgeable, and articulate teachers should be able to develop a strong curriculum that meets the needs of the children and families enrolled in their program. While we encourage teachers to draw upon the strengths of the various curriculum models presented in this chapter, we also encourage them to adapt any program to the specific Canadian milieu. As we have outlined elsewhere (Howe and Jacobs 1995), the Canadian context presents some interesting challenges for those in the early childhood education field. In particular, we must emphasize Canadian ideas regarding multiculturalism and our official bilingual status. Since culture plays a definitive role in children's development, teachers must be aware of the way particular cultural values regarding development may influence their own teaching style. They must also be aware of the worth placed on specific aspects of children's behaviour by parents from different cultures (Bernhard et al. 1996; Kilbride 1997). Clearly, the need to build collaborative partnerships with parents is paramount to this issue (Potter and Jacques 1997), as is the recognition that we work in a country of recent immigrants whose mother tongue is neither English nor French. Thus specific curriculum models should be employed or adapted to reflect these concerns.

Moreover, a significant percent of Canadian children speak French in a majority culture, (i.e., in Quebec) or as a minority group in predominantly English-speaking milieus (i.e., in Ontario, Alberta, and New Brunswick). Special efforts must be made to ensure that not only is the curriculum sensitive to the needs of such children and families, but that these communities have a direct role in creating curricula used in early childhood settings in their communities. Clearly, there are other special groups or geographic, economic, or social circumstances that dictate careful reflection and consideration of the way the curriculum can best be developed or adapted. Here we refer to children and families living in rural communities widely dispersed across our large country, inner-city children, Aboriginal children, children with special needs, and immigrant children. The challenges to the field of early childhood education are diverse and demanding, but we believe that they are not insurmountable.

Note

The writing of this chapter was supported by grants from the Social Sciences and Humanities Research Council of Canada and the Fond pour la Formation de Chercheurs et l'Aide à la Recherche to the first author, and Child Care Visions, Human Resources Development Canada, to the second author. We wish to thank Christie Bemister and Nadine Gariépy for editorial assistance.

References

Bereiter, C., and S. Engelmann. 1966. *Teaching disadvantaged children in the pre-school.* Englewood Cliffs, NJ: Prentice-Hall.

Berk, L., and A. Wensler. 1995. *Scaffolding children's learning: Vygotsky and early childhood education.* Washington, DC: NAEYC.

Bernhard, J.K. 1995. Child development, cultural diversity, and the professional training of early childhood educators, *Canadian Journal of Education* 20:415-36.

–. 1998. Culture and developmentally appropriate practice. *Canadian Journal of Research in Early Childhood Education* 7(1):81-90.

Bernhard, J.K., G. Chud, M.L. Lefebvre, and R. Lange. 1996. Linguistic match between children and caregivers. *Canadian Journal of Research in Early Childhood Education* 5:5-18.

Blatz, W.E. 1944. *Understanding the young child.* Toronto: Clarke, Irwin.

–. 1966. *Human security: Some reflections.* Toronto: University of Toronto Press.

Blaxall, J., K.M. Kilbride, D. McKenna, C. Warberg, and M. Yeates. 1996. *Children at the centre: Principles of early childhood education in Canada.* Toronto: Harcourt Brace.

Bobrow, B., and F. Hellstrom. 1998. Predicting and preventing early school failure: Classroom activities for the preschool child. *Canadian Journal of Research in Early Childhood Education* 6:369-72.

Bredekamp, S. 1993. Reflection on Reggio Emilia. *Young Children* 5:13-7.

Bredekamp, S., and C. Copple. 1997. *Developmentally appropriate practice in early childhood programs.* Washington, DC: NAEYC.

Brown, J.S., A. Collins, and P. Duguid. 1989. Situated cognition and the culture of learning. *Educational Researcher* 18:32-42.

Budgell, R. 1998. Aboriginal Head Start and Native American Head Start: Hands across the border? Paper presented at the annual conference of the National Association for the Education of Young Children, Toronto.

Canadian Psychological Association. 1996. *Predicting and preventing early school failure: Classroom activities for the preschool child.* Ottawa: Canadian Psychological Association.

Carmichael, L. 1956. Introduction to J. Dewey, *The child and the curriculum* and *The school and society,* 1902 and 1915. Chicago: University of Chicago Press.

Clarke-Stewart, A., and G. Fein. 1983. Early childhood programs. *In Handbook of child psychology,* vol. 2, ed. P.H. Mussen, 917-1000. New York: Wiley.

Corbett, B.E. 1989. *A century of education in Ontario.* Mississauga, ON: Froebel Foundation.

Crittenden, B.S. 1970. A critique of the Bereiter-Engelmann preschool program. *School Review* 78:145-67.

DeVries, R., and L. Kohlberg. 1987. *Constructivist early education: Overview and comparison with other programs.* Washington, DC: NAEYC.

Dewey, J. [1902 and 1915] 1956. *The child and the curriculum* and *The school and society,* ed. L. Carmichael. Chicago: University of Chicago Press.

Evans, E.D. 1975. *Contemporary influences in early childhood education.* New York: Holt, Rinehart and Winston.

Fyfe, B. 1998. Questions for collaboration: Lessons from Reggio Emilia. *Canadian Children* 23:20-4.

Goodman, Y.M., and K.S. Goodman. 1990. Vygotsky in a whole language perspective. In *Vygotsky and education,* ed. L.C. Moll, 223-50. Cambridge, UK: Cambridge University Press.

Greene, M. 1965. Dewey and American education, 1894-1920. In *John Dewey: Master educator,* ed. W.W. Brickman and L. Lehrer, 75-92. New York: Atherton.

Heafford, M. 1967. *Pestalozzi.* London: Methuen.

Hendley, B.P. 1986. *Dewey, Russell, Whitehead: Philosophers as educators.* Carbondale, IL: Southern Illinois University Press.

Hohmann, M., and D.P. Weikart. 1995. *Educating young children.* Ypsilanti, MI: High/Scope.

Howe, N., and E. Jacobs. 1995. Child care research: A case for Canadian national standards. *Canadian Psychology* 26:131-48.

Humphryes, J. 1998. The developmental appropriateness of high-quality Montessori programs. *Young Children* 54(4):4-16.

Hunt, J.M. 1964. *Introduction to M. Montessori, The Montessori method.* New York: Schocken.

Kamii, C., and R. DeVries. 1973. Piaget-based curricula for early childhood education: Three different approaches. Paper presented at the meeting of the Society for Research in Child Development, April, Philadelphia.

Kilbride, K.M. 1997. *Include me too! Human diversity in early childhood.* Toronto: Harcourt Brace.

Knudsen-Lindauer, S.L. 1993. Montessori education for young children. In *Approaches to early childhood education,* ed. J.L. Roopnarine and J.E. Johnson, 243-60. New York: Merrill.

Lave, J., and E. Wenger. 1991. *Situated learning: Legitimate peripheral participation.* New York: Cambridge University Press.

Lillard, P.P. 1972. *Montessori.* New York: Schocken.

McKinnon, J., S. Flieger, and M. Patterson. 1982. *A comparative study of the effects of preschool education on middle-class children.* Puce Ontario Area Development Project. ERIC document no. ED 220 179.

Marcon, R.A. 1992. Differential effects of three preschool models on inner-city 4-year-olds. *Early Childhood Research Quarterly* 7:517-30.

Mayhew, K.C., and A.C. Edwards. [1936] 1965. *The Dewey School.* New York: Atherton.

Meyer, J. 1997. Entering the child's world of make-believe. *Interaction* (Summer):18-20.

Miller, L.B., and R.P. Bizzell. 1984. Long-term effects of four preschool programs: Ninth- and tenth-grade results. *Child Development* 55:1570-87.

Miller, L.B., and J.L. Dyer. 1975. *Four preschool programs: Their dimensions and effects.* Monographs of the Society for Research in Child Development 40:5-6, serial no. 162.

Montessori, M. [1912] 1964. *The Montessori method.* New York: Schocken.

–. 1965. *A Montessori handbook.* New York: G.P. Putnam's Sons.

Morrison, G.S. 1997. *Fundamentals of early childhood education.* Upper Saddle River, NJ: Merrill.

Munroe, W.S. [1907] 1969. *History of the Pestalozzian movement in the United States.* New York: Arno Press and New York Times.

New, R.S. 1997. Reggio Emilia's commitment to children and community: A reconceptualization of quality and DAP. *Canadian Children* 22(1):7-12.

Orem, R.C., ed. 1974. *Montessori: Her method and the movement.* New York: G.P. Putnam's Sons.

Panofsky, C.P., V. John-Steiner, and P.J. Blackwell. 1990. The development of scientific concepts and discourse. In *Vygotsky and education,* ed. L.C. Moll, 251-67. Cambridge, UK: Cambridge University Press

Pellegrini, A. 1991. *Applied child study: A developmental approach.* Hillsdale, NJ: Lawrence Erlbaum.

Pence, A.R. 1998. On knowing the place: Reflections on understanding quality child care. *Canadian Journal of Research in Early Childhood Education* 7:71-80.

Pence, A., V. Kuehne, M. Greenwood-Church, and M.R. Opekokew. 1993. Generative curriculum: A model of university and First Nation co-operative post-secondary education. *International Journal of Education Development* 13:339-49.

Pence, A., and McCallum, M. 1994. Developing cross-cultural partnerships: Implications for child care quality research and practice. In *Valuing quality in early childhood services: New approaches to defining quality,* ed. P. Moss and A. Pence, 108-22. London: Paul Chapman.

Perret-Clermont, A.N., J.F. Perret, and N. Bell. 1991. The social construction of meaning and cognitive activity in elementary school children. In *Perspectives on socially shared cognition,* ed. L.B. Resnick, J.M. Levine, and S.D. Teasley, 41-62. Washington, DC: American Psychological Association.

Peters, R.D., and C.C. Russell. 1996. Promoting development and preventing disorder. The better beginnings, better futures project. In *Preventing childhood disorders, substance abuse, and delinquency,* ed. R.D. Peters and C.C. Russell, 19-47. California: Sage.

Piché, C., B. Roy, and G. Couture. 1992. Le projet Apprenti-Sage: Une expérience d'intervention précoce et à long terme auprès d'enfants à haut risques psychosociaux. *Apprentissage et socialisation* 15(2):145-58.

Potter, A., and M. Jacques. 1997. Developing an inclusive approach to preschool education: A discussion of issues and strategies, with implications focussing on Quebec. *Canadian Journal of Research in Early Childhood Education* 6:85-104.

Quebec. 1998. *Jouer, c'est magique.* Montreal: Government of Quebec.

Rawl, R.K., and F.S. O'Tuel, 1982. A comparison of three prereading approaches for kindergarten students. *Reading Improvement* 19:205-11.

Reich, C. 1971. *Preschool education for inner city children: Preliminary results of an experimental Montessori programme.* Toronto Board of Education (Ontario), Research Department. ERIC document ED 066 219.

Reynolds, G. 1996. How teachers support master players. *Canadian Children* 21:9-12.

Schweinhart, L.J., H.V. Barnes, and D.P. Weikart. 1993. *Significant benefits: The High/Scope Perry Preschool study through age 27.* Ypsilanti, MI: High/Scope.

Schweinhart, L.J., D.P. Weikart, and M.B. Larner. 1986. Consequences of three preschool curriculum models through age 15. *Early Childhood Research Quarterly* 1:15-45.

Shapiro, J. 1987. A retrospective look at the return to child-centred instruction in reading. *Journal of the Canadian Association for Young Children* (Fall):25-33.

Simner, M.L. 1997. CANSTART: A new Canadian primary prevention program. *Canadian Journal of Research in Early Childhood Education* 6:287.

–. 1998. Predicting and preventing early school failure: Classroom activities for the preschool child. A reply to reviewers Barbara Bobrow and Fiona Hellstrom. *Canadian Journal of Research in Early Childhood Education* 7:101-5.

van der Veer, R., and J. Valsiner. 1991. *Understanding Vygotsky: A quest for synthesis.* Cambridge, MA: Blackwell.

Vygotsky, L. 1978. *Mind and society.* Cambridge, MA: Harvard Press.

Weber, E. 1984. *Ideas influencing early childhood education.* New York: Teachers College Press.

Weikart, D.P., L. Rogers, C. Adcock, and D. McClelland. 1971. *The cognitively-oriented curriculum: A framework for teachers.* Urbana, IL: ERIC-NAEYC.

Wertsch, J. 1979. From social interaction to higher psychological processes. *Human Development* 22:1-22.

Wien, C.A. 1997. A Canadian in Reggio Emilia: The May 1997-study tour. *Canadian Children* 22:30-8.

Wright, M.J. 1983. *Compensatory education in the preschool.* Ypsilanti, MI: High/Scope.

Zimilies, H. 1993. The Bank Street approach. In *Approaches to early childhood education,* ed. J.L. Roopnarine and J.E. Johnson, 261-73. New York: Merrill.

8

The Child Care Provider

Donna White and Davina Mill

The increase in dual-earner and single-parent families in recent years has resulted in a record number of women in the labour force (E. Beauchesne, Families pay the price, Montreal *Gazette*, 25 October 1991, A1-A2; Health and Welfare Canada 1992). Greater numbers of children are being looked after in a variety of child care contexts. In Canada, the most rapid increase of children in group child care is at the toddler and preschool levels (Health and Welfare Canada 1992). In the United States, the use of infant care as well as toddler and preschool care is increasing (Hoffman 1989). Given the growth of what has been called "other than mother" care (Scarr 1984), there is a need to ask how child care affects children and who is looking after them. It is also necessary to pay attention to the working conditions of child care providers. Unfortunately, there are a large number of child care settings about which we know very little. These include sitter care, relative care and, to some extent, family day care (see Chapter 6). This chapter, of necessity, must draw largely on research with child care providers who work in group settings or centres, although information on child care providers in other settings is included when it is available.

This chapter has four objectives. The first is to describe the background literature on child care attendance and quality of care in relation to child development outcomes. In reviewing this literature, we argue that research must focus on identifying specific variables related to high-quality care, and we emphasize the need to examine several variables in a multivariate framework. We argue further that caregiver-child interactions provide an important, process-guided definition of quality.

The second objective and focus of this chapter is to describe child care providers. Three categories related to caregiving are discussed – namely, caregiver characteristics, work environment, and job perceptions. The first set of variables deal with the background and personal characteristics of child care providers. Several national studies in both the United States and

Canada provide information about the gender, age, marital status, and training of group child care providers. Some studies focus on family day care providers, and a few studies describe care from relatives, often within family day care settings. Very few studies have examined personal characteristics such as caregiver self-esteem, stress, or neuroticism.

The second set of variables are the working conditions of caregivers. Wages, health benefits, paid preparation time, and professional status form an important domain in the work environment of child care workers; however, so do many other variables that are often discussed under the label of environmental quality. These variables include group size, staff-child ratios, adult needs, materials, staff relations, and staff-child interactions.

The third domain of variables are related to the way staff perceive themselves and their jobs. Are they satisfied or dissatisfied with their work? Do they experience burnout or feelings of exhaustion, negative attitudes toward work, and a poor sense of personal achievement?

The third goal of the chapter is to examine how caregiver characteristics, working conditions, and job perceptions are related to three educator behaviours: turnover (leaving the job or the field), caregiver anger and negative interactions with children, and caregiver warmth in interactions with children in day care centres. Although few studies focus on the prediction of caregiver behaviour, it is important to examine the existing literature and to provide directions for research in this area.

Finally, this chapter will compare parallel research trends in elementary schools and preschool child care centres and will use this work to provide directions for future research in both areas.

Child Care Attendance, Quality of Child Care, and Child Development

Early ideas about child care advocated the view that child care not provided by the mother would be uniformly harmful to children. This fear was based largely on psychodynamic theory and the work of Bowlby (1969, 1973) on attachment and separation. These theories held that a single mother-child bond was critical to optimal child development. It was thought such a bond could not be formed if mothers were away from their children, particularly during infancy, for long periods of time. Furthermore, it was originally believed that children could not form multiple attachment bonds (e.g., could not be attached to both mothers and fathers or mothers and caregivers). Thus, it was feared that prolonged separation from the mother might weaken mother-child attachment, and child care providers might replace mothers as primary attachment figures. Research has refuted all these premises. Maternal employment per se does not impair the mother-infant or mother-child bond (Belsky and Steinberg 1978) or lead to a replacement of maternal attachment by caregiver attachment (Belsky and Steinberg 1978; Etaugh 1980). Research shows that infants can and do develop multiple attachments – some of them with caregivers (Ainslie and Anderson 1984; Farran and Ramey 1977; Howes et al. 1988). The types of attachments formed are related to children's development. For example, Howes et al. (1988) found that additional secure attachment to a caregiver other than the mother was related to higher levels of children's social competence with peers and adults, and that, in fact, day care may compensate for insecure mother-child attachment.

Given that children may become attached to their caregivers and that positive caregiver-child attachment enhances children's development, it is very important to examine the behaviour of child care providers toward children and the conditions that contribute to the caregiver's behaviour. However, research on the effects of day care and school programs has investigated variations in quality using criteria that rarely included measures of caregiver behaviour (Zaslow 1991). These studies focused on regulatable characteristics of child care or on global indices of quality. When regulatable characteristics such as teacher training, class size, or caregiver-to-child ratio were examined, it was noted that studying centre characteristics individually did not advance our knowledge of factors contributing to optimal child development. Simply noting that group size is high, rather than measuring other variables such as staff-to-child ratios, does not provide complete information about quality (Ruopp et al. 1979). Instead, it was necessary to study several group characteristics simultaneously in order to describe the quality of a centre. Quality can be defined, at least in part, as a combination of several regulatable characteristics. Such definitions of quality, however, provide little information on caregiver-child interactions and their relationship to child development.

Global measures do include ratings of caregiver-child interactions. However, these measures embed several dimensions of quality, including staff-child interactions, in a single measure and often in a single item (e.g., Harms and Clifford 1980; Harms, Cryer, and Clifford 1986). In such global measures, staff-child interactions are confounded with many other variables.

When either regulatable or global measures are used, the consensus is that low quality is related to poor performance on developmental indices and high quality is related to improved child outcomes (McCartney et al. 1982; McCartney 1988; Schliecker, White, and Jacobs 1991). These studies have made a valuable contribution to the definition and measurement of quality child care and have demonstrated that high-quality care is essential to positive child development. However, because regulatable and global measures combine environmental and caregiver components, it is difficult to use them to isolate the role of the child care provider. There are several reasons to separate caregiver characteristics from other dimensions of quality. First, the caregiver has a unique role in providing child care. The caregiver's spontaneous interactions with the children are considered by many to be the critical factor in determining the quality of care received by the child (Kaplan and Conn 1984; Scarr, Phillips, and McCartney 1990; Snider and Fu 1990). To highlight this point, two studies using all three approaches to defining quality (regulatable, global, interactions) have concluded that interactions may best predict child outcome (Howes, Phillips, and Whitebook 1992; Love 1993). Second, understanding caregivers and their work context is essential for improving child care. For example, child care providers who are stressed, unhappy or poorly trained may be more likely to leave their positions and less likely to form secure attachments with children in their care. For these reasons, the child care worker in the day care setting becomes an important focus of study.

A Profile of Those Who Work in Child Care

Background and Personal Characteristics

This section reviews factors such as gender, age, marital status, and training of child care providers. Several important studies in Canada and the United States have reported highly consistent results about the people who work in group child care settings. These studies include the early report of Ruopp et al. (1979) entitled *Children at the Center;* the later National Child Care Staffing Study (NCCSS) conducted in the United States by Whitebook, Howes, and Phillips (1990); the *Canadian National Child Care Study* (CNCCS) conducted by Lero et al. (1988); the CNCCS provincial and territorial reports by Pence et al. (1992); and the national study of the Canadian Day Care Advocacy Association (CDCAA) and the Canadian Child Day Care Federation (CCDCF) (CDCAA/CCDCF 1992) entitled *Caring for a Living.* A replication of *Caring for a Living* was conducted in 1997-8 and preliminary results of the "You Bet I Care!" study were recently presented (Doherty et al. 1998).

To summarize, child care staff are almost exclusively young women. In 1990, the NCCSS study (Whitebook, Howes, and Phillips 1990) surveyed a large national sample of 1,309 child care staff in five metropolitan areas in the United States. They noted that 97 percent of staff were female, and 81 percent of staff were forty years old or younger. The Canadian study *Caring for a Living* (CDCAA/CCDCF 1992) found that 98 percent of caregivers were women, and 58 percent of staff were under thirty years old. According to the NCCSS study, only 46 percent of the staff were married. Sixty-five percent of married staff members, and 21 percent of single staff members had children. *Caring for a Living* reported that 57 percent of child care providers in its sample were married, and 41 percent of staff had children living at home.

Both studies reported that child care staff working in group centres were relatively well educated. For example, the NCCSS study reported that 42 percent of the directors and 31 percent of caregivers had some college education, compared with 23 percent of the female civilian labour force in the United States. *Caring for a Living* reported that 68 percent of Canadian child care providers had a postsecondary certificate, diploma, or college degree compared with 41 percent for the national employed labour force.

In addition to studies of caregivers who work in centres, several studies of family child care providers are available. These include two studies conducted in the United States: the National Day Care Home Study (Fosburg 1981), and a study of family and relative care (Galinsky et al. 1994); and one Canadian study (Pence and Goelman 1987). In the United States, it was reported that family child care was used by 37 percent of children younger than five: 15 percent were cared for by grandparents and other relatives, and 22 percent by non-relatives (US Bureau of the Census 1987). Galinsky et al. (1994) reported similar data – 33 percent of children under five years old with employed mothers used family care: 13 percent were cared for by relatives, and 20 percent by non-relatives. Given that only 28 percent of children were in group care (Galinsky et al. 1994), family day care was used slightly more frequently than centre-based care. More than 90 percent of family day care homes in the United States were operating outside any regulatory system (Corsini, Wisensale, and Caruso 1988).

The National Day Care Home Study (NDCHS) (Fosburg 1981), though somewhat dated, noted that 100 percent of home child care providers were women. The median age for their sample of over 300 settings in three US cities (Philadelphia, San Antonio, and Los Angeles) was 41.6 years, and most providers were between twenty-five and fifty-five years of age. Stevens (1982) reported that "most" of these women were married and caring for at least one related child. Fifty-seven percent had completed high school and the median years of schooling completed was 11.3, slightly under the average of 12.5 years for the general adult population.

A Canadian study (Pence and Goelman 1987) found that family care providers sometimes differed according to whether homes were licensed or non-licensed. This Canadian study found that licensed homes had somewhat older care providers (thirty-nine years) than non-licensed homes (33.5 years). However, the caregivers from licensed and non-licensed homes were similar in that more than 90 percent of both groups were married, more than 75 percent of both groups were Canadian by birth, and only about 12 percent had a university degree.

In conclusion, child care in both group and family settings remains women's work. Family child care providers were more likely to be married and caring for a related child than were group care providers. They were somewhat older than group care providers, and possibly less educated. It may be difficult to describe family care providers as one group. In fact, the NDCHS study (Fosburg 1981) identified three groups of family caregivers. The first group consisted of middle-aged women who provided care for friends and neighbours, but generally not for relatives. The second group was composed mainly of Hispanic and Black women in their 40s and 50s who cared for a relative's child, often their own grandchildren. The third group included white women in their 20s and early 30s who cared for their own children as well as others'. It may be necessary to identify several groups of family day care providers on the basis of ethnicity, whether they work in licensed or non-licensed care, and their reasons for providing care.

Wages and Working Conditions

Caring for a Living (CDCAA/CCDCF 1992), which included data from 969 Canadian day care centres and over 7,200 child care staff, indicated that "the wages of many Canadian Child Care Workers hover close to, or fall below, Statistics Canada poverty line." The average national wage reported was $18,870 per year in 1991. Doherty et al. (1998) reported that the average hourly wage of Canadian child care providers is $12. Interestingly, this means that wages in the field have not increased significantly since 1991. Whitebook, Howes, and Phillips (1990) found that average annual income for full-time work (thirty-five hours per week, for fifty weeks per year) was $9,431 (US dollars). Medical coverage and benefits were minimal. Unpaid overtime was common and some child care providers subsidized the centres by contributing money for supplies that would not otherwise be available.

Even more appalling were estimates of wages paid to family day care providers. Stevens (1982) estimated average provider net income between $2,614 and $3,229, well below the 1977 US poverty line. In a Canadian study conducted in British Columbia, Pence and Goelman (1987) reported that 89 percent of family child care providers working in unlicensed homes and 58 percent of family child care providers in licensed homes earned less than $5,000 per year. Galinsky et al. (1994) noted that the average annual income for family child care providers in regulated homes was substantially higher, $15,649 (US dollars), than for those in non-regulated homes, $8,026 (US dollars), or relative care, $2,993 (US dollars). These figures say it all: child care providers are underpaid.

It has been noted that higher wages are related to other quality indices. Whitebook, Howes, and Phillips (1992) found that quality, as defined by ratio, group size, and developmentally appropriate practice, was related to wages paid: higher wages were related to lower ratios (fewer children per educator), smaller group size, and better developmentally appropriate practice. Mill, Bartlett, and White (1995) reported a relationship between wages, auspice, and global quality of centres: non-profit group centres paid higher wages, had staff with better training, and had higher ratings on global quality than for-profit centres. While it is difficult to know whether better child care providers select or are selected for higher-paying jobs in higher-quality centres, it seems certain that providers who are paid higher wages work in better quality environments, whereas those paid lower salaries have poorer work environments.

Child Care Providers' Perceptions of Their Work

One way of conceptualizing feelings about one's work is often called burnout (Maslach and Pines 1977; Pines and Maslach 1980). Burnout is a condition often found in professions with a high degree of people contact, such as child care. In the lay literature, burnout is a term used frequently to describe any negative feelings toward work and is generally thought to be a cynical, drained work orientation. In the research literature, Perlman and Hartman (1982) define burnout as a multidimensional construct with three parts: (a) emotional exhaustion or a feeling of being drained of energy and the inability to give to others; (b) depersonalization or having a negative attitude toward oneself and one's work; and (c) low personal accomplishment or lack of a sense of achievement in the workplace. These constructs were operationalized in the *Maslach Burnout Inventory* (Maslach and Jackson 1986). Using this inventory, Schneider and Boyd (1996) provide some Canadian data on burnout in child care providers. Investigators compared a sample of 137 child care providers in Winnipeg, Manitoba, with a sample of child providers in the United States (Boyd and Pasley 1989) and a sample of 11,067 other (i.e., non-child care) workers (Maslach and Jackson 1986). In short, neither Canadian nor US child care providers showed higher levels of burnout than other workers. Canadian providers scored about the same as US providers and other workers on emotional exhaustion, lower than other workers on depersonalization (they had fewer negative attitudes toward work and self), and lower on personal accomplishment than US providers and other workers.

Though Canadian providers may be particularly at risk for feeling that they lack a sense of achievement, these data do not support the notion that child care providers experience higher levels of burnout than other workers. There are several possible explanations for such findings. First, it is possible that the samples studied do not accurately reflect burnout rates in child care because those with high burnout have already left their positions or the field. Finding other jobs may be easier for young, well-educated women than for other workers. Furthermore, in the Schneider and Boyd (1996) study, age was related to burnout, with older providers reporting less exhaustion and less depersonalization than younger providers. It may be that older providers have come to terms with the difficulties in their field, have better coping strategies, or have limited options for change, whereas younger child care providers are able to find other positions or careers. In order to examine this problem, research is needed on child care providers who leave their jobs.

Another explanation of the failure to find high rates of burnout among child care workers is that researchers have found that child care providers are satisfied with some aspects of their jobs and dissatisfied with others. Interestingly, the very dimension thought to define burnout – excessive people contact – seems to be a source of satisfaction to child caregivers. For example, Phillips, Howes, and Whitebook (1991) reported that child care providers viewed their work environment as positive, and expressed high levels of career orientation and satisfaction with day-to-day demands. Canadian child care providers reported being satisfied with, interested in, and loving those aspects of their work that involved daily contacts with children (CDCAA/CCDCF 1992). According to this Canadian study, child care staff saw their jobs as careers, and indicated that they would choose to work in child care again. In the US study, satisfaction was related to paid preparation time, reduced-fee child care for one's own children, and provisions for adult needs at the centres (Whitebook, Howes, and Phillips 1990). At the same time, child care providers expressed dissatisfaction with low salaries, and the low status and support accorded them. Further, the US study found that low pay, poor working conditions, unpaid overtime, and lack of benefits were related to dissatisfaction in child care providers. The CDCAA/CCDCF (1992) study found that most caregivers ranked being paid a better salary as the most important variable for increasing job satisfaction and ranked promoting more respect for caregivers as second.

Finally, at least one study of family day care providers in British Columbia (Pence and Goelman 1987) noted that satisfaction was related to enjoying being with children, at least for licensed family care providers. Low pay and interference with one's own family were related to dissatisfaction of unlicensed care providers. Demanding work and lack of parental reliability were related to dissatisfaction of licensed family day care workers.

In summary, the majority of caregivers are young females with good educational levels. In spite of their education, they are poorly paid for working in child care. Their working conditions vary considerably, but those earning the lowest wages are often in centres that rate low on regulatable quality and global quality indices. While they are satisfied with some aspects of their jobs, such as caring for children, child care workers are dissatisfied with their salaries, the societal view of their job status, and the lack of parental, co-worker, and supervisor support they receive. Given this description of child care providers, we next examine predictors of staff turnover (leaving jobs), negative caregiver behaviours toward children, and positive caregiver behaviours toward children. In particular, we ask if there are specific variables that can predict the type of person who leaves the job, who directs anger at children, and who maintains warmth in interacting with children.

Turnover, Anger, and Warmth in Child Care Providers

Studies have consistently found high rates of turnover in the child care field (see also Chapter 10). Data from studies conducted in the United States place annual turnover rates at somewhere between 20 percent and 70 percent in the years from 1985 to 1989 (Hartmann and Pearce 1989). Phillips, Howes, and Whitebook (1991) noted that high turnover rates characterize preschool group child care workers and that the US Department of Labor estimated that annually between 1980 and 1990, 42 percent of all centre-based child care workers would need to be replaced to maintain an adequate and stable number of staff. In Canada, there is less research, and turnover rates in group settings are reported to be somewhat lower than in the United States. For example, the CDCAA/CCDCF study (1992) reported a national turnover rate of 26 percent among Canadian child care providers.

According to Phillips, Howes, and Whitebook (1991), poor wages were the strongest predictor of turnover among child care providers. While wages may provide a pre-condition for long-term satisfaction and tenure in child care, the support offered to staff, paid preparation time, good co-worker relations, advancement and professional development opportunities, and provision of space for adult needs were also related to higher satisfaction and lower turnover. Fleischer (1985) also found that caregivers who left their jobs were more dissatisfied with their supervisor's technical competence and lack of support for career development than caregivers who remained in their jobs. Although more extensive research is needed, it seems that both work environment (wages, adult needs, paid preparation time) and job perceptions (satisfaction, co-worker relations, supervisor support) are related to turnover among child care providers. Caregivers may be less apt to leave their jobs if wages were higher and they felt supported and satisfied at the centres. Research is needed to examine whether background (e.g., less training) or personal (e.g., non-job related stress, low self-esteem) characteristics are related to greater turnover among child care providers. Furthermore, it seems theoretically sound to suggest that lack of stability of care or high turnover might be related to poorer attachment of children to their caregivers. Consistency of caregiving or low turnover rates seem critical to children's sense of security. There is little research examining the effects of turnover on children, but two studies seem to offer empirical support for the relation between low turnover, adjustment in children, and quality of care. Howes and Hamilton (1993) found that children who experienced frequent losses of their primary caregiver became increasingly aggressive. High staff turnover was associated with poor quality as measured by the ECERS (Early Childhood Environment Rating Scale) and less responsive teacher behaviour (Kontos and Fiene 1987; Phillips and Howes 1987).

Although caregivers often leave their jobs, it is important to describe those who stay in their jobs and the type of affective environment they create in the classroom, particularly whether caregivers are generally angry or engage in negative behaviour toward children or are generally warm and positive with children. It is also important to know whether those who remain on the job are influenced by background or personal characteristics, the work environment, and job perceptions in the way they deal with children. It is also of interest to examine the relationship of caregiver anger or affection to child outcomes. There is very little research that deals with any of these aspects of caregiver behaviour.

In a recent study by Mill and White (1999), about 12 percent of 78 caregivers observed for two hours in their classrooms displayed angry behaviour toward children. The "angry behaviour" observed was that defined by codes developed by Cummings and Vittenberga (1991) and included (a) handling children in a rough manner, (b) insulting or threatening children, or (c) inappropriately taking something away from the child. Mill and White's findings are both reassuring and startling. While it is true that most educators showed no angry behaviour toward children, 12 percent displayed between one and thirteen angry acts in a two-hour period, even though they knew that the observers were present.

Mill and White (1999) also examined the prediction of angry caregiver interactions from four groups of variables: background characteristics, personal characteristics, work environment, and job perception. Only job perception, such as whether the job was seen as non-rewarding or a cause for concern and lack of supervisor support, was directly related to the expression of caregiver anger. Job perception was also related to work environment – for example, wages, class size, number of children on government subsidies, and profit or non-profit status of the centre. Low wages, large class sizes, a high number of children on subsidies, and profit status were related to feelings of dissatisfaction, reports of lack of supervisor support, and few job rewards. Finally, poor job perception was related to personal resources such as low self-esteem, more problems at home, and a lower sense of well-being.

A somewhat different picture emerges when affectionate or warm caregiver behaviour was observed. In the same study, Mill and White (1999) used a coding system developed by Twardosz et al. (1979) to measure caregiver affection. On average, educators displayed 124 affectionate acts toward children per hour. Smiling was the most common manner in which educators expressed affection. Affectionate words were next, followed distantly by passive and affectionate physical contact. The same four sets of variables used to predict angry behaviour were used to predict affectionate behaviour or warmth. Only variables from the work environment category (e.g., wages, global quality) were related to warmth.

Although correlational, the results of this study indicate that changes in work environment such as increasing wages may have dramatic effects on caregiver warmth. Caregiver anger, on the other hand, seems to be related to caregivers' feelings about their jobs and support on the job. Furthermore, personal stress and self-esteem outside the job are related to angry caregivers' feelings about their job. Either such personal resources erode perceptions of support and job rewards or negative job perception affects the caregiver's feelings outside her job. Furthermore, poor work environments seem to act through poor job perception to increase angry caregiver behaviour. More research is certainly needed to replicate Mill and White's findings with a larger sample, and to utilize path analysis statistical procedures to better understand the relationships among variables that predict angry caregiver behaviour.

Finally, there are little data at present linking caregiver warmth and anger to child development outcomes. There is an extensive body of literature that deals with parental anger, harshness, and poor developmental outcomes in children. In addition, parental warmth has been related to positive developmental outcomes (Adessky 1996; Belsky 1984, 1993). A few studies have linked caregiver behaviour to child behaviour. Using the Caregiver Interaction Scale developed by Arnett (1989), Love (1993) found that children were more stressed – that is, they exhibited more nail biting, stuttering, fighting, and complaining of feeling ill, and were less involved in classroom activities – when caregivers were harsher, more critical, and more detached. Howes, Phillips, and Whitebook (1992) found that the effects of regulatable characteristics were mediated by the caregiver's style of relating to and disciplining the children. For example, teacher training may lead to positive outcomes only if more training in early childhood education is combined with affectionate caregiving. Such a hypothesis requires multivariate studies of several factors, which might be related to child care providers' interactions with children.

Comparing Research on Child Care and Elementary School

The situation of elementary school teachers differs in many respects from that of preschool child care providers. Teachers are required to have university degrees; they receive significantly higher wages, and benefits are considered part of their work conditions. Elementary school classrooms are more uniform in terms of equipment and resources available to teachers and tend to be of good quality (Baillargeon et al. 1993). Yet the research questions asked about the effects of child care are similar to those asked about school as an intervention (McCartney and Jordan 1990). These investigators point out that in the early stage of studies of school effects, there was considerable debate about whether school had a strong impact on children's achievement. It was argued that family rather than school was the dominant factor predicting achievement. Similarly, day care was not always found to influence development, and many studies concluded there were no differences between children who attended day care and those in home care. McCartney and Jordan (1990) argue that in both fields, research needed to identify and evaluate variables associated with quality and good developmental outcomes rather than to ask whether a multidimensional variable such as school or child care attendance affected child development.

When those variables were identified and included in the research, it was found that many variables affected development and that these variables had to be considered in the same study in a multivariate framework, whether teachers or child care providers were being considered. Finally, McCartney and Jordan (1990) note that an ecological model – one that considers the joint influences of family, community, child care, and school – is needed to understand and integrate findings. In short, say McCartney and Jordan (1990), "Child-care research and school effects share similar pasts. We expect that these two areas will share similar problems and triumphs as the fields continue to develop. The parallels illustrate the value of each field monitoring the progress of the other. In this way, each may benefit from the conceptual and methodological advances made by the other" (26).

In the current chapter, we present an important variable that has not received sufficient systematic study in either field – namely, factors related to teacher-child interaction. It is our contention that work in both fields should begin to examine the issue of variables related to teacher warmth and anger. This type of study may well be seen as another way in which school and child care research are parallel and, in fact, may benefit each other.

Is Change Probable?

Paying a fair wage and providing supervisor support would seem to be at least two important steps that could be taken immediately in an attempt to facilitate caregiver warmth and reduce caregiver anger directed at children. Such relatively simple suggestions for change have been made in the current chapter and in previous work (Phillips, Howes, and Whitebook 1991). In addition to increased salaries and support, professional development opportunities, paid preparation time, and health benefits (in the US) are recommended. However, though we have been aware of these needs for several years, significant changes have not occurred. One reason for the failure to make these changes has been suggested by Scarr, Phillips, and McCartney (1990), who note that our society remains ambivalent about shared childcare and mothers who work outside the home. "The cost of our reluctance to shed fantasies about children's needs and parental obligations is the failure to develop constructive social policy" (26). As long as we are ambivalent, we will not be able to move forward in the child care field.

In an intriguing article, Friendly and Rothman (1995) examine Canadian goals and policies in child care. They outline four goals: (a) alleviating poverty, (b) fostering women's equality, (c) optimizing child development, and (d) promoting economic well-being. Although neither the federal nor the provincial governments endorse all these goals, and although many federal and provincial strategies to meet such goals have been unsuccessful, it is of interest that the child care provider is rarely a target of suggested policies or interventions. Social policy largely ignores that child care providers may live below the poverty line, are females without equality in either wages or status, are primarily responsible for optimizing child development in centre care, and work to promote economic well-being by providing safe, warm care for our children. Our ways of thinking about quality child care must change. It must be recognized that the child care provider's well-being is the key to the future development of our children, and social policy must integrate goals for child care providers as well as for users.

In the meantime, it seems reasonable to thank women who elect to remain child care providers despite universally poor wages, lack of status, and less than excellent regulatable or global environmental quality. The fact that under these conditions, they can produce 124 displays of affectionate behaviour each hour toward children in their care is a remarkable achievement!

References

Adessky, R. 1996. The relationship of group and family experiences to peer rated aggression and popularity in middle class kindergarten children. Doctoral thesis, Concordia University, Montreal.

Ainslie, R.C., and C.W. Anderson. 1984. Day care children's relationships to their mothers and caregivers: An inquiry into the conditions for the development of attachment. In *The child and the day care setting,* ed. R.C. Ainslie, 98-132. New York: Praeger.

Arnett, J. 1989. Caregivers in day-care centers: Does training matter? *Journal of Applied Developmental Psychology* 10:541-52.

Baillargeon, M., R. Betsalel-Presser, M. Joncas, and H. Larouche. 1993. One child, many environments: Continuity or discontinuity in kindergarten and school-based day care programs? *Alberta Journal of Educational Research* 39:127-42.

Belsky, J. 1984. The determinants of parenting: A process model. *Child Development* 55:83-96.

–. 1993. Etiology of child maltreatment: A developmental-ecological analysis. *Psychological Bulletin* 114:413-34.

Belsky, J., and L.D. Steinberg. 1978. The effects of day care: A critical review. *Child Development* 49:929-49.

Bowlby, J. 1969. *Attachment and loss: Volume 1, Attachment.* New York: Basic Books.

–. 1973. *Attachment and loss: Volume 2, Separation.* New York: Basic Books.

Boyd, B.J., and B.K. Pasley. 1989. Role stress as a contributor to burnout in child care professionals. *Child and Youth Quarterly* 18:243-58.

CDCAA/CCDCF (Canadian Day Care Advocacy Association/Canadian Child Day Care Federation). 1992. *Caring for a living: A study on wages and working conditions in Canadian child care.* Ottawa: CDCAA/CCDCF.

Corsini, D.A., S. Wisensale, and G. Caruso. 1988. Family day care: System issues and regulatory models. *Young Children* 43:17-23.

Cummings, E.M., and G. Vittenberga. 1991. Contexts of children's exposure to adults' anger: Day care and the way conflicts end. Paper presented at the Society for Research in Child Development, April, Seattle, WA.

Doherty, G., A. LaGrange, H. Goelman, D. Lero, and J. Tougas. 1998. You bet I care! Paper presented at Linking Research to Practice: A Canadian Forum, October, Banff, AB.

Etaugh, C. 1980. Effects of nonmaternal care on children: Research evidence and popular views. *American Psychologist* 35:309-19.

Farran, D., and C. Ramey. 1977. Infant day care attachment behaviors toward mothers and teachers. *Child Development* 48:1112-6.

Fleischer, B. 1985. Identification of strategies to reduce turnover among child care workers. *Child Care Quarterly* 14(2):130-9.

Fosburg, S. 1981. Family day care in the United States: A summary of findings. *Final report of the National Day Care Home Study.* DHHS Publication No. 80-30282. Washington, DC: Department of Health and Human Services.

Friendly, M., and L. Rothman. 1995. Miles to go ... The policy context of child care in Canada. *Child Welfare* 74:503-24.

Galinsky, E., C. Howes, S. Kontos, and M. Shinn. 1994. *The study of children in family and relative care.* New York: Families and Work Institute.

Harms, T., and R. Clifford. 1980. *The Early Childhood Environment Rating Scale.* New York: Teachers College Press.

Harms, T., D. Cryer, and R. Clifford. 1986. *The Infant/Toddler Environment Rating Scale.* New York: Teachers College Press.

Hartmann, H.I., and D.M. Pearce. 1989. *High skill and low pay: The economics of child care work.* Washington, DC: Institute for Women's Policy Research.

Health and Welfare Canada. 1992. *Status of day care in Canada*. Ottawa: Health and Welfare Canada, National Child Care Information Centre, Child Care Programs Division, Social Programs Branch.

Hoffman, L.W. 1989. Effects of maternal employment in two parent families. *American Psychologist* 44:283-9.

Howes, C. and C. Hamilton. 1993. The changing experience of child care: Changes in teachers and in teacher-child relationships and children's social competence with peers. *Early Childhood Research Quarterly* 8(1):15-32.

Howes, C., D. Phillips, and M. Whitebook. 1992. Thresholds of quality: Implications for the social development of children in center-based care. *Child Development* 63:449-60.

Howes, C., C. Rodning, D.C. Galluzzo, and L. Myers. 1988. Attachment and child care: Relationships with mother and caregiver. *Early Childhood Research Quarterly* 3:403-16.

Kaplan, M.G., and J.S. Conn. 1984. The effects of caregiver training on classroom setting and caregiver performance in eight community day care centers. *Child Study Journal* 14:79-93.

Kontos, S., and R. Fiene 1987. Predictors of quality and children's development in day care. In *Quality indicators of child care,* ed. D. Phillips, 57-79. Washington, DC: National Association for the Education of Young Children.

Lero, D.S., A.R. Pence, H. Goelman, and L. Brockman. 1988. *Canadian national child care study*. Ottawa: Statistics Canada and Health and Welfare Canada.

Love, J.M. 1993. Does children's behavior reflect day care classroom quality. Paper presented at the Society for Research in Child Development, March, New Orleans, LA.

McCartney, K. 1988. Effect of quality of day care environment on children's language development. *Developmental Psychology* 20:244-60.

McCartney, K., and E. Jordan. 1990. Parallels between research on child care and research on school effects. *Educational Researcher* 19(1):21-6.

McCartney, K., S. Scarr, D. Phillips, S. Grajek, and J.C. Schwarz. 1982. Environmental differences among day care centers and their effects on children's development. In *Day care: Scientific and social policy issues,* ed. E. Zigler and E. Gordon, 126-51. Boston: Auburn House.

Maslach, C., and S. Jackson. 1986. The measurement of experienced burnout. *Journal of Occupational Behavior* 2:99-113.

Maslach, C., and A. Pines. 1977. The burnout syndrome in the day care setting. *Child Care Quarterly* 6:100-13.

Mill, D., N. Bartlett, and D.R. White. 1995. Profit and non-profit day care: A comparison of quality, caregiver behaviour and structural features. *Canadian Journal of Research in Early Childhood Education* 4:45-53.

Mill, D., and D.R. White. 1999. Correlates of affectionate and angry behavior in day care educators of preschool-aged children. *Early Childhood Research Quarterly* 14:155-78.

Pence, A.R., and H. Goelman. 1987. Who cares for the child in day care? An examination of caregivers from three types of care. *Early Childhood Research Quarterly* 2:315-34.

Pence, A.R., S. Griffin, D. Crozier-Smith, L. McDonell, and L. Lewis. 1992. *Canadian child care in context: Perspectives from the provinces and territories*. Ottawa: Statistics Canada and Health and Welfare Canada.

Perlman, B., and E.A. Hartman. 1982. Burnout: Summary and future research. *Human Relations* 35:283-305.

Phillips, D., and C. Howes. 1987. Indicators of quality in child care: Review of research. In *Quality in child care: What does research tell us?* ed. D. Phillips, 1-19. Washington, DC: National Association for the Education of Young Children.

Phillips, D., C. Howes, and M. Whitebook. 1991. Child care as an adult work environment. *Journal of Social Issues* 47:49-70.

Pines, A., and C. Maslach. 1980. Combatting staff burnout in a day care center: A case study. *Child Care Quarterly* 9:5-16.

Ruopp, R.R., J. Travers, R. Glantz, and C. Coelen. 1979. *Children at the center.* Final report of the National Day Care Study. Cambridge, MA: Abt Associates.

Scarr, S. 1984. *Mother care-other care*. New York: Basic Books.

Scarr, S., D. Phillips, and K. McCartney. 1990. Facts, fantasies and the future of child care in the United States. *Psychological Science* 1:26-35.

Schliecker, E., D.R. White, and E. Jacobs. 1991. The role of day care quality in the prediction of children's vocabulary. *Canadian Journal of Behavioural Science* 23:12-24.

Schneider, N.I., and B.J. Boyd. 1996. Burnout in Canadian child care providers. *Canadian Journal of Research in Early Childhood Education* 5:3-11.

Snider, M.H., and V.R. Fu. 1990. The effects of specialized education and job experience on early childhood teachers' knowledge of developmentally appropriate practice. *Early Childhood Research Quarterly* 5:69-78.

Stevens, H.H. 1982. The National Day Care Home Study: Family day care in the United States. *Young Children* 37(4):59-66.

Twardosz, S., S. Schwartz, J. Fox, and J.L. Cunningham. 1979. Development and evaluation of a system to measure affectionate behavior. *Behavioral Assessment* 1:177-90.

Whitebook, M., C. Howes, and D. Phillips. 1990. *Who cares? Child care teachers and quality of care in America: Final report of the National Child Care Staffing Study.* Oakland, CA: Child Care Employee Project.

Whitebook, M., C. Howes, and C. Phillips. 1992. The social policy context of child care: Effects on quality. *American Journal of Community Psychology* 20:25-49.

US Bureau of the Census. 1987. *Who's minding the kids? Child care arrangements.* Washington, DC: US Government Printing Office.

Zaslow, M. 1991. Variation in child care quality and implications for children. *Journal of Social Issues* 47:125-38.

9
Child Care as a Social Policy Issue

Martha Friendly

Since the inception of Canadian child care more than 150 years ago, in the form of charitable nurseries run by religious institutions, it has evolved without the support of a national social policy. This point is often cited as perhaps the single most influential factor that has defined the way child care has developed in Canada (Friendly 1994).[1] Between the 1960s and 1990s, the federal government assumed some responsibility for child care through several separate funding schemes, the most significant of which was the child care provision of the Canada Assistance Plan. At the same time, most provincial governments began to assume a primary role in child care through regulation, funding arrangements, and provision of training. Throughout the 1970s and 1980s, both the federal government and the provincial governments maintained an interest in developing and expanding child care policy and improving child care services; the supply, variety, and quality of services thus grew across the country.

In the 1990s, however, even the limited role the federal government assumed in the preceding twenty-five years has shrunk. After several tentative attempts at developing national child care policy, federal involvement in child care has diminished considerably, with a reduced policy role and reduced funding (Bach and Phillips 1997). As federal withdrawal from child care and other social programs continued in the 1990s, the funding and regulation commitments of provincial governments began to dwindle as well. Today the child care situation across Canada is characterized by increasing reliance not only on provincial and territorial governments but also on the local level and on parents (Doherty, Friendly, and Oloman 1998).

Although child care in Canada has a long history as a service, it is only within the past twenty-five years that an intense debate has been carried on about its place in social policy. This debate has taken place among policy makers, child care advocates, and early childhood professionals, as well as in a number of arenas such as government commissions and task forces; federal, provincial, and even local election campaigns; and the media. Although the debate has revolved around a variety of topics, the fundamental question that has been debated, and upon which most of the other topics turn, is whether child care is a matter of public concern or a private family responsibility. The answer to this question will determine whether child care is treated as a private commodity within a market model or as a public service within the framework of social policy. This is a fundamental point because whether child care is considered a private responsibility or a "public good" is central to the design of child care policy and, ultimately, to service delivery.

A second key social policy question, whose answer also very much shapes Canadian early childhood education and care, is "What (and who) is child care for?" The answer to "What is child care?" ranges from "healthy child development" and "readiness to learn" to "a tool to support parental employability," and from "equality for women" to "reduction of reliance on social assistance" and to "early intervention for children at risk." The answer to "Who is child care for?" varies from "children" to "parents," and from "families" to "women."

Almost all Western European nations have developed relatively coherent systems of publicly supported, universal early childhood education and care services to meet a range of needs. In contrast, Canada has a multiplicity of discrete early childhood education and child care services and programs that have evolved arbitrarily, each with its own goals, objectives, and funding arrangements (see Chapter 6). These include a rarely coordinated array of regulated child care, kindergarten, Head Start, and other children's services as well as vouchers and tax deductions. While fragmentation has historically prevailed in child care, the inability to resolve the key questions as well as increased targeting of low-income and at-risk children and parents have accelerated the proliferation of disjunctive early childhood education and care programs in the 1990s.

Social policy has been characterized as involving "acts of government undertaken for a variety of reasons to provide for a range of needs that the market does not or cannot satisfy for certain segments of the population" (Zimmerman 1979). A social policy approach, distinguished from a market approach to social programs by government's integral role in their conception and implementation, is generally concerned with questions of redistribution and fairness. Social policy includes principles and procedures that guide intervention in an otherwise arbitrary social system through use of regulation, constraints, and rewards. Social policy "helps shape the quality of life and determines the well-being of members of society" (Zimmerman 1979, 488).

Like other social issues, child care exists within a set of connections between the child, the child care program, the family, the community, and the social/cultural/political/economic environment. Thus child care both has its own context and is part of a broader context. For child care and child care policy, the broader context includes labour force participation and labour policy, education and schooling, women's employment issues, other family policy issues such as parental leaves and child benefits, taxation, and other economic issues. This holistic, multilayered approach to social systems was first applied to child care by Urie Bronfenbrenner who described how child care policy is influenced by the social, political, and economic factors that shape its development and, in turn, influences the way child care develops and is delivered (Bronfenbrenner 1979).

This chapter places child care within the context of social policy. It first proposes that it is appropriate to treat child care within a social policy framework because, if it is of high quality, child care is a "public good," of benefit not only to individual children and families but also to the community and the society at large. Indeed, it is suggested that not only is it inappropriate to treat child care as a private, marketable commodity but that, from the perspective of service provision, it is also ineffective. (For a discussion of child care's "market failure," see Krashinsky and Cleveland 1997). The chapter goes on to present child care within the framework of Canadian social policy, and then describes the current responsibilities for child care in Canada among the various levels of government and individual families.

What Is the Public Interest in High Quality Child Care?

A paradigm for exploring whether child care should be an issue of public concern was supplied by a 1994 federal government discussion paper. The paper, published as background for the federal government's Social Security Review, identified child care as pivotal to three areas of concern: security, work/employment, and learning. Child care, it was observed in the paper, is "at the heart" of the three areas, a "critical support for employment ... but more than an employment measure" and a way to "provide children with a good environment in which to grow and learn" (Canada 1994b).

The federal discussion paper recognized that child care has a wide range of interconnected goals associated with a diversity of purposes. Thus, a well-conceived system of child care has the potential to meet a range of needs simultaneously. In this way, child care has social value as an instrument for enhancing children's healthy development (regardless of their socio-economic status); as part of a strategy for reducing poverty; as a tool to assist parental employability; as a support to families; and as key to women's equality.

The benefits of child care, if it is of high quality, is financially and practically accessible, and reflects parents' needs for care, primarily arise from two propositions:

- *Proposition 1.* High-quality child care promotes the healthy development, safety, and well-being of children regardless of parental work status or socio-economic group.
- *Proposition 2.* Access to reliable child care allows parents, especially mothers, to participate in the paid labour force, training, or education.

Proposition 1 is supported by the growing body of child development literature pertaining to child care. This research suggests that if the program is of high quality, it can strengthen the intellectual and social competencies that promote positive social behaviour and relationships as well as good school performance. These characteristics can persist into the elementary school years, laying the groundwork for later personal, school, and work success. Conversely, poor-quality child care has been demonstrated to have negative impacts. These findings pertain regardless of social class. (For recent reviews of this literature, see Doherty 1996; Lamb 1997).

US research also shows that economically disadvantaged children (who are, for a variety of reasons, less likely to succeed in schooling, and more likely to become involved in negative social activities later on) can derive substantial benefit from child care/early childhood education programs. Examinations of programs like Head Start and the Perry Preschool Project – both of which focused on highly disadvantaged at-risk children in the United States – show that for this population, high-quality early childhood education and care programs enriched with supports such as parent education, enhanced health care, health and nutrition, and social services may help to ameliorate the effects of disadvantage (Zigler and Styfco 1994).

It is now widely acknowledged that healthy development in the early years serves as a solid foundation for lifelong good health and as the underpinning for later school success (National Forum on Health 1997; Doherty 1997). In addition, benefits to children are mediated through the impact of child care on their parents; children can benefit from reduced poverty and family stress as well as from competent parenting skills. At the community level, healthy social development enhanced by high-quality child care can, over the long term, serve as a foundation for a competent, civil citizenry by fostering prevention of crime and supporting healthy, cohesive communities (Zigler and Styfco 1994; National Crime Prevention Council 1996). Child care services can promote equity among classes, levels of ability, racial and ethnic groups, and generations. It can also strengthen communities by solidifying respect for and appreciation of diversity in the early years. These are benefits not only for local communities, but also for society at large.

Proposition 2 is related to demographic changes in our society that have occurred over the past twenty or thirty years. In the industrialized countries in the past few decades, women with young children have entered the paid labour force in large numbers. Today about 65 percent of Canadian women with children under the age of six work outside the home (Statistics Canada 1996). Without reliable, affordable child care, women – both those who are single parents and those in two-parent families – may be obliged to stay out of the labour force, to work at poorly paid part-time employment, or be unable to take opportunities for advancement (Akyeampong 1988; Powell 1997).

A sizable proportion of social assistance recipients are sole-support mothers who may be driven into long-term reliance on public assistance and poverty if child care is not accessible. US research found that access to affordable child care plays an important role in the decision whether or not low-income mothers enter the paid workforce (US General Accounting Office 1994). Canadian data show that families headed by a sole-support mother who is not in the labour force almost invariably fall below the poverty line. Canadian data also show that for many two-parent low-income families, the mother's income is the factor that lifts the family above the poverty line and that without the mother's income, more than 500,000 families would fall into poverty (Kitchen et al. 1991). Thus accessible, reliable child care must be a central component of strategies that permit low-income families to rise above the poverty line and that allow single parents (usually mothers) to become self-reliant by participating in employment, training, and education.

Reliable child care can also contribute to parents' effectiveness at work, regardless of their economic situation, by diminishing tension between work and family responsibilities. Research has found that poor-quality or unstable child care can have multiple effects on parents' work performance, including absenteeism, tardiness, and on-the-job stress.

From these two propositions follow a number of subsidiary short-term and long-term benefits to children, to their families, to mothers, to local communities, and to society at large:

- enhancing school readiness and success
- providing equal opportunities for children with special needs

- providing equity for lower socio-economic groups
- promoting lifelong good health
- supporting women's equality
- helping families balance work and family responsibilities
- enhancing effective parenting
- supporting parental economic self-reliance
- valuing diversity
- creating employment
- promoting crime reduction and healthy communities
- promoting social cohesion and social unity.

Most of these positive attributes of child care are, in part at least, beneficial for the community and the larger society as well as to the individual child or family. A recent Canadian cost-benefit analysis calculated a ratio of 2:1 – that is, an eventual return of two dollars for every public dollar – for investments in high-quality child care services that simultaneously allowed maternal employment and promoted healthy child development (Cleveland and Krashinsky 1998).

Accordingly, the larger society gains if high-quality child care programs contribute to child development as well as family and community formation and maintenance. However, in the 1990s, the question of whether child care should be treated as a private family responsibility or as a public service has yet to be resolved in Canada. Resolution of this question is inextricably connected to the outcome of the question of whether future expectations for child care are resolved by social policy or by the marketplace.

The Historical Role of the Federal Government

Like other Canadian health, education, and social services, child care is under provincial or territorial jurisdiction. Nevertheless, the development of these programs in Canada has almost always been influenced by the federal government. The government of Canada's function in programs under provincial jurisdiction has ranged from a historical role in moulding the shape of elementary and secondary education, to a strong principle-determining function in health care, to a funding role, as in postsecondary education. Historically, not having a national policy, the federal government's role has been more indirect than direct in child care policy although its role as a funder of early childhood education and care and child care–related programs has been somewhat larger.

Although there was organized child care in many of Canada's provinces as early as the 1910s, the federal government had no role in child care until the Second World War. The Authorization of Agreements with

Provinces for the Care of Children initiated the first federal intervention in child care; 50 percent cost-sharing would be available to allow provinces to provide child care for children whose mothers were working in war-related industries. Only Ontario and Quebec participated in this agreement. After the war, the federal government withdrew, and all six of Quebec's child care centres, and many of Ontario's, closed (see Chapter 1).

The federal government's second foray into child care began in 1966 with the introduction of the Canada Assistance Plan (CAP), which was intended to ameliorate or prevent poverty. For the purposes of offering 50-50 federal/provincial cost-sharing, CAP treated child care like other welfare services or items of social assistance, stipulating that federal funds were available only for needy or potentially needy families and setting some conditions for cost-sharing (to be eligible for cost-sharing, welfare services had to be regulated and not-for-profit). Although CAP's cost-shared funding primarily took the form of fee subsidies for low-income families, the introduction of CAP provided a new catalyst for child care services to develop across Canada.

In the 1970s, the federal Local Initiatives Projects (LIP) provided a significant impetus to the expansion of non-profit child care centres in many provinces, and in 1971, child care expenses were included for the purpose of a tax deduction under the Income Tax Act. Although a national child care policy did not materialize as a result of federal interest, throughout the 1980s, the federal government acknowledged its role in child care by establishing two federal task forces (the Ministerial Task Force headed by Dr. Katie Cooke and the Special Parliamentary Committee on Child Care), by increasing its funding role through expansion of the federal training-related Dependent Care Allowance, and by increasing the Child Care Expense Deduction several times (Friendly 1994). In the mid-1980s, the federal government adopted a new role in research and demonstration projects through the Child Care Initiatives Fund.

In the 1990s, renewed federal interest in child care was signalled by its inclusion in the 1993 Liberal *Red Book* as an election commitment; the *Red Book* specified a commitment to significantly expand funds for regulated child care (Friendly and Oloman 1996). At the same time as Health and Welfare Canada was restructured into Health Canada and Human Resources Development Canada (HRDC), and regulated child care was assigned to HRDC, early childhood programs other than regulated child care began to emerge through Health Canada's responsibility for young Community Action Program for Children (CAP-C), a 100 lly funded program, was initiated by the federal government 990s, as was a new Aboriginal Head Start program.

Policy Incoherence, Program Fragmentation, and Targeting: The "Least Bang for the Buck"

Historically, regulated Canadian child care has, in general, been viewed primarily as a marketable service, treated as a private commodity to be purchased at the going rate in the marketplace. Within this model, the role of government in Canadian child care has been limited to intervening where the market fails (Cameron 1994). As economists Michael Krashinsky and Gordon Cleveland point out, the market model fails to ensure that either parents or children secure the benefit of funding for child care (1997). It should be noted that other early childhood education and care services – kindergarten and early childhood programs for children at risk – have not been treated as marketable commodities. Cameron suggests that the funding and organizational mechanisms for developing and maintaining child care services are intrinsically connected with the issue of whether child care is viewed as a public good or a marketable commodity: direct public funding and universality is associated with a public-good approach, and payments directly to parents and targeting appropriate to a marketplace approach. "In the case of child care [services], government intervention is directed at those too poor to afford the market costs. It does this through subsidisation of parent fees ... Other than this, the role of government is limited to regulating the private market" (Cameron 1994, 3).

Canada's failure to resolve whether child care is a public good or a marketable commodity means that instead of the adoption of a social policy solution, the existing market model is maintained by default. Without a deliberate, coherent social policy approach, there prevails a policy vacuum in which there is no mechanism to answer the questions "What is child care?" and "Who is it for?" As a result, a confusion of early childhood education and care services, supplemented by direct payments to parents, concentrate on different populations with somewhat different but related purposes. Thus, although child care's multiplicity of goals are met through a variety of services and funding programs, appropriate services are not sufficiently available in most regions; even if they are available, services may be too costly for most parents, have restrictive eligibility requirements, or may be inappropriate from a scheduling point of view to even begin to meet the full range of community needs. Consequently, the array of early childhood education and care services and programs are devised in such a way that Canadians get the "least bang for the buck," as economist and child care policy analyst Ruth Rose has described it (Rose 1997).

Canadian child care resembles what child care policy analysts have called policy incoherence, or, more popularly, a "patchwork quilt" (Lero

1997; Friendly 1997; Child Care Advocacy Association of Canada 1994). Canada's array of disjunctive child care services and programs, goals, and target groups manifest what Moss has described as "three specific discourses about child care" or, to use Moss's term, early childhood services. These discourses, or "silos," are *"the child care for working parents' discourse* used by groups primarily interested in labour market, gender equality and welfare benefits issues, *the nursery education (or kindergarten) for over 3s* used by groups interested in education and child development, and *the day care for children in need discourse"* (Moss 1997, 28 [italics in original]). Moss points out that, individually, each of these three approaches is narrow, restrictive, and thus insufficient. He proposes a fourth discourse, focused more broadly on a holistic view of the needs of young children and their families. This discourse views child care (or early childhood services) as "institutions of cultural, social and economic significance" and "as an important part of the economic and social infrastructure" (Moss 1997, 28). Moss's conception of a fourth discourse advances the idea that inclusive child care programs can enhance social solidarity and cohesion, first, by uniting families of all social strata and cultural origins in common activities related to the well-being of children, and second, by demonstrating to children in early childhood that cooperation among racial and ethnic groups and social classes is possible and valued.

The Social Policy Context of Child Care: Who Is Responsible for Child Care in Canada?

Under Canadian constitutional arrangements, the federal government has no direct jurisdiction over education, health, or social welfare. Although at the time of Confederation, social welfare as we know it did not exist, later the courts assigned the responsibility for developing and administering education, health, and social welfare programs to the provinces/territories.[2] As these programs developed in the years following the Second World War, it became obvious that the provinces did not have the financial resources to meet this responsibility, and grant programs were established to allow the federal government to provide the provinces with the necessary funds. Thus postsecondary education, health care, and social welfare programs have been developed by the provinces and territories using both their own and federal funds; health care and social welfare programs were developed by the provinces within the framework of national policies. It was through the exercise of what was called the "federal spending power" that the federal government had a role in shaping these areas, which were acknowledged to be within exclusive provincial jurisdiction. In this way, child care has generally been viewed as being within the jurisdiction of provincial governments, although it has long been assumed by both federal and provincial governments that the federal government could play a role in shaping child care policy as it has health care. (See Beach, Bertrand, and Cleveland 1998; Cooke et al. 1986; Canada 1994b; Doherty, Friendly, and Oloman 1998).

In the twentieth century, Canadian approaches to social programs have been characterized by two main shifts in perception and treatment. In the nineteenth century, health and education were considered to be private responsibilities; and at the time of Confederation, social welfare had not yet developed as an issue. When there was a need for social assistance outside the nuclear and extended family, it generally fell within the domain of churches; later, non-religious charitable institutions assumed responsibility for assisting the deserving poor and needy. A good example of an early foray into what had previously been in the private realm were mothers' pensions, originally introduced to provide support to needy mothers of young children who were "deserving" because they had been widowed in the First World War (Guest 1990).

The first conceptual shift was that from the original individualistic, family-centred or, at most, charitable view to one of increased collective responsibility. This first shift occurred between the end of the Second World War and the early 1970s, when Canada's main social programs – health care, unemployment insurance, pensions, and social welfare – were emerging. Over this period, governments, both federal and provincial, assumed a major responsibility for these functions, with the federal government assuming a policy-shaping role, and the provinces becoming the program managers and deliverers (Doherty, Friendly, and Oloman 1998).

Most of Canada's health, educational and social programs were developed as universal or inclusive programs (sometimes called "institutional"). National health care, or medicare, is perhaps the best example of the way a social policy has defined its target group as *all* Canadians, rather than the poor or needy; postsecondary, elementary and secondary education, Unemployment Insurance, and Canada Pension were also developed as universal programs.

The main national social program that was designed not as a universal but as a targeted or non-inclusive "residual" program was Canada's main social welfare program, the Canada Assistance Plan. It was introduced by the federal government in 1966 and terminated in 1996. The CAP included provisions for general welfare or social assistance, child welfare, and child care. Its provision of public funding for these services was restricted to those defined as needy or "likely to become needy," reflecting CAP's conception of social welfare as "alleviating or preventing poverty."

The second conceptual shift in Canadian social policy occurred in the 1990s, and, at the end of the 1990s, has come to be described as "the new social union." For child care (and, indeed, for health and social programs generally), the social union has been exemplified by the Canada Health and Social Transfer (CHST), introduced by the federal government in 1996. The CHST replaced the Canada Assistance Plan and Established Programs Financing (EPF); EPF provided federal funds for postsecondary education and health care as a block fund. The end of CAP and the introduction of the CHST formalized the federal government's withdrawal, which had begun in the 1970s, from cost-sharing social programs. The conclusion of federal/provincial/public discussions about the social union is still far from certain, but the kind of model Canadians may expect from provincially driven social programs in a "social union" is previewed by the new National Child Benefit. This is a payment available to low-income families earning up to about $25,000 only if parents are in the labour force (the provinces may "claw back" the payment if parents are relying on social assistance). (For fuller analysis of the effects of the social union on social programs and programs for children, see Boismenu and Jenson 1998; Banting 1998; and Doherty, Friendly, and Oloman 1998.)

The differences between cost-shared programs and block-funded programs have significant implications for services such as child care. The block fund leaves the provinces much freer to spend the funds as they wish, choosing among postsecondary education, health care, and social welfare services. The block-fund mechanism employed by the CHST means an end to the federal government's traditional role in shaping programs under provincial jurisdiction through its use of the "spending power." As the Caledon Institute of Social Policy and others have noted, the federal government's shift from CAP's open-ended cost-sharing to the CHST's block-funding mechanism, together with the substantial cuts to federal funds transferred to the provinces, has had a major impact on the federal government's ability to shape national social programs such as child care (Battle and Torjman 1995).

At the same time, in the 1990s, almost all provincial and territorial governments have retreated from the affirmative role in improving accessibility and quality that many had adopted throughout the 1980s (Friendly and Oloman 1996). As the federal/provincial jurisdictional shift occurred and the federal government cut back on funds, more and more provinces have been either unable or unwilling to finance expansion or even maintenance of child care services. Thus provinces have moved toward an even more targeted and market-driven approach to child care. As child care moved off the agenda (except in Quebec), federal/provincial discussion about child care became focused on the targeted use of Reinvestment Funding, clawed back from social assistance recipients under the National Child Benefit (Boismenu and Jenson 1998). Provincial early childhood education and care programs, never strong, have become more market-driven, more targeted, more fragmented, and in some jurisdictions – Ontario, for example – the responsibility for child care has devolved not only to the local level but also to individual families (Bach and Phillips 1997).

It was not until the 1980s that child care became a national issue, and so during the period of federal leadership in shaping national social programs (from 1945 to the 1970s), it had not yet come onto the public agenda. By the time recognition was given to the benefits of early childhood programs to children's development, and mothers of young children in the paid workforce constituted the majority of those needing care for their young children, fiscal and political factors had begun to militate against the introduction of a potentially expensive social program, or, indeed, by the mid-1990s, any kind of new national social program (Doherty, Friendly, and Oloman 1998). One could say that child care, still in its infancy as a social program, failed to "catch the wave" of federal social policy development in Canada.

Who Does What? Governments, Parents, and Child Care

As the previous sections describe, assumption of responsibility for child care in Canada has undergone two major shifts, with governments first beginning to assume a greater role in child care development and maintenance in the 1980s, and later, in the 1990s, moving away from responsibility.[3] At present, even the limited role of the federal government in sharing some of the provincial child care expenditures for regulated child care for the needy has diminished considerably with the end of the Canada Assistance Plan. Yet although provincial governments have argued throughout the 1990s for more authority for social programs vis-à-vis the federal government, their enthusiasm appears to have diminished as well (Doherty, Friendly, and Oloman 1998). The child care situation across much of Canada today can be characterized by three trends: first, increasing reliance on provincial and territorial governments; second, some provincial and territorial governments downloading responsibility to local or regional governments; and third, devolution of responsibility from federal to not only provincial and local governments, but also to parents (Bach and Phillips 1997).

This section describes in detail aspects of current child care policy across Canada, including service provision, funding, regulation, training, and data and research. One of the most conspicuous aspects of Canadian child care is its significant variation in accessibility and quality of services across the country. As Friendly and Oloman (1996) pointed out, "It is sometimes suggested that provincial variation in child care is an appropriate response to regional variation in conditions as well as in families' and children's needs. If child care had been tailored to meet these needs, diversity might have been a virtue, rather than a shortcoming of Canada's child care situation. However, Canada's regional child care diversity has not developed in response to the local and unique needs of families and communities. Instead, due to differing economic realities and political will, and the absence of a national policy framework, what has developed is disparity and inequity" (274). And as a Senate committee studying child care in the late 1980s observed, "Provincial child care systems resemble each other ... in what they lack." (Standing Senate Committee on Social Affairs, Science and Technology 1988, 1)

There are some things, however, that are common to all provincial and territorial jurisdictions. Each of Canada's ten provinces and two territories has an assortment of early childhood education and care services with regulated child care under provincial or territorial child care legislation and regulations. Although services and programs vary considerably, each jurisdiction has a program of regulated child care services, a scheme of funding arrangements, and a child care policy, whether more or less developed. In all provinces and territories, there are other early childhood services and funds available to parents as well, usually with purposes and approaches that overlap those of regulated child care.

Service and Program Provision

Over the years, each province and territory has developed a variety of early childhood education and child care services:

- All provinces and territories have regulated full- and part-time centre-based and family day care (usually called child care or day care centres and nursery schools or preschools (see Chapter 6). Each jurisdiction has legislation that determines the operating characteristics of these services, including types of services, staff-to-child ratios, group sizes, required early childhood training, physical characteristics, health and safety, and monitoring and enforcement. Some provinces and territories have policy – usually not written policy – that is pertinent to inclusion of or provision of services for children with special needs and Aboriginal communities. Provinces also have funding policies pertaining to capital funding, fee subsidies for low-income families, and operating and salary grants that have an impact on the affordability, availability, and quality of services in that jurisdiction.
- All provinces and territories provide universal kindergarten under ministries of education except Prince Edward Island, where it is regulated as child care. Canadian kindergarten is usually a part-time service (but a full school-day in Quebec since 1998 and in New Brunswick) for all five-year-olds (and some four-year-olds in Ontario and Quebec), for which parents pay no fee. Kindergarten services fall under each jurisdiction's

education act, but attendance at kindergarten is not compulsory in any jurisdiction except New Brunswick. Provincial and territorial governments pay 100 percent of the kindergarten costs, under education ministries; there is no federal funding.

- Community Action Programs for Children (CAP-C) for children at risk are fully funded by Health Canada and established through bilateral federal-provincial/territorial agreements. CAP-C programs have a wide range of priorities, including child development and parent education under a loosely defined federal program. These services are not required to be provincially regulated and do not fall under provincial legislation; nor are they publicly operated.
- Aboriginal Head Start is 100 percent federally funded under Health Canada for Aboriginal children in urban centres and northern communities. It was expanded in 1998 to include services on reserves. Aboriginal Head Start programs include regulated nursery schools, other part-day programs, family resource centres, and other services. Some Aboriginal Head Start programs are provincially regulated under child care legislation.
- Aboriginal on-reserve child care services are federally funded under two separate federal programs (Human Resources Development Canada and Indian and Northern Affairs) for First Nations on reserves and Inuit communities. In some jurisdictions, on-reserve Aboriginal child care is regulated under provincial and territorial legislation. First Nations and Inuit communities have assumed the responsibility for implementing the Human Resources Development Canada First Nations/Inuit Child Care Initiative at the regional level.

Other early childhood education and care services may be specific to particular provinces (e.g., in Ontario, there are many provincially funded family resource centres), and in some provinces, child care or child care–related services that do not fall into any of the above categories but may have some of the same purposes receive support from school boards, local governments, or voluntary agencies. Generally, policy regarding these services is relatively undefined.

In addition to early childhood education and child care services, several funding arrangements direct funds to parents to pay for child care for purposes related to employment, education, or training. These funding schemes ("demand subsidies") include the following:

- the Child Care Expense Deduction (federally and provincially funded tax deduction under the Income Tax Act for employment-related, receipted child care expenses)

- the Dependent Care Allowance (federally funded cash allowance in connection with participation in federally sponsored training programs; now in the process of being devolved to the provinces with labour force training programs)
- other "demand-side" financial supports that may be available to parents for child care regionally. All provinces and territories have "demand subsidy" programs – for example, to support parents in training or involved in workfare, or through student loan programs. No reliable information exists about the amount of these public expenditures, nor how they are spent, but recent key research suggests that the amounts may be considerable (Jane Beach, personal communication 1997).

Public Funding

Although accurate national figures are not available for some of the public expenditures on these programs (for public kindergarten, for example), considerable funds are spent by federal, provincial, and territorial governments; the total has been estimated at more than $3 billion annually (Child Care Advocacy Association of Canada 1994).

Moreover, federal contributions to regulated child care that were, before 1996, visible in the Canada Assistance Plan have become invisible with the introduction of the block-funded Canada Health and Social Transfer. Furthermore, with the development of Health Canada's early childhood development programs and the First Nations/Inuit Child Care Initiative in Human Resource Development, the nature of federal spending for early childhood development and care services has become less coherent than it was previously.

Since the beginning of the 1990s, the regional variation in provincial and territorial policy pertinent to child care funding has become even more pronounced, with most provinces reducing or cancelling operating and salary funding, reducing or limiting fee subsidy arrangements for low-income families, and/or reducing regulation. At the same time, one jurisdiction, Quebec, has introduced and implemented policy designed to consolidate disjunctive early childhood education and child care services and make them accessible to more families through public funding policy. (For detailed information about each province and territory and its arrangements for regulated child care, and Quebec's new child care program, see Childcare Resource and Research Unit 1997, and in press).

Note, too, that in Canada most spending for regulated child care is not public, but private spending by parents through parent fees for regulated child care and payment by parents for the unregulated child care arrangements that most parents in the labour force use. Various ways of estimating the parental contribution to early childhood education and care have been attempted; one approach calculates that parents pay the cost of child care for labour force–related purposes (Brit Task Force on Child Care 1991).

Regulation

It is widely accepted, and supported by research, that a good system of regulation is an important contextual component of a policy framework for high-quality child care (Doherty 1995), at least when child care is delivered by the private (voluntary, not-for-profit, or for-profit organizations), rather than the public (government) sector. Cameron (1994) suggests that when child care is publicly operated, as it is in Western Europe, the public administration of the services is assumed to do the job of regulation. In an environment like that in North America, where the free market prevails as it does in regulated child care, regulation by government – using licensing or permitting to signal compliance with minimum standards – is appropriate. Child care centres are subject to regulation in every province and territory, although not all nursery schools are. Kindergarten in almost every province and territory (except Prince Edward Island where, as mentioned above, it is regulated as child care) is publicly operated under school boards and under each jurisdiction's Education Act. Some of the early childhood education and care services provided in Canada, however, are neither regulated nor publicly provided; CAP-C, funded by Health Canada, is not required to be regulated, nor is it publicly operated. Aboriginal Head Start services are not publicly operated.

The management and delivery of regulated child care programs are considered to be a provincial responsibility. Thus each of the provinces and the two territories has specific legislation that includes

- funding arrangements
- a legislated set of standards for the provision of care
- a mechanism for monitoring whether the standards are met
- a mechanism for enforcing compliance with the standards.

The standards set by each jurisdiction are concerned with detailed aspects of the provision of child care including staff-to-child ratios, group size, staff qualifications, physical indoor and outdoor environment, and health and safety. (For detailed information about each province's child care regulations, see Childcare Resource and Research Unit 1997, and in press). The standards, monitoring, and enforcement established by provincial and territorial child care regulations are assumed to set a minimum baseline standard, not to ensure high quality; it is generally agreed that Canadian child care standards are considered to be less than adequate as minimum standards (Doherty et al. 1995).

Training and the Profession

Early childhood specific training and education has been demonstrated as being key to the provision of high-quality child care (Doherty 1995) (see Chapter 2). Generally, most pre-service early childhood training in Canada is at the postsecondary level, usually in community colleges, or in Quebec, in CEGEPs. There are a small number of undergraduate university programs available, and a very limited number of postgraduate certificates and postgraduate degree programs (see Chapter 2). In several provinces, there are private, not-for-profit early childhood training programs and in a few provinces, proprietary or for-profit early childhood education training companies (Beach, Bertrand, and Cleveland 1998).

Thus early childhood training, like other postsecondary education, falls within provincial jurisdiction and, like other college and university programs, is funded both by provincial governments and by the federal government, now through the Canada Health and Social Transfer's block fund described earlier. Two research studies carried out in 1997 suggest that federal and provincial cutbacks to postsecondary education have begun to limit access to early childhood training programs (Doherty, Friendly, and Oloman, 1998).

Conclusion

This chapter has considered several questions about child care as a social policy issue. It has, first, discussed what social policy is, and why and how a social policy approach, in contrast to a market approach, applies to child care as a public good. It suggests that the absence of a national, pan-Canadian policy for early childhood care and education is the single key factor that has shaped the way these programs have developed in Canada. It examines the policy vacuum that has developed in Canada in the absence of such a policy, and describes the disparate, often disjunctive, array of services, programs, and policies (federal, provincial, and local) that have emerged in the vacuum.

The author suggests that the emerging, decentralized federal and provincial arrangements known as the social union are likely to militate against the emergence of coherent child care policy. If one wanted to take a perspective contrary to this point of view, it could be argued that a national policy exercise led by the federal government is only one of a variety of ways in which effective, coherent child care policy could develop. A 1998 policy research study considered that possibility and arrived at five options, each with associated strengths and weaknesses for ways in which a national child care policy could emerge:

- *Option 1.* Each province and territory develops its own approach without federal involvement (the status quo).
- *Option 2.* The federal government takes a leadership role and uses its spending power to shape provincial and territorial programs with Canada-wide principles (the approach applied in a limited way under the Canada Assistance Plan and under discussion until 1995).
- *Option 3.* The provincial, territorial, and federal governments collaborate as equal partners to develop a Canada-wide framework (the model that developed the National Child Tax Benefit, an income program not a service).
- *Option 4.* The provinces and territories, in the absence of the federal government, work together to develop a Canada-wide approach.
- *Option 5.* One province undertakes a strong child care initiative, thus setting an example for the rest of Canada. The federal government contributes to the program's cost, and eventually, other provinces follow suit (the first part of this option has been undertaken by Quebec, acting unilaterally. However, the federal government has not contributed to the program's cost nor have the other provinces, to date, showed signs of following suit).

The study concluded that the status quo is unlikely to produce a child care system that would be able to support national objectives across Canada. Any of the other options would require considerable cooperation, commitment, and teamwork by federal, provincial, and territorial governments to create a child care system that meets national objectives (Doherty, Friendly, and Oloman 1998). As was pointed out earlier in this chapter, however, neither the federal government nor the provinces have demonstrated these characteristics vis-à-vis child care in the late 1990s.

In Canada today, however, there is broad agreement among experts, policy makers and practitioners that public investment in children in their early years is vital to our collective future. Groups as diverse as trade unions, the health care community, educators, and anti-poverty groups recognize that healthy development in the early years sets the stage for readiness to learn, lifelong good health and well-being, and competent citizenship. The early years are especially critical for establishing healthy development because the learning curve is highest at this stage of life. Thus investment at this time is likely to yield the greatest returns. At the same time, it is recognized that multiple social goals – fostering healthy development, supporting parents in the labour force, alleviating child poverty, developing a healthy economy, and furthering women's equality – can be attained through well-conceived early childhood education and care programs (Campaign Child Care 1993; Canada 1994a). Clearly, it can be argued that assurance of high-quality early childhood education and care services is an issue of national importance that is in the public interest and that should be met through coherent social policy. Furthermore, our inability to provide children and families with this assurance presents a problem of significance for all of us. At the turn of the new millennium, the challenge to Canada will be to solve this problem by devising a coherent solution.

Notes

1 Discussion of child care within a social policy framework almost invariably leads to the question "What is child care?" It seems most useful to answer this question and to assign definitions to the words prior to analyzing child care as a social policy issue. If the term "early childhood education and care" or "early childhood development service" had been used, the historical "silos" that have developed over the years in Canada (and in the United States too) and that encompass day care, kindergarten, Head Start, and other early childhood services might not have developed. The Canadian situation is further complicated by the presence of several schemes that provide funds to parents so that (presumably) they can purchase their own child care. The situation of service and policy incoherence and the assortment of policy objectives associated with the various programs are analyzed in the chapter. This having been said, for consistency with current usage, the term "child care" is used in this chapter to refer to regulated centre-based full- and part-time services and provincially regulated family day care services unless it is otherwise specified.

2 It should be noted that at the time that education was assigned to the provinces as a responsibility, there was really no concept of "early childhood education." Thus, it can be argued that early childhood education is, de facto, a provincial responsibility. Historically, kindergarten has been part of provincial education systems (except in the case of Prince Edward Island, which instead provides kindergarten within the regulated child care system under the Ministry of Health and Community Services. Parents pay fees as they do for other child care services).

3 At the beginning of the new century, the political terrain for child care may be shifting again. The federal government and the provinces have embarked on development of a National Children's Agenda, which will mark the 2000 federal budget as a "children's budget." Expectations for child care have risen and early education care and education have returned to the public and political agenda. A more detailed analysis of child care and the National Children's Agenda can be found in Friendly (1999).

References

Akyeampong, E. 1988. *Women wanting work, but not looking due to child care demands.* Household Survey Division: The labour force, 123-9. Ottawa: Canadian Government Publishing Centre.

Bach, S., and S.D. Phillips. 1997. Constructing a new social union: Child care beyond infancy? In *How Ottawa Spends,* ed. G. Swimmer, 235-58. Ottawa: Carleton University Press.

Banting, K. 1998. Social citizenship and the social union in Canada. *Policy Options.* November, 33-6. Montreal: Institute for Research in Public Policy.

Battle, K., and S. Torjman. 1995. *How finance re-formed social policy.* Ottawa: Caledon Institute of Social Policy.

Beach, J., J. Bertrand, and G. Cleveland. 1998. *Our child care workforce: From recognition to remuneration.* Ottawa: Child Care Human Resources Steering Committee.

Boismenu, G., and J. Jenson. 1998. A social union or a federal state? Intergovernmental

relations in the new Liberal era. In *How Ottawa spends: Balancing act: The post-deficit mandate,* ed. L. Pal, 57-80. Don Mills, ON: Oxford University Press.
British Columbia Task Force on Child Care. 1991. *Showing we care: A child care strategy for the 1990s.* Victoria: Ministry of Government Services.
Bronfenbrenner, U. 1979. *The ecology of human development.* Cambridge, MA: Harvard University Press.
Cameron, B. 1994. *Child care: Whose responsibility? Putting the pieces together: A child care agenda for the 90s,* 18-33. Toronto: Ontario Coalition for Better Child Care.
Campaign Child Care. 1993. Information package. Campaign Child Care, Ottawa.
Canada. 1994a. *Agenda: Jobs and growth. Improving social security in Canada.* Ottawa: Human Resources Development of Canada.
–. 1994b. *Child care and development: A supplementary paper.* Ottawa: Human Resources Development of Canada.
Child Care Advocacy Association of Canada. 1994. *Taking the first steps. Child care: An investment in Canada's future.* A brief to the Standing Committee on Human Resources Development. Halifax, Nova Scotia, December.
Childcare Resource and Research Unit. 1997. *Child care in Canada: Provinces and territories 1995.* Toronto: University of Toronto, Centre for Urban and Community Studies, Childcare Resource and Research Unit.
–. In press. *Early childhood care and education in Canada, 1998.* Toronto: University of Toronto, Centre for Urban and Community Studies, Childcare Resource and Research Unit.
Cleveland, G. and M. Krashinksy. 1998. *The benefits and costs of good child care: The economic rationale for public investment in young children.* Toronto: University of Toronto, Centre for Urban and Community Studies, Childcare Resource and Research Unit.
Cooke, K., J. London, R. Edwards, and R. Rose-Lizee. 1986. *Report of the Task Force on Child Care.* Ottawa: Supply and Services Canada.
Doherty, G. 1995. *Quality matters: Excellence in early childhood programs.* Don Mills, ON: Addison-Wesley.
–. 1996. *The great child care debate: The long-term effects of non-parental child care.* Occasional paper no. 7. Toronto: University of Toronto, Centre for Urban and Community Studies, Childcare Resource and Research Unit.
–. 1997. *Zero to six: The basis for school readiness.* Ottawa: Human Resources Development, Applied Research Branch.
Doherty, G., M. Friendly, and M. Oloman. 1998. *Women's support: women's work: Child care in an era of deficit reduction, devolution, down-sizing and deregulation.* Ottawa: Status of Women Canada.
Doherty G., R. Rose, M. Friendly, D.S. Lero, and S. Irwin. 1995. *Child care: Canada can't work without it.* Occasional paper no. 5. Toronto: University of Toronto, Centre for Urban and Community Studies, Childcare Resource and Research Unit.
Friendly, M. 1994. *Child care policy in Canada: Putting the pieces together.* Don Mills, ON: Addison-Wesley.
–. 1997. What is the public interest in child care? *Policy Options* 18(1):3-6.
–. 1999. *Canary in a coal mine: Child care and Canadian federalism in the 1990s.* Paper presented at Good child care in the 1990s: Preparing the policy map. National conference, 23 May 1999, Toronto. http://www.childcarecanada.org.
Friendly, M., and M. Oloman. 1996. Child care at the centre: Child care on the social, economic and political agenda in the 1990's. In *Remaking Canadian social policy,* ed. J. Pulkingham and G. Ternowsky, 273-85. Halifax: Fernwood Press.
Guest, D. 1990. 2nd ed. *The emergence of social security in Canada.* Vancouver: UBC Press.
Kitchen, B., A. Mitchell, P. Clutterbuck, and M. Novick. 1991. *Unequal futures: The legacies of child poverty in Canada.* Toronto: Child Poverty Action Group and Social Planning Council of Metropolitan Toronto.
Krashinsky, M., and G. Cleveland. 1997. Rethinking the rationale for public funding of child care. *Policy Options* 18(1):16-9.
Lamb, M.E. 1997. Nonparental child care: Context, quality, correlates, and consequences.

In *Child psychology in practice,* I.E. Sigel and K.A. Renninger (vol. eds.), *Handbook of child psychology,* 4th ed., W. Damon (gen. ed.). New York: John Wiley.

Lero, D.S. 1997. Principles for sound child care policy development. *Policy Options* 18(1):38-41.

Moss, P. 1997. Early childhood services in Europe. *Policy Options* 18(1):27-30.

National Crime Prevention Council Canada. 1996. *Preventing crime by investing in families.* Ottawa: National Crime Prevention Council Canada.

National Forum on Health. 1997. *Canada Health Action: Building on the Legacy.* Vol. 1: *Final report of the National Forum on Health.* Vol. 2: *Synthesis reports and issues reports.* Ottawa: Health Canada, National Forum on Health.

Powell, L. 1997. Family behaviour and child care costs: Policy implications. *Policy Options* 18(1):11-5.

Rose, R. 1997. For direct public funding of child care. *Policy Options* 18(1):31-3.

Standing Senate Committee on Social Affairs, Science and Technology. 1988. *Report of the Subcommittee on Day Care.* Ottawa: Standing Senate Committee

Statistics Canada. 1996. *Labour force annual averages.* Household Surveys Division (18-B-29). Ottawa: Author.

United States General Accounting Office. 1994. *Child care: Child care subsidies increase likelihood that low income mothers will work.* Report to the Congressional Caucus for Women's Issues, House of Representatives. Washington, DC: US General Accounting Office.

Zigler, E., and S.J. Styfco. 1994. Is the Perry Preschool better than Head Start? Yes and no. *Early Childhood Research Quarterly* 9:269-87.

Zimmerman, S.L. 1979. Policy, social policy, and family policy: Concepts, concerns, and analytic tools. *Journal of Marriage and the Family* 41(3):487-95.

10

The Business of Child Care: The Issue of Auspice

Susan Prentice

A significant proportion of Canada's licensed child care spaces is operated as profit-making businesses. Commercial care ranges from single owner/operator centres to large chains and franchises traded on major stock exchanges. Today, 30 percent of Canada's 323,000 licensed child care centre spaces are commercial, and the free-enterprise day care industry is lobbying to increase its market share (Prentice 1988). Many provincial governments are increasingly supporting for-profit human services, including child care, and see privatization as a fiscal policy to reduce government spending. Research into quality of care, on the other hand, demonstrates that privatized care is generally of lower quality (see Chapter 6 for a discussion of quality issues). This research has persuaded many early childhood education professionals and most child care advocates that a non-profit child care system is superior. These forces – services, politics, research, and advocacy – have generated a debate over who should be in the business of child care.

The question "Who should be in the business of child care?" is – relatively speaking – a very recent one. Although the specific question about sponsorship has only recently arrived on the policy scene, Canadian parents, politicians, journalists, and others have nevertheless thought about child care for a much longer period. For at least 150 years, they have grappled with the question "Who is responsible for child care?" The answer to this longstanding question has not changed much, despite the many differences between families of the nineteenth and late twentieth centuries. The steady answer is that *parents* are, and should be, responsible for child care.

Until recently, it has been assumed that the answer to "Who should be responsible for child care?" automatically solved the question "Who should pay for child care?" which in turn satisfied those who wondered "Who should be in the business of child care?" In fact, these different dimensions are so closely linked that they are almost invariably conflated into one giant question and tend to be considered as a single debate.

This entanglement is especially problematic today, in an era when social policy is driven by debt and deficit-reduction concerns. In the 1990s, federal and provincial governments have been attracted to policy approaches that rationalize private family responsibility and minimal public spending. In this chapter, I argue that good public policy must desegregate and carefully reconsider the issues of who is responsible for child care, who should pay for child care, and who should be in the business of child care. To disentangle this debate, we must first review the history of child care services in Canada on questions of sponsorship, and place their development in the broader context of Canadian public policy.

The Development of Child Care Services in Canada

Mothers have always worked, many for pay outside the home. Since the earliest days of Confederation (and before), families have required non-parental care for their children. Today, like a century ago, parents rely on older children to mind younger siblings or meet the child care needs of their families through babysitters, relatives, latchkey children, or other ad hoc arrangements. In the 1990s, the need for child care vastly outstrips the supply of licensed group or family home day care: fewer than 1 in 13 children has access to a regulated child care space (Childcare Resource and Research Unit 1994). Today, huge numbers of Canadian families need child care: over 2.8 million children under the age of twelve have mothers in the paid labour force (Childcare Resource and Research Unit 1994). Over 60 percent of Canada's preschool children need care because their parents are in the labour force (Mill, Bartlett-Pawsey, and White 1994). An unknown additional number of non-working parents would also like to use licensed care, either to help them enter the labour market or to support them in their caregiving responsibilities. Corresponding to the growth in demand, the supply of service has increased dramatically over the past two decades. Between 1971 and 1991, the number of regulated child care spaces grew nineteenfold (Friendly 1994). Despite the recent rapid growth in the number of licensed spaces, demand has grown faster and so the supply of regulated child care is even more inadequate today than it was twenty years ago (Friendly 1994).

Conditions and quality of care have improved since the turn of the century, however. The earliest suppliers of group child care were religious and philanthropic societies. In 1858, the Grey Nuns of Montreal opened a *salle d'asile* with the dual purpose of caring for the children of working mothers and of providing religious education. Other centres opened in close succession, supplying custodial care with scant regard for child development (Schulz 1978). Like their counterparts in other countries, Canadian child care centres sprang up as a response to changing social conditions, the pressures of industrialization, and women's need to work outside the home. From the mid-1800s to the middle of this century, group day care service was provided nearly exclusively by educational, philanthropic, or religious organizations (see Chapter 1).

In 1942, at the height of the Second World War, the federal government made a bold intervention with the passage of the Dominion-Provincial Wartime Day Nurseries Agreement. The Act provided 50-50 cost-sharing for child care centres in participating provinces – although only Quebec and Ontario signed on (Pearson 1986). In retrospect, it seems clear that Canada's first (and to date only) national child care act was designed to serve the war effort, not the needs of parents or children. In Ontario, the new cost-shared programs were publicly operated, usually by the municipality but occasionally through voluntary agencies and local groups that received public funding (Prentice 1993). During the war years, auspice or sponsorship status (commercial or non-profit) was not an issue for government or those providing child care.

The federal government stopped funding child care at the end of the war. Ottawa resumed child care spending only in 1966, with the establishment of the Canada Assistance Plan. In the intervening years, numerous nursery schools and child care centres had sprung up independently. By 1968, this pattern of development resulted in three-quarters of Canada's child care centres and nursery schools being commercially operated (Friesen 1995).

Under the 1966 Canada Assistance Plan (CAP), the federal government began to share some costs of child care with provincial and territorial governments for families who were either in need or likely to become in need of the service. Although CAP was not designed explicitly to fund child care services, it was a broad and elastic funding program and could accommodate them. Under both streams of CAP funding, child care was a strictly residual welfare service. Provinces could choose which funding route they preferred, but an important caveat was that under the welfare provision route for families in need, only non-profit and regulated services were eligible for cost-sharing. CAP funds were pivotal to the development of child care in Canada (Friendly 1994).

In 1971, four years after CAP was established, the federal government began to use the income tax system as another vehicle for supporting child care expenses (Friendly 1994). Currently, the Income Tax Act allows the Child Care Expense Deduction, the Young Child Supplement and the Dependent Care Allowance, for both non-profit and commercial child care. Together, these three tax-related benefits to individuals cost approximately

$736 million in 1993-4, almost twice as much as the federal government spent on funding to services through CAP and smaller programs (Canadian Child Care Advocacy Association 1996). Arguments against using tax dollars are widespread and familiar: they benefit high-income rather than low-income earners, do not distinguish between regulated child care and unregulated babysitting, require parents to pay cash up front, and do nothing to increase the supply of service. The federal government's choice of tax-based spending accommodates one of the peculiarities of the political division of power in our federal system: the Canadian government has no direct jurisdiction over education, health, or social services such as child care.

Provinces have the lion's share of control over child care services. Provinces establish the licensing requirements, set the standards and determine which forms of child care are regulated. Across the country, provincial control and discretion have resulted in a patchwork of services. For example, nowhere in Newfoundland is there licensed infant group care or regulated family day care (Child Care Research and Resource Unit 1994). The governments of three provinces directly operate licensed child care centres. Some provinces make direct grants available to child care facilities (such as operating subsidies, start-up, repair and expansion grants, and funding for children with special needs). A few provinces augment child care worker salaries through wage supplement grants or a direct operating grant (e.g., Nova Scotia). Provincial discretion determines whether such funding is restricted to non-profit programs or whether commercial programs are also eligible.

In 1996, the federal government terminated CAP and replaced it with the Canada Health and Social Transfer (CHST). Under CHST, provinces receive a block grant representing the federal government's total contribution to all social service and health care spending. Provinces are free to disburse the block grant to any child care programs they wish to support, whatever their auspice status; provinces are even free to stop funding child care altogether. The total amount of CHST funding to provinces is substantially lower than previous payments through CAP, which means that each province has much less money – a particularly devastating loss to the historically poorer regions of Canada.

Federal funding policies and provincial discretion have produced wide differences in the distribution of non-profit, commercial, and government-operated spaces. In 1993, slightly less than one-third of Canada's 323,000 licensed child care centre spaces were commercial, operated on a for-profit basis (Child Care Research and Resource Unit 1994). The proportion of proprietary child care ranges from a high of 88 percent in Newfoundland to a low of 6 percent in Saskatchewan. Publicly operated day care, found only in Quebec, Ontario, and Saskatchewan, makes up less than nine percent of the total regulated child care spaces in Canada (Child Care Research Resource Unit 1994).

Commercial child care has emerged as a key policy issue for policy analysts and child care advocates, especially in the light of the proprietary sector's willingness to start up badly needed services at minimal or no public cost. Commercial child care has also been the focus of numerous research studies conducted by early child education specialists and others concerned about child development. From across the social sciences, research shows that commercial child care tends to produce lower-quality care for children than non-profit or directly operated public services (see Chapter 6).

The Relationship of Quality of Care to Auspice

Since the first US national study in 1972, research has consistently shown the superiority of non-profit care (Keyersling 1972). On every known index of quality – age-appropriate programming, staff-to-child ratios, health considerations, wages and working conditions, turnover rates, group size, and administration – there are significant differences between the two forms of care, with non-profit care scoring better than commercial care.

One problem emerges with the very definition of what exactly constitutes non-profit or commercial care. Technically speaking, the differences between commercial and non-profit care are legal – that is, whether a program is incorporated as a profit-making business or not. Researchers generally agree that non-profit includes organizations that are incorporated as non-profit or are part of a larger incorporated non-profit organization (like the YWCA's child care programs), and may include services directly operated by government such as municipal child care centres (Friendly 1986). A common factor uniting non-profit centres is that they are legally governed by a board of directors; and some provinces (New Brunswick, Quebec, Manitoba, Saskatchewan, Northwest Territories) mandate parent involvement on the board (Child Care Research and Resource Unit 1994). Nova Scotia, for example, requires that full-time centres hold parent meetings every three months.

By contrast, commercial centres are legal entities that may or may not have a board of directors. Some researchers have noted important grey areas in respect of commercial auspice (Friendly 1994). Potential grey areas relate to both non-profit and commercial programs – for example, a lucrative child care centre operated as a subsidiary of a larger non-profit corporation and whose profit is returned to the large non-profit organization, or a non-profit workplace child care centre operated by an employer. Although the majority of the research literature tends to consider auspice as a straightforward variable, some findings suggest that an equally important factor may be the governance or accountability structure of a program. Various studies hint at the importance of parental involvement in enhancing quality of care (Fuquya and Lagenshoh 1986). For example, a Toronto study found that centres that were officially non-profit but had an owner-appointed board were more similar to commercial centres than to other non-profit centres in terms of the likelihood that they would violate the ratios (West 1988).

Friendly argues that some commercial centres may masquerade as non-profit centres. She cites the concerns of the Special Committee on Child Care, which also noted the problem of operators who "make a nominal switch of auspices to nonprofit status, but retain the essential characteristics of the prior for-profit operation." (Friendly 1994, 239). For example, Wee Watch, a national commercial day care chain has used the tactic of incorporating as non-profit. "For our franchisees, that's no problem," report the owners, "all nonprofit means is that you're incorporated without share capital and all money in excess of expenses must be taken as salary" (McGugan 1989).

Child care can be operated at a significant profit. Profits come from an excess of total revenue (from fees and public monies) over total costs (salaries, rent, equipment, food, etc.). Fees tend to be relatively fixed, since there is a limit to the amount parents can pay and what the current market will bear. To generate profits, commercial operators must therefore lower costs, and the major cost in child care is wages – which are directly linked to quality of care for children and quality of work experience for staff (see Chapter 8). In a non-profit centre, labour constitutes a significantly higher proportion of costs than in commercial centres – 77 percent of the total versus only 63 percent, according to one study (Mukerjee and Witte 1993). Profits in commercial programs can be as high as 25 to 30 percent of total revenue, or even higher (Ross 1978). The *Calgary Herald* once calculated that a 100 percent profit margin was possible (Friendly 1994).

Economic logic predicts that profits are achieved through sacrificing quality. William Pierce argues that it is quite simple: "All other things being equal, it simply costs more, or one must deliver less, if one offers the same thing at the same price as a competitor who need not show a profit" (Pierce 1975, 101). For-profit organizations have both "legal sanction and motivation" to exploit customers (Phillips, Howes, and Whitebook 1992). Early childhood education research has indicated that the main criteria of quality include staff-to-child ratios, group size, consistency of staffing, and caregiver education and training. Other evidence of quality may include working conditions (including remuneration), licensing violations, and parental involvement.

Three major Canadian studies in the 1980s determined that commercial care tended to fare poorly when measured on staff-to-child ratios, turnover rates, and quality of programming (SPR Associates 1986). A Calgary study showed that over half of commercial centres but only 15.4 percent of non-profit centres were rated as providing poor quality; furthermore, over 60 percent of non-profit centres were rated as providing good care versus only 15.6 percent of commercial centres (Friesen 1995). Research in the Atlantic region also showed significant differences in quality rating between commercial and non-profit centres (Lyon and Canning 1995).

Friendly's 1986 review of regulations and standards relating to group size and staff-to-child ratios revealed that commercial programs regularly failed to meet or, more frequently, just met the minimum requirements; non-profit and directly operated programs, on the other hand, more regularly met or exceeded the minimum standards. In a study of Metropolitan Toronto, West (1988) reported that "grey area" and commercial centres had significantly higher average total capacities than non-profit centres with parent boards of directors. US research showed that commercial programs are more likely to be large overall, and in particular are more likely to have larger preschool groups than non-profit day care centres (Sassen and Avrin 1974; Phillips, Howes, and Whitebook 1992). In terms of child-to-staff ratios, Friendly (1986) reported that low-quality centres (all of which were for-profit programs) showed poorer ratios than high-quality care. West (1988) argued that commercial centres were "more likely to have staff-child ratio violations than non-commercially operated centres" and had a "higher average number of months short the required number of ECE staff and assistant staff than non-commercially operated centres" (1).

As a condition of licensing, all centres are required to meet or exceed minimum standards. Whereas non-profit child care regularly meets or exceeds government regulations, commercial child care more frequently fails to meet legislative standards (Maxwell 1992). A major Canadian study found that 80 percent of government-operated centres and 50 percent of non-profit centres exceeded basic regulations versus 32 percent of independent commercial centres and only 29 percent of commercial chains (SPR Associates 1986). West's 1988 study in Toronto revealed that commercial centres were less likely to meet legislative requirements and were consequently more likely to receive a more restrictive type of licence than non-profit centres. In addition, commercial centres were more likely to have spaces that were not licensed because of lack of staff and/or equipment than non-profit centres. Commercial centres, moreover, had significantly higher than average total visits and monitoring visits by program advisors than other types of operators, and were more likely to have a complaint lodged against them than any other type of operator. "Roughly 54 percent (over half) of commercially operated centres had a violation, while only 15 percent of non-profit parent/community board operated centres had a violation" (West 1988). The Toronto study showed that only 13 percent of commercial centres had a clear licence (West 1988). In Edmonton, a survey by city health inspectors "showed almost half the commercial centres were not giving the children adequate care" (Ross 1978). In Quebec, investigators upheld complaints made in 9.7 percent of the commercial centres versus only 1.9 percent of complaints against non-profit centres (Doherty 1991). The Quebec Office des services de garde à l'enfance reported that most complaints they receive are lodged against commercial establishments.

The United States is one of the few other industrialized countries, in addition to Canada, that supports a for-profit child care sector. US data is revealing since there is much wider variation in public regulations between states than between Canadian provinces. US research shows that quality differentials are most dramatic in states with the most lax regulations. States with more demanding licensing standards have fewer poor-quality centres (Cost, Quality, and Child Outcomes Team 1995). Interestingly, large child care chains (whose reputations are made on standardization) avoid states with weak regulations, because "the economics simply don't work out," according to one industry analyst (Neugebauer 1996). The difficulty for large child care corporations is that independent commercial centres or small chains can make a competitive advantage of lax state regulations; large chains that operate in a standardized way across several states must meet the highest standards, and hence are more expensive.

In the United States, where centres receiving publicly subsidized children must meet federal as well as state standards, more non-profit than commercial centres enrol subsidized children. This income-segregated system has a number of corollaries: studies reveal that over half the children in non-profit centres live in single-parent households, and most of them are visible minorities. In 75 percent of commercial centres, more than three-quarters of children were white. In acknowledging this income- and race-segregated system, one analyst takes comfort in the observation that needy children are at least benefiting from the best ratios in the industry (Kagan 1991).

Wide discrepancies exist within commercial care (SPR Associates 1986). While commercial day care consistently scores lower in quality than non-profit day care, small owner-operated commercial day care experiences the wildest fluctuations in quality. Chain day care (like franchised fast food) offers a standardized and often higher quality of care than small commercial centres. Evidence that owner-operated "Mom and Pop" operations may be the least safe places for children flies in the face of much commonly accepted wisdom. Most critics of commercial care reserve their harshest criticism for chain, franchised care, and tend to be less concerned about single-owner centres. Evidence suggests this criticism should be precisely inverted: in the strictest terms of quality, chain day care is not the most troubling.

Since the quality of care rests so heavily on the staff-child relationship, important indexes of quality can be found by examining staffing issues. Here again, commercial child care emerges as inferior to non-profit care. The Canada-wide *Caring for a Living* study found that fewer than 50 percent of caregivers in commercial centres had a certificate or diploma in early childhood education versus 75 percent in government-operated programs and 57 percent in other non-profit centres (Doherty 1993). An Alberta study showed that non-profit centres had both more trained staff and fewer untrained staff than commercial centres (Friesen 1995). US studies reveal the same pattern of superior training and education among staff of non-profit centres.

Another important axis of quality concern is the turnover rate (see Chapter 8). Low turnover rates ensure caregiver consistency – a key determinant of high-quality care. Further, "a system with high staff morale and cohesiveness and low staff turnover is likely to provide consistently better care for its children" (Sassen and Avrin 1974). Research shows higher staff turnover rates in commercial than in non-profit programs, for reasons related to working conditions, job-related decision making, and job structures. A Canadian study reports that turnover rates are 5 percent higher in for-profit programs than in non-profit programs (Friendly 1986). One US study concluded: "Turnover rates were highest for staff in private proprietary centres, which are the ones with the poorest ratios, worst reported working conditions, fewest benefits, and most stated tension. The high degree of tension in proprietary centres may well be a response to the high rate of turnover, as well as a cause of it" (Whitebook et al. 1982, 222).

Child care staff earn significantly lower salaries in commercial centres than in non-profit centres. A 1992 national Canadian study determined that the national average wage was $8.07 per hour in commercial centres compared with $10.07 per hour in non-profit care and $13.88 per hour in publicly operated centres (Maxwell 1992). The commercial sector also offers lower levels of benefits and fewer professional development opportunities than the non-profit sector (Baynham and Russell 1986). A 1994 Quebec study reported that staff in commercial day care centres earned an average of 20 percent less than staff in non-profit centres (despite similar education and experience), cost per week was significantly higher than in non-profit centres, and overall quality was much lower (Mill, Bartlett-Pawsey, and White 1994). The same study showed that child care staff in commercial centres reported significantly more job concerns, fewer job rewards, and less supervisor support than staff in non-profit centres. Like Canadian commercial care, proprietary US services are also characterized by high annual turnover rates, poor working conditions, caregivers who are less satisfied with their jobs, lower levels of caregiver education, and harsher care (Doherty 1991).

The degree of worker participation – or workplace democracy – also varies by auspice and unionization rates. Unionization rates are consistently highest in directly operated programs and lowest in commercial programs. The Association of Early Childhood Educators of Ontario concluded that "unionization is often a positive factor in the area of wages and work experience" (Baynham and Russell 1986, 24). Working in a commercial centre has a negative effect on job satisfaction, according to one study, which found staff in commercial centres had less paid and unpaid time for program planning or preparation compared with workers in the non-profit sector (Baynham and Russell 1986, 22).

The empirical data conclusively demonstrate that for-profit status is associated with inferior quality. Prominent Canadian researcher Martha Friendly (1986) states definitively that "for-profit status is a main predictor of poorer quality." She concludes that there is a definite "distribution skew in the continuum of program quality." While both commercial and non-profit day care varies in quality, commercial care is disproportionately represented in poor-to-fair quality care, and non-profit care is disproportionately represented in good-to-superior quality care. It is apparent from a survey of the research literature on quality that commercial care generally fails the test of providing the most developmentally appropriate service for children and their families. Even aside from philosophical questions about the ethics of commercialization, these findings cause most child care advocates to support non-profit care.

Politics, Policy, and Free Enterprise Child Care

Provinces develop, monitor, and enforce provincial child care regulations within the specific framework of that province. The differences that characterize Canada's child care system are reflected in provincial variations with regard to regulations, monitoring, and enforcement. Regulations such as those concerning training requirements, ratios, group size, and parental involvement vary widely across the country. Further research shows there is a correspondence between low standards, weak monitoring, and the proportion of commercial child care centres, just as there tends to be an association between high levels of commercial care and low staff salaries. Moreover, provinces with strong requirements for parental involvement generally have a lower proportion of commercial care, both cause and effect of the policy (Ferguson and Prentice 1999).

In Newfoundland and Alberta, the two Canadian provinces with the highest percentage of commercial care (at 88 percent and 65 percent, respectively, of the total regulated centre-based spaces), regulations are relatively lax (Child Care Research and Resource Unit 1994). In Alberta, child care centre directors are required to have only the equivalent of a two-year community college early childhood education certificate (Childcare Resource and Research Unit 1994). One in four staff is required to have the equivalent to a one-year certificate; the remaining 75 percent of staff are required to have only a fifty-hour orientation course. Staff who work with special-needs children are not required to have additional training. There are no requirements for regulated family day care providers. In 1991, the mean hourly wage of staff in Alberta child care centres was $6.76. Alberta has no statutory requirement for parent involvement on boards of directors. Newfoundland has no licensed infant group care, no regulated family day care, no specified role for parent involvement, and the lowest mean hourly wage for staff of any province in Canada at $6.03 (Child Care Research and Resource Unit 1994). Alberta permits a maximum centre size of eighty spaces, with infant ratios of 1:3 in day care centres, 1:5 in drop-in centres, and 1:6 in nursery schools.

By way of contrast, Saskatchewan (at 6 percent) and Manitoba (at 10 percent) have the lowest proportion of commercial child care in Canada. Manitoba requires that all staff must be at least eighteen years old and have first-aid training. Two-thirds of a centre's staff must have a minimum of a one-year certificate program in early childhood education, and supervisors must have a two-year degree or advanced certificate and a minimum of one year's experience. In both occasional and full-day preschool centres, ratios for infants are 1:3. Licensed family day care providers must have taken first-aid and CPR courses; they are screened for any criminal record and their personal references are checked. In Saskatchewan, supervisors must have at least a one-year certificate in child care or equivalent, and 100 percent of staff must either hold a one-year certificate in child care (or equivalent) or take a 130-hour child care orientation course provided through regional community colleges. All Saskatchewan staff working with children who have special needs must have additional training. Mean hourly wages in Manitoba are $9.29 per hour and $7.52 per hour in Saskatchewan (Child Care Research and Resource Unit 1994).

How can these differences be explained? A key difference between provinces is their approach to funding commercial care: some provinces restrict public funds to non-profit services, whereas others make funds available to commercial centres as well. In the mid-1970s, the Saskatchewan provincial government passed legislation to prohibit the expansion of commercial care (Ross 1978). Alberta's policy, by contrast, created a level playing field so there is no distinction in any way between commercial or non-profit programs. In jurisdictions where proprietary services are eligible for funding, we find a greatly increased percentage of commercial care. When commercial day care centres receive ongoing operating funds, their profitability is greatly enhanced. This lucrative environment for day care results in the expansion of commercial services. In such provinces, commercial operators tend to be well organized as a lobby group, thereby being both cause and consequence of the province's policy of supporting commercial care. Where commercial operators have organized to lobby for access to public funding and more profitable standards, regulatory standards tend to be lower.

Profit-making day care is thus doubly troublesome: as well as providing lower quality of care along every index, it prompts the growth of the politically powerful free-enterprise day care lobby. In the United States, the commercial sector has traditionally opposed state and federal efforts to upgrade child care regulations, thereby "adding to the potential negative effects of privatization on the quality of care" (Phillips, Howes, and Whitebook 1992, 48). Ontario and Alberta provide the clearest and best-documented Canadian examples of this tendency. The high degree of commercial care in Alberta is directly attributable to policy that made both commercial and non-profit programs eligible for a direct operating grant. One commentator has noted about the role of commercial day care operators in Alberta: "The government has acceded to the lobbying of the independent operators that the raising of standards be supported by appropriate funding increases. It is perhaps the essence of the free enterprise position to seek *maximum* government subsidies, combined with *minimum* government control or interference in day-to-day operations" (Ontario Coalition for Better Daycare 1987, 3). Several examples illustrate the political power of the free-enterprise day care lobby in Ontario. In 1974, the province proposed changes to the Day Nurseries Act, through a series of measures known as the Birch proposals, after provincial secretary for social development, Margaret Birch. The province was secretive about how the proposed regulatory changes were developed, although the *Globe and Mail* reported, on 31 July 1974, that "members of the Task Force have stated that they agreed to ease regulations after being lobbied by large, private operators." A key player defending corporate interests in free-enterprise day care was John Christiansen (a former Conservative minister in Manitoba), president of Mini-Skool, a small commercial chain. Mini-Skool organized a pressure group that eventually became the Association of Day Care Operators of Ontario (ADCO) (Ross 1978).

ADCO was formed in 1977 when a group of operators realized "that the growing voice of certain groups who would like to see all Child Care operations completely Government operated, could soon falsely taint the public's image of private operators. Unless they spoke out as a group, they could be seen as uncaring, profit-oriented entrepreneurs" (ADCO 1987, 3). ADCO is primarily a lobby group to "promote and defend" proprietary day care. ADCO has a number of goals. Among them are the following:

- to present a strong and united voice for everyone involved in commercial child care services in the day care community
- to promote and safeguard the interests of proprietary tax-paying providers of child care
- to assist legislative, regulatory, standard-setting, and other Government or private bodies in the development of laws, regulations and policies affecting Child Care services in Ontario and Canada
- to enhance the development of Child Care services with caring, responsible, logical and economical management policies (ADCO 1987, ii).

ADCO declared, "Today, we are one of the leading voices of child care advocates in this country" (Canadian Child Care Management Association 1986). Its national counterpart is the Canadian Child Care Management Association (CCCMA). CCCMA defines itself as a "national association representing the free enterprise system of child care services throughout Canada" (ADCO 1987). Its motto is "Your bottom line is our bottom line." The free-enterprise lobby finds an ally in a well-known conservative think tank, the Fraser Institute, which argues that subsidized day care "distorts private decisions" and household choices, as well as "distorting labour market participation decisions" (Carr 1987).

More evidence of the political influence of the commercial lobby can be seen in Ontario's 1987 New Directions policy. One aspect of the new policy was a direct operating grant to centres, a response to user fees, a Catch-22 situation in which fees must rise if day care worker wages are to increase. Under the 1987 Ontario policy, commercial centres were made eligible for the direct operating grant, although the new grant was restricted to existing commercial centres. Commercial operators received only 50 percent of the grant for which non-profit centres were eligible, owing to CAP restrictions on services eligible for cost-sharing between the two levels of government. In the absence of matching federal dollars, Ontario chose to provide only its 50 percent share to proprietary centres. Mini-Skools Ltd., a division of Kinder-Care Inc., was "stopped dead in [its] tracks," according to one business magazine report, and decided against expansion in Ontario. According to the Toronto district manager, "it would be tough to compete against people who were getting government support" (McGugan 1989). The commercial sector bitterly protested its lesser eligibility, but the fact that they received any public support at all is testimony to their effective lobbying.

In late 1996, under the leadership of Conservative Premier Harris, Ontario again proposed changes to its child care regulations (Rudd and Rothman 1996). The province moved to lower staff-to-child ratios, reduce staff wages (through elimination of a wage supplement grant instituted by the former NDP provincial government), and decrease monitoring. In an unprecedented move, the province agreed to permit public funds to go the building of centres owned by commercial operators. Taxpayers will thus subsidize the capital assets of small businesses. Ontario will now permit publicly funded fee subsidies to be spent on unlicensed programs and babysitters (Ontario Federation of Labour Women's Committee 1996). With lower ratios, reduced monitoring, and increased access to scarce public funding, commercial operators can be predicted to increase their presence and market share in Ontario.

The commercial day care sector's business interests meshed neatly with the pro-business approach of the reigning Conservative Ontario government. This meshing of corporate interests and public policy is providing increasingly fortuitous opportunities for promoters of for-profit human services. The pro-free-enterprise alignment means that advocacy organizations, which argue against privatization (in child care, as well as other human services, such as health care), are unlikely to be successful in persuading governments to promote non-profit child care even though it provides better quality, greater fiscal accountability, and more efficient use of public dollars. US child care researchers Kate Ellis and Rosalind Petchesky noted this trend over twenty years and predicted the following: "We should expect, therefore, to see an increased partnership between business and government ... with private expenditures underwritten by government subsidization and encouraged by government contracts. Indeed, it would seem this 'partnership' is already the dominant pattern in the financing of social welfare programs, even while the media are transmitting the message that 'the private sector' is dipping into its own pocket ('because we care') to lend a hand in alleviating 'social ills'" (Ellis and Petchesky 1972). As they point out, this ideology of "partnership" conceals the characteristic way in which neo-liberal governments operate on the home front, "underwriting corporate investments and risks with public revenue, and at the same time delegating policy-making and administrative authority to the same special interests that reap high profits from the programs underwritten."

Conclusion

How one answers the question "Who should be in the business of child care?" is connected to a much larger set of concerns. Beliefs about whether child care should be operated commercially are connected to a cluster of other attitudes, including ideas about whom child care is for and who should pay for it. Elsewhere I have demonstrated that those who support commercial care are also likely to believe that child care should be targeted to needy children instead of universally available, that public funds should not be provided for universally accessible child care, and that child care funds should be paid to parents through the tax system (Prentice 1987).

On the one hand, rigorous research into early childhood education demonstrates conclusively that non-profit care is superior in quality, offers better wages and working conditions, and experiences lower staff turnover. On the other hand, there is political and public resistance to reducing or eliminating the commercial sector. Instead, a more prevalent tendency in Canadian public policy is to promote a level playing field and hence invite a commercial sector. This promotion takes place despite research evidence showing that where legislation discourages commercial child care, the proportion of proprietary care is lower and the quality of care is higher; where legislation supports commercial child care, the proportion of proprietary care is higher and the quality is lower. Moreover, in pro-corporate provinces that are sympathetic to commercial care, the commercial sector tends to form a well-organized lobby, which further entrenches its interests. Across Canada and in the United States, jurisdictions with a high percentage of commercial child care are associated with poor staff-to-child ratios, larger group size, low educational requirements for staff, and inferior physical and administrative environments in comparison with jurisdictions with a low percentage of commercial care. It is thus hard to avoid the conclusion that public policy is an intensely political phenomenon.

"If provision of high-quality care for children is a goal, the promotion of child care-for-profit is a false solution," asserts Martha Friendly (1994). Provincial and federal policies that support for-profit care are not based on the best interests of children, their parents, or child care staff. Such policies instead are premised on the belief that child care is simply a market good that can be bought and sold like any other commodity. Evidence shows that few governments seem troubled by the fact that their legislation condones or even promotes poor-quality care. Some proponents of commercial care contend that parents who are dissatisfied can simply shop for better care. Because there are so few licensed child care spaces in the country, parents are rarely free to shop for higher-quality care. This dilemma is magnified in provinces such as Alberta, where two out of every three spaces are commercial. The free market of child care is, therefore, not a realm of free choice, and arguments about consumer choice are misleading.

The problem rests with the very connection of child care with the market. In a system where child care is only a market commodity, parents and children are simply consumers, and caregiving by staff is merely a labour cost. If Canadians conceived of child care as a public good and a public investment, we would see very different policy orientations – the relationships would be ones of community-building, citizenship, and entitlement. Child care would then be seen as a right, much as we see health care and education as a right of all Canadians. Child care as a universal public good would lead to a fundamental reordering of claims in our society. In such a society, the answer to the question "Who should be in the business of child care?" would be that child care should not be a business at all – it is far too important to be left to the market.

References

ADCO (Association of Day Care Operators of Ontario). 1987. *Deputation to the Select Committee on Health.* Toronto.

Baynham, P., and L. Russell. 1986. *Wages and work experience survey of child care staff in an Ontario community.* Toronto: Association of Early Childhood Educators of Ontario.

Canadian Child Care Advocacy Association. 1996. Federal child care spending, 1993-1997. *Vision* 22:5.

Canadian Child Care Management Association. 1986. *Deputation to the Special Committee on Child Care.*

Carr, J. 1987. *The daycare dilemma.* Vancouver: Fraser Institute.

Childcare Resource and Research Unit. 1994. *Child care in Canada: Provinces and territories, 1993.* Toronto: University of Toronto, Centre for Urban and Community Studies.

Cost, Quality, and Child Outcomes Team. 1995. *Cost, quality, and child outcomes in child care centres.* Denver: University of Colorado, Economics Department.

Doherty, G. 1991. *Factors related to quality in child care: A review of the literature.* Toronto: Ministry of Community and Social Services.

–. 1993. *Quality child care: Contextual factors.* Prepared for the Canadian Child Care Federation, Toronto.

Ellis, K., and R. Petchesky. 1972. Children of the corporate dream: An analysis of daycare as a political issue under capitalism. *Socialist Revolution* 2(6):22.

Ferguson, E., and S. Prentice. 1999. Parent involvement in child care: The Canadian example. In *Early childhood landscapes: Cross-national perspectives on empowerment and restraint,* ed. J. Hayden. New York: Peter Lang.

Friendly, M. 1986. *Daycare-for-profit: Where does the money go?* Toronto: Parliamentary Committee on Child Care.

–. 1994. *Child care policy in Canada: Putting the pieces together.* Don Mills, ON: Addison-Wesley.

Friesen, B. 1995. *A sociological examination of the child care auspice debate.* Occasional paper no. 6. Toronto: University of Toronto, Centre for Urban and Community Studies, Childcare Resource and Research Unit.

Fuquya, R., and D. Lagenshoh. 1986. Parents as consumers of child care. *Family Relations* 35(2):295-303.

Kagan, S. 1991. Examining profit and nonprofit child care: An odyssey of quality and auspice. *Journal of Social Issues* 47(2):87-104.

Keyersling, M.D. 1972. *Windows on daycare: A report based on findings of the National Council of Jewish Women.* New York: National Council of Jewish Women.

Lyon, M., and P. Canning. 1995. *Atlantic day care study.* Halifax: Department of National Health and Welfare.

McGugan, I. 1989. Franchised referrals ease day care dilemma. *Small Business* 8(11):14-20.

Maxwell, A. 1992. Auspice in CCDCF/FCSGE. *Interaction* 6(2):18-21.

Mill, D., N. Bartlett-Pawsey, and D. White. 1994. Profit and nonprofit daycare: A comparison of quality, caregiver behavior and structural features. Concordia University, Department of Psychology, *Research Bulletin* 13(3).

Mukerjee, S., and A. Witte. 1993. Provision of child care: Cost functions for profit-making and not-for-profit day care centres. *Journal of Productivity Analysis* 4:141-57.

Neugebauer, R. 1996. How's business? Status report #9 on for-profit child care. *Child Care Information Exchange* 108:60-9.

Office des services de garde à l'enfance. n.d. *Executive summary: Profit-making daycare centres and nonprofit day care centres. Towards an evaluation of quality.* [Translation]. Ontario: Child Care Branch.

Ontario Coalition for Better Day Care. 1987. *Newsletter* 3.

Ontario Federation of Labour Women's Committee. 1996. *Women's Rights Bulletin* 1.

Pearson, R. 1986. *They're still women after all: The Second World War and Canadian womanhood.* Toronto: McClelland and Stewart.

Phillips, D., C. Howes, and M. Whitebook. 1992. The social policy context of child care: Effects on quality. *American Journal of Community Psychology* 20:25-51.

Pierce, W. 1975. Profiting from day care. In *Rationale for child care services: Programs vs. politics,* ed. S. Auerbach and J.A. Rivaldo, 91-110. New York: Human Sciences Press.

Prentice, S. 1987. The politics of care: Child care in Ontario. Master's thesis, York University.

–. 1988. Kids are not for profit: The politics of profit-making daycare. In *Social movements, social change: The politics and practice of organizing,* ed. F. Cunningham, S. Findlay, M. Kadar, A. Lennon, and E. Silva, 98-128. Toronto: Between the Lines.

–. 1993. Militant mothers in domestic times: Toronto's postwar daycare struggle. Ph.D. diss., York University, Toronto.

Ross, A. 1978. Corporate care. In *Good day care: Fighting for it, getting it, keeping it,* ed. K. Gallagher Ross, 89-96. Toronto: Women's Press.

Rudd, K., and L. Rothman. 1996. Ontario report: Child care is under attack. *Visions* 22:9.

Sassen, G., and C. Avrin. 1974. Corporate child care. *Second Wave* 3(3):21-144.

Schulz, P. 1978. Day care in Canada: 1850-1962. In *Good day care: Fighting for it, getting it, keeping it,* ed. K. Gallagher Ross, 137-58. Toronto: Women's Press.

SPR Associates. 1986. *An exploratory review of selected issues in for-profit versus not-for-profit child care.* Prepared for the Special Committee on Child Care, Ottawa.

West, S. 1988. *A study on compliance with the Day Nurseries Act at full time child care centres in Metropolitan Toronto.* Toronto: Ministry of Community and Social Services.

Whitebook, M., C. Howes, R. Darrah, and J. Friedman. 1982. Caring for caregivers: Staff burnout in child care. In *Current topics in early childhood education,* ed. K. Katz, 4:211-35. Norwood, NJ: Ablex.

Part 3
Future Directions

11

Early Childhood Care and Education in Canada: An Overview and Future Directions

Nina Howe

> The direction in which education starts a man will determine his future life ... Let early education be a sort of amusement; you will then be better able to find out the natural bent.
>
> Plato, *The Republic*

The importance of early childhood education has been recognized since ancient times, as demonstrated by the above quotation from Plato. The notions that early education will help establish the foundation for future achievements and that it should be a sort of "amusement" are ancient and fundamental ideas in Western thought. By "amusement," Plato advocated the need for a relaxed, non-academically oriented beginning to education, perhaps more like the activity- and play-based programs that we see so frequently in modern early childhood settings. In these kinds of educational contexts, children have the opportunity to learn about their own interests, strengths, weaknesses, other people, and the world around them. Given the realities of the modern world for our children, how can we ensure that these goals will be maintained? It is made evident in this chapter that there are no simple answers to this question. In addition, as some critical issues are highlighted during the review of where we have come from, where we are today, and where we might be in the future, it seems that more questions arise than answers. But such is the nature of intellectual enterprise.

Where Have We Come From?

Let us turn back for a minute before we look at the present and future. It is always important to know one's historical roots so that one can take past information into account in considering future directions. As the chapters in Part 1 have indicated, Canada has a long and rich history in the field of early childhood care and education. An examination of the historical and social events, personalities, and builders of the field provides us with an excellent perspective on current events and developments in Canadian child care.

In Chapter 1, Larry Prochner examines the history of both formal early childhood education (e.g., kindergarten) and informal arrangements (e.g., day care) over the past 200 years in Canada. Although these two streams have had a distinct history, several important and overlapping themes are apparent in the history of both types of settings. The view that early childhood care and education should have a social benefit is one that remains with us today. Prochner has traced the roots of early care as provided by charitable institutions to provide safe, secure, healthy environments for young children so that they would be under proper adult supervision rather than being left unsupervised at home or to run wild in the streets. Many advocates of early care saw this as a means to ameliorate the effects of early poverty and it was an important part of the progressive or social reform movement of the late nineteenth century. Thus the stress on early intervention was a prominent motivation in the creation of a number of kindergartens and day nurseries in both the nineteenth and early twentieth centuries. As Prochner points out, this rationale for early childhood programs is still with us today; it can be seen in a variety of Head Start types of intervention programs (e.g., Better Beginnings in Ontario or Aboriginal Head Start). In addition, recent initiatives by the province of Quebec to provide full-day kindergarten for all children, half-day prekindergarten programs, and $5.00/child care for children under the age of five fit into this interventionist model.

The debate in the nineteenth century regarding the role of parents versus the role of the state or private charity in the care and education of children is still a prominent issue today. The continuing discussion about whether young children should be placed in child care and its effect on their development is also a current manifestation of this historical theme.

Prochner's history of both the kindergarten and the day nursery movements charts their disjointed progress and reflects the ambivalent view of society regarding the need for early childhood care and education – an ambivalence that endured over the last 200 years and that is still with us today. By discussing the history of specific programs, centres, and kindergartens in cities across Canada, Prochner provides us with a realistic view of developments in the field. This history is marked by many starts and stops in the provision of child care across the country. As Prochner points out, the reason for the disjointed history of child care emanates partly from the ambiguous roles of mothers and teachers that Canadians have grappled with over the years. The popular view of the ideal mother as a person who devotes all her time and energy to the care of her young children has never coincided with the reality of life for many Canadian women – that is, many Canadians women have chosen to work either for personal reasons or to support their families. This fact has always been part of the fabric of Canadian society, as argued by a number of authors in the current book. Thus, in many ways, framing the issue as mothers versus educators forces an unnecessary and false dichotomy in terms of who has responsibility for raising children. We can all agree that parents have primary responsibility, but others such as educators or grandparents may act as supports in the child's life. Furthermore, as current research has demonstrated, the quality of both home and out-of-home care is the critical factor influencing children's development. We know that children thrive in high-quality environments, both at home and in early childhood education and care settings, whereas less optimal environments may not be beneficial for children's development.

The ambivalent view of both the general public and governments toward early childhood care and education is seen in the slow reaction of the authorities to enact legislation to regulate child care centres, specifically teacher training, teacher-to-child ratios, and health and safety. In contrast, kindergarten has achieved a greater sense of importance in the minds of politicians and government officials, perhaps because kindergartens have been co-opted by the teachers' unions, school boards, and provincial ministries of education, and are now integrated into the more formal education system. However, even funding for kindergartens has often been precarious over the century. As governments attempt to deal with economic downturns and deficits, cuts to education budgets have been seen as inevitable; unfortunately, kindergarten is often viewed as a frill. As a result, kindergarten is frequently on the cutting block – for example, cutbacks in Alberta in the early 1990s vastly reduced the funding available for kindergarten programs.

Chapter 2, by Donna Varga, is an excellent history of teacher training in Canada since the nineteenth century. She clearly outlines the dual streams in training programs for elementary school teachers and early childhood educators. Over time, provinces became more involved in the certification and licensing of elementary school teachers. This led to greater homogeneity in the training of these individuals as well as in the conceptions of what constituted proper classroom behaviour for teachers and students, methods of instruction, appropriate curriculum, and so forth. It is important to remember, however, that conceptions of appropriate teacher practice have also changed dramatically over the decades of the twentieth century. Eventually teacher training for primary education was offered only at the university level and thus has acquired a professional status in the eyes of the public. Professional status, along with provincial certification and unionization of teachers, has created better working conditions, wages, and benefits for teachers who are employed by powerful and active institutions – namely, school boards.

In contrast, as Varga outlines, the training of early childhood educators has taken a separate route, which has resulted in a different outcome for this group of individuals. In the 1950s, the training of early childhood educators became a mandate of community colleges across the country, including schools such as Ryerson Polytechnic Institute (now Ryerson Polytechnic University), and CEGEPs in Quebec. Note, however, that there were some exceptions to the placing of training for early childhood education at the community college level, as Kathleen Brophy describes in the history of university laboratory schools, Chapter 4. The creation of early childhood education programs both at community colleges and at universities reflected the recognition by some in the field that child care workers required specialized training; it was not enough to love children, to be patient, and to be "a natural" with children. Rather, educators needed training in child development, curriculum planning, behaviour management, evaluation, communicating with parents, and working as a member of a team.

The expansion of early childhood education programs at community colleges has been dramatic, partly because of the growing need for well-trained child care educators. Nevertheless, a number of factors have had a detrimental effect on the early childhood field – namely, the placement of training at the community college level, the slowness of many provinces to require that child care workers be trained in early childhood education, the poorer working conditions and wages compared with elementary school teachers, and the lack of power that comes from not being unionized or organized. Specifically, child care is considered a low status job by the public, and governments are reluctant to grapple with the issues of regulation, licensing, and working conditions, as outlined in this book by a number of authors, such as Martha Friendly (Chapter 9), Donna White and Davina Mill (Chapter 8), and Susan Prentice (Chapter 10). The most important role for professional and advocacy organizations is, at present, probably in promoting greater understanding of the nature of work in the child care field. To their credit, organizations such as the Canadian Child Care Federation and the Canadian Child Care Advocacy Association have actively lobbied for more stringent regulations and legislation governing child care. Nevertheless, reading the history of child care as outlined in this publication provides us with a good sense of how far the field has come; however, one is still left with the realization that much territory remains uncharted.

The history of academic child study at both the University of Toronto and McGill University, described by Mary Wright (Chapter 3), conveys a sense of the rich heritage that we can reach back into for a sense of the origins of Canadian early childhood care, education, and developmental psychology. Wright has the striking advantage of having been trained at the Institute of Child Study in Toronto in the 1940s, with William Blatz as her teacher. Thus her understanding of Blatz's ideas and his importance to Canadian child care comes from personal experience and knowledge as well as from the vantage point of historical analysis. In addition, Wright had the opportunity to apply some of Blatz's ideas, as well as many of her own, in the University of Western Ontario Laboratory Preschool, which she founded in 1973. She describes these experiences in an important book (Wright 1983), and they are also discussed in Chapter 7 here.

While research was a primary concern for Blatz and others, such as Mary Northway, at the institute, the melding of theory with practice was also a major focus. The institute played an active role in parent education and public health in informing the public about optimal child-rearing and child-development issues. Moreover, as Varga outlines, the institute was the primary institution for training Canadian early childhood educators for much of this century, and its methods had an impact on many generations of teachers. In fact, its influence can also be seen in the establishment of other laboratory nursery schools. For example, as Brophy points out, Ryerson modelled its nursery school on the one at the Institute of Child Study. One unanswered question concerns the long-term influence of Blatz's ideas on early childhood education programs offered by many community colleges, some of which probably fit into a child study model of early education. During the 1970s the Institute of Child Study was integrated into the Faculty of Education at the University of Toronto, and one of its diploma programs resulted in an elementary school teaching certificate. Wright does not say whether Blatz's ideas continued to hold currency for early-childhood-teacher education at the institute after his retirement or in what ways his ideas might have been integrated into or influenced models of elementary school teaching advocated in the Faculty of Education. It would be interesting for historians to examine whether Blatz's ideas were incorporated into provincial curriculum guides for junior and senior kindergarten developed in Ontario in the 1960s and later.

Brophy outlines the history of university laboratory schools in Canada, focusing on English institutions and indicating their varied history and the reasons for their founding, as well as the different purposes that they retain today. Some laboratory schools were designed in the more traditional nursery school format, where preschool children attended for two or three hours each day; others evolved into group child care settings, providing care for children of working or student parents. These different facilities varied in their original mandates and some, such as the Child Development Centre at the University of Manitoba, have roots in home economics or domestic science programs. Others were associated with early childhood or elementary education programs and were conceived as model schools to train future teachers – for example, the University of Calgary Elementary School. Still others arose out of a need for the provision of child care for students, faculty, and staff associated with the university (e.g., Child Study Centre at Mount Saint Vincent University).

The mandate of the laboratory schools also varies, from providing a research environment for faculty and graduate students in different disciplines (e.g., education, psychology, family studies) to internship sites for student-teachers. In the latter case, these laboratory schools have been regarded as model programs exemplifying high-quality teaching, offering an optimal learning environment for the children, and providing a site for the application of particular curriculum models (e.g., High/Scope, developmentally appropriate practice). Currently, some laboratory schools are associated with teacher-training programs for kindergarten and elementary education (e.g., University of Calgary), whereas others service the training of early childhood educators (e.g., University of Waterloo, Ryerson Polytechnic University). Although not always explicitly noted by Brophy, it is clear that laboratory schools provide important functions beyond their main teaching and research roles. For example, the listing of demonstration and resource goals in the description of the University of Calgary Elementary School is embedded in the mandate of other laboratory schools. By acting as models of excellent early childhood practice, these centres have historically played an important demonstrative role for students, parents, the early childhood community, and the university community. This role continues today and may become increasingly important.

Brophy's description of the laboratory schools notes the resource role provided by many of these programs – for example, providing for at-risk and special-needs children. Moreover, the staff associated with these programs are often active in local, provincial, and national early childhood education associations and are well placed to take leadership positions in advocating for high-quality care and education. The laboratory schools, whether at community colleges or universities, also provide opportunities for classroom teachers to teach and supervise advanced students. In addition, they provide opportunities for faculty to renew their own practical and pedagogical skills on a regular basis. Thus the blending of theory and practice remains alive today for both the classroom teacher and the course instructor.

The multiple roles of teaching, research, and educating parents and the public have made the mandate of laboratory schools precarious and the schools themselves sometimes an easy target for institutional administrators who might consider them frills in difficult financial times. Brophy's description of the events at the University of Guelph to integrate the two centres and recast their role indicates the determination, hard work, and imagination required to provide a continuing life and role for early childhood care and education in these times of fiscal restraint. Although the laboratory school is one of the mainstays of any teacher-education program, it also adds to the expense of such programs, whether in universities or community colleges. In fact, laboratory schools should be considered as the "natural laboratory" in which students observe, practise, and evaluate their own and others' teaching practice, in addition to the development and learning of children. Universities or colleges would not consider closing down a research laboratory in the natural sciences because they recognize the critical links between research and teaching, and that these activities cannot be conducted without proper laboratory facilities. For many administrators, however, the same understanding of the critical relationship between the classroom and the laboratory for teacher education is apparently not as clear. Future efforts must be directed at educating others about the value of having model schools in which to help students learn about appropriate and high-quality pedagogy.

Laboratory schools such as the Institute of Child Study at the University of Toronto have historically played active roles in the promotion of teacher training, public and parent education, and research, although it is less clear whether they have such a prominent role today. Certainly part of the visibility of the Institute of Child Study had to do with the character of Blatz himself and specifically with his involvement with the Dionne quintuplets. The worldwide fascination with the Dionnes is hard for us to comprehend today, but they were considered a marvel in 1934, particularly given the rural and unsophisticated setting of their birth. One interesting part of the Dionne story was the focus on promoting optimal physical development, apparently at the expense of their emotional security and attachment to others. The focus on the Dionne girls as research subjects – bringing greater public awareness about the nature of research – is a story of its own (see Prochner and Doyon 1997). The relationship between research and public policy is another issue brought to the fore by the Dionne story, and is an issue that the field continues to debate today; we will return to this issue later in the chapter.

Alan Pence and Allison Benner provide, in Chapter 5, an insightful review, or life story, of child care research over the past thirty or more years in Canada. This extensive bibliographic project allows us to understand the changes and developments in the field from the perspective of research, which is quite widely defined by these authors to include government-sponsored studies, surveys, and quasi-experimental work. Pence and Benner have classified the search by decade (1965-75, 1976-85, 1986-95, along with a postscript), by theme of the research, type of research, and where the work was published. This review of the literature leads to several major conclusions. First, there has been an impressive increase in the amount of child care research over this thirty-year period. Second, the orientation of the research has changed over the three decades. The first decade was characterized mostly by the desire of governments to understand the child care scene. Thus a large number of surveys and needs assessments were commissioned, but little quasi-experimental research was conducted. The second decade was a time of great debate concerning child care, and this was reflected in a more complex approach to research. Thus child development outcomes, auspice, child care workers, and quality were all issues given more attention. Moreover, the social policy issues concerned with child care were explored by a number of authors. During the third decade, the amount of research doubled over the previous ten years, and researchers continued to investigate the complex ecology of child care. Studies focused on specific types of child care in this decade – for example, school-age care, special-needs children, and Aboriginal child care. However, issues related to quality became one of the dominant themes in this period.

As Pence and Benner note in their postscript, the diversity in types of research and the nature of the issues being examined generally appear to have been maintained, although they also discuss some philosophic reorientations in approaches to research and in the questions posed. In particular, social constructivist critiques highlight the diverse needs of many communities with regard to child care and their varied philosophic approaches. Finally, while the number of Canadian publications most likely increased in the past decade or more – for example, through the founding of the *Canadian Journal of Research in Early Childhood Education* – Pence and Benner argue strongly that Canadian researchers need to look beyond the national scene and publish more work in international journals. In this way, Canadian research will become more widely known and gain greater acceptance and respectability. Clearly, there is the need for high-quality national as well as international publication outlets that encourage both traditional research papers and articles that translate research findings into practical guidelines for teachers, thus bridging the gap between theory, research, and practice.

As Varga notes, the history of teacher training has been greatly influenced by changing trends in curriculum and, in fact, the fads and fashions in curriculum have been diverse, as outlined in Chapter 7 by Nina Howe, Ellen Jacobs, and Lisa Fiorentino. These authors describe the theoretical models of curriculum that have been important in the last 200 years or so.

In addition to examining the primary focus and components of each model, they trace how the major ideas have survived over time and have often been integrated into later models of curriculum. For example, Montessori's cognitive materials and child-sized furniture are now such an integral part of any early childhood education setting that many teachers may not be aware of their origins. Dewey's emphasis on child-centred and child-initiated learning are certainly integral parts of more current developmentally appropriate practice and the Reggio Emilia approach. Chapter 7 also focuses on the way these international models of curriculum have been adapted and modified for Canadian settings. For example, the authors outline the influence of US Head Start programs, as models of early intervention, on Canadian approaches; these models are most recently seen in the Better Beginnings program (Ontario), $5 per day universal day care (Quebec), and Aboriginal Head Start (federal government). Teacher-training programs in early childhood education have not been immune to the changing emphases in curriculum over the decades, and as Varga notes, one can trace the focus on different approaches from a maturationist perspective in the earlier years to a more cognitively oriented approach to current methods emphasizing developmentally appropriate practice and constructivist perspectives.

The important issue for those in the field is to recognize that any particular curriculum model has a long tradition and roots; so while one approach may be the current rage, awareness of our history will provide us with a more critical and analytic eye in determining how new or innovative a particular approach may actually be in practice. Moreover, as Howe, Jacobs, and Fiorentino argue, there is no single curriculum model that is superior to others. The needs of the children and families, the philosophical orientation of those involved, the investment of the community, and the practical issues are only some of the factors that must be taken into account. These authors also argue that the choice of a particular curriculum model should be a joint one – that is, teachers and parents should all contribute to this process. This approach apparently works successfully in the Reggio Emilia system, as well as in recent Canadian attempts by some Aboriginal communities to develop their own generative curricula.

Where Are We Today?

With the great increase in both dual-income and single-parent families in Canada in the last few years, early childhood care and education has become an important feature of Canadian society. There is probably no returning to the traditional family of the 1950s, where Mother stayed home to look after the children and Dad went out to work. In any case, many mothers, even in the 1950s, worked outside the home to help support the family or because they enjoyed doing so. Currently, more young women than young men take postsecondary education, thus we can expect women's presence in the workplace to continue and to increase. Clearly, the need for high-quality care and education for our young children is paramount.

As should be evident, families have a wide variety of preferences in the type of care and education they choose for their young children, ranging from grandparent care to group child care settings to nursery school programs. As Jacobs has outlined in Chapter 6, a number of types of child care are in fact available to families, but perhaps the most important aspect of choice is that parents and children feel comfortable with the decision concerning the care of children when the parents are working. Moreover, what may be desirable for a child at one age may be less so at an older age. For example, some parents may feel that Grandma is the best person to look after their infant, but as the child becomes more active and desiring of playmates, then a family day care home or a group child care centre may be more appropriate. Thus it seems that parents should take the developmental needs of their child into consideration, as well as their own preferences.

In terms of preferences, many factors are integral to a decision about the choice of child care, some of which are more obvious than others, as Chapter 6 demonstrates. Certainly, availability of the type of child care is one criterion, but parents also factor into their decision accessibility, cost, their child's temperament or personality, how well the child might adapt to various kinds of situations, and cultural values and attitudes. For some parents, the ability to place their child in the care of someone who holds similar cultural or ethnic values may be paramount in their decision. Thus, for example, we have seen an increase in Aboriginal child care and French immersion kindergarten programs. Of course, availability of the different types of child care and educational programs varies across the country, depending on province, location (urban, rural), funding, and social policies. For example, group settings may be found less frequently in some rural areas, where relative or family day care may be the norm, and French immersion kindergarten may not be as easy to find in Newfoundland as it obviously would be in Montreal.

Canadians have come to recognize diversity in the population, but have perhaps been slower to accept that preferences and needs for child care are diverse and that, as a society, we need to make a variety of choices available to parents. The question is no longer whether particular kinds of child care are beneficial or detrimental to children's development, but rather, given the reality of Canadian society, how we can ensure that all types of child care are beneficial and of high quality. Certainly, we want our children to be happy and in the best situation possible. To this end, we need to ensure that children receiving non-parental care are in safe, healthy, stimulating, and developmentally and culturally appropriate environments with adults who know how to facilitate optimal child development. While it may be feasible to regulate group child care settings and license family day care, how do we ensure that all children receive high-quality care – from neighbours and relatives too, who may be convenient and inexpensive, but may not all provide high-quality experiences for children? The question becomes then, "What is the process needed to accomplish this goal?"

Jacobs explicitly considers the question of quality of child care, and the various definitions and measures of quality. In addition, she reviews the research on the influence of such quality on children's development and its relationship to licensing regulations. In a nutshell, higher-quality centres are more likely to facilitate optimal child development, and more stringent licensing regulations are more likely to produce high-quality environments for children. In fact, we know which structural parameters predict quality; they include group size, teacher-to-child ratio, and trained teachers. These concrete elements are easy to regulate, whereas optimal teacher behaviour may be more difficult to determine (although White and Mill have provided some excellent direction here) and thus to regulate. Nevertheless, as both Jacobs and Prentice outline in Chapters 6 and 10, respectively, provincial regulations concerning such regulatable factors vary considerably across the country. Child care may be a provincial responsibility, but one has to ask why the children in Newfoundland should be in centre or family child care that must meet standards lower than those for children in Manitoba? As Howe and Jacobs (1995) have argued, it may be time for some national standards that will ensure the highest levels of care for our children. Nevertheless, as Friendly says in Chapter 9, current trends in federal-provincial relations toward devolution of federal control over social policies and programs increasingly diminishes the likelihood of national standards.

The issue of the relationship between quality, regulatable variables, and optimal child outcomes is complicated by the issue of auspice, or who should be in the business of group child care. Prentice has raised some challenging and provocative questions for us to consider and debate. For example, the business of child care is complex and to a large degree reflects our social and political preferences. Prentice outlines very succinctly the convoluted history of the federal-provincial funding relationship and its impact on auspice. Some provinces such as Manitoba and Saskatchewan have taken the view that child care should be operated by non-profit or government-operated boards, frequently run by parents. In contrast, other provinces such as Alberta and Newfoundland have allowed the service of child care to become a private business – for-profit child care.

Prentice argues convincingly and strongly, on the basis of the research literature, that for-profit centres offer lower quality care for children than non-profit or government-operated centres. Furthermore, provinces that encourage for-profit child care have laxer regulations with respect to group size, numbers of trained teachers, teacher-to-child ratios, etc. In comparison, provinces that restrict for-profit centres have considerably more stringent regulations. Naturally, entrepreneurs would prefer to establish for-profit centres in provinces with laxer standards because they do not have to hire as many trained staff, can have larger groups of children with fewer teachers, and so forth. Thus, laxer standards promise a higher level of profit for the business operator, whereas, as pointed out in both Chapters 8 and 10, non-profit centres do not keep the profit but return the money in the form of higher wages and better working conditions for staff, employ more trained and well-qualified staff, buy new and up-to-date equipment, and have lower staff-to-child ratios.

Interestingly, in Chapter 10, Prentice points out that many advocates of non-profit child care are vehemently opposed to franchised child care centres, when it is the "Mom and Pop" centres owned by individuals in which the quality of care varies most widely. In fact, the franchises tend to provide a more consistent level of care across their centres; thus advocates of non-profit care may be partly targeting the wrong businesses. However, Varga's caution, in Chapter 2, against the homogeneity of care may be pertinent here. We know that franchised child care centres tend to look alike in terms of physical environments, but we do not know how similar they are in terms of the quality of experiences provided to children, the style of teacher behaviour, or the way the curriculum models are applied in practice.

We need to ask whether it is possible to encourage for-profit centres to improve the quality of care. Probably most business entrepreneurs would be unwillingly to do so unless required to by provincial regulations. As Prentice says, in some provinces the owners of for-profit centres constitute a powerful lobby and are politically and socially aligned with the government. Thus the push by child care advocates for more stringent regulations is an uphill battle. Will more stringent regulations put some owners of child care centres out of business? Probably. But we need to ask ourselves where we stand on this issue and how we can make the lives of young Canadian children in all types of child care a high-quality experience. For some individuals, the notion of making money from the care of children is repugnant; for others, it is not. These are all serious questions for debate in the early childhood education community. Constructive means need to be developed to correct the inequities in care that are evident across the country.

As a society we do not sanction the education of school-aged children by untrained individuals, except in rare cases such as home schooling; but even in these situations, parents are typically required to follow the provincial education curriculum. Why do we allow untrained individuals to work with our youngest children at a critical period of their development – namely, when they are learning at an incredibly fast rate and are developing attitudes toward learning and education, and the ability to get along with others? We know that teachers play a critical role in determining the quality of the child care environment and the kinds of experiences that children continually undergo. Nevertheless, as White and Mill point out in Chapter 8, we need further research delineating exactly which aspects of teacher behaviour are critical. Presumably warm, accepting teachers who employ constructive management techniques and plan interesting and developmentally appropriate curricula would facilitate optimal child development. Moreover, the Mill and White (1999) study demonstrating associations between caregivers' working conditions and their warmth or anger during daily interactions with children raises some critical questions. When adults' feelings regarding their working conditions spill over into their exchanges with children, what kind of environment are these individuals creating for the youngsters in their care? Do we want our children exposed to angry, frustrated, overworked adults or to warm, caring, supportive adults, especially over long periods of time? What is the long-term effect on children's development of experiencing angry or warm interactions with adults? These questions are of paramount concern whether children are in group care, family day care, school-age care, sitter care, or relative care.

In fact, we know little about the specifics of teacher behaviour – for example, how does the teacher's management of emotional situations, such as separation from the parent, influence both the child's and the parent's adjustment to the particular child care setting? Presumably a warm, calm, sensitive approach by the teacher, accompanied by discussion of the child's emotional experience both with the parents and the child, would facilitate the adjustment to non-parental child care in a more optimal way than a disapproving, cool, and dismissive approach (White and Howe 1998). In conclusion, we would probably not take our car to an unlicensed auto mechanic for repair; so why would we leave our children in the care of non-professionals? Clearly, there is much work to be done in promoting the value of trained, well-paid, professionally satisfied, and well-adjusted teachers in the eyes of the public, our politicians, and the civil servants who develop the regulations for child care.

Varga raises some provocative questions concerning the move, in recent years, toward a more homogenous approach to the training of early-childhood teachers, particularly with the emphasis on developmentally appropriate practice and the lack of information about alternative models (except perhaps as historical asides). Is current teacher training flexible enough to accommodate the diverse needs of different children and families? A related question is how well students actually implement the theory and practice they have been taught in community college or university programs when they are on the job? Do teachers manage their classrooms and interact with children in ways that reflect high-quality teaching practice and the theoretical models of curriculum advocated by the teacher-training program they attended? How well do teachers adapt their training to their own preferred style and to the needs and abilities of the children and families in their care? These are serious questions for those in the field to address.

As White and Mill reveal, child care is a female work ghetto that attracts young women who work long and arduous hours, usually for shamefully low salaries, yet report high levels of satisfaction with the nature of their work. Many are relatively well educated and have community college or university degrees in early childhood education or a related field. The work conditions in for-profit child care are significantly poorer than in non-profit centres, as Prentice says. This raises the issue of auspice once again. Some provinces – for example, Nova Scotia and Prince Edward Island – have instituted programs of salary enhancement for child care workers in an attempt to ensure that child care workers receive a more equitable salary (Lyon and Canning 1997). In addition, as White and Mill note, the low prestige accorded the profession worries many child care workers. They view their work as important and as supporting families and society; yet the public generally does not recognize their contribution. Certainly we can expect professional organizations and advocacy groups to become increasingly active on this issue, and for teachers in the field to become better organized and more outspoken about their views. Child care workers tend to work in small settings and in isolation from other centres or family day cares. They have not felt they have much power. Nevertheless, the attempts of women in similar kinds of jobs, such as nursing, to become better organized and unionized have created higher salaries and better working conditions.

In some jurisdictions, the growth in school-age care has meant that school boards are now in the business of child care. Generally, child care workers are not paid at the same level as elementary school teachers, but they may be eligible for similar kinds of benefits. Some have argued that as school boards expand their full-day kindergarten and pre-kindergarten programs, the lines between the primary school teacher and the early childhood educator become blurred. In fact, many early childhood educators may be better trained to work with four- and five-year-olds than teachers who receive elementary education training, where the focus is typically on delivering the academic curriculum more appropriate for children in grades 1 to 6. Some have expressed concern that elementary school teachers may attempt to push the academic curriculum down from the primary grades into the kindergarten and pre-kindergarten levels (Doherty 1996), rather than providing a more child-centred curriculum that is typically advocated by early childhood care and education programs. Certainly this is a concern that warrants close attention by those in the field, particularly those responsible for the more traditional teacher-training programs for elementary school. Nevertheless, as the lines become blurred between child care workers and pre-kindergarten teachers, the public perception of the value of child care work may increase. As school boards take over the school-age centres, they may be more likely to pay decent salaries and begin to put pressure on other centres to increase the wages of workers. In addition to financial considerations, there may be opportunities to develop a more child-oriented curriculum that bridges the child's experiences across both child care and kindergarten settings.

Does it all come down to money? In Chapter 9, Friendly raises a number of important issues that revolve around funding, but, as she argues, these issues really can only be understood within the context of social policy. Child care in Canada has evolved without the benefit of a coherent national social policy. Thus the present situation is often confusing to the newcomer attempting to study the Canadian situation. As Friendly points out, the debate about the role of government in child care comes down to a fundamental philosophical issue that has haunted those in the field for decades: specifically, should the provision of child care services and early childhood education programs be the responsibility of the public or a private family matter? The implications of this debate are reflected in our discourse about child care services (see also Kyle 1997). If we believe that early childhood services are a matter of public concern, governments should develop coordinated, coherent social welfare policies to provide the needed services (i.e., accessible, financially supported, regulated, non-profit group and family child care). On the other hand, if we believe that child care should be a matter of private responsibility, services should be provided as a private commodity within a market model (e.g., for-profit child care, neighbourhood babysitters). Prentice also discusses this issue in the chapter on auspice of child care. This debate is fundamental and not easily resolved, yet it has coloured the provision of early childhood care and education for a long time. Interestingly, to a large degree this is no less of an issue for formal education programs (kindergarten programs), which many agree should be provided as a public responsibility; however, the provision of pre-kindergarten programs is more a matter for debate. In sum, various perspectives on the public versus private responsibility debate are evident today. On the one hand, we note the attempt by the province of Alberta to cut funding for kindergarten programs, an action that was based on the view that early childhood education is a family responsibility. On the other hand, the province of Quebec has taken the view that early education should be a matter of public responsibility. It has therefore made expansions to full-day kindergarten programs and introduced pre-kindergarten programs and universal $5 per day child care for all children under the age of five.

Friendly raises a second critical issue – namely, what is child care and whom is it for? Although these seem like simple questions, an analysis of the answers indicates a complicated picture. What is the purpose of child care? It has been promoted as beneficial for any of the following reasons: healthy child development; support for working parents; equality for women; reducing the reliance of families on social assistance; and early intervention for children considered at risk for future social, health, and economic problems. These are all admirable goals and ones that most members of society would probably support, at least to some degree. Whom is child care for? Everyone, of course: children, parents, families, women. Nevertheless, the implications of the answers to these questions have an immediate and direct impact on the kind of social services that have been provided by governments. Moreover, is child care really available for all Canadians and does it meet the diverse needs of our multicultural, multilingual, and geographically diverse nation?

Friendly concisely outlines the history of the federal government's role in creating various social welfare programs – for example, the Canada Assistance Plan (CAP) in the 1960s and, more recently, Aboriginal Head Start and Aboriginal child care. She also discusses the federal government's patchwork approach to social policy and tracks several major shifts in thinking from the nineteenth century view that child care was a charity service to the 1960s view that universal programs (although child care was not really included in this) were needed, and then to the more recent withdrawal from cost-sharing social programs. Having made a serious commitment to universal health and education programs, the federal government could apparently do no more than flirt with the notion of universal child care. Many in the early childhood community gasped when the Liberal party's now-famous *Red Book* committed, as part of the 1993 federal election campaign, a huge increase in funding for child care. Was this going to be the beginning of a publicly supported universal system of early childhood care and education, like the social policy programs in many Western European and Scandinavian countries? As with so many election promises, it appears that this one was made only to be broken.

Where Do We Go from Here?

What is the future of early childhood care and education in Canada? There is a strong sense that Canada is at a crossroads with respect to early childhood care and education. The lack of a national consensus on the public-versus-private role for child care, combined with the present economic conditions and social attitudes, leaves one with a feeling of uncertainty over the future. As Friendly points out, the current situation is a fragmented, confusing array of services that vary across provinces and territories. Friendly notes three current trends that will have a major impact on the early childhood care and education field in the years to come. First, as the federal government has moved from the cost-sharing programs (shared 50-50 between national and provincial governments) of the 1970s and 1980s to block grants for social services in the 1990s, the result has been a diminishing role for the federal government in shaping a national policy on child care. Consequently, there has been a greater reliance on provincial and territorial governments to articulate policies and programs for early childhood care and education. We thus have a myriad of programs (or lack of programs) and great variation in licensing standards and regulations for the provision of care and teacher training. Second, there has already been some downloading of financial responsibility for child care by provinces and territories onto local governments, many of whom are heavily strapped by having to provide a wide range of other social services. Third, the devolution of responsibility for child care continues as the federal government placed it in the hands of provincial and territorial governments, who then shifted responsibility onto local levels of government. Who is left? Final responsibility is now being shifted onto parents, some of whom may be better equipped than others to find and pay for high-quality care and education for their children. Already we see charitable organizations stepping in to develop programs for those in need. Are we about to go full circle and return to the days when child care was offered as a charitable service by well-meaning wealthy ladies?

We can speculate that there are a number of directions in which the field will move. On the one hand, we can cite recent efforts by the province of Alberta to cut funding for kindergarten and child care services as one possible direction. However, it should be noted that this province has restored some funding to education and social services after a massive outcry from the public, teachers unions, and child care advocates concerning the need for these kinds of early childhood services. Clearly, a significant portion of the Canadian population recognizes the importance of these services.

In contrast, Quebec has taken a different approach. Its recent initiatives show that it now regards early childhood education as an important means to increase young children's readiness for formal schooling; in particular, we note the move to introduce full-day kindergarten, pre-kindergarten programs, and $5 per day child care for all three- and four-year-olds. The proposal includes a plan to add younger age groups on a yearly basis until all children from birth to age four will be eligible for $5 per day child care. Quebec's initiatives also support Prochner's contention that education, health, and social services have become integrated over the past thirty years. As part of these initiatives child care centres will have to provide other social service functions for families, such as after-school programs, a family day care registry, or a parent drop-in centre. This integrative approach recognizes that child care is of great benefit to children who are at risk and their families; it also directs such children into early education (e.g., full-day kindergarten). Nevertheless, implicit in this view is that the charity stigma is still with us. Private charities may no longer be in charge of providing care and moral instruction; instead the government has assumed some share of this responsibility, albeit somewhat uneasily. The burden placed on the early childhood community is a heavy one, particularly when the amount of provincial funding provided does not easily allow for high-quality service to children and families. Moreover, the move toward funding child care may have come at the expense of relaxing licensing standards. For example, the teacher-to-child ratio for four-year-olds has been increased from 1:8 to 1:10, a move that raises concerns about the quality of care that teachers will be able to provide for children.

As the numbers of educated and qualified early childhood educators increase, the push for greater recognition of the value of their work is also likely to increase. Thus we can expect professional organizations (e.g., Canadian Association for Young Children) and advocacy groups (e.g., Canadian Child Care Federation, Canadian Day Care and Advocacy Association) to become increasingly vocal, sophisticated, and well organized in their public education campaigns and efforts to organize educators into a more powerful force. We can expect such groups to lobby extensively for more stringent provincial licensing and regulations for both child care and early childhood programs (e.g., teacher-training qualifications, maximum group size in kindergartens). But above all, these organizations are likely to attempt to push child care back onto the national agenda by asking for a coherent, national, and universal system of care for young children. This will not be a short or easy battle, but when the future of children and families is in question, the high stakes suggest a concerted campaign is required.

The question of the diverse needs of Canadian families is a complex one, as a number of authors have noted in this book, and we can expect the development of a greater range of services to be available to families. The needs of many kinds of families are currently not being met by the child care system, so the demand for greater flexibility is apparent. We can point to a few examples to illustrate this point: the lack of group care in some rural areas; seasonal care (e.g., at crop-harvesting time); care available while parents do shift work (i.e., day, evening, night); early education that reflects the cultural and ethnic make-up of the families enrolled; greater availability of family day care; and half-day as well as full-day kindergarten. Flexible services will help ensure that the developmental needs of children are more likely to be met, as well as providing solutions for the practical issues and problems faced by parents. More than likely, the move to remedy these concerns will come from the grassroots (i.e., parents, local advocates) rather than from provincial governments.

The need for greater flexibility in, and control over, the kinds of early care and education experiences that our children encounter is also integral to the types of curricula employed in different kinds of programs. As Howe, Jacobs, and Fiorentino point out, there are few uniquely Canadian curricula. Rather, most Canadian programs have modified curriculum models developed in other countries for children living in other times, or in different cultural or economic circumstances. Thus we must ask ourselves whether transplanting these models without a critical analysis of their basic premises, goals, and characteristics is the best approach. In other words, does it make sense to employ a curriculum designed for one specific population living in one specific context to another context without due consideration for the cultural and economic circumstances of Canadian families? While the High/Scope model has certainly demonstrated its value for the inner-city children of Ypsilanti, Michigan, it seems rather naïve to expect it to have the same value for the children of Quebec without considering the characteristics of the local milieu. In the absence of a deep understanding of the basic premises and goals of a particular model, we would be foolish to expect that teachers who are arbitrarily mandated to implement such a curriculum will do so faithfully or knowledgeably. These are the kinds of government policies that invite disaster.

In contrast, the generative curriculum models that have been developed by some First Nations are more promising. By developing a cross-cultural curriculum that draws upon the knowledge, expertise, and needs of two cultures, we can see the beginnings of a more culturally sensitive and community-centred approach to developing child care and early education programs. This is an exciting approach and one that allows communities to become involved in and develop a sense of ownership over the programs; it allows communities to have direct input into the kinds of experiences and development their children and families will undergo. It is a model that many other Canadian programs would do well to consider, particularly those designed for immigrant children, rural children, children with special needs, minority francophone or anglophone youngsters, and so forth. By employing a generative model of curriculum, the voices of the community, the parents, the teachers, and the children can be heard. Perhaps in this way, we will move forward in the development of a number of unique Canadian curriculum models.

Quality: this word recurs in many aspects of the early childhood care and education field. It is employed in terms of quality experiences for young children and families, working conditions for staff, well-conducted research, well-articulated social policy, and so forth. With regard to children, we can conclude that high-quality care is beneficial for children's development in all kinds of settings (e.g., family day care homes, group centres, kindergartens). We need to ensure that the quality of present programs continues and improves, and that quality reaches into the lives of children presently outside the more organized parts of the system – for example, children who are cared for by relatives, babysitters, and family day care providers. Part of this process involves increasing public awareness and education, as well as improving the standards of teacher training, at both the community college and the university level. In the twenty-first century, an admirable goal would be to ensure that all persons who work with young children are properly trained, highly qualified, appropriately supervised on a regular basis, and well paid. This will help to ensure that our children have the best possible kinds of early care and education experiences.

Teachers are the framers of quality experiences for children, whether in formal or informal child care or kindergarten settings. Since we know that teachers with higher qualifications provide higher-quality care, all persons who work in child care should have college diplomas or university degrees. Moreover, it is equally important that the salaries of such individuals be commensurate with their qualifications and take into account both the professional nature of their work and their level of training and experience. Perhaps as school boards become more involved with child care and after-school care programs, a movement toward greater professional and financial recognition, as well as better working conditions, will be seen in the next few years. Furthermore, if schools become more closely linked to the community, as are the Reggio Emilia or generative models, the community school may become the child care and education centre of the community. Clearly, this will require greater integration of the education, health, and social services ministries of government, as well as a greater willingness to fund such projects.

The development of a national, universally accessible, high-quality early childhood care and education system is possible. Canada has the theoretical and applied expertise to organize, establish, and maintain such a system; however, there are several impediments. One stumbling block is the perception of many Canadians that mothers should remain at home with their young children and not be in the workforce. We know that this is not a realistic option for many Canadian families, nor the desire of many women. As noted, we do need a flexible system and the availability of many kinds of options for women and families. Another large impediment is the lack of funding. The late 1990s has been a period of government cutbacks, and so often health care and education have been the main target of funding restraints. The recipients of health care and education (i.e., the old and the young) are generally not powerful members of society and require others to speak out for them. Thus parents need to become stronger advocates and lobby actively for high-quality care and education for their children.

Of course, so much of our knowledge concerning the development of high-quality experiences for children can be traced directly back to the quality of the research conducted. Although we expect a variety of studies to be conducted, an increasing emphasis is likely to be placed on identifying parameters of quality care and education. We thus need to know more about the determinants of quality (e.g., teacher training, group size, teacher behaviours) in different kinds of settings (e.g., family day care, group care, kindergarten, relative care, school-aged care, for-profit and non-profit centres), as well as the influence of the context (e.g., socioeconomic status, culture, geographic location). In addition, we need to understand the role of the employer in providing quality experiences (e.g., working conditions, salaries, benefits, decision making). Some of this research will be done by academics working together or in conjunction with both practitioners and social policy makers. The opportunities and questions are limitless, but the link between research and social policy must be maintained: well-informed social policy must be based on rigorous and valid research.

As we move forward to consider the possibilities and the directions that we would like Canadian society to take, it is always important to keep an eye on our history. As should be apparent, Canada has a rich and varied history in early childhood care and education, much of which we can confidently examine with pride. However, there are many low points, which we would do well to keep in mind as we move forward. After all, our goal should be to ensure that the next generation faces the world with the deep desire to learn, explore, create, reflect, solve problems, and laugh.

Note

The writing of this chapter was supported by grants from the Social Sciences and Humanities Research Council of Canada and the Fond pour la Formation de Chercheurs et l'Aide à la Recherche.

References

Doherty, G. 1996. School for three- and four-year-olds: What does the research tell us? *Canadian Journal of Research in Early Childhood Education* 5:135-42.

Howe, N., and E. Jacobs. 1995. Child care research: A case for Canadian national standards. *Canadian Psychology* 36:131-48.

Kyle, I. 1997. Private and public discourse: The social context of child care. *Canadian Journal of Research in Early Childhood Education* 6:203-22.

Lyon, M.E., and P. Canning. 1997. Auspice, location, provincial legislation and funding of day care in Atlantic Canada: Relationships with centre quality and implications for policy. *Canadian Journal of Research in Early Childhood Education* 6:139-55.

Mill, D., and D.R. White. 1999. Correlates of affectionate and angry behavior in day care educators of preschool-aged children. *Early Childhood Research Quarterly* 14(2):155-78.

Prochner, L., and P. Doyon, 1997. Researchers and their subjects: William Blatz and the Dionne quintuplets. *Canadian Psychology* 38(2):103-10.

White, D.R., and N. Howe. 1998. The socialization of children's emotional and social behavior by day care educators. In *Improving competence across the life-span,* ed. D. Pushkar, W.M. Bukowski, A.E. Schwartzman, D.M. Stack, and D.R. White, 79-90. NY: Plenum.

Wright, M.J. 1983. *Compensatory education in the preschool.* Ypsilanti, MI: High/Scope.

Contributors

Allison Benner is a writer and policy consultant based in Victoria, British Columbia.

Kathleen Brophy is an associate professor at the Department of Family Studies at Guelph University.

Lisa M. Fiorentino is a graduate student at the Department of Education at Concordia University, Montreal.

Martha Friendly is director of the Childcare Resource and Research Unit, Centre for Urban and Community Studies, University of Toronto.

Nina Howe is an associate professor at the Department of Education at Concordia University, Montreal.

Ellen Jacobs is a professor at the Department of Education at Concordia University, Montreal.

Davina Mill is a clinical psychologist and research coordinator at Concordia University, Montreal.

Alan R. Pence is a professor at the School of Child and Youth Care at the University of Victoria.

Susan Prentice is an associate professor at the Sociology Department at the University of Manitoba.

Larry Prochner is an associate professor at the Department of Education at Concordia University, Montreal.

Donna Varga is an associate professor at the Department of Child and Youth Study at Mount Saint Vincent University, Halifax.

Donna White was an associate professor at the Department of Psychology at Concordia University, Montreal.

Mary J. Wright is professor emeritus at the Department of Psychology at the University of Western Ontario, London.

Index

UNIVERSITY OF WALES COLLEGE NEWPORT
LIBRARY
AND
INFORMATION
SERVICES
CAERLEON

Set in Stone by First Folio Resource Group
Printed and bound in Canada by Friesens
Copy editor: Robyn Packard
Proofreader: Margaret Williams
Indexer: Jin Tan

UNIVERSITY OF WALES COLLEGE NEWPORT
LIBRARY
AND
INFORMATION
SERVICES
CAERLEON